A Theory of Intergenerational Justice

For Finn

A Theory of Intergenerational Justice

Joerg Chet Tremmel

earthscan

publishing for a sustainable future

London • Sterling, VA

First published by Earthscan in the UK and USA in 2009

ISBN: 978–1-84407–826–4

Typeset by Saxon Graphics Ltd, Derby
Cover design by Andrew Corbett

For a full list of publications please contact:

Earthscan
Dunstan House
14a St Cross St
London, EC1N 8XA, UK
Tel: +44 (0)20 7841 1930
Fax: +44 (0)20 7242 1474
Email: earthinfo@earthscan.co.uk
Web: **www.earthscan.co.uk**

22883 Quicksilver Drive, Sterling, VA 20166–2012, USA

Earthscan publishes in association with the International Institute for Environment and
Development

A catalogue record for this book is available from the British Library

Library of Congress Cataloging-in-Publication Data
Tremmel, Joerg, 1970–
  A theory of intergenerational justice / Joerg Chet Tremmel.
      p.cm.
  Includes bibliographical references and index.
  ISBN 978-1-84407-826-4 (hardback)
  1. Justice. 2. Intergenerational relations. I. Title.
  JC578.T74 2009
  320.01′1–dc22

                                              2009010093

At Earthscan we strive to minimize our environmental impacts and carbon footprint
through reducing waste, recycling and offsetting our CO_2 emissions, including
those created through publication of this book. For more details of
our environmental policy, see www.earthscan.co.uk.

This book was printed in the UK by CPI Antony Rowe.
The paper used is FSC certified.

Mixed Sources
Product group from well-managed
forests and other controlled sources
www.fsc.org Cert no. SGS-COC-2953
FSC © 1996 Forest Stewardship Council

Contents

List of Figures and Tables

Figures

Tables

Acknowledgements

This book is dedicated to my son Finn Christof who was born during the course of writing. He influenced my reasoning more than he is aware, as he constantly reminded me (even before he saw the light of day) of my obligations to him. The rest of my family helped me more explicitly, and I wish to thank them all for that, especially my wife Laura and my parents. Hardly any expression of gratitude on my part could repay the debts that I have been fortunate enough to incur.

I am further deeply indebted to Professor Birnbacher from the University of Düsseldorf, Germany, but for whom this book would maybe not have been begun. He wrote on the same topic 20 years ago and his works, together with Ernest Partridge's, inspired me to conduct a study on intergenerational justice. Dieter Birnbacher supervised my second PhD thesis and was a guide, disputant and friend in these years.

Between submitting my thesis to the university and the deadline of the publisher, over a period of a year, I had time to improve the text whenever I gained new insights. I am grateful for critical remarks, inspirations, ideas and comments on earlier versions of this study to Burns Weston, Bryan G. Norton, Marcel Wissenburg, Axel Gosseries, Lukas H. Meyer, Simone Dietz, Richard Hauser, Peer Ederer, Oliver Goetz and a number of anonymous referees. They are not to be blamed for inconsistencies and deficiencies that have withstood their efforts.

Leila Kais was my main, and a great, sparring partner when it came to language issues. The discussions with Hannah Taylor Kensell about the most accurate formulations also helped me a lot to get my message across and make the text more readable. Hannah helped me also in formatting the text, together with Dan Sylvain.

These acknowledgements would be incomplete without recognizing the support I received from the publisher, especially from Rob West, Camille Bramall, Claire Lamont and Dan Harding. They helped make a tight timetable work and a demanding schedule look easy.

Some philosophers might raise their eyebrows when I say that philosophy, as it is presently taught at universities and set out in relevant journals and books, could be improved by three simple methodological and stylistic rules. First, refrain from using arguments and examples that are too detached from reality. Leaving empirical facts aside to too great a degree involves the risk of proposing normative theories that cannot be applied in a real society. However, a good ethical theory, for instance on questions of just distribution, should be of benefit for real decision makers.

Secondly, do not use 'isms' too readily. Some experts make the mistake of immediately pigeonholing (e.g. as utilitarianism, contractualism, naturalism, liberalism, etc.) any new theory they come across. But catchwords can cover contents.

The third bad habit is to develop own theorems, abridge them, and then use a kind of secret language for the rest of the text, largely made up of homespun abbreviations.

I will refrain from giving examples for these three nuisances. They even occur in my own texts (even if my list of abbreviations on the following page is rather short and contains no neologisms). Nevertheless, it would be worthwhile for the philosophical community to discuss whether we should all subscribe to these three methodological or stylistic principles. I think we should.

Joerg Chet Tremmel

List of Acronyms and Abbreviations

AU	average utilitarianism
c.p.	ceteris paribus (all other variables stay equal)
ESI	Economic Sustainability Indicator
GDP	gross domestic product
HDI	Human Development Index
HDR	Human Development Report
HWI	Human Well-being Index
LDC	less developed countries
MDC	more developed countries
MRI	magnetic resonance imaging
NGO	non-governmental organization
NPT	Nuclear Non-Proliferation Treaty
OECD	Organisation for Economic Co-operation and Development
OSL	overall satisfaction of life
PET	positron emission tomography
PWI	personal well-being index
QALY	quality adjusted life years
R&D	research and development
TAC	Treatment Action Campaign
TDC	time-dependence claim
TRIPS	Trade-Related Aspects of Intellectual Property Rights
TU	total utilitarianism
UNDP	United Nations Development Programme
UNEP	United Nations Environment Programme
UNESCO	United Nations Educational, Scientific and Cultural Organization
UNO	United Nations Organization
WHO	World Health Organization
WISP	Weighted Index of Social Progress

1

Introduction

Mankind's increasing powers

In the past decades, systematic concepts and theories on justice between non-overlapping generations have been developed for the first time ever – 2600 years after the first theories on justice between contemporaries had been articulated. This delay can be explained by the different impact of mankind's scope of action, then and now.

In his epoch-making book *The Imperative of Responsibility* (first published in German in 1979), the philosopher Hans Jonas points to the fact that the potential to irreversibly impair the future fate of mankind and nature by actions and omissions is increased by modern technology. Jonas clearly works out what held true throughout all ages up to the 20th century:

> *With all his boundless resourcefulness, man is still small by the measure of the elements, precisely this makes his sallies into them so daring... Making free with the denizes of land and sea and air, he yet leaves the encompassing nature of those elements unchanged, and their generative powers undiminished... Much as he harries Earth, the greatest of Gods, year after year with his plough – she is ageless and unwearied; her enduring patience he must and can trust, and to her cycle he must conform. (Jonas, 1980, p25)*

Jonas can be criticized for considering nature stable and indestructible. Such a concept is surely one-sided and is no longer advocated by ecologists in such general terms. In view of the five geological phases of global extinction of animal species (Cincotta and Engelmann, 2001, p31) and the cycles of ice and warm ages, nature must be seen as far more vulnerable to catastrophes.

However, Jonas' decisive and indisputable point is that, throughout history, man had relatively little influence on global, supra-regional nature before the modern age. Man was not able to throw the ecosystem he lived in off balance. He did not adapt to nature on grounds of reason, but simply because he had no choice. Under these circumstances, there was no need for an ethics of responsibility to nature. Rather, man was well advised to approach nature with as much cleverness and efficiency as possible to sufficiently benefit from its seemingly boundless resources.

But, things he had to accept as his fate in earlier times gradually came within his scope of influence in 20th century. The long-term effects of nuclear energy were not conceivable in the past, except in utopias with a science-fiction character. The same applies to the magnitude of climatic changes – which are, after all, an influence on the basic biophysical conditions of our planet itself.

As the comparison of standards of mankind and nature in Figure 1.1 shows, we are able now to shape the future by intervening in the household of nature to a great extent, for millions of years.

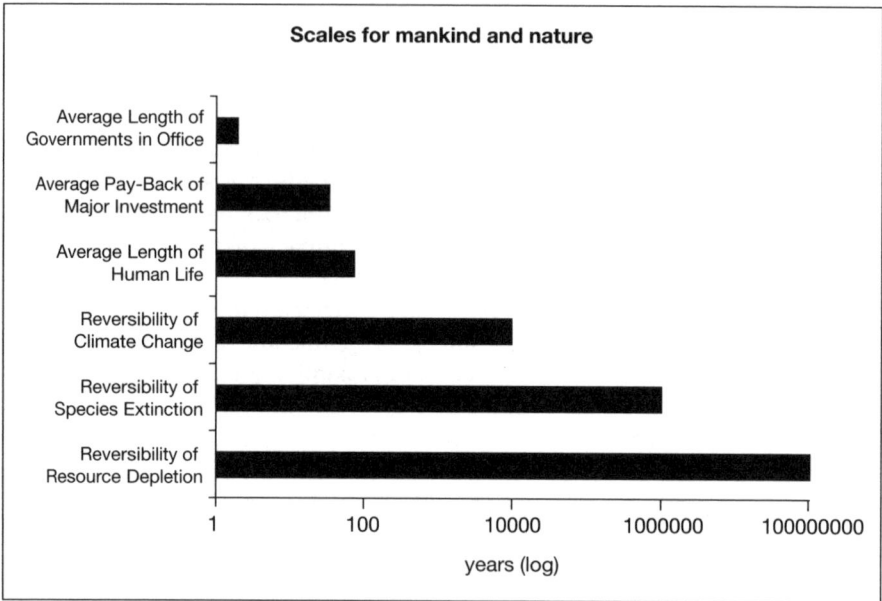

Source: Tremmel (2006b, p188)

Figure 1.1 *Relevant timescales for mankind and the environment*

Let us take nuclear waste as an example. A country like Germany (which is not a nuclear power and thus does not reuse plutonium for military purposes) has produced in its nuclear power plants 118 tonnes of plutonium (Pu-239) as a waste substance until now.[1] Plutonium has a half-life period of 24,110 years. So, according to our present state of knowledge, 1 gram (g) of our present waste plutonium will still be left in 310,608 years, and 1g can be lethal for a human being.[2]

If we consider that our written history is only 10,000 years old, the permanence of the burden present generations are placing on the shoulders of future generations becomes quite clear. The Berlin semiotician Roland Posner explains:

> *In all three fields [nuclear, genetic and space engineering; annotation J. T.], we are dealing with time spans that go beyond that of human history up to*

now. The science, literature, and art of earlier centuries become unintelligible if they are not re-interpreted and translated into new languages every few generations. In the same way, state institutions have rarely existed for more than a few centuries, and they are constantly threatened by war and subversive movements. Even present-day religions are not much older than a few thousand years, and they have not primarily handed down scientific information to us, but myths and rituals. (Posner, 1990a, p8)[3]

The man-made climatic change, the depletion of the oceans through unsustainable fishing, the clearing of the wilderness for plantations and the loss of biodiversity are by no means new phenomena. But in earlier times, they were limited to certain areas, whereas they are now taking place on a global scale and at a far greater pace (Knaus and Renn, 1998, pp37–43).

The enormous increase in mankind's powers that has taken place in the 20th century explains why even the most important moral philosophers of the past hardly paid any attention to our responsibility towards posterity. Kant, for instance, writes the following:

What remains disconcerting about all this is, firstly, that earlier generations seem to perform their laborious tasks only for the sake of later ones, so as to prepare for them a further stage from which they can raise still higher the structure intended by nature; and, secondly, that only later generations will in fact have the good fortune to inhabit the building on which a whole series of their forefathers (admittedly, without any conscious intention) had worked, without themselves having been able to share in the happiness they were preparing. (Kant, 1949, p6 et seq.)

According to Jonas, the universe of traditional ethics is limited to contemporaries, that is, to their expected lifespan. This 'neighbour ethics' is not sufficient anymore. 'The new territory man has conquered by high technology is still no-man's-land for ethical theory', he writes (Jonas, 1979, p7).

If Jonas is correct, moral philosophy still lives in the Newtonian age.

The no-man's-land of ethics

This convincing plea for a fundamental and radical extension of the scope of ethics is in stark contrast to the opinion of many moral philosophers who believe that all important moral principles have essentially already been brought forth and discussed in the long history of ethics, so there can be no fundamental changes. Here, for example, is Robert Spaemann's witticism: 'In questions of how to live life rightly, only wrong ideas can truly be new' (Spaemann, 1989, p9). For millennia, ethics have dealt with future generations with the confidence that the future is likely to resemble the past. Therefore, the idea of generational justice[4] might be a discontinuity in the history of ethics. Vittorio Hösle points out:

that a certain model of justification of moral standards, namely that of a reciprocal consideration of interests for egoistic reasons, has been impeached by the idea of the rights of future generations...: those living in one hundred can hardly impose sanctions on us for the harm we are doing to them today. Now, to believe our moral obligations are a function of our own selfish interests is by no means the only existing approach to a justification of morals in modernity, but since Hobbes it has been a particularly popular one that has greatly influenced the leading social sciences economics and political science. Therefore, it can be said that one line of modern ethics – a decisive one – is being challenged and probably even impeached by the idea of generational justice. (Hösle, 2003, p132 et seq.)[5]

Rawls – much like Kant a few hundred years before him – takes an 'autonomous social savings rate' (Rawls, 1971, pp319–335) for granted, a type of natural law by which the living conditions of future generations will continuously improve. But the image of the 'spoilt heir' has now been replaced by the concern that future generations might become the ecological, economic and social victims of the short-sighted politics of today's generations. That extends the range of responsibility of those living today. Under our present circumstances, responsibility for future generations, which is more or less included in the traditional concept of responsibility, must be interpreted in a completely new light (Birnbacher, 2006a, p23).

However, such 'remote ethics' often meet with numerous objections, which are discussed later on. First of all, the difference between inter- and intragenerational ethics requires clarification. Depending on the definition of the term 'generation', generational justice is conceivable as justice between the present and future generations (intertemporal generations), also as justice between the young and the old (temporal generations) and between family generations. But basically, intergenerational justice is not conceivable between persons of the same age. Questions of justice between persons of the same age – be they of a different social standing, sex, race, sexual orientation or nationality – are matters of intragenerational justice (see Figure 1.2).

Ethics of the future – in a double sense

The concept of generational justice is likely to play a greater role in future philosophy. Ever more social actors are demanding new ethics of future responsibility. Ever since the beginning of the global ecology movement, the interests of future generations have been advanced as an argument. Avner de-Shalit even claims: 'In fact, the most important element in the question of intergenerational justice is the environmental issue, to which almost every aspect of intergenerational justice is related' (De-Shalit, 1995, p7). If, however, the shifting of ecological burdens to the future is an ethical problem, so is the shifting of burdens in other areas. Therefore, such ethics would necessarily have to include not only ecology but also other political fields. Already by the 19th century, Thomas Jefferson called national debts a problem of intergenerational ethics.[6] Compre-

Intergenerational Justice: Justice *between* generations:	Intragenerational Justice: Justice *within* generations:
Temporal focus depending on definition of the term 'generation' – temporal – intertemporal – family-related	**Social Justice** Justice between the poor and the rich within a country
Spatial level – global – national – regional	**International Justice** Justice between different countries, independently from the revenue repartition in those countries
	Gender Justice Justice between men and women
	Other Forms Justice between the ill and the healthy, those with and those without children, persons of different ethnic and religious backgrounds, etc.

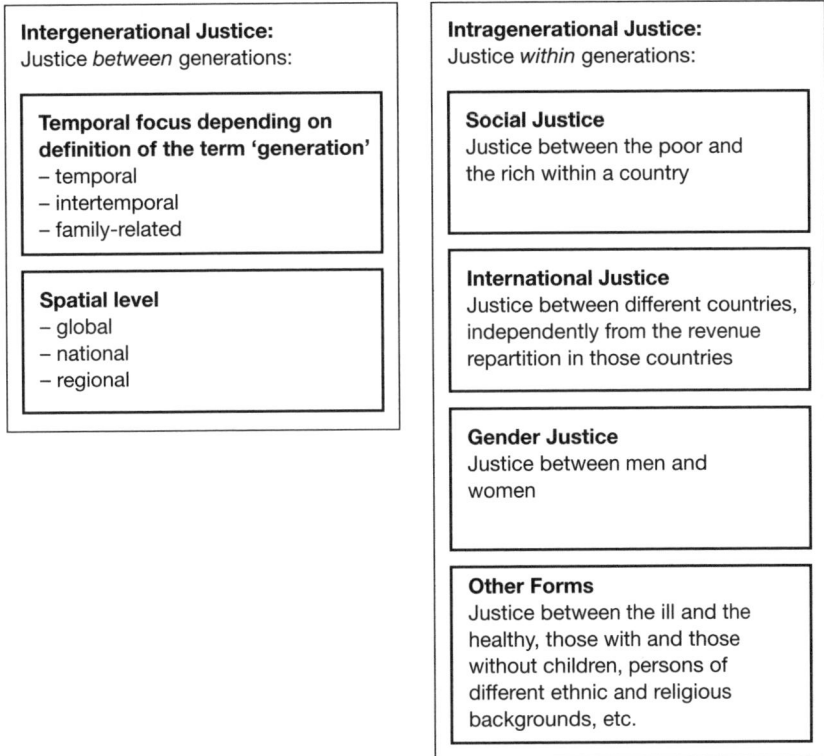

Figure 1.2 *Spheres of intergenerational and intragenerational justice*

hensive generational accounting methods are now being developed to determine the burdens on future generations (Auerbach at al, 1999). A fresh impetus has been given to the debate on generational justice in the more developed countries (MDCs)[7] by the demographic development in the last quarter of the 20th century, which has prompted forecasts of a 'turn toward less'. Numerous representative studies prove the widespread fear of, particularly younger, people that they will not be better but worse off than their parents. In the US, the term 'boomerang generation' has come into use; the German version is '*Generation Praktikum*', and the French version is the '*génération précarité*'.

In the medium term, the question of justice between the young and the old or between present and future generations might become as important in philosophy as the question of social justice, i.e. justice between the poor and the rich. But, as yet, it is still being worked out. In 1980, Ernest Partridge, one of the first editors of an anthology on responsibility for the future, criticizes:

> *The lack of manifest philosophical interest in the topic is further indicated by the fact that of the almost 700,000 doctoral dissertations on file at University Microfilms in Ann Arbor, Michigan, only one has in its title either the words 'posterity', 'future generations' or 'unborn generations. (Partridge, 1980a, p10)*

Here, a lot has changed. Taking into account the new publications in English and German over the past decades, the list has grown quite long, as Table 1.1 shows.

Table 1.1 *Number of publications on generational justice in the widest sense*

British Library/Library of Congress[8]		Deutsche Bibliothek[9]	
intergenerational justice/generational justice/justice between generations	37	Generationengerechtigkeit/ intergenerationelle Gerechtig-keit/intergenerative Gerechtigkeit/Gerechtigkeit zwischen Generationen	39
intergenerational equity/generational equity	29		
future generations/ succeeding generations	175	zukünftige Generationen/ künftige Generationen/ nachrückende Generationen	10
future ethics/future ethic	188	Zukunftsethik	18
unborn generations	3	ungeborene Generationen	0
posterity	n/a	Nachwelt	n/a
environmental justice/ environmental philosophy/ environmental ethics	639	Umweltethik/Naturethik/ Ökologische Ethik	367
Sustainable development/ sustainability	6536	Nachhaltige Entwicklung/ Nachhaltigkeit	2673

A few notes on the results are:

- 'Intergenerational justice'/'generational justice'/'justice between generations' is only included in 37 titles or subtitles.[10] Many of the most important English publications were already written in the 1980s. There are 39 German publications with the term '*Generationengerechtigkeit*' included in their title or subtitle. Many of them were written after 1990.
- The hits for 'intergenerational equity'/'generational equity' mainly refer to philosophical or economic texts on discounting and to economic texts on pension schemes and national debts. These results partly overlap with 'generational accounting', a special procedure for balancing national debts that is now used in many countries.
- The number of hits for the term 'future generations' was originally far higher but many of them had a different context and were excluded. Many of the remaining publications concerned future studies, forecasts or projections and hopes that certain material things or contents of consciousness will be preserved for future generations. The remaining hits also include numerous audio documents. The number of publications in the field of political philosophy is rather low.
- Many hits were found for the term 'posterity', used by Partridge, but they belong to other contexts. It is not a very useful search word for finding literature on just relations between generations. That also applies to the German translation '*Nachwelt*'.

- Of course, questions of generational justice might also be dealt with under other terms. Therefore, the terms 'environmental justice' (or 'environmental philosophy' and 'environmental ethics') and 'sustainable development' (or 'sustainability') were also searched. Here, there were very many hits in total, those for 'sustainable development' (or 'sustainability') numbering higher by one power of ten. However, all newly introduced search topics apparently do not match the topic of this study. Therefore, a clear distinction must be drawn between 'intergenerational justice' and these two topics.
- The national libraries in the US and UK have formed the search terms 'environmental justice', 'sustainable development', 'intergenerational relations' and 'common heritage of mankind (international law)'.
- The Deutsche Nationalbibliothek has formed the search terms '*Zukunftsethik*', '*Umweltethik*', '*Nachhaltige Entwicklung*' and '*Generationenvertrag*'.

There can be no doubt that there is, nowadays, a significant literature on the subject of the nature of our obligations to posterity. But the growing library of studies still has its deficiencies. As Bryan Norton puts it:

> *the problem is that little attempt has been made to relate the abstract philosophical arguments of the 1970s and 1980s to the more practical problems of stating operational criteria for sustainable living in the 1990s. Especially, philosophers have had little to say about specifying a* metric *by which progress – or lack thereof – toward sustainability can be measured. (Norton, 2003, p420, emphasis original).*

If you replace 'sustainability' by 'intergenerational justice' here, it is precisely this lacuna that Chapter 5 of my study intends to fill.

Distinguishing generational justice from sustainability

It is best to draw a distinction between 'generational justice' and 'sustainability' at this early point. According to my earlier studies (Tremmel, 2003a, 2003c, 2006a), sustainability can be defined as a concept that gives intergenerational justice the same weight as intragenerational justice on a normative level. The demand for intergenerational justice leads to two fields of activity: ecology and finances ('ecological' and 'financial' sustainability). Intragenerational justice mainly aims at international justice (adjustment of the living conditions in the North and the South), justice between the poor and the rich within a country, and justice between men and women. These contexts are referred to in Figure 1.3.

International justice is implicitly demanded by all scientists who speak of 'sustainable development', thus emphasizing the necessity to attach the development interests of the less developed countries (LDCs) to the environmental interests of the planet. Many scientists consider social justice – as a normative counterpart of the social pillar – an important constituent of the sustainability concept. Many scientists also use the term 'sustainability' to refer to gender justice (an individual chapter deals with women in the Agenda 21).

This definition of sustainability also makes it clear why far more publications can be found on sustainability than on generational justice. A theory of generational justice does not focus on questions of social justice, gender justice or international justice, but deals at best with interactions between generational justice and these other fields.

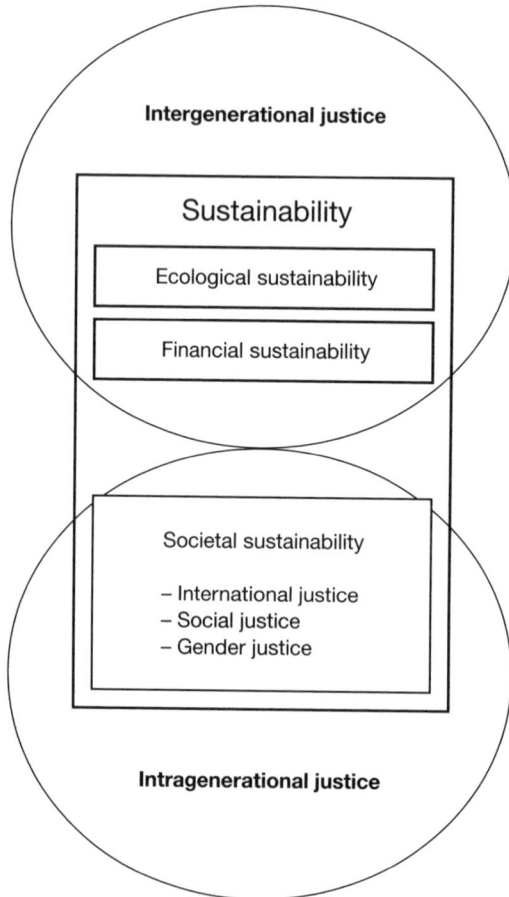

Figure 1.3 *The analytical definition of sustainability*

This study does not primarily deal with sustainability, but with generational justice.

The role of philosophy

Public debate on generational justice often centres on environmental policy, pensions policy, financial policy or even – albeit less often – on cultural or educational policy. Obviously, individual sciences such as environmental sciences, history, jurisprudence, economics, sociology or political science also deal with aspects of generational justice. What is distinctive of the philosophical approach?

Philosophy is the only science that deals directly with the question of justice. Only philosophy can give answers to questions like: what is justice and to what extent can established principles of justice be applied to the intergenerational context?

The question of generational relations reaches far. It actually involves all aspects of life within a society. It deals with the basic relations within a society that are normally taken for granted and therefore hardly reflected. It inevitably touches on the most fundamental ethical questions, for example regarding the obligations of each individual or even of mankind altogether. This brings us to the second special philosophical approach to the subject: philosophy tries to focus on the entire issue, thereby distinguishing itself from the individual sciences. Economics may determine financial bequests, but only philosophy asks: what will actually be important for future generations? Can we recognize the needs and preferences of future generations? How can the entire bequest that a generation will pass on to its successors be determined?

Furthermore, the subject 'generational justice' gives rise to certain theoretical questions regarding the identity and personality of man, discussed under the term 'non-identity paradox'. These questions can certainly not be ascribed to any individual science, but are a matter of metaphysics.

Also, epistemology is required to develop criteria for defining terms. An occasionally discussed question is whether future generations will have 'rights' or whether we have obligations to them (Beckerman, 2006, pp56–60). How can we react if one scientist claims that these questions are two sides of the same coin whereas another scientist has a different understanding of the terms and therefore disagrees? Here, epistemology is called on.

These are good reasons to include this research project in the field of philosophy. But the research topic 'intergenerational justice' certainly requires philosophy to open up towards history, jurisprudence, economics and social sciences; it is fascinating for the very reason that it defies single-discipline answers (Auerbach, 1995, pxiii). Political science (and related social sciences) can help outline a generationally just policy in various political fields. Jurisprudence may help to clarify how a long-term responsibility can be institutionally anchored. Economics can contribute generational financial balances and economic facts to support the debate on generationally just social systems. Of all sciences that are needed in addition to philosophy for a theory of generational justice, history is probably the most important one. We cannot write about generational justice without a basic knowledge of history and the living conditions of various generations.

Hence, this study is multidisciplinary. It tries to offer a fairly complete, systematic overview of the scattered literature in ethics, political science, economics and the environmental disciplines.

Outline of the book

The following chapter is a brief epistemological discussion on scientific criteria for definitions; I refer to it whenever controversial terms require clarification. In brief, the book is then divided into four main chapters: Chapter 3 focuses on comparisons between 'generations'; Chapter 4 presents arguments against theories of generational justice and their refutations; Chapter 5 asks what we should sustain – capital or well-being as an axiological goal?; then Chapter 6 asks how much we should sustain and discusses the demands of justice in the intergenerational context.

Chapter 3 deals with the fact that statements on generational justice require comparisons between generations. Yet, the term 'generation' is ambiguous. Distinctions will be drawn between 'societal', 'family-related' and 'chronological' meanings of the term 'generation'. Also, there is an examination of which of these meanings are relevant for statements on generational justice.

Before starting to develop my own theory of generational justice, I inquire in Chapter 4 if *any* theory of generational justice can be possible. In this context, the 'non-identity paradox' is discussed, as it is considered by some authors to be the most important argument against a theory of generational justice.[11] Strong objections to this argument are presented.

Afterwards, the claim that future generations cannot have rights is dealt with. Special attention is devoted to the nature of rights in general and the relationship between rights and obligations.

Chapter 5 focuses on the fact that a basic distinction must be drawn when evaluating possible alternative conditions under which future generations may have to live, that is to say whether one intends to discuss: first, which 'societal end' can be considered the axiological goal for the construction of social orders; in other words: *what* should we leave for future generations?; and second, how the described 'societal end' can be distributed in a just way; put differently, *how much* should we leave for future generations?

Let us suppose the following statement were up for discussion: 'A generationally just society is a society that satisfies its present needs without risking that future generations will not be able to satisfy theirs.'[12] First, one could ask whether 'needs' are actually the ultimate goal that matter, or second – and that would be a completely different angle of attack – one could doubt whether the distribution of possibilities to satisfy needs is just if the present generation is able to satisfy them to the same degree as future generations will be able to.

Let us turn to the first question: the term 'capital' is often used in an intergenerational context. A capital model can establish the fair bequest package we should try to leave behind for future generations if we want to maintain generational justice. 'Capital' is used as a generic term for, for example natural capital, real capital, cultural capital, social capital and other forms yet to be determined. A special aspect of the debate is whether natural capital can be replaced by artificial capital (strong vs. weak sustainability). But is capital what ultimately matters to people?

While axiological considerations are the first major topic of this book, justice theories are the second. Like many others, I put forward in Chapter 6 the view that our obligations to succeeding generations are a matter of justice, rather than of charity or supererogation (cf. De-Shalit, 1995, p11). It will be argued, however, that none of the traditional notions of justice – egalitarianism, performance-oriented, effort-oriented, need-oriented distribution or contractarian theories – can easily be applied to the intergenerational discourse. The reasons why shall be explained in detail.

Any good theory of intergenerational justice must meet two criteria: first, it has to be applicable for overlapping and non-overlapping generations. Many existing theories are limited to non-overlapping generations. They make interesting theoretical thought experiments possible, but in reality, however, generations overlap. Second, a comprehensive theory of generational justice must not be limited to only one political field such as environmental policy. Rather, it should also be applicable to financial policy, labour market policy, or educational policy. Many existing theories on generational justice are focused on environmental issues, or even limited to them.

2

Criteria-based Definitions
of Scientific Terms

Repeatedly, throughout this book, we will encounter the problem that key terms are contested. The well-considered definition of core concepts is an indispensable part of a scientific study. Nevertheless, some scientists neglect it. They spend only a few lines on justifying why they define their core concepts the way they do. The definition process is then somewhat like a black box. It takes place spontaneously, and not on the basis of intelligible criteria. Instead, this study takes a closer look at the whole object of definitions in science.[1] Among others, the terms 'generation', 'justice', 'future', 'well-being', 'happiness' and 'needs' are defined, so clear criteria will be needed.

Should scientists try to develop precise definitions at all? Definitely; it is more difficult to constructively criticize theories if they include terms that remain imprecise or ambiguous (von Savigny, 1980, p8; Opp, 2002, p131). However, the scientific community should never treat an agreed definition as final, because every definition is preliminary inasmuch as the definition process has to be repeated from time to time. Max Weber puts it this way:

> *Therefore, the history of social sciences is and remains a continuous back-and-forth movement between trying to mentally order facts by forming definitions... and the regeneration of terms on the bases altered thereby... The terms are not the* end, *but the* means *to insight regarding the important coherences from individual standpoints:* for the very reason *that the content of historical terms could change necessarily, it is important to formulate them exactly. (Weber, 1904, p207, emphasis original)*

Take for instance the term 'generation'. It is certainly one of the main topoi of humanities and social sciences. As a third category next to 'stratus' (or similar terms such as 'class' or 'background') and 'gender', the term is indispensable for mentally ordering a society. But as we will see, the sciences using this term are still in an orientation phase, according to Weber's phase model. It is often unclear what the basic concept of 'generation' is meant to designate. To pave the way for fruitful theories, the term 'generation' needs to be defined sharply, or at least more sharply than it has been defined up to now.

Four criteria for definitions

Etymologically, the term 'definition' is derived from '*fines*' (Latin for 'limit'). It means delimiting things from one another, so reality becomes describable by words. We can only cope with the world by learning to name things. As though touched by a magic wand, each thing that is given a name emerges from the wavering, undivided and incomprehensible mass that surrounds us (cf. Kamlah and Lorenzen, 1967, p5). Language opens the world up, so to speak. It greatly influences what we see as reality and the way we grasp it. This can be observed in the development of each and every child. Each new thing it learns to call by a name becomes accessible to its mind.

The following parts of a definition can now be distinguished (cf. Pawlowski, 1980, p10 et seq.):

- the definiendum (the thing to be defined), i.e. the phenomenon that needs a new name;
- the definiens (the thing that defines), i.e. the combination of words with a known meaning that determines the term to be defined;
- the definition copula that links the definiendum to the definiens and creates the equivalence.

All parts of the sentence together form the definition. For instance, in the sentence: 'Social roles are demands society makes on the holders of positions' (Dahrendorf, 1971, p13), 'social roles' is the definiendum, and 'demands society makes on the holders of positions' is the definiens. In this example sentence, the word 'are' is the copula.

In explicit definitions, the definiens includes only terms that are known or have previously been defined. A definition is much like an equation with an unknown x, the definiendum being that unknown quantity.

According to which criteria can we define terms in humanities or social sciences? If we could agree on such criteria, we would be able to exchange more sound arguments in the debate on the proper definition of contested terms than hitherto. Authors could then criticize the definition criteria of others, or their application. The most important criteria[2] are:

- the common use by a majority in the scientific community;
- the adequacy;
- the fruitfulness;
- the etymological meaning.

The common use

Many people believe that whoever wants to know what a word means must find out how it is used – that is the only way to gain insight into its meaning. Indeed, a scientist's definitions should, to a certain degree, comply with what most scientists associate with them. That is not the only criterion, but it is the most important one, because it includes all the others. Other scientists who use a term form a kind of Delphi panel on the other criteria. But is such a list of definitions truly an analytical study, or is it merely a study in the sociology of knowledge? That would insinuate that other scientists do not proceed analytically, which would surely be a daring statement. Rather, the analytical considerations of all scientists are summarized in this criterion. A definition used by a *single* scientist may be inadequate, unfruitful and contrary to its etymological meaning, but it is very unlikely that the entire scientific community should make such a mistake.

So, evaluating definitions of existing terms (and redefining them, if need be) requires knowing how these terms are commonly used. That will also reveal how ambiguous or unambiguous they are.

Adequacy

A definition should identify the essence of a concept, so it should neither be too narrow nor too broad (von Savigny, 1980, p24). To explain when a definition is too narrow or too broad, the term 'extension' must be introduced. The extension of a word is the totality of the things it designates. The extension of the term 'Cubist picture' is the totality of all Cubist pictures. So, a definition is adequate if it is neither too narrow nor too broad. In other words: the extension of the definiens must be the same as that of the definiendum. A definition is too narrow if all the objects that belong to the extension of the definiens also belong to the extension of the definiendum, but only a few of the objects that belong to the extension of the definiendum also belong to the extension of the definiens. That means that the extension of the definiens is smaller than that of the definiendum.

Here is an example for a too narrow definition: 'A dog is a poodle.' There are of course dogs that are poodles, but because of all other dog races, this definition is not adequate.[3] An example for a too broad definition, where the extension of the definiens is (far) greater than that of the definiendum, is: 'A dog is a living being.' That is true, of course, but it is too broad. A child would get a completely wrong idea of a 'dog' if it were given this definition. Third, the extension of the definiendum can cross that of the definiens. In that case, the definition would be too narrow *and* too broad at the same time. In the sentence: 'A car is an electrically driven vehicle' (cf. Pawlowski, 1980, p41), the extension of the definiendum is broader than that of the definiens because there are cars – in fact, most of them – that are driven by an internal combustion engine. However, the extension of the definiens is broader because there are electrically driven vehicles that are not cars (for example trams).

So, all three example definitions are imprecise and inadequate.[4]

Fruitfulness

The main question of each science is that of *fruitfulness*. How shall the phenomena in the world be classified, and how shall these classifications be allocated to the scientific terms in a way that patterns can be discovered that apply to the phenomena? (Pawlowski, 1980, p84). For three reasons, the task of categorizing and classifying is far more difficult in humanities and social sciences than in natural sciences.

First, in humanities, knowledge develops in a less cumulative manner than in natural sciences. Second, the phenomena humanities deal with are abstract and not corporeal. Often, intangible contents of consciousness one cannot directly observe are concerned, such as 'truth', 'control', 'democracy', 'society' or 'sustainability'. Third, the question of which of the competing definitions is the proper one is often more grimly debated in humanities and social sciences. Whoever enforces his definition gains the supremacy of interpreting – and thus the power of explaining – a phenomenon.[5]

The fruitfulness of a set of terms should therefore be examined in natural sciences first. Whether terms used in physics, chemistry and other nomological sciences are useful depends on whether they are suitable for formulating general laws that make it possible to explain and predict events.

In botany, the concept of 'anemogam (wind-dispersed) grasses' has proven very useful because it leads to many conclusions and theories. By contrast, the concept of 'tetramers' in Linné's system, describing plants with four stamens, is not very useful (Pawlowski, 1980, p89) because the fact that a plant has four stamens hardly leads to any conclusions that would imply general laws. So, this term is adequately defined (neither too broad nor too narrow), but it is barely fruitful as far as the number of theories is concerned that can be derived from it (cf. Carnap, 1959, p13).

What would be comparable examples in social sciences? After the end of the East–West conflict, there were various attempts to combine research on the 'environment' on the one hand and 'conflicts' on the other, and to introduce new terms such as 'ecological safety'. Here, too, the question is how fruitful that can be, i.e. whether such a neologism is based on a complex of problems or whether it is rather an accidental combination of problems (Brock, 1998, p39). Only in the first case would it make sense to further pursue theories that are based on the new term; otherwise, the newly developed terminology would be unfruitful. Nevertheless, if we compare this example with that of the term 'tetramer', it becomes clear that it often takes longer and is more difficult to evaluate the fruitfulness of a concept in social sciences than in natural sciences.

But in many cases, at least a preliminary evaluation is quite easy in humanities and social sciences. It surely made sense to invent the word 'sociology'[6] and thereby delimit a new science from the mass of the undivided. But it would certainly not be fruitful to create the science of 'human society and rock formations' and name it 'geo-sociology'. Such definitions are not untrue (because definitions cannot be true or false), but they are a waste of time.

Often, the play with words replaces the analysis of a complex of problems. Some peace researchers believe it is enough to link the terms 'violence' and 'poverty' to 'structural violence' instead of analysing the nexus between them. This is a shortcut to criticizing the conditions concerned but it leads to superficial scientific results. The question of the nexus between political stability and justice is neutralized in a similar definition-based way by distinguishing 'negative' and 'positive' peace, as is the analysis of the nexus between armament and economic interests by distinguishing 'military' and 'economic' security.

How can the fruitfulness of terms and concepts be determined? Only by trial and error (Opp, 2002, p135). Theories are developed by means of terms and concepts based on an intuitive supposition, and these theories must then prove resistant against attempts to falsify them.[7] The theories can only be fruitful if the concepts are, too.

Etymological meaning

To a certain degree, the definiens should comply with the original meaning of the definiendum. 'Conservative' is derived from the Latin word *'conservare'* (conserve, preserve), so it would not make sense to call a political party that seeks a radical and comprehensive change 'conservative'. Nevertheless, this criterion is rather weak because there are many words that are now used in a completely different sense than they used to when they were coined. According to the etymological meaning of the word, a 'chancellor' is a 'fence maker' (cf. Pawlowski, 1980, p45). Even the term 'philosophy', which literally means the 'love of wisdom', describes something that all individual sciences would nowadays claim for themselves. Here, too, the first definition criterion (common use in the scientific community) deviates from the fourth one (etymological meaning).

Sometimes, a term remains valid even after its original meaning turns out to be inapplicable, such as the term 'atom'. The Greek philosopher Democritus (470–360 BC) developed the theory that space consists of innumerable bodies that are too small to be perceived. He called them 'atoms', based on the Greek word *'átomos'* (the indivisible) because he considered them the smallest (and therefore indivisible) bodies.[8] But atoms are made up of even smaller particles (or elements that behave like waves). But it was not Democritus who made the mistake. What he called 'atom' should have been renamed by his successors.

It would be too hasty to draw the conclusion that the etymological meaning is irrelevant for definitions. But the examples do show that, first, the etymological meaning is only one of several criteria for definitions, and second, a discoverer ought to be careful when naming new phenomena.

A final note will lead us to the next chapter: a concept can very well be used in various scientific disciplines and be adequate and fruitful in all of them, for instance the word 'force' in physics and political science. The word 'generation' is especially tricky because there are four meanings, all of which are fruitful: the family-related, the societal, the chronological–temporal and the chronological–intertemporal meaning.[9] Let us take a closer look at them.

3

Comparisons between Generations

The ambiguity of the term 'generation'

'Generational justice' consists of the two words 'generation' and 'justice'. 'Justice' is definitely the more difficult one to define. However, the term 'generation' is also used in many different contexts and is likewise ambiguous. This chapter is an attempt to reduce its vagueness and find out how a scientific definition of the term 'generation' can be arrived at.[1]

Family generations

The etymological roots of the term 'generation' (in Latin, *'generatio'* is procreation, procreative capacity) refer to family relationships. Family generations are the members of a lineage (Kohli and Szydlik, 2000, p11; Veith, 2006, pp24–38). Therefore, they are also called 'genealogical' generations. Kin relationships are not the same as cohorts, that is why the terms 'children' and 'parents' belong to a different context than the terms 'younger' and 'older' generation. After all, there are younger and older parents. Aunts and uncles can be younger than their nieces and nephews (Laslett and Fishkin, 1992, p9). Even family members born in the same year can belong to different (family) generations, for example if a woman gives birth at the age of 36 while her twin sister gives birth at the age of 18 and her daughter does the same.

Relationships between family members can be analysed on a micro-level, for instance in psychoanalysis. Yet, the relationships between parents and their children are also examined on a macro-level with empirical social research methods, for example by family sociologists.

This first meaning of the term 'generation' is undisputed. The terms 'genealogical', 'family-related' and 'family...' are used as synonyms by the scientific community. The definition is neither too broad nor too narrow. But, apart from the family-related meaning, as I shall call it hereinafter, the term 'generation' has other meanings that cannot be explained by its etymological roots.

Societal generations

The term 'societal generation' refers to a group of people whose beliefs, attitudes or problems are homogenous.[2] In many cases, the members of the group have undergone similar fundamental political, economic or cultural experiences[3] within a certain period of time (for instance, the 'Silent Generation', the 'Flower-Power Generation', the 'Generation Jones', the 'Generation X', the 'Generation of 89', the 'Net Generation', the 'Boomerang Generation', the 'Generation Internship' and the 'Generation of 9/11').[4]

Only if there is a perception of peer personality are neighbouring age groups regarded as a single generation (Bude, 2000a, p187). Such a collective 'generation' identity can even exist among people of different origin, religion or ethnicity. Paradoxically, such people feel close without even knowing each other. 'Generations' in this sense that existed before the Second World War are also referred to as 'historical generations'. The term also plays an important role in the field of arts (e.g. the 'Romanticists') and literature ('Generation of 1898'[5] or the 'Lost Generation'[6]). In this context, the term 'generation' indicates a common style and common topics. Age is not a decisive factor in a 'societal generation'. Nevertheless, the age difference between its members is rarely more than a decade. And yet, in arts and literature, 20-year-olds can belong to the same generation as 50-year-olds.

Chronological generations

Last, but not least, there are two chronological meanings of the term 'generation'.[7] They are common in English, German and other languages:

1 **Chronological–temporal**
   First, 'generation' can refer to an age group, i.e. the young, middle-aged or old people in a society. In this sense, several generations always live at the same time.[8] People below 30 are usually considered 'the young generation', whereas those between 30 and 60 represent 'the middle-aged generation'. Seniors aged 60 and above are referred to as 'the old generation'. Smaller time brackets (years, decades, etc.) are also common. The criterion is not whether the cohorts are large or small, i.e. whether the time brackets comprise one year or 35 years, but that there are several contemporary generations. Richard Easterlin has this meaning of 'generation' in mind when he states that he uses 'generation' and 'cohort' interchangeably (Easterlin, 1980, p7). De-Shalit defines 'generation' as follows: 'A generation is a set of people who are more or less the same age and who live at the same period in history, usually regarded as having a span of thirty years' (De-Shalit, 1995, p138). And Thomson writes: 'Generation, in the sense of a birth cohort or a group defined by having been born in the same era' (Thomson, 1992, p207).
2 **Chronological–intertemporal**
   Second, the term 'generation' can refer to everyone alive today. Used in that sense, there is only one generation at a time.[9]

In Table 3.1, temporal generations are marked grey whereas intertemporal generations are marked with a double frame.

For simplification, it is assumed that generation 1 is the first generation in the history of mankind, a generation without predecessors. For further simplification, the point of time at which the considered populations are dying is assumed to coincide with point of time at which their great-grandchildren are born.

Irrelevance of societal generations for intergenerational justice theories

It is evident that theories of intergenerational justice based on a chronological meaning of the term 'generation' are possible. But what about the family-related and societal meanings of 'generation'? It does not make sense to discuss justice between societal generations because, unlike chronological or family generations, they cannot be clearly distinguished from each other. Lüscher puts the difference between societal and family-related generations this way:

> *Sociocultural-historical applications are mostly focussed on... proving the existence of generations and examining the processes that led to them. In genealogical-family discourses, on the other hand, their existence... is considered natural, and one concentrates on the way relationships are led. (Lüscher, 2005, p71).*

In Germany, there are different labels for today's young generation. Sociologists call cohorts born in Germany between 1965 and 1990 'Generation Berlin', '89er', 'Generation X', 'Generation @', and 'Cyber-', 'Techno-', 'Golf-' or 'Ally-Generation' (cf. Kohli and Szydlik, 2000, p7; Bude, 2000b). Obviously, there is no consensus about the characteristics of these cohorts. The names of earlier societal generations are also disputed. When scientists (in the UK, the US or Germany) speak of the 'Flower-Power Generation', it is not clear whether they mean only those who were between 20 and 30 in the year 1968 or those who were between 18 and 35. Or, does the term only refer to the students of the year 1968? And where did they have to study to belong to the '68er Generation'? Is the term limited to students at all? Or does it include those who read the news-papers, occasionally took part in a demonstration and were below 30 in the year 1968 (Landweer, 1996, p89)? Generational justice theories require comparisons between clearly defined generations. Birth years are suitable criteria; attitudes are not.

Moreover, 'responsibility for future generations' would certainly not be a reasonable operational concept if it referred to future *societal* generations. After all, we have no idea whether a future societal generation will be labelled the 'Generation of 2011' or perhaps the 'Generation of 2020'.

Relevance of family-related generations for intergenerational justice theories

Differently from 'societal generation', the family-related meaning of the term 'generation' is relevant to the topic of generational justice. The discourse on what children owe their parents has been going on ever since ancient times, as the fourth commandment in the bible shows. What are the links between family-related and chronological generational conflicts? People who have experienced an upsetting generational conflict with their own parents do not necessarily criticize the behaviour of the old generation in general, and vice versa. A 20 year old complaining about the injustice of the fact that the adult generation does not protect the environment probably does not mean his parents in particular. When David Thomson deplores the selfishness of the Baby Boomers in New Zealand (Thomson, 1991), he certainly does not mean to call his parents selfish. The fact that the members of the pressure group Americans for Generational Equity demand redistribution from old to young does not mean that they shun their parents at Christmas.[10] In our present society, there are fewer family-related generational conflicts than 30 years ago (cf. Haumann, 2006), whereas the collective distribution conflicts between chronological generations are becoming fiercer. According to several studies, young people believe they will receive less from the statutory pension scheme than their parents and grandparents (Opaschowski, 2004, p199; Dallinger, 2005), but that does not keep anyone from enjoying breakfast with their grandfather. A contradiction? Not if one distinguishes between chronological and family generations. I will concentrate now on chronological generations.

Temporal and intertemporal generational justice

The chronological definitions 1 and 2 are clearly relevant for the debate on generational justice. The difference between the two definitions can be illustrated by the following statement of a 61 year old: 'All around the world, my generation's high quality of life is unprecedented! The next generation will be less well off.' Given a temporal meaning, the term 'my generation' would encompass the 672 million people on earth who are currently over 60 years old. Given the wider intertemporal meaning, 'generation' would refer to the total world population.

Therefore, it is imperative to distinguish the two definitions. Unfortunately, the scientific debate on generational justice has failed to do so for a long time.

In this book, I use the term 'temporal justice between generations' for justice between young, middle-aged and old people *alive today*. Intertemporal generational justice is defined by me as justice between people who lived in the past, people alive today and people who will live in the future.

Table 3.1 *Temporal and intertemporal generations*

	Period 1	Period 2	Period 3	Period 4	...
1st generation	Young (0–30)	Middle (31–60)	Old (61–90)		
2nd generation		Young (0–30)	Middle (31–60)	Old (61–90)	
3rd generation			Young (0–30)	Middle (31–60)	Old (61–90)
4th generation				Young (0–30)	Middle (31–60)

Should we use the term 'age groups' instead of 'temporal generations'?

Some philosophers prefer to use the term 'generation' only in a chronological intertemporal sense and otherwise speak of 'age groups'.[11] Laslett, for example, writes:

> *The three age-groups into which cohorts are traditionally marshaled for the purposes of the discussion of rights, duties, and welfare flows are also, somewhat unfortunately, frequently called generations... Generations defined in this way as existing within a population of all coevals have to be held distinct from removed generations linked by the generational tricontract. (Laslett, 1992, p30)*

This proposed definition, however, is impractical. Further on, Laslett speaks of 'age-groups of the generational kind' – a rather awkward expression (Laslett, 1992, p37 et seq.). And his terminology excludes many other common expressions. For example, it would no longer be possible to say 'young generation' in scientific language. A great number of scientists refer to the question of justice between young and old as 'intergenerational justice'. Laslett's terminology does not allow him to do the same. Instead, he is forced to use the cumbersome expression 'justice between age groups and generations'. Although it makes sense to distinguish between the two chronological meanings of the term 'generation', Laslett's terminology is too artificial because it is too distant from everyday language *and* scientific language. Therefore, it violates the first criterion for the definition of scientific terms (common use).

Definition of 'future' generations

In this book, a generation is referred to as a 'future generation' if none of its members is alive at the time the reference is made. We are all subject to time's flow, so statements referring to future generations can only be made in relation to a point in time. That is illustrated by this example: as I write the following sentence, it is 2:04 pm[12] on 27 June 2009: 'On average, the first future generation will live a life that is worse than that of my generation.' The 'future generation' it refers to includes baby B that is born immediately after I have finished writing my sentence. If reader R reads the sentence two years after it was written, B no longer belongs to a 'future generation'. As shown in Table 3.1, the young generation of period 2 is a 'future generation' for the generation of period 1, namely a future temporal generation or the first third of the first future intertemporal generation. Consequently, 'future generations' should not be defined as generations that will not overlap with the lifetime of contemporaries. It is better to define 'future generations' as generations that did not exist at a certain time t_0. This definition is used here, although it differs from Golding's definition of 'future generations':

> *Obligations to future generations are distinct from the obligations we have to our presently living fellows... What is distinctive about the notion of obligations to future generations is, I think, that it refers to generations with which the possessors of the obligations cannot expect in a literal sense to share a common life. (Golding, 1980, p61 et seq.)[13]*

Whom does Golding mean by 'we'? Let us assume, a 1988-born philosophy student in Western Europe reads Golding's definition. According to life-expectancy statistics, she will live until 2069. Based on Golding's definition, she would have no moral obligations to persons born in 2050 or 2065, not even to her own children, grandchildren or great-grandchildren.

In Table 3.1, it was assumed that people die on the day their great-grandchildren are born. Considering the increasing life expectancy, however, it is more realistic to assume they live to see their great-grandchildren, at least for a few years. Table 3.2 shows the number of generations for which obligations are excluded by Golding's definition (from the vantage point of the first generation in period 1).

Table 3.2 *Generations for which obligations are excluded by Golding's definition*

	Period 1	**Period 2**	**Period 3**	**Period 4**
1st generation	Young (0–30)	Middle (31–60)	Old (61–90)	Very old (+90)
2nd generation		Young (0–30)	Middle (31–60)	Old (61–90)
3rd generation			Young (0–30)	Middle (31–60)
4th generation		No obligations exist according to Golding's definition of 'future generations'		Young (0–30)

At the time of writing this (8 April 2009), the oldest person alive is 115-year-old Gertrude Baines of the US, who was born on 6 April 1894.[14] Should life expectancy continue to rise as it has over the last 150 years, the oldest person of the birth cohort 2009 will live to an age of 130 and die in the year 2139.[15] If we were to apply Golding's definition, questions of intergenerational justice would only concern distant future generations, to be exact, people who will be born 2138 or later.

Whenever Golding's definition of 'future generations' is used, issues of inter-generationally fair social insurance systems, employment opportunities, education chances or national debt distribution are by definition banned from the realm of intergenerational justice.[16] The scope of a theory of intergenerational justice is unnecessarily restricted. The definition used in this study is more fruit-ful than that of Golding. And it is more realistic: in reality, generations overlap. Non-overlapping generations are a construct. A universally applicable theory of generational justice should include all possible comparisons between genera-tions, i.e. it must include non-overlapping generations, but not be limited to them. A theory of intergenerational justice that excludes overlapping generations is not comprehensive.

Direct and indirect comparisons of chronological generations

Obviously, the concept of generational justice involves drawing comparisons between generations. However, that is often done improperly in the scientific (and all the more in the public) debate. Basically, we must distinguish between direct and indirect comparisons (see Figure 3.1).

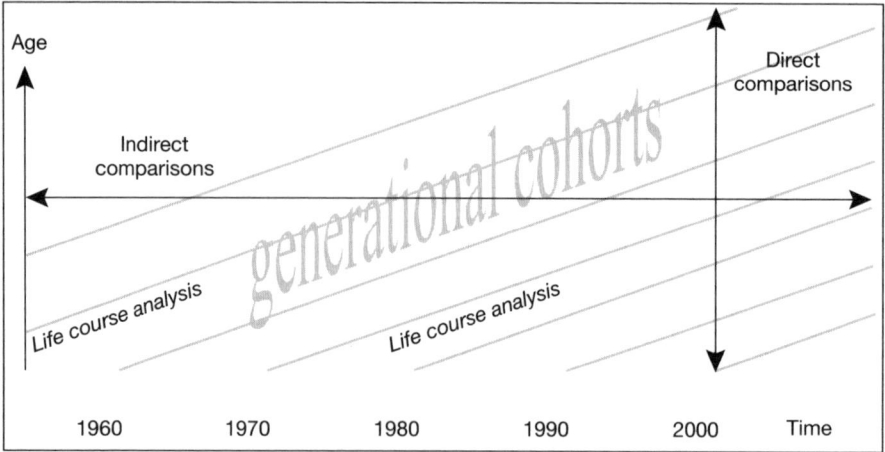

Source: Author (following the Lexis diagram)[17]

Figure 3.1 *Comparisons between generations in the Lexis diagram*

In the Lexis diagram, the vertical axis shows the age and the horizontal axis shows the flow of time. The diagonal line that starts above the birth year of a certain cohort represents its life course. The cohort born in 1960 is symbolized by the diagonal line that starts in that year; it is 10 years old in 1970, 20 years old in 1980, etc. Comparisons can either be drawn between generations at a certain point in time (for example in the year 2000)[18] or between certain age groups (for example 50 year olds). This fundamental difference is illustrated here by a two-generations model. The two hatched grey generations are compared respectively.

The direct (here: vertical) comparison is between today's 'young' and 'old', for example the percentage of members of the second (31–60 years old) and third (0–30 years old) generation who live on social security at a certain point in time (for example in 2007). This procedure is the same as with a cross-section study (see Figure 3.2).

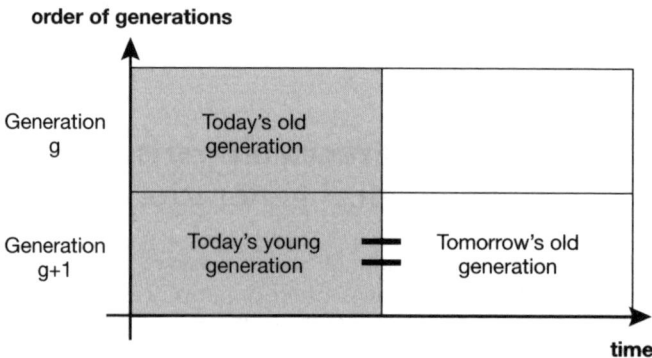

Figure 3.2 *Direct comparisons between generations*

Unlike the direct comparison, the indirect comparison (here: diagonal) compares the old with the old (see Figure 3.3) or the young with the young (see Figure 3.4).

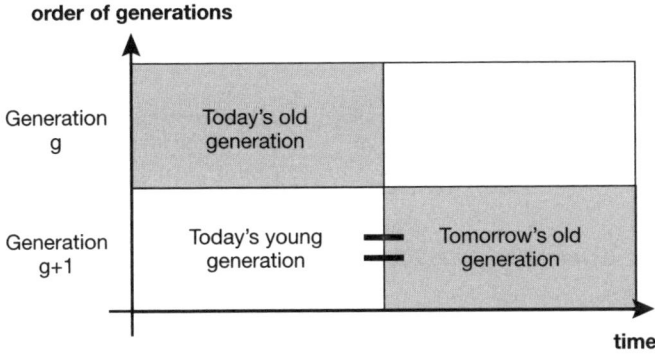

order of generations

	Today's old generation	
	Today's young generation	Tomorrow's old generation

Generation g — Today's old generation

Generation g+1 — Today's young generation ▬ Tomorrow's old generation

time

Source: Adapted from Bomsdorf (2004, p87 et seq.)

Figure 3.3 *Indirect comparisons between generations (old/old)*

For instance, Figure 3.4 might be used to show the share of young persons on social security in 2007 is compared with that in 1977 – when today's older generation was young. If less young persons were on social security 30 years ago than today, it would mean that less young people were relatively poor back then.

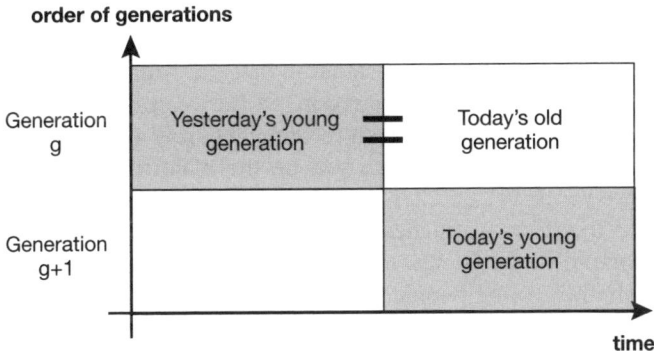

order of generations

Generation g — Yesterday's young generation ▬ Today's old generation

Generation g+1 — Today's young generation

time

Source: Adapted from Bomsdorf (2004, p87 et seq.)

Figure 3.4 *Indirect comparisons between generations (young/young)*

Neither direct nor indirect comparisons are the same as a longitudinal study in which individuals are monitored over a relatively long period of time. In the two-generations model, Figure 3.5 would be a longitudinal study. It is not a comparison between different generations. Instead, it is an observation of the same generation over time. Statements about intergenerational justice cannot be drawn directly from longitudinal comparisons.

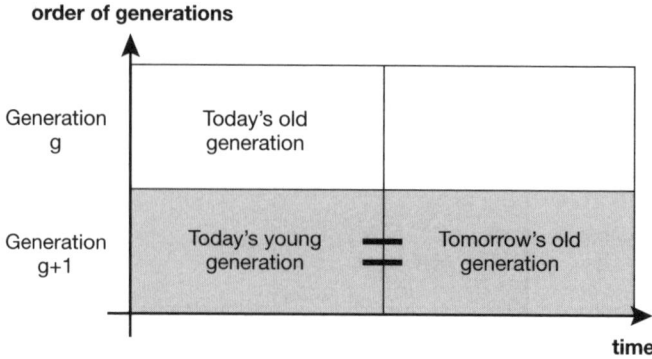

Source: Adapted from Bomsdorf (2004, p87 et seq.)

Figure 3.5 *Longitudinal comparison*

Comparisons between generations in various fields

If we apply the methods to various political fields to find out which generation is better or worse off, the results differ (see Table 3.3).[19]

Usually, questions concerning a comprehensive theory of generational justice will focus on indirect comparisons. Direct comparisons are the exception. The reason is that we age (Daniels, 1988, p18), so we belong to different age groups over the course of our life.

Unlike the sex and race groups we belong to, the (temporal) generational group we belong to changes. Over the course of our life, we are all sometimes better off, sometimes worse. Let us assume that the young generation has only half as many voters as the old generation, so they can only rarely assert their interests at elections. It would be rash to claim that it is a generational injustice. After all, in 50 years, today's youth will be the majority and dominate those people who are young in 2060. Or is it unjust that the old generation is normally wealthier than the other two generations? Not necessarily, unless young people have no chance to be in the same situation when they grow older. The crucial question is whether young people will attain the same wealth as senior citizens, once they have reached their age.

Comparisons: The field of ecology as an example

We shall now examine whether famous, exemplary statements on generational justice take the complexity of comparisons between generations into account. Ever since the beginning of the ecological movement, generational justice has been considered the most important reason for protecting the environment and nature. A famous statement by the well-known biologist Edward O. Wilson is:

> *The one process now going on that will take millions of years to correct*
> *is the loss of genetic and species diversity by the destruction of natural*

Table 3.3 *Comparisons between generations in various fields*

	Indirect comparison	Direct comparison	Background
Environmental policy Indicator: number of animal and plant species	Today's young generation is worse off than previous ones	Young and old generations are in the same situation	The number of species worldwide which people can enjoy has constantly been shrinking during the last 100 years[20]
Financial policy Indicator: total debt /GDP	Today's young generation is worse off than previous ones	Young and old generations are in the same situation	With rare exceptions, the total amount of public debt has been on the rise since the 1960s in Germany
Youth policy Indicator: suffrage (right to vote)	Today's young generation is better off than previous ones	The young generation is worse off than the old generation	Between 1949 and 1972, the voting age was 21 years, since then it has been 18 years
Labour market policy Indicators: unemployment rate among those below 25 and unemployment rate among those between 25 and 65	Today's young generation is worse off than previous ones	The young generation is slightly better off than the old generation	In Germany, the youth unemployment rate is at present (2007) much higher than 30 years ago, but it is presently slightly lower than the unemployment rate of the total population
Educational policy Indicator: percentage of GDP spent on school education	Today's young generation is worse off than previous ones	The young generation is better off than the middle-aged and old generations	The share of GDP spent on education is lower today in Germany than 30 years ago. But of course, the major part of the public resources that is channelled into education benefits the young generation, not the older ones

> habitats. *This is the folly our descendants are least likely to forgive us...*
> *For if the whole process of our life is directed toward preserving our*
> *species and personal genes, preparing for future generations is an expres-*
> *sion of the highest morality of which human beings are capable. (Wilson,*
> *1984, p121)*

To examine which meaning of the term 'generation' Wilson uses here, let us assume that the past, present and future numbers of animal species differ on account of man's interventions in nature.

The number of animal species we leave behind is part of the natural assets we pass on. The extinction of a species deprives present and future generations of its economic, medical or scientific use, as well as of the aesthetic pleasure we take in its existence.

On the assumption that the past, present and future numbers of animal species differ on account of man's interventions in nature, the situation of today's young, middle-aged and old generations would be the same (6:6:6) inasmuch as all of them would be living in a world with a smaller number of animal species than in former times (for example in the year 1700) (see Table 3.4).[21]

Table 3.4 *Comparisons between generations (example of biological diversity, millions of species)*

	18 years old	50 years old	70 years old
1700	12	12	12
1957	9	9	9
1977	8	8	8
2009 (present)	6	6	6
2041	4	4	4
2300	1	1	1

Note: Numbers are chosen randomly.

An indirect comparison leads to the following result: when those who are now 50 years old were 18, there were more animal species than today, and when those who are now 70 years old were 18, there were again more (9:8:6). An indirect comparison involving the future will show that those who are now 50 years old are better off than those who are now 18, because the latter will presumably be able to enjoy even less biodiversity when they are 50 years old (6:4).

The intertemporal perspective makes the injustice even clearer, because those living in the future (for example in the year 2300)[22] will live in a world with far less biodiversity than those living today, who are already experiencing less biodiversity than the generations that lived around the year 1700[23] (12:6:1). This is an indirect comparison because we are comparing the situation of each member of a generation at different points in time (the years 1700, 2009 and 2300). Direct comparisons cannot refer to intertemporal, non-overlapping generations because there is no reference year by which the situation of present, past and future generations could be compared.

To sum it up, the result of this example is:

- Direct comparison
  - Temporal generations: 6:6:6
  - Intertemporal generations: n/a
- Indirect comparison
  - Temporal generations: 9:8:6(:4)
  - Intertemporal generations: 12:6:1

So, we can conclude that Wilson's statement is most provoking if it is based on an *indirect* comparison between generations and an *intertemporal* meaning of the term 'generation'.

Comparison of life courses

Indirect comparisons between generations must still be refined by comparing life courses.[24] We can compare two birth cohorts by just looking at one year of their lifetime (for example a comparison of the newborns of the years 1700 and 1900); we can compare a birth cohort by looking at 30 years of their lifetime (like the 0–30 year olds who were living in 1700–1730 and 1900–1930); or we can compare two birth cohorts by looking at their total lifetime. All these are indirect comparisons, but the last one is usually the most meaningful.

A life-course analysis is a longitudinal study and will not by itself produce any statements on generational justice. But if two or more life courses are compared, statements can be derived. In Table 3.4, the number of animal species a person who is 70 years old in the year 2009 was able to enjoy dropped over the course of his life. But the *average* number (for example 7.75 million) of species she will have been able to benefit from at the end of her life will inevitably be higher than that of a person who is now 50 (for example 5.8 million) or 18 years old (for example 3.7 million). Therefore we can say that also in a comparison over the whole life course, the birth cohort of 1927 is better off than the birth cohort of 1957 or the one of 1989 (regarding the indicator of benefiting from biological diversity).

Usually life courses are compared in the debate on generational justice regarding pension schemes or health policy (Ohsmann and Stoltz, 2004, p59).[25] For instance, the statement 'The young generation is worse off, because it has a lower yield in the public pension system than the old generation' does not see a 30 year old as a 30 year old. Rather, it includes his entire estimated life expectancy, taking him into account as a 90 year old and as a 1 year old. The yield is the interest rate based on which the cash value of all payments a person has made for the statutory pension scheme during his working life equals the cash value of all payments he will receive from the statutory pension scheme when he is a pensioner.

Today, the yield is quite commonly used as an indicator for generational justice in pension systems. The Sachverständigenrat zur Begutachtung der Gesamtwirtschaftlichen Entwicklung (German Council of Experts on Economic Development) in Germany has recently published yield calculations according to which the yield of a newborn will be roughly 25 per cent lower than of a person who was born 1940 (Sachverständigenrat zur Begutachtung der Gesamtwirtschaftlichen Entwicklung, 2004, p304). The calculations by the Bundesversicherungsanstalt für Angestellte (German Federal Insurance Institute for Salaried Employees) also indicate that the yield of the younger generation in Germany will be significantly lower than that of earlier generations. According to calculations by the Bundesversicherungsanstalt für Angestellte, the yield of an unmarried man who became a pensioner on 1 January 2004 at the age of 65 is 3.96 per cent (Ohsmann and Stoltz, 2004, p62).[26] A man who is 30 years old today and will retire round about the year 2040 will only obtain a yield of 3.0 per cent (see Table 3.5).

Table 3.5 *Comparisons between life courses (example of pension scheme yields, %)*

	30 year old	40 year old	50 year old	60 year old
1975	4.0	5.0	6.5	7.6
1985	3.7	4.0	5.0	6.5
1995	3.5	3.8	4.0	5.0
2007 (present)	3.3	3.5	3.7	4.0
2015	3.2	3.3	3.4	3.5
...	...			
2035	3.0			

Note: Figures approximated.

The situation is similar in other aging welfare states, especially if they have pay-as-you-go pension schemes. In all those countries, it must be assumed that the succeeding generations will be worse off than their predecessors (Thomson, 1991).

Summary

The term 'generation' is ambiguous. Four different meanings must be distinguished. A detailed examination reveals that no meaningful statements on generational justice can be made on the basis of the societal meaning of the term 'generation'. Only the family-related and chronological meanings offer fixed reference points from which various cohorts can be compared. On the basis of the chronological meaning of the term 'generation', direct and indirect comparisons for statements on generational justice can be made. These two forms of comparison must be distinguished from simple longitudinal studies. The system developed here helps to assess the consistency and relevance of statements on generational justice.

An important result is that comparisons of life courses – a special form of indirect comparisons between generations – can grant the most meaningful information on generational justice. Here, the argument of the moral philosopher Norman Daniels (1988) comes into play, stating that we all start out young and end up old, so we belong to different temporal generations over the course of our lives.

4

Objections to Theories of Generational Justice

Before starting to develop my own theory of intergenerational justice, I want to find out whether any theory of intergenerational justice is possible at all. In this context, the 'non-identity paradox' will be discussed, as it is considered by some authors to be the most important argument against us having obligations to posterity. Strong objections against this line of reasoning will be brought forward. Afterwards, the claim that future generations cannot have rights will be dealt with. Special attention is devoted to the nature of rights in general and the relationship between rights and obligations.

Non-identity problem

Ever since the late 1970s,[1] a special problem has been discussed under the keywords 'non-identity problem' (Parfit, 1987, p359) or 'future individual paradox' (Kavka, 1982). According to Unnerstall (1999, p20), this problem is so substantial that it has made the philosophical discussion on our obligations to future generations ebb in the 1980s.[2] Mulgan (2002, p8) states that the 'non-identity challenge' is still 'plaguing present-day Western theories of intergenerational justice'.[3]

The 'non-identity thesis' reads as follows: not only do our present actions affect the conditions of life of future persons, they also affect which people (if any) will exist. We might say that the trouble with individual future persons is not that they do not exist *yet*, it is that they might not exist at all (Kavka, 1978, p192). The same action to alter the conditions of distant future life changes the roster of individuals who exist in the distant future; this is the genetic case of 'disappearing victims' and of 'disappearing beneficiaries' (Partridge, 2007, p3).

A 'same-people choice' occurs whenever our actions do not change the number and the identity of people who live (Parfit, 1987, p356). This is usually the case when we make decisions regarding our contemporaries in an intragenerational context. We make a 'different-people choice' whenever our actions determine who will exist, that is, when our decisions affect who mates with whom and when, and thus which individuals will be born in the future (Page, 2007, p133). Parfit makes the 'time-dependence claim (TDC)', which he initially formulates as: 'TDC 1: If any person had not been conceived when he was in fact conceived, it is *in fact* true that he would never have existed' (Parfit, 1987, p351, emphasis original).

Parfit wants to make his argument as strong as possible, so he takes into account that if an embryo were conceived a few days earlier or later, it would most probably be the result of a different sperm, but of the same egg. He writes: 'TDC 2: If any particular person had not been conceived within a month of the time when he was in fact conceived, he would in fact never have existed' (Parfit, 1987, p352). Parfit therefore claims that the identity of a person is at least in part constituted by his or her DNA. This can be called the 'genetic dependence claim'. '"The Genetic Dependence Claim": If any particular person had not been created from the particular genetic material from which they were in fact created, they would never have existed' (Mulgan, 2002, p6).

In this context, the debate on 'wrongful life' and 'wrongful birth' cases comes into play.[4] The former cases concern interests of children in not being born into existence under certain circumstances whereas the latter cases concern interests of parents in not giving birth to a defective child.

A standard example is that of a practitioner who is asked by prospective parents whether there is any chance that a given disease could be genetically transmitted to their child if they were to decide to conceive one at a certain point in time (Gosseries, 2004a; 2004b, p10). The doctor makes a mistake and says 'no'. The parents then decide to conceive a child. The child then turns out to be affected by the disease after all, so the parents sue the practitioner for breaching their rights. In return for the examination fee they paid, he should have informed them correctly. If we apply the 'genetic-dependence claim', the practitioner did harm the parents, but not the child because the parents would not have conceived *this* child, had they been informed correctly. In this example, it shall be assumed that the child's life is still worth living, despite the hereditary disease. It is difficult to say whether there is any such thing as a life not worth living.[5] For now, we shall assume there *is*, for instance a short life that was made of nothing but atrocious suffering. The 'non-identity problem' applies if a person has a life worth living, but claims to have been harmed by actions without which he would not have been born at all. A 'compensation for damage' requires comparing the present situation of the person concerned with the condition he would be in if the harmful action had not taken place.[6] If the former is worse than the latter, the person has been harmed. Parfit himself speaks of a 'two-state requirement' (Parfit, 1987, p487), Meyer more accurately calls this the 'better-or-worse-for-the-same-person requirement' (Meyer, 2003, p6). In the example given above, such a comparison cannot be drawn because the person would not exist without the allegedly harmful action. If we accept that non-existence cannot be considered a condition of a person, it follows that the usual concept of damage and compensation is not applicable in such cases. 'We can no longer say that the persons harmed are worse off than they otherwise would have been. Had the harmful action not occurred, the persons in question would never have come into existence', conclude Laslett and Fishkin (1992, p4).

But what has that got to do with generational justice? Gosseries establishes a connection quite clearly by describing a father who drives home from his office every evening by car and thereby pollutes the environment (Gosseries, 2004b, p11). Should his daughter reproach him for that one day, he could answer that the time he arrived home also influenced the time he had sexual intercourse with his wife. Had he commuted by bike, he would not have polluted the environment, but his daughter would not have been born, because a different sperm would have probably fused with the egg (Gosseries, 2004b, p10). The person x would have been born instead of y. According to representatives of the 'non-identity argument', it is not possible to harm future individuals (or generations made up of future individuals) as long as their lives are worth living. For, if the members of generation A would have acted differently, generation C would exist instead of generation B. If the morality of our actions depends on their consequences for particular individuals, it becomes impossible to compare the effects of two actions if two different people exist because of them (Muñiz-Fraticelli, 2005, p413). Of all of our actions, this is a key question because the 'non-identity problem' leaves intact duties to those of our descendants whose identities are beyond our influence (Page, 2007, p134). Parfit thinks 'very many' of our actions affect, directly or indirectly, our reproduction choices, without listing the actions he would not include, i.e. the decisions he believes would not influence reproduction decisions.[7] We return to this question later on.

Unconvincing arguments against the 'non-identity problem'

The 'non-identity problem' seems highly esoteric to many. It may indeed have dominated the debate on generational justice too much, but it is still a serious objection. Every theory on generational justice must meet this 'challenge'. The following arguments, however, are *not* suitable to confute the claim.

'Humans are more than their DNA'

One might object that the 'non-identity argument' only takes the genetic assets of a human being into account, but not her socialization. Without recapitulating the 'nature vs. nurture' debate, it is surely beyond dispute that a personality is not defined by its genetic code alone. But the representatives of the 'non-identity argument' do not deny that. All they say is that a person's genes *also* go into making him who he is. If, for instance, a mother had an abortion and gave birth to another child one year later, the two children would be different, even if the second child experienced the same education and socialization as the aborted one would have, had it been born. Almost certainly, it would be different in looks, height and perhaps even sex.

'There will be enough people in the future to justify our responsibilities to them'

A second objection is that there will always be enough future individuals to justify responsibility of the present generation to them. Given the current global population growth rate, it is indeed realistic to assume that there will be at least some people in the future. Provided we accept that these people, once they exist, will *then* be rights-bearers, it is justified to speak of obligations of the current generation. According to this argument, we should care for the well-being of future individuals, independently of their identities. This train of thought is correct, but in my opinion it does not solve the 'non-identity problem' because it confuses indeterminacy with contingency. The 'non-identity argument' is based on contingency rather than indeterminacy. To show that we can have responsibilities towards future people even if we do not know their identities does not disprove the claim that we cannot harm future persons that are contingent on our present actions. The indeterminacy argument is dealt with at length in the next main section of this chapter, entitled 'Future individuals cannot have rights'.

'The snowball effect of the non-identity problem is minimal'

As hinted at before, a 'non-identity problem' requires concrete actions or policies that are hostile to posterity to actually (and not only theoretically) affect the time of a conception. Using our common sense, let us ask couples with children which events made them meet. The answers will be: 'Oh, we were in the same dance class' or 'We met watching a soccer game'. Such anecdotes seem to indicate that actions or state policies hostile to posterity hardly affect times of conception.

Parfit realizes that his might be a weak point in his theory and emphasizes:

> *Suppose that we are choosing between two social or economic policies. And suppose that, on one of the two policies, the standard of living would be slightly higher over the next century... It is not true that, whatever policy we choose, the same particular people will exist in the further future. Given the effects of two such policies on the details of lives, it would increasingly over time be true that, on the different policies, people married different people. And, even in the same marriages, the children would increasingly over time be conceived at different times. (Parfit, 1987, p361 et seq.)*

But is it true that a policy can alter the 'genetic shuffle' of future meetings, matings and births in a way that the earth is soon repopulated by different individuals (Partridge, 1990, p44)? Let us do some calculations. In the last century, people decided to build nuclear power plants to largely cover our energy demands, which nowadays is often considered hostile to posterity from an environmental point of view. In how many cases did that change the time people met and conceived children? In hardly any, so it seems, except for nuclear industry workers themselves. But what about effecting an even larger scale event, say global warming?[8] Even if the greenhouse effect had directly or indirectly made a quarter of a population change its conception plans, it would take 180 years (one generation = 30 years) for a population of 80 million to be made up of different individuals completely.[9]

So, for that period of time, the 'non-identity argument' would not be fully applicable. Are 180 years a long time or not? Anyway, not long enough to get rid of the 'non-identity argument'. And the argument can be made stronger by referring to cases that might have influenced the lives and marriages of even more people, for example Hitler's decision to lead Germany into the Second World War. Between 1939 and 1945, that might have changed the time when children were conceived in more than 90 per cent of all cases in Germany.

To summarize, these three objections, like many others,[10] cannot defeat the 'non-identity-argument'.

Convincing objections against the 'non-identity challenge'

The 'your neighbour's children' argument

A generation's nuclear or energy or war policies, as described in the examples given above, are political programmes.[11] By referring to the entire generation, we speak as if every individual were jointly and severally liable for the deeds of its generation. But ultimately, the actions of identifiable individuals, not of generations, are to be judged to what extent they harmed future generations. The rejoinders against the 'non-identity argument' are much more obvious if we look at actions of individuals instead of actions of generations.

If someone pours toxic waste into a river that supplies drinking water for children, he will harm those children. If the river is contaminated for a long time, even children who have not yet been conceived will be harmed. If the polluter's own child is affected, the 'non-identity problem' will apply, but not with all the other children (see Figure 4.1). In Gosseries' example, too, not only the car driver's own daughter but all her friends are likewise harmed. The 'non-identity problem' does not apply to them, so the man's behaviour is immoral towards the members of future generations.

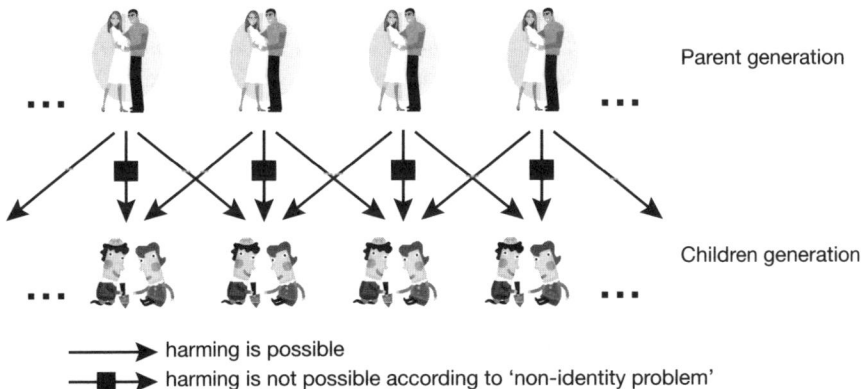

Parent generation

Children generation

harming is possible
harming is not possible according to 'non-identity problem'

Figure 4.1 *The 'your neighbour's children' argument*

To distinguish collective actions of a whole generation (political programmes) from actions of individuals reduces the scope of the 'non-identity problem' enormously, but does not refute it completely.

The 'butterfly-effect' argument

The flapping of a butterfly's wing

The above objection merely reduced the scope of the 'non-identity argument', whereas the second objection will explode it, at least with regard to theories of intergenerational justice. The 'non-identity thesis' can be rephrased as follows:

> Because of *an action by a present agent, a future individual came into existence. This action cannot have harmed this person if without it she would never have existed.*

The 'butterfly-effect' argument deals with the 'because'. The question of which egg and sperm fuse depends on countless actions, so it is misleading to pick out only one that is detrimental to a future person and hold it responsible for the conception and birth of a child. In other words: the 'non-identity argument' describes causalities that cannot be proven. That does not mean that they do not exist. In chaos theory, the flapping of a butterfly's wing in Asia can set off a tornado in the Caribbean. In the same way, one of the countless developments that take place on the day a child is conceived might have an effect on its genetic code.[12] But it is misleading to construe a monocausal relationship on the basis of such a weak multicausal connection. Let us get back to Gosseries' example. It suggests that the father could justify his ecologically harmful behaviour to his daughter with the 'non-identity argument'. Gosseries imagines the fictive dialogue between the father and his daughter to be as follows:

> *The car-driver example: Having grown 17 and having become a green activist, she asks him: 'why did you not choose the bike rather than the car? The atmosphere would be much cleaner today! And given your circumstances at that time, you had no special reason not to take the bike!'. The father may well answer: 'True. Still, had I done so, you would not be here. Since your life in such a polluted environment is still worth living, why blame me? I certainly did not harm you. Which one of your rights did I violate then?'. (Gosseries, 2004b, p11)*

But his daughter would have no reason to fall silent. She could reply:

> *Are you actually trying to tell me that your car drive was responsible for the fact that I was conceived on 14 March 2007 at 8:11 p.m. and 43 seconds? Okay, it made you get home half an hour earlier than you would have, had you gone by bike. But remember that you were running late that day anyway, because you had thrown a party the night before. And on the*

day I was conceived, you got stuck in a traffic jam for half an hour on your way home. And if you hadn't patted the cat, you would have gotten home five minutes earlier, too. And if you hadn't gone to the fridge just before you had sex with my mother, the conception would have taken place at a different point in time than it actually did. And, anyway, you wouldn't have worked such long hours, had the government not dropped a limit on working hours shortly before. And that, in turn, was done to keep up with Chinese competitors. All that, and a billion other things, is responsible for the fact that I was conceived at 8:11 p.m. and 43 seconds, far more than your taking the car. So don't try to talk your way out of it. There is no excuse for you having polluted the atmosphere.

Our existence is highly sensitive to even the most negligible antecedent events (for example looking out of the window, yawning, coughing). For at each second, a man's genetic deck of 200 million gametes is reshuffled (Partridge, 2007, p3). The proponents of the 'non-identity problem' suggest that a certain action (for example one that is hostile to posterity) of person A was causal for the identity of his successors. But the fusion of a certain egg with a sperm is the result of countless independent actions and chains of actions. It is impossible to assign identifiable effects on concrete personal identities to *certain* acts of polluting the environment. All the more, it is impossible to assign an identifiable influence on the conception of certain future persons to concrete political programmes.

The flapping of the wings of eagles and mosquitoes
We have examined the soundness of the statement 'Our present actions affect which people will exist'. With reference to the 'car-driving example', we have found that this statement is as right or wrong as the statement that the flapping of a butterfly's wings in Asia sets off a tornado in the Caribbean.

However, there are indeed cases in which there is a clear connection between a present action and the procreation of a child. Procreation requires intercourse or in-vitro fertilization, just as a clone requires cloning. The 'non-identity argument' only applies in the narrow field of reproduction medicine, for example with regard to genetic ailments of children that can (more or less) be traced back to deliberate acts of their parents.

But theories of intergenerational justice deal with other cases, namely with actions such as depleting valuable resources, incurring national debts or causing a war. In these cases, the causal link is usually as weak as the butterfly effect. However, there are cases in which the causality seems more plausible – such as the statement that the flapping of an eagle's wings can set off a tornado, so to say. And there are others in which an action that is hostile to posterity would seem to have even less influence on the identity of a future person than in the car-driving example, such as the flapping of a mosquito's wings compared to that of a butterfly's wings, if you will.

Examples comparable to the 'flapping of an eagle's wings' are mostly found in catastrophic events such as nuclear wars or other situations that cause massive repopulations, especially if there are many refugees. The causality is not strong: even a minor flu, or the alcohol consumption, of the parents at the day of conception is a more decisive factor for the genetic identity of a person than a world war. But they constitute a *stronger* causality than cases comparable to the 'flapping of a mosquito's wings'. The latter are much more common. Consider:

> *The ecological booby-trap: an irresponsible entrepreneur has toxic indus-
> trial waste buried outside the city, in an unpopulated area. Fifteen years
> later, his ten-year old son goes hiking, comes into contact with pollutants
> and falls seriously ill.*

The causality between the cause (burying industrial waste) and the effect (genetic identity of the son) is even less plausible than in the car-driver example. The circumstances on the day of the boy's conception (e.g. a romantic dinner) have a far greater effect on his genetic identity than the fact that his father had committed an ecological crime long ago.

The 'no-difference view'

We have seen that the 'non-identity paradox' only applies in reproduction cases in a narrow sense. But, would it make a moral difference if it also applied in connection with generationally just or unjust behaviour (although we have seen that it does not)? Parfit claims:

> *We may be able to remember a time when we were concerned about effects
> on future generations, but had overlooked the Non-Identity Problem. We
> may have thought that a policy like depletion would be against the inter-
> est of future people. When we saw that this was false, did we become less
> concerned about effects on future generations? (Parfit, 1987, p367)*

Parfit is mistaken in thinking that the 'non-identity problem' applies to policies such as depletion or conservation of resources. But let us ignore that and ask whether the 'non-identity paradox' makes a moral difference in strict reproduc-tion cases, in which it does apply. He says no and calls his standpoint the 'no-difference view' (Parfit, 1987, pp366–371). Consider the following example:

> *Nuclear power plant example: on account of an incident in a nuclear
> power plant, a territory is contaminated for a certain period of time with
> an isotope that can harm embryos during pregnancy. The isotope will
> disintegrate after one year; afterwards, pregnancies will be safe again. The
> government asks the entire population in that territory (1000 people) to
> refrain from procreation for one year. A woman forgets to take the pill and
> becomes pregnant. She gives birth to a slightly disabled child.*

According to the non-identity argument, the disabled child cannot reproach its parents. But the parents may still be stung with self-reproach. And other members of the community could also rightly reproach them. In their moral judgement, the people would be comparing the fate of the child with that of another child that might have existed instead and been better off. As the nuclear power plant example shows, a reproduction decision can be morally wrong, even if the conceived person would otherwise not exist and therefore cannot criticize it. But it would be *more* wrong if the harmed person could *also* criticize it. If the 'non-identity view' applies, 1000 people would have the right to criticize the woman's negligence; if not, 1001 people would (the child, too). This 1001st person is a decisive person. That the no-difference view does not hold up becomes all the clearer if we think of a scenario in which the 'non-identity problem' could not apply at all – neither to matters of generational justice, nor to strict matters of reproduction. That would be the case if we take the reincarnation view of many followers of Eastern religions, such as Hinduism, Buddhism and Jainism, as a basis. There are certain differences in the various metempsychosis notions of the religions mentioned that are too complex to be explained in detail here. Also, the element that is reincarnated (Atman) is not necessarily identical with the Western notion of 'self awareness'.[13] What matters is that, in Eastern traditions, the notion of reincarnation is dominant, whereas Western cultures primarily know and accept the 'person = body' notion. Mulgan describes one possible form of the reincarnation view:

> *each currently existing person has died and been reborn innumerable times prior to this life and will be reborn many times in the future. When a new human body is formed, a new person is not created. Rather, an already existing person is reborn. (Mulgan, 2002, p6)*

'Non-identity claims' presuppose that humans are not reborn. But if we adopt the reincarnation view, the 'non-identity paradigm' is no longer applicable. Then, the disabled child could very well reproach its parents for having harmed it, because the same person might have been born with a healthy body if it had been born one year later. That shows that 'non-identity claims' are morally relevant. To what extent must remain unanswered here, but they are certainly not irrelevant. Therefore, the 'no-difference view' is implausible. Figure 4.2 shows the overall nexus of these matters, the area of applicability of the 'non-identity argument' and its moral relevance.

Other arguments against the 'non-identity challenge'

The 'your neighbour's children' argument reduces the scope of the 'non-identity problem' significantly by distinguishing individual actions from collective actions of generations. The 'non-identity argument' only applies to an actor's own children, not to their peers in other families.

The 'butterfly-effect argument' shows that it is wrong to construe a mono-causal relationship on the basis of a weak multicausal connection. The causality

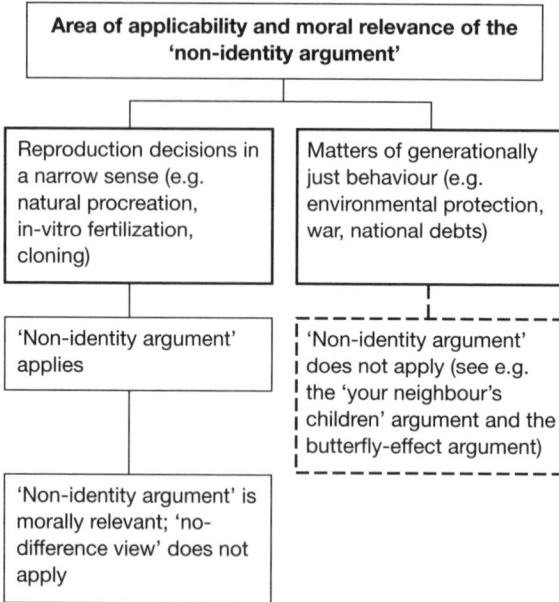

Figure 4.2 *Area of applicability and moral relevance of the 'non-identity argument'*

between concrete actions that are hostile to posterity, for example initiating a war or dumping toxic waste at sea, and the genetic identity of children is no stronger than that of the 'butterfly effect'.

I consider these two objections against the 'non-identity problem' the strongest ones, which is why I discussed them in detail. There are, however, further arguments, for example Dieter Birnbacher's 'quasi-harm argument', Axel Gosseries' 'catching-up argument' and different new interpretations of the term 'harm'.

The 'quasi-harm argument' proves that an action of reproduction in a narrow sense can be reprehensible, even if the 'non-identity argument' does not allow the reproduced child to criticize it. Up to now, we have discussed cases of individuals conceived by the fusion of a sperm with an egg, be it naturally or by artificial fertilization. Birnbacher brings up an interesting argument concerning the moral admissibility of the most controversial form of reproduction: cloning (Birnbacher, 1998, p57). Normally, a clone will accept his or her existence and find it better than not existing at all. According to the 'non-identity argument', one cannot say that a cloned person has been harmed as long as he or she has a life worth living. Birnbacher writes:

> *Surely, no one can be* harmed *by the fact that he exists... But that does not render a quasi-harm (i.e. a disadvantage without harm) bound up with the mere existence or procreation of a person morally irrelevant. One could even go further and ask whether it makes a moral difference if I (case 1) procreate A first and put him at disadvantage afterwards or if I (case*

2) procreate A under conditions that will make A end up with the same disadvantage he would have ended up with in case 1. If I clone A, knowing that A will have a major disadvantage on account of this specific way of procreation, it seems morally irrelevant whether I can say that I am harming A. Not only harming A, but his procreation with the risk of putting him at a disadvantage is also morally questionable. Therefore, it seems that the procreation of A can be reprehensible ex ante *to the degree to which there were alternatives to procreating A that would have resulted in the procreation of an individual B with significantly less disadvantage or in refraining from having genetically own children. This is even so if A does not wish to have been born without his disadvantage* ex post. *(Birnbacher, 1998, p58, emphasis original)*

Birnbacher points out that actions can be reprehensible, even if the individual who is procreated as a result will not criticize them.

Gosseries suggests an avenue that applies in some cases, for instance in the case of the father who uses the car instead of the bike:

If we consider that the fulfillment of the obligation to bequeath a 'clean' environment should be assessed at the end of each person's life (complete-life obligation), the following strategy can be envisaged. As long as the father's pro-car choice was a necessary condition for his daughter's existence, it remains unobjectionable. However, as soon as the daughter was conceived, all his subsequent polluting actions were no longer falling within the ambit of the non-identity context. Nor is there any reason to hold the view that given his pre-conceptional polluting behaviour, the father's obligation to bequeath a clean environment should be attenuated accordingly. In principle, we should expect the father to catch up as soon as his daughter has been conceived in order to be able, at the end of his life, to eventually meet the requirements of his constitutional obligation. This 'catch up' argument relies on the existence of a generational overlap. (Gosseries, 2004b, p11)[14]

Lukas Meyer's 'subjunctive-threshold' interpretation introduces a new reading of the term 'harm': 'An action (or inaction) at time t_1 harms someone only if the agent thereby causes (allows) this person's life to fall below some specified threshold' (Meyer, 2003, p7). A similar view has been defended by Woodward (1986)[15] and Page (2007). For Page, 'actions can harm (and therefore wrong) a person even if they do not render that person worse off than they would otherwise have been. This is because such actions might violate a person's specific interests and rights without endangering that person's overall well-being' (Page, 2007, p147).[16]

It is a legitimate strategy to broaden the term 'harm'. If we adopt a new interpretation, future people could indeed be wronged by a policy that is inimical to posterity, notwithstanding the fact that the policy determines their existence.

But, as shown in Chapter 2, terms, for example 'harm', cannot be redefined arbitrarily, but only according to certain criteria. Whether or not these suggested definitions meet the criteria cannot be discussed here.

One more is the fact that the Western 'body = person notion' is not the only possible way of thinking. Non-Western reincarnation views should not be ruled out from the start.[17] If they constitute what John Rawls dubs 'reasonable comprehensive doctrines' (Rawls, 1993, p59; 1999, pp573–615), the 'non-identity problem' would only apply to a possible, but by no means certain, state of affairs.[18]

To sum things up, it can be said that the 'non-identity argument' is an interesting theoretic argument that is applicable to a limited number of cases in reproductive behaviour and reproduction medicine. But it would be grossly misleading to apply it beyond this field, for instance by claiming that we cannot harm future generations by a resource-depletion policy or by driving a car instead of riding a bike. The 'non-identity problem' is not an insurmountable difficulty for a theory on generational justice.

'Future individuals cannot have rights'

So far, I have not invoked the term 'rights of future persons', instead, I spoke of 'intergenerational justice'.[19] I did not couch my line of argument in human rights language, which is so often employed when it comes to future persons. I believe it is possible to formulate a theory of intergenerational justice without employing the term 'rights'. Compare the sentence 'We should respect the rights of future persons' with the following sentences:

- 'We should respect the just claims (the interests, the needs, the preferences) of future persons.'
- 'We should not be unjust (unfair) to future persons.'
- 'We should meet our obligations to future persons.'
- 'We should not harm future persons.'
- 'We should not wrong future persons.'
- 'We should not act immorally towards future persons.'

If it could be ascertained that at least a few of these sentences constitute valid ethical norms, a theory of intergenerational justice would be possible. Even if it were true that future generations cannot be said to have rights, it does not follow that it would be morally permissible to harm them.

Part 3 of Partridge's anthology *Responsibilites to Future Generations* (1980a) discusses whether future generations can be said to have rights.[20] The editor puts paramount importance on this question:

> *Thus, if future generations have rights-claims against us, they will have no cause to be 'grateful' to us for preserving a viable ecosystem; for they will have received their due. On the other hand, if we violate this duty, their*

appropriate response will be not simply regret *but moral* indignation.
Moral duties born of rights *weigh more heavily upon the duty-bearers.*
Thus, to the degree that our policy-makers and legislators respond to valid
moral arguments, the interests of future generations will be far better
served if we can succeed in defending the notion that succeeding genera-
tions have rights-claims against the living who, in turn, have the moral
duty to respect and respond to these rights. (Partridge, 1980b, p136,
emphasis original).[21]

I do not agree that the attribution of rights makes all that much difference with
regard to duties to future generations, and I will explain why. In this chapter,
how far the 'rights approach' carries with regard to future persons is nevertheless examined.

Human rights discourse and ethical discourse

According to Feinberg, 'to have a right is to have a claim *to* something and
against someone, the recognition of which is called for by legal rules or, in the
case of moral rights, by the principles of an enlightened conscience' (Feinberg,
1980, p139; see also Gosepath, 2004, p231). Today's widespread concept of
rights as claim-rights goes back to Hohfeld (1919), for whom it was only one of
three concepts of rights, however. The legal theorist Jeremy Waldron writes in his
book *Theories of Rights*: 'Hohfeld's claim-right is generally regarded as coming
closest to capturing the concept of individual rights used in political morality'
(Waldron, 1984, p8). To understand rights as claims is not limited to positive
rights or entitlements. This concept also applies to negative rights (i.e. liberties)
because the rights-bearer can claim that no one should interfere with her rightful action. Thus all types of rights impose duties on others, be it duties to assist
the rights-bearer, or duties to not interfere when he exercises these rights.

Bentham puts forward the opinion that real (or enforceable) rights come
from real (or legislated) law, recognizable by the duties imposed on others, not
by normative contents of aspirational documents (Bentham, 1824; see also
Stark, 1952, p334). But most ethicists nowadays employ the term 'rights' in the
ethical sphere ('moral rights') and the legal sphere ('legal rights'). The legal and
the ethical discourse overlap, but they should be distinguished. The two intersecting circles in Figure 4.3 show the relationship between laws and ethical
norms.

Three cases are possible. First, there are ethical norms that are not embedded
in positive law – some will be non-contextualized, others could be codified into
legal terms, but the political majority is reluctant to do so. Norms that have not
(yet) been codified are depicted by the non-overlapping part of the 'ethical
norms circle'. Second, there is the group of ethical norms that are at the same
time laws and vice versa (intersecting part of the two circles). The third case
(non-overlapping part of the 'law' circle) refers to legal norms that are not
ethical. For example, the Nuremberg Racial Laws of Hitler's 'Third Reich' were
blatantly unethical. Nevertheless, they were codified in positive law. Another

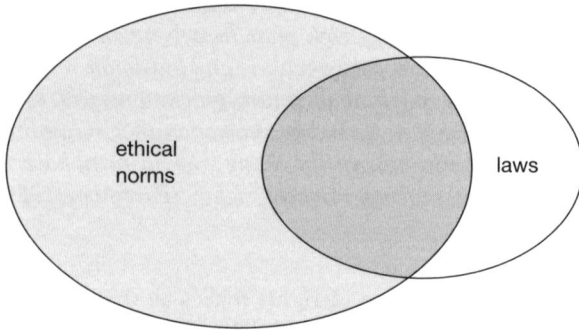

Source: adapted from Tremmel (2006b, p199)

Figure 4.3 *The relationship between ethical norms and laws*

example (still not comparable to the Nuremberg Racial Laws, but bad enough) are the apartheid laws in South Africa until 1994. They made apartheid legal, but not moral.

Can future people be said to have moral rights?

Taking a bird's-eye view, codified law is usually adjusted according to the changes in the moral convictions of a society, sooner or later. If there were a consensus that future people had moral rights, it would probably only be a question of time for these rights to be enshrined in law. So, if we could justify that future persons have moral rights, we could conclude that their moral rights will probably be embodied in a law one day. But many writers have denied that future people can have moral rights (De George, 1980, p161; Macklin, 1980, pp151–52). Winfred Beckerman (1994, 2003, 2004, 2006; Beckerman and Pasek, 2001) has long been considered the most renowned critic of all concepts based on 'rights' of future generations. Over the past years, he has also criticized theories on generational justice. As mentioned above, those are two different things. Even if one could not speak of 'rights of future generations' in a meaningful way, a meaningful theory on generational justice would be conceivable. Beckerman sums up his theses as follows:

> My argument is really very simple and can be summarized in the following syllogism:
>
> (1) Future generations – of unborn people – cannot be said to have any rights.
>
> (2) Any coherent theory of justice implies conferring rights on people.
>
> Therefore, (3) the interests of future generations cannot be protected or promoted within the framework of any theory of justice. (Beckerman, 2006, p54)

Let us first examine statement 1: the conceived but unborn child has the legal capacity to hold rights, for instance the right not to be killed if the conditions for a legal abortion are not fulfilled. But below we will exclusively deal with non-fathered, 'potential' individuals. According to Beckerman, the general proposition that future generations cannot have anything, including rights, follows from the meaning of the present tense of the verb 'to have'. 'Unborn people simply cannot *have* anything. They cannot have two legs or long hair or a taste for Mozart', Beckerman writes in the *Intergenerational Justice Review* (2004, p3, emphasis original). Beckerman's argument is correct, but of minor importance. It reminds us that we should use future tense instead of present tense, that is, to say: 'future generations will have rights' instead of 'future generations have rights'. We normally use future tense when we refer to characteristics and attributes of future people, their rights or even their noses, and rightly so. But Beckerman's argument cannot be used to denounce the term 'rights', or to replace 'rights' by 'just claims', 'needs', 'interests', 'wishes' or the like. If future generations do not have 'rights', they do not have 'interests' and so on, either. They *will* have interests, just as they will have rights. If we want to favour the term 'interests' over 'rights', we must find other arguments (Tremmel, 2004b, 2006b). The hint that we should use the future tense instead of the present tense is just a minor aspect;[22] of more importance is which nouns, verbs or adjectives are chosen. Beckerman's argument has been misunderstood in the literature as a substantial issue. In fact, it is insubstantial and would only have required some semantic clarification. His statement, the headline of this article, only needs to be rephrased.

Will future people have moral rights?

The substantial, correctly formulated questions are: 'Will future people have moral rights?' or 'Can unborn people have rights in the future?'. These questions are easy to answer, prima facie: if present people have human rights during their lifetime, so will future people. Annette Baier puts it this way: 'No one doubts that future generations, once they are present and actual, will have rights, if any of us have rights' (Baier, 1980, p171).[23] But do we believe that any of us have rights? And if yes, why? The answers to these questions will shed some light on the question of the future rights of future generations.

The origin and nature of 'rights'

The language of the human rights discourse was coined during the Age of Enlightment (Ishay, 2004, p8). It must be distinguished from older ethical concepts, for example the notion of 'justice'. The great Greek philosophers never spoke explicitly of individual or human rights. The concept of rights also does not appear explicitly either in the Hebrew Bible or the New Testament. The duties that these documents mention are owed to God. Human rights took centre stage only in the 17th and 18th centuries, in the writings of Thomas Hobbes, John Locke or Jean-Jacques Rousseau. The idea of rights gained broad acceptance during the 18th century when the *American Declaration of Independence* (1776) proclaimed that all men are endowed by their Creator with certain unalienable rights, that among these are life, liberty and the pursuit of happiness. A few years later, the French revolutionists drew up the *Declaration of the Rights of Man and Citizen* (1789). Of course, there were important documents before, such as the British *Bill of Rights* (1689),[24] but in her pathbreaking book *Inventing Human Rights*, the historian Lynn Hunt (2007) argues that the idea of unalienable rights only became convincing to political philosophers and theorists in the 18th century.[25] Not to all of them, however. The essayist and member of parliament, Edmund Burke, supported the American Revolution and agreed with the *purpose* of the human rights talk during these days, namely to protect the individual from all political games and governments (MacDonald, 1984, p21). But Burke puts his finger on the crucial question of *justification* when he writes in his pamphlet *Reflections on the Revolution in France* (1790): 'We know that we have made no discoveries, and think that no discoveries are to be made, in morality' (cited in Hunt, 2007, p17). The French enlightener Marquis de Condorcet holds the opposite point of view: '[T]hese rights that are at once so sacred and so long forgotten' (cited in Hunt, 2007, p17).

Now, was the concept of rights invented or discovered? The question of whether people have rights is not comparable to the question of whether people have noses, because rights are abstract matters (De George, 1980, p159; on this question, see Gewirth, 1982). Are there natural rights? If human rights are self-evident, as claimed in the documents of 1776 or 1789, then why does this assertion have to be made at all, and why was it made only under certain conditions, thousands of years after philosophers had started debating moral questions? These questions lead us into epistemological territory that cannot be explored here. It suffices to remember that theories of justice existed long before the concept of rights was invented (or discovered) to show that the second statement in Beckerman's syllogism ('Any coherent theory of justice implies conferring rights on people') is indefensible. A theory of intergenerational justice, or of any other kind of justice, does not necessarily require employing a certain rights language. The idea that the rights of man could be a *starting point* for political morality in general, and theories of justice in particular, has never gone unchallenged. 'Even in the liberal tradition, some philosophers insisted that rights could be taken seriously only if they were understood to be based on a prior theory of social and political morality such as the theory of utilitarianism', writes Waldron (1984, p1).[26] Yet, a third possible starting point for theories of justice is Kant's deontological position that bases norms on duties. The realm of morality is not confined to rights alone. That is emphasized by contemporary critics of the moral rights narrative such as Annette Baier who states:

> We do of course have legal rights, but to see them as backed by moral rights is to commit oneself to a particular version of the moral enterprise that may not be the best version. As Hegel and Marx pointed out, the language of rights commits us to questionable assumptions concerning the relation of the individual to the community, and, as Utilitarians have also pointed

out, it also commits us more than may be realistic or wise to fixing the details of our moral priorities in advance of relevant knowledge that only history can provide. (Baier, 1980, p182, footnote 1)

In fact, whatever one may think of it, in utilitarianism the criterion of utility determines whether an action is right or wrong. That is a consistent and technically advanced metaethical justification. With rights-based approaches, actions are wrong if they violate rights. But who is to decide whether there are rights in the first place? Just think of the lengthy dispute on the priority of either political and civil rights or socio-economic rights between capitalist and socialist countries (both conceptions of rights are enshrined in the *Universal Declaration of Human Rights*, published by the United Nations in 1948). In Jefferson's days, the unalienable rights did not apply to those without property, slaves, free blacks, a number of religious minorities and women (Hunt, 2007, p18). Later, a majority attributed moral rights to women. By this shift in consciousness, women 'received' these rights. The underlying conditions had not changed, but according to the collective social awareness, these 'rights' now exist. Kant says, man can and must decide by himself what is morally correct and *rightful*. Hence, the attribution of (moral) rights is only a semantic step and does not require physical changes. The attribution of rights, and thus their existence, depends on emotions as much as on reason. The claim of self-evidence of a human right strikes a chord if we feel horrified by the violation of the right in question. Up to today, it all depends on determining what is 'no longer acceptable' for a majority of people (Hunt, 2007, p26). Does that mean there are no limits to claiming new rights, as long as people are sympathetic? Could a general right to a minimum income of €2000 per month soon see the light of day? Hunt (2007, p29) writes: 'Rights remain open to question because our sense of who has rights and what those rights are constantly changes. The human rights revolution is by definition ongoing'. But people's emotions might move forward *or* backward, so we cannot be sure that ever more rights will be established. As we have seen, rights are not self-evident but a matter of convention.

Apart from empathy, are there any logical criteria for ascribing rights? It is commonly believed that an individual must have interests before he or she can become a rights-bearer (Hart, 1973, pp171–179; see also Feinberg, 1980, p142 et seq.; and Partridge, 1990). The basis for interests are needs. That is why we can ascribe rights to animals or even aliens, but not to rocks or to artifacts such as the Taj Mahal. Interests must somehow be compounded out of conations. A rights-holder must be capable of being a beneficiary in his own person, and an object without needs is incapable of being harmed or benefited. This is an important logical criterion for ascribing rights.

Needless to say, future people are not able to renounce their rights in the present. But the same applies to many contemporaries, and that does not mean they have no rights. Babies or people in a coma cannot waive their rights, but according to a broad consensus they still have rights, for example the right to live. If a starving person is too weak to express himself, he has by no means forfeited his right to be fed:

> *The fact that future subjects are not able to assert any rights they may have towards the present generation for logical reasons whereas contemporary subjects may not be able to do so for contingent reasons, cannot reasonably justify denying moral rights from the former, but not to the latter. (Birnbacher, 1988, p98)*

Thus, it would be wrong to assume that the ability to waive a right is a precondition for ascribing a right. Nor is the ability to understand what a right is and to set legal machinery in motion by one's own initiative a prerequisite for having rights (Lamont, 1946, pp83–85). For instance, the rights of infants are normally claimed and defended by appointed counsels or public agencies. Therefore, the (future) rights of persons who have not yet been born can be represented by proxies or attorneys empowered to speak in their names.

Do we have present obligations to people who will exist in the future?

Persons with indeterminate identities

It is almost undisputed that we have present obligations and responsibilities towards future persons, even if their identities are 'not yet determined'. Even critics of the rights of future persons such as Beckerman or De George freely admit that we have obligations towards them. In many respects, the distance in time resembles distance in space. Many ethically minded people feel obliged to relieve the suffering and despair of people on the other side of the earth. The enormous outpouring of aid in Europe and the US after the tsunami on 26 December 2004 with its roughly 230,000 victims is proof of this long-distance ethics. 'Location in space is not a morally relevant feature of a person, determining his worthiness for considerations or aid. Why should location in time be any different?' asks Kavka (1978, p188). In the case of future persons, indeterminacy is a result of non-actuality. In the tsunami case, we donate to people who are indeterminate to us because we believe that the agencies know best who needs the money most urgently. We often feel obligated towards indeterminate people, and it is irrelevant whether they are already born or not. I should refrain from leaving broken glass on the beach, not for the 'sake' of a particular beneficiary of that duty but to prevent possible harm to anyone (Partridge, 2007, p6).[27] Or, if I dig a mine shaft in a remote hiking area, I am obliged to cover it so no one gets hurt (Partridge, 1990, p56). In the same way, I am obliged to leave a very remote campsite neat and tidy when I leave (Pletcher, 1980, p168). And that has nothing to do with whether or not the person who might get harmed if I do not meet my obligations has already been born. If we take the moral point of view, we should care for the well-being of present *and* future individuals, independently of their identities. Muñiz-Fraticelli adds an important point:

> *Most laws, for instance, are not written with specific, identifiable individuals in mind but rather in generic language which is not identity depend-*

ent. We may not know whether Anna or Ben has bought the house on the corner, but we can be sure that whoever is now the owner is equally obligated to pay taxes on the property. Why then, to contemplate a harm to a future person, must we identify the particular individual who will actually exist in the future and not merely point out that... the category of 'future person' will not be an empty set? (Muñiz-Fraticelli, 2005, p413)

The same applies to case law: when a case is before a court, the judgement is passed to the individual, but it affects the way everybody else in the same situation would also be treated (Weston and Bach, 2009). And Partridge convincingly argues that moral principles apply to individuals by description and not denotatively; that is, due to shared general qualities and relations rather than qualities that distinguish persons as individuals, such as their genetic codes or personalities (Partridge, 2007, p6).

To cut a long story short: the indeterminacy argument does not relieve us from our obligation to take the interests and rights of future, yet-to-be-determined persons into account in our present actions.

Today, there is a broad consensus in the ethical literature (as well as in the general public opinion) that we are obliged to leave behind an intact world for future persons. Any objections against that must be well justified. One objection might be that future persons are contingent on our actions. But this objection – the 'non-identity paradox' – has already been discussed and refuted.

As mentioned, future people don't yet have rights because of their 'non-actuality'. But this does not necessarily imply that we, the present generation, cannot violate future individuals' rights today (Unnerstall, 1999, p450). That would only be the case if we conceded that present rights alone can constrain present actions (Meyer, 2003, p4). But *future* rights can also constitute *present* obligations. Imagine a freshly married couple, both of them physically able to have children, discussing whether they should stop using contraceptives in order to have a baby. It would be absurd to say that they have no obligations for the child at present. The fact that they have not picked a name for the baby yet does not affect their duties and responsibilities. Supposing the husband has travelled around the world and enjoyed himself instead of finding a job and earning money. His wife could rightly ask him to take measures to support his family when she is pregnant or on maternity leave. The unborn child will have needs, for example food and shelter, and it will have corresponding rights, such as the right to life. The parents are obliged to make sure *now* that it has a home and can be fed after birth.

An indeterminate number of future persons

If it were unlikely that the child will ever exist, the couple would have less present obligations. The same applies on a global scale. In order to assess our obligations towards future persons, we must make some assumptions about the number of future persons. How do we know if there will be any at all?

The convincing rejoinder is: probability. Excellent scientists have made state-of-the-art forecasts regarding the global population. Given the current global population growth rate, we can safely assume that there will be many people on earth over the next centuries. According to the medium scenario of the United Nations' long-range population projections, the world population will rise from nearly 7 billion in 2009 to a maximum of 9.2 billion in 2075 and then decline to 8.3 billion in 2175. The return to replacement level fertility coupled with increasing longevity in the medium scenario will produce a steadily increasing population after 2175 that will reach 9 billion by 2300 (cf. UN Population Division, 2003, p7). According to demographers, that is the most likely scenario. Demographers are still discussing whether there might be 8, 9 or 10 billion, but none of them assigns any probability to a scenario in which there will be zero people on earth in the year 2300. Let us take 9 billion as a starting point, since that is the best prognosis of the scientific community at the moment. Provided we accept that these people, once they exist, will *then* be rights-bearers, we are justified to speak of obligations of the current generation. The event that could wipe out human beings from the face of the earth to the greatest degree is a nuclear catastrophe. But that (or other man-made catastrophes) can scarcely release us from our responsibility towards future generations, because it is up to us to avoid it (Partridge, 1990, p53). We would only be relieved from our obligations if we could assume that an act of *force superieure* will eliminate mankind (for example a cataclysmic meteorite). But up to now, no such meteorite impact has ever taken place in the history of mankind.

The relationship of rights and obligations

It is undisputed that rights are somehow related to obligations or duties (Waldron, 1984, p2).[28] There are four possible relationships between rights and obligations:

1   Whenever party A[29] has an obligation in relation to party B, B has a right in relation to A. Whenever party A has a right in relation to party B, B has an obligation in relation to A (positive/positive). In this conception, rights and obligation are just two sides of a coin. They are strictly correlative.
2   Whenever party A has an obligation in relation to party B, B does not necessarily have a right in relation to A. Whenever party A has a right in relation to party B, B has an obligation in relation to A (negative/positive).
3   Whenever party A has an obligation in relation to party B, B has a right in relation to A. Whenever party A has a right in relation to party B, B does not necessarily have an obligation in relation to A (positive/negative).
4   Whenever party A has an obligation in relation to party B, B does not necessarily have a right in relation to A. Whenever party A has a right in relation to party B, B does not necessarily have an obligation in relation to A (negative/negative).

Obviously the relationship is complex. Which definition is preferable? The problem is that the community of philosophers have not yet agreed on a final definition of the terms 'moral right' and 'moral obligation'. So the definition criterion 'common use in the scientific community' (see Chapter 2) yields no clear result. There is a wide variety of opinions on these definition options among philosophers.[30] For Beckerman, it is not possible to deduce that all obligations imply rights from the proposition that all rights imply obligations (this is option 2): 'One can think of innumerable situations in which one's behaviour will be influenced by some conception of what our moral obligations are, without necessarily believing that somebody or other must have some corresponding rights' (Beckerman, 2004, p4; see also Macklin, 1980, p151).

Waldron considers but does not adopt option 3: 'I can say, for example, that a child in Somalia has a right to be fed, meaning not that some determinate individual or agency has a duty to feed him' (Waldron, 1984, p10).

I see no logical criteria that would make any of the four definition options more compelling than the others, so it is a matter of language convention.

I personally tend to opt for a strict correlation (option 1). Most authors who cling to other options do this because of moral 'in rem' rights. Bandman explains:

> *A right in personam is made against a specific or determinate person or group such as one finds in the right of a creditor against a debtor. Such rights correlate with specific duties of determinate individuals. In rem rights are not against specific nameable persons, but against the world at large. The right of an accident victim to assistance implies a duty by anyone who happens to be in a position to help is an in rem right. (Bandman, 1982, p99)[31]*

I would not speak of a 'right' of the accident victim in such a context. If we search for analogies in the sphere of legal rights (which we will treat in detail later), I see a clear correspondence between 'legal rights' and 'legal obligations' that makes definition 1 appear most conclusive (Birnbacher, 1988, p100). If an orphan has a legal right to be raised in a family, then the state is obliged to make sure he or she is adopted as soon as possible. The orphan can call on the power of the state. The alleged moral rights against 'the world in general' or rights 'in rem' correspond either to legal rights against state authorities (then legal measures can be directed to their representatives) or they are no legal rights at all. In a society, people use different wordings for their moral principles, but the language of law applies to all alike. In this particular case, this seems to be an argument to choose option 1 in the definition-making process.

Parenthetically speaking, that does not mean that party A only has rights if it also has obligations. One does not have to be a duty-bearer to be a rights-bearer. Even new-born babies have rights, but they have no obligations yet (cf. Feinberg, 1980, p141).

Unusual wordings

So far, I have listed a series of points that indicate that it makes sense to say: 'Future people will have moral rights. We are obliged to respect these rights, today.' Nevertheless, that leads to unusual wordings that shall now be discussed in more detail. We are used to employ 'rights talk' if there is at least a theoretical chance of enforcing the rights, be it by convincing others by means of moral arguments or by taking legal action.

Consider the following: tigers are now a threatened species. Suppose the people alive today were obliged to preserve them because future people will have a right to experience them. If the people alive today do not meet their obligation and tigers become extinct, will future people – perhaps in 300 years from now – have the right to see tigers in *their* present? Beckerman does not think so, and his example – slightly modified – is as follows:

> *In the case of rights to particular physical objects, like a right to see a live tiger, it is essential that the tiger exist... Thus for the proposition 'X has a right to Y' to be valid, where Y refers to some tangible object, two essential conditions have to be satisfied. First, X must exist, and second, it must be possible, in principle, to provide Y. In the case of the right of a future person to see live tigers, for example, one of these two conditions is not satisfied. He exists in* his *present (in* our *future), but tigers do not exist. And before tigers became extinct, the tigers existed but the future person did not exist. Hence, insofar as it is implausible to say that the future person* had *the right to the preservation of live tigers before this future person existed it must be implausible to say that a member of a non-existent unborn generation will have any rights to inherit any particular asset. (Based on Beckerman, 2006, p55)*[32]

It is unusual, but is it implausible? Imagine a world in which human rights *cannot* be respected. Do the people in that world have no human rights anymore? If human rights are an inherent, unalienable attribute of man, then they will not disappear the day after a disaster. Suppose members of today's generation 1 caused a nuclear catastrophe and made many future generations live in a nuclear winter. It would take roughly 1000 years (but not forever) for the radiation to drop. The radiation would reduce life expectancy to 25 to 30 years, and everyone would suffer from illness and deformity. Could future people in generation 2 only deplore the fact that they have been harmed, or could they complain that their right to live a better life has been violated? I think, they continue to have a right to a life under conditions that are fit for human beings, even if it cannot be enforced.

This is the very point that makes it difficult for many to speak of rights of future generations. Speaking of 'needs' or 'interests' of members of generation 2 would not pose a problem for many in this example. But rights that cannot be enforced, so lawyers cannot do anything about them, appear strange to many. Beckerman concludes that it would be wrong to speak of rights in such a context. I would not call it 'right' or 'wrong', but simply 'usual' or 'unusual'.

Today, there are examples of cases in which we speak of rights even if these purported rights cannot be enforced at all or at least not for a long time. Article 1 of the *Universal Declaration of Human Rights* (1948) starts as follows: 'All human beings are born free and equal in dignity and rights.' This is, of course, counterfactual. There is still a long way to go before we all live with the same dignity. Article 24 reads:

> *Everyone has the right to a standard of living adequate for the health and wellbeing of himself and of his family, including food, clothing, housing and medical care and necessary social services, and the right to security in the event of unemployment, sickness, disability, widowhood, old age or other lack of livelihood in circumstances beyond his control.*

Even in developed countries, there are many homeless people, people without health insurance, or without insurance against unemployment.

To sum it up, we often avoid allocating rights in cases in which they cannot be enforced. But there is no compelling logical reason for this language habit.

Can future people be said to have legal rights?

National constitutions

The question of whether there are legal rights of future people is an empirical one. It is correct to speak of their legal rights (and of our legal obligations to them) insofar as these rights are codified in positive law. The task is therefore to browse all national constitutions and the bodies of international law.[33] The increasing acceptance of our responsibility for posterity[34] has resulted in the fact that constitutions and constitutional drafts, especially the ones that were adopted in the last few decades, verbatim refer to generations to come. Among the countries that only recently changed their constitutions are France, Germany, Argentina, Brazil, South Africa and many Eastern European countries.[35] All these constitutional clauses of different states, worldwide, can be grouped into three categories: general provisions to protect future people, provisions to protect them in the field of ecology and provisions to protect them in the field of finances. Many states obviously deem the fields of ecology and finances so prone to intergenerational misconduct that they want to mention them explicitly (Tremmel, 2006b, p190).

If we analyse all constitutional provisions on rights, duties and responsibilities, we will notice that some speak of basic rights of each citizen while others speak of obligations (or objectives) of the state. These are two diametrically opposed positions. The first position is based on the assumption that conditions for a good life must primarily be maintained for today's generation. If that is achieved, future generations will also benefit from them (harmony thesis). According to this thesis, there should be an individual basic right to environmental protection, for example, to fortify the rights of today's citizens. This attitude is reflected by the constitutions of Argentine, Brazil, Finland, Hungary,

Latvia, Portugal and South Africa, for instance. The latter does not explicitly mention future generations, but gives every inhabitant of the country the right to a healthy and well-balanced environment. This harmony thesis basically says: 'whatever is good for today's generations is also good for future generations' (cf. Beckerman, 2006; Wallack, 2006).

The second position is based on the assumption that here is a conflict of interests between the present and future generations with regard to many environmental aspects, for instance nuclear energy or global warming (competition thesis). Today's generations can benefit by burdening future generations. In this case, a regulation would ideally mention future generations explicitly and underline our responsibility to them. If this competition thesis applies, it would be more appropriate to make the state the guardian of the interests of future people than to introduce a basic right for today's citizens. The German article 20a is based on this approach (similar in the Czech Republic, France, Greece, The Netherlands, Lithuania, Spain, Sweden and Switzerland).

In analysing the protection clauses for future generations in national constitutions, further criteria could be applied, for instance anthropocentrism vs. biocentrism. But hardly any constitutional clause is based on a biocentric world view, saying that nature has an intrinsic value, irrespective of its usefulness for man. Finally, it should be pointed out that especially countries with a very rich and glorious history, such as Italy or Greece, often mention the preservation of natural and cultural heritage in one breath.

Only three constitutions explicitly grant rights to future generations (Gosseries, 2008, p448). Article 11 in the Japanese Constitution of 1946 states that 'these fundamental human rights guaranteed to the people by this Constitution shall be conferred upon the people of this and future generations as eternal and inviolable rights'. Second, Norway's article L 110 b, al 1, as amended in 1992, specifies that:

> *every person has a right to an environment that is conducive to health and to a natural environment whose productivity and diversity are maintained. Natural resources should be managed on the basis of comprehensive long-term considerations whereby this right will be safeguarded for future generations as well.*

Third, article 7 of the Bolivian Constitution, as amended in 2002, states that all citizens have the right 'to enjoy a healthy environment, ecologically well balanced, and appropriate to their well-being, while keeping in mind the rights of future generations'.

Just recently, there have been a number of new attempts to explicitly include the rights of future generations in constitutions. During discussions on a revision of article 20a of the German Basic Law in the year 2000, Herta Däubler-Gmelin, then the Federal Minister of Justice, proposed the following supplement (new words not in italics):

To meet its responsibility towards the rights *of future generations, the state shall protect* the animals *and the natural bases of life within the framework of the constitutional order by legislation and in accordance with the law by means of the executive and legislative power. (Däubler-Gmelin, 2000, p27)*[36]

In Israel, four members of parliament applied for a basic law that should start as follows: 'The objective of this Basic Law is to protect the rights of all people, including those of future generations' (Shoham and Lamay, 2006, p280 et seq.). No matter whether these applications will be accepted or not, the trend indicates that national constitutions will increasingly include rights of future generations.

Of course, such clauses should not speak of *present* legal rights of future people (and none of them does). But all wordings such as 'the state should protect the rights of future persons' are unproblematic and avoid the 'present tense/future tense problem' that Beckerman addresses.

'Succeeding' instead of 'future' generations

Another legal innovation is the replacement of the term 'future generations' by 'succeeding generations'. Unlike the term 'future', the term 'succeeding' generations includes not only unborn generations but also present children and adolescents. In many respects, it makes no difference for a theory of an intergenerationally just distribution of resources and life-chances whether a child was born yesterday or will be born tomorrow. In both cases, it has a life to live and should be protected against intergenerational injustice. The temporal generations wielding power today (the middle and the old generation) have the option to use or conserve resources, save or dispose of wealth, secure or neglect institutions – the unborn, as much as the young, do not (Muñiz-Fraticelli, 2002, p4).[37] Imminent future generations and today's infants are on an similar level of powerlessness, thus one could talk about 'succeeding' instead of 'future' generations. If this term 'succeeding generations' were adopted in constitutional provisions or international law, children and adolescents or their parents would have the right to take legal action. The clauses would then have a concrete and judicially guaranteed effect. Then the achievement of the Filipino lawyer Antonio Oposa could be repeated; he successfully sued his government because it did nothing to stop the destruction of the rain forest in the Philippines. Forty-three children (representing succeeding generations) appeared as petitioners. The Federal Constitutional Court of the Philippines upheld the claim of the petitioners on 30 July 1993:

This case, however, has a special and novel element. Petitioners minors assert that they represent their generation as well as generations yet unborn. We find no difficulty in ruling that they can, for themselves, for others, in their generation and for succeeding generations, file a class suit. Their personality to sue on behalf of succeeding generations can only be cased on the concept of inter-generational responsibility insofar as the right to a balanced and healthful ecology is concerned. [38]

Subsequent cases did not follow into the footsteps of this one (Westra, 2006, p135). But this might change in the future.

International law

It is beyond the scope of this study to provide a comprehensive overview of the provisions to protect future generations in international law (see Brown-Weiss, 1989, pp45–119; Westra, 2006, pp135–155; Weston and Bach, 2009). However, a few important legislative landmarks shall be mentioned. Until the Second World War, international law allowed that new territories were introduced according to the principle 'first come, first serve'. Since the 1950s, this principle has been replaced by the doctrine of the common heritage of mankind with regard to a number of territories such as the high seas and the deep seabeds, outer space and the moon. The doctrine has five principal elements: non-ownership of the heritage, shared management, shared benefits, use exclusively for peaceful purposes, and conservation for mankind (Brown-Weiss, 1989, p48; Agius, 2006, pp317–323). This shift from a Hobbesian to a Kantian element in international law (Cassese, 1996, p31) is an important landmark on the way to legal clauses for the protection of the interests of future generations.[39] In 1972 in Stockholm, coming generations were explicitly mentioned at the first UN conference on environmental protection. The Stockholm Declaration (principle 1) reads:

> *Man has the fundamental right to freedom, equality and adequate conditions of life, in an environment of a quality that permits a life of dignity and wellbeing, and he bears a solemn responsibility to protect and improve the environment for present and* future generations. *(Emphasis added)*

Ever since then, international declarations have essentially included a reference to the needs of future generations, including those adopted in Rio in 1992 and Johannesburg in 2002. However, we should distinguish such references made in preambles and other non-binding sections of declarations (soft law) from those made in litigable articles of international agreements (hard law). The *UN Convention on Biological Diversity* (1992) is an example of the latter:

> *Art. 2.: 'Sustainable Use' means the use of components of biological diversity in a way and at a rate that does not lead to the long-term decline of biological diversity, thereby maintaining its potential to meet* the needs and aspirations of present and future generations. *(Emphasis added)*

Recently, the principle of 'intergenerational justice' has also been mentioned for the first time, perhaps in order to avoid the question of whether future generations have rights. In the *Berlin Commitment for Children*, the closing document of the Conference on Children in Europe and Central Asia preparing for the United Nations General Assembly Special Session on Children (May, 2001), the term 'intergenerational justice' appears in a document on international law.[40]

On 12 November 1997, United Nations Educational, Scientific and Cultural Organization (UNESCO) adopted a *Declaration on the Responsibilities of the Present Generations Towards Future Generations* at its 29th meeting.[41] It deals primarily with environmental issues (art. 4 and 5). But the protection of the human genome (art. 6), the preservation of peace (art. 9) and education (art. 10) can also be derived from it as objectives of a policy based on generational justice. The declaration was triggered by an initiative of the late French marine biologist and ecologist Jacques-Yves Cousteau, who had collected several million signatures for a 'Bill of Rights for Future Generations'.[42]

Group rights

It should not go unnoticed that the legal clauses mentioned above speak of 'future generations', thereby referring to groups of people instead of individuals. So, if 'rights' of future generations are mentioned, are these 'group rights'? Let us take a closer look at the concept of group rights.

Group rights are legal rights that all members of a group have in certain countries, solely by virtue of belonging to that group. Affirmative action programmes that grant more 'rights' to members of a particular gender, race or ethnicity (for instance in the US) are a topical example. If candidates with the same qualification apply for a job, members of certain groups must be given preference. It is important to note that this concept of group rights is not suitable for the rights of future generations.

In a second view on group rights of future generations, it suffices to think of the rights of future generations as aggregated individual rights. It is not necessary to extend the concept of rights beyond its paradigm application (Partridge, 1990, p41). The concept of rights is usually based on the needs and resulting interests of individuals. Therefore, the rights of a future generation are the same as the rights of the individual members of that generation. There is no difference between the rights of 'all those who live in the year 2300' and the rights of 'the intertemporal generation of the year 2300', because the people alive then are defined as a generation (see Chapter 3). In this view, the rights of groups are the aggregation of the rights of their members (Page, 2007, p150; cf. also Kymlicka, 1995).

A third articulation of group rights is grounded in the claim that groups possess interests – and therefore rights. Page explains:

> *Many people believe, for example, that the destruction of entire communities or cultures is bad over and above the fact that this is often accompanied by the deaths (or reductions in well-being) of their individual members. On the other hand, people are disposed to view a natural, or human originating, disaster as being more regrettable if it involves the destruction of a whole community than if it involves an identical amount of human misery though dispersed amongst strangers in different communities. (Page, 2007, p153)*

One of the leading representatives of a concept of rights of future generations in this sense of group rights is Edith Brown-Weiss. The UN commissioned her to find out whether international law must be adapted to the global ecological challenges. Her conclusion:

> *The thesis of his study is that each generation receives a natural and cultural legacy in trust from previous generations and holds it in trust for future generations. This relationship imposes upon each generation certain planetary obligations to conserve the natural and cultural resource base for future generations and also gives each generation certain planetary rights as beneficiaries of the trust to benefit from the legacy of their ancestors... For these obligations and rights to be enforceable, they must become part of international law, and of national and subnational legal systems. (Brown-Weiss, 1989, p2)*

Brown-Weiss proposes a new kind of rights, the 'planetary' or 'intergenerational' rights:

> *They are the rights which each generation has to receive the planet in no worse condition than that of the previous generation, to inherit comparable diversity in the natural and cultural resource bases, and to have equitable access to the use and benefits of the legacy (Brown-Weiss, 1989, p95; see also Delattre, 1972).*

And then: 'The planetary rights proposed here for future generations are not rights possessed by individuals. Rather they are generational rights, which can only usefully be conceived at a group level' (Brown-Weiss, 1989, p96). To explain the nature of this type of rights, Brown-Weiss continues:

> *Members of the present generation also possess planetary rights, which are rights derived from membership in the present generation to enjoy the natural resources of earth and our cultural heritage. They derive from intergenerational rights, but are enforced on an intragenerational basis. These rights are associated with corresponding duties, which members of the present generation have toward other members of the same generation. At this stage, they could be viewed as individual rights in the sense that there are identifiable interests of individuals that the rights protect. However, the remedies for violations of these rights will often benefit the rest of the generation, not only the individual, and in this sense they may be said to retain their character as group rights (Brown-Weiss, 1989, p96).*

Brown-Weiss explains that by introducing the concept of group rights she wants to evade objections (like the indeterminacy argument) against rights of future generations.[43]

We have already dealt with the two objections that the number and identity of the members of a future generation is yet unknown (glass on a beach example, mineshaft example, campsite example), and we saw that the indeterminacy argument is untenable. Since I see no convincing objections against the concept of rights of future generations in the sense of rights of individual future people, I do not think the other two interpretations of group rights of future generations are necessary. But as long as there are no inherent contradictions, group rights are also a matter of convention, not of right or wrong. Ultimately, the opinion of the majority is decisive for the allocation of rights.

Summary

No logical or conceptual error is involved in speaking about rights of members of future generations. Whom we declare a rights-bearer with regard to a moral right is a question of convention. Whom we declare a rights-bearer with regard to a legal right is an empirical question. But moral rights precede legal rights, thus the former must first be justified. To whom we ascribe such rights is a question of our empathy, of convention and definition. What we define as a moral right is largely a matter of personal sentiment and speculation. I would not go as far as Mulgan who states: 'The language of rights is problematic, although not impossible with regard to future generations' (Mulgan, 2002, p5). But I agree that rights-talk is a sometimes tricky way of discussing intergenerational justice. There are rights-based conceptions of justice (Vlastos, 1984) but they are not necessarily the most appropriate ones. Not enough effort has been made to frame theories of intergenerational justice in other terms, for instance needs-based language. After all, justice questions had been discussed before rights were invented (or discovered).

There are more important intergenerational justice issues than the question of whether future people will have 'rights'. Imagine again our newly married couple discussing whether it should stop using contraceptives in order to have a baby, and the wife saying: 'Once the baby is born, remember not to come home from work too late. Our baby has a right to spend time with you.' Is it worthwhile discussing whether or not she should have said 'need' instead of 'right' (or 'will have' instead of 'has')? In my opinion, it would make more sense to discuss how much of his time and other resources the father should spare for his child. The same applies to generations at large. Therefore, the next chapter is dedicated to the question *what* future generations will want from us. After that, we will ask *how much* we owe future generations.

5

What to Sustain? Capital or Well-being as an Axiological Goal?

Societal targets and concepts of justice

When it comes to evaluating alternative conditions under which future generations might have to live, we must distinguish whether we want to discuss, first, which 'societal end' can be considered the axiological goal for constructing social orders, or second, how the identified 'societal end' can be distributed in a *just* way.

Let us suppose, the following statement were up for discussion:

> *A society is intergenerationally just if it meets the needs of the present generation without compromising the ability of future generations to meet their own needs.*

Then, first, one could ask whether the satisfaction of 'needs' is actually the ultimate target that matters. And, second, one could doubt whether the distribution of possibilities to satisfy needs is just if the present (intertemporal) generation is able to satisfy them to the same degree as future generations will be. The former is an axiological problem, whereas the latter is a normative one.

This chapter deals with the axiologicial question of what can be considered the desirable 'societal end' when a social order is constructed. A capital-based approach is pitted against a well-being-based approach. My preliminary thesis is that the latter is preferable. But let us take a look at the capital approach first.

The capital approach

In the intergenerational context, the 'societal end' is often designed as the total value of various types of capital – far more often than in the intragenerational context. Gosseries, for instance, writes that the basket that is transferred by each generation to the next one 'contains a capital, broadly understood, which consists of a variety of elements, namely physical ones, but also technological, cultural, relational, political and other elements' (Gosseries, 2005, p40).[1] It is crucial to distinguish 'natural' from 'artificial' capital (Knaus and Renn, 1998, p45). Natural capital includes all the natural resources man can use or enjoy. Artificial capital refers to man-made values. That includes marketable goods and services, for example all technical plants, production methods, consumer goods, consultation services and financial assets. Furthermore, all social arrangements such as laws, institutions, courts, parliaments, administration systems, as well as economic and social principles are also part of the artificial capital. Then there is the so-called social capital: the quantity and quality of social contacts.

According to the capital-based approach, the quantitatively measurable heritage of each generation can be depicted as the total amount of all types of capital (for example natural, real, financial, social, cultural, human and knowledge capital) passed on from one generation to the next. That means the 'savings rate' is positive (negative) if the transferred *total* capital has increased (decreased). See Table 5.1 for an example of a balance sheet from one country in which the total captial has increased by five units in the year under review,

Which capital?

The capital-based approach poses a number of problems that do not exist with the well-being-based approach. First of all, it is heavily disputed which types of capital should be distinguished. Some authors identify the category 'knowledge capital' in addition to human capital and define it as economically relevant but non-person-bound knowledge (Kopfmüller et al, 2001, p60; Ott and Döring, 2004, p100; Hauser, 2007). This knowledge can be either be free of charge (knowledge stored in libraries) or be accessible against a fee (intellectual property rights, patents stored in patent offices). Most authors, however, do not identify knowledge capital as a separate form of capital.[4]

Furthermore, the question arises whether cultivated natural capital belongs to the category 'natural capital' or 'real capital' (which is part of the artificial capital). Cultivated natural capital is natural capital modified by man (Knaus and Renn, 1998, p446), for example aqua farms, farm animals, farmland, commercial forests in the form of monocultures, zoos, laying batteries with genetically modified chicken and so on. Cultivated as well as non-cultivated natural capital serves man in many ways, yet cultivated natural capital does not fulfil the other purposes of non-cultivated natural capital, for instance of being a habitat for wild animals.[5] In many cases, it will not be possible to answer the question of whether something is artificial or natural with a clear 'yes' or 'no', but only with 'more' or 'less' (see Birnbacher, 2006b, p7).

As far as human capital is concerned, the question is whether it includes only people's education or their health condition as well.

Heritage or legacy?

Before we take a closer look at the individual types of capital, we ought to discuss a methodological problem that affects all of them. It seems obvious that the

Table 5.1 *Forms of capital*

Type of capital	Description	Method of calculating the value at the end of the period	Example calculation	
			Year under review	Previous year
Natural capital	Biodiversity, renewable and non-renewable resources, sinks, atmosphere, ozone layer	Value at the beginning of the period – losses/ consumption + newly created natural capital	24–3+1=22	27–4+1=24
Real capital	Consumer goods, investment goods, infrastructure, buildings[2]	Value at the beginning of the period – depreciation + investments	15–1+2=16	14–1+2=15
Financial capital	Financial claims vis-à-vis foreign countries Debts vis-à-vis foreign countries[3]	Consolidated value (assets – debts) at the beginning of the period +/– changes to both	Assets: 7+2–1=8 Debts: 3+2–1=4 Financial capital (consolidated): 8–4=4	Assets: 6+2–1=7 Debts: 2+2–1=3 Financial capital (consolidated): 7–3=4
Social capital	Quality and quantity of social contacts	Value at the beginning of the period +/– changes	6–2+1=5	7–2+1=6
Human capital	Abilities and knowledge, health condition (person-bound)	Value at the beginning of the period +/– changes	14–1+5=18	11–1+4=14
Cultural capital	Institutions (political system, economic system, legal system)	Consolidated value (positive – negative cultural heritage) +/– changes to both	Positive cultural heritage 11–2+1=10 Negative cultural heritage 7+1–1=7 Cultural capital (consolidated): 10–7=3	Positive cultural heritage 12–2+1=11 Negative cultural heritage 7+1–1=7 Cultural capital (consolidated): 11–7=4
Knowledge capital	Knowledge that is not person-bound	Value at the beginning of the period +/– changes	23–1+5=27	20–1+4=23
Total			**95**	**90**

Source: Adapted from Tremmel (2006a, p12)

value at the end of the accounting period is a result of the initial value, plus the increase, minus the decrease. The structure of the initial value of some types of capital might already be heterogeneous, however. In other words, it may have positive and negative elements (that both change during the period under review). Therefore, starting with the initial capital value, we must distinguish between 'heritage' as an asset and 'legacy' as a burden.

This double character of capital becomes clear if we think of the financial and cultural capital that each generation inherits (that is why the example calculation in Table 5.1 shows consolidated values). The initial value of the financial capital, for instance, must be consolidated. That means the debts must have been deducted from the assets. Likewise, the cultural capital (especially the political order, the constitutions, the legal and economic structures) cannot be regarded as a *bonum per se*. In some respects, this form of capital is also a tough legacy. The cultural capital may appear to be relatively high in liberal democracies at the moment, but would we feel the same if we were in the shoes of a young Persian woman? She would probably not regard the institutions she has inherited from the older generation (including the lack of equal rights, political repression and dictatorial structures) as purely positive. Not all social arrangements make living together more pleasant, nor do they all pave the way for peace. Some do the exact opposite. Each constitution, legal system and tradition is a blessing for the young generation on the one hand, because it represents the achievements of the past chain of generations, but on the other hand, it is a burden, because this type of capital often has to be modernized by the young generation, a process that often triggers the resistance of the older generation.

The question of 'heritage or legacy' also has to be discussed with regard to real capital, natural capital and social capital, even if it was assumed that these types of capital can be considered pure assets in Table 5.1 without inherent negative elements (that is why the example calculation does not show consolidated values).

The standard accounting by governmental statistical offices takes all manufactured goods and services into account, but can land mines, cigarettes or violent pornography truly be regarded as positive real capital in the sense of a heritage? And what about goods (rather: bads) that are not only unethical but outright illegal, for example narcotics? Do they belong to the positive real heritage? If representatives of the capital-based approach answer in the negative, they are in for a lengthy methodological discussion on which goods are useful and which are not.

The question of whether natural capital is purely a heritage (or a legacy to a certain extent) also arises: AIDS viruses are definitely a part of nature. But aren't they rather a legacy for coming generations than a heritage? Can elements of natural capital be considered negative? The more deadly viruses are eliminated, the better? This leads us to evaluation problems between the instrumental and intrinsic value of nature that shall not be discussed any further here.[6] Nevertheless, whoever advocates the capital-based approach should be aware of them. Anti-naturalists have always pointed to the cruel side of nature; more people died of the Spanish influenza of 1918 alone than were killed during the entire First World War.

Finally, with regard to the social capital, the question is not so much whether it has a mixed structure and includes positive as well as negative elements. Rather, it is whether the same elements that can be considered positive can also be seen as not positive from a different viewpoint. If social capital were something neutral or even negative, it would not belong in the generational balance at all.

Substitution of different types of capital

The substitutability of individual types of capital by others has been broadly discussed among representatives of the capital-based approach. The extreme positions of the parties to the debate can be called 'strong sustainability' vs. 'weak sustainability'.

'Weak sustainability'

The advocates of 'weak sustainability' believe an equal or greater amount of capital is a fair intergenerational heritage, *independent of how it is composed.*[7]

The intergenerational justice maxim could then be described as follows:

> *The capital available to mankind shall increase/shall stay equal/may decrease over the course of time,*[8] *no matter which types of capital make up the total capital.*

In particular, a decrease in natural capital is considered ethically justifiable as long as it is compensated or even overcompensated by an increase in the other types of capital. It shall be possible to offset all things against each other – from coal and oil to the ozone layer, the biodiversity of wild animals, roads, cigarettes or beach shoes. That allows us to consume natural capital as long as our real-capital investments are high enough.[9] The cardinal approach makes the concept particularly appealing for economists. In principle, the extinction of an animal species and the depreciation of a car over the course of four years are treated equally.

At first sight, this approach seems to meet the manifold, plural preferences of individualized societies. But there are serious arguments against the hypothesis of unlimited substitutability.

Basic measuring problems

It is difficult to quantify social, cultural, knowledge or human capital. Therefore, the concept of 'weak sustainability' is in its practical application not based on offsetting natural against artificial capital, but only natural capital against real capital.

But can at least that be done adequately? In actual fact, real capital is fully evaluated, but of natural capital, only the elements considered appraisable are taken into account. Many economists simply put 'natural capital' on a level with non-renewable resources because, first, they are tradable and, second, they are dead matter, and many people shrink back from evaluating a living being. However, 'natural capital' comprises more than that. The following segments of nature should definitely be included in the natural capital: the atmosphere, the ozone layer, global substance cycles, the climate system, soil, individuals of animals and plants, genetic and species diversity, the groundwater, streams, lakes, forests and other ecosystems, mineral resources and fossil energy carriers.[10]

As this list shows, pricing most elements of natural capital is bound up with problems that may never be solved. Unlike real capital, most elements of natural capital are not tradable (Costanza, 2001, p126). Moreover, natural capital is complex and its components are intertwined, so it is not possible to set up a list of clearly distinct elements. The natural resource 'forest', for instance, supplies wood that can be used as production or construction material, or to obtain energy. In addition, forests protect land and water, prevent erosion and avalanches, and they have a positive influence on the regional climate. Not least, we can also use the forest as a recreation area. This multifunctionality makes it difficult to substitute it. It would be ideal if we had one or more 'replacement goods' that could adequately fulfil all the environmental purposes of each of our present multifunctional environmental goods. Realistically, however, we can at best have substitutes for fulfilling individual purposes: it is relatively easy to find construction material to replace wood, but almost impossible to replace the climate-stabilizing function of the forest (Knaus and Renn, 1998, p47).

Despite these basic difficulties, there are some approaches for evaluating natural capital.[11] 'Objective' approaches try to determine the value of natural goods on the basis of the costs of a change, while 'subjective' approaches try to derive the appreciation for natural goods from statements regarding individual preferences. In the framework of 'objective' methods, the costs for replacing the performance of a natural good by an artificial good or by another natural good are determined. With the 'subjective' methods, the money a visitor is prepared to pay to see a certain natural good is counted ('travel cost method'). Another 'subjective' method is the 'contingent valuation method'. Here, it is determined how much a test person would be willing to pay for the improvement of an environmental condition (e.g. the quality of breathable air) or, alternatively, for the prevention of a certain environmental deterioration or destruction (Kopfmüller et al, 2001, p58). To find out how much the survival of the last tigers is worth for us, for instance, one could ascertain how much mankind would be prepared to pay, i.e. our readiness not to hunt tigers and destroy their natural habitat (Weimann at al, 2003). To be consistent, however, we would also have to take future individuals into account in this calculation. After all, future generations will suffer a complete loss if the species became extinct because of our present activities. Empirical surveys examining the present intertemporal generations' readiness to pay would have to be multiplied by the number of generations that will pass until evolution has brought forth a new species. That would make most species so expensive that they would have to be preserved under all circumstances. 'Most neoclassical economists, however, have serious reservations against giving any good an "exorbitantly" or prohibitively high price', criticize ecological economists (Costanza, 2001, p127). Instead, neoclassical economists frequently discount future costs and benefits. In doing so, they implicitly suppose there was an immortal, myopic individual who would represent the continued existence of the society, and they derive a 'social discount rate' from that assumption. Yet, that is inadmissible: an individual can discount his own benefit without violating moral obligations (except maybe for obligations towards himself). But it would be immoral to discount the benefit of *others*.[12]

Probably none of the hitherto known pricing methods for non-tradable natural capital elements is right – but it would definitely be wrong not to price them at all.

Irreplaceable goods

Another argument against the substitutability thesis is that certain elements of our natural capital are essential for human life on this planet, and we will probably never be able to manufacture them artificially. There will never be substitutes for such 'primary values'. As long as there was no hole in the ozone layer, it was justified from an economic point of view to regard the ozone layer as a 'free good'. As we understand now its value for mankind's survival, we could be inclined to put a price tag on it. But what could this price tag be other than: 'indefinitely high'.[13] Pricing only makes sense with regard to marginal quantities of natural resources (Hampicke, 2001, p157).

It is clear that goods such as air and water can never be artificially manufactured but it is controversial whether it will ever be possible to artificially manufacture substitutes for non-renewable raw materials and energy carriers (Kopfmüller et al, 2001, p63). We may assume that technological progress and market processes will one day lead to substitution goods that yield the same output with a lower input. Since the outdated model assumptions in the Club of Rome bestseller *The Limits to Growth* (Meadows et al, 1972), fears of an imminent raw-material scarcity have diminished. Yet, natural resources will definitely have to be replaced by other elements of the same or of other natural resources, and not by real capital. The production or preservation of real capital depends on complementary performances of nature, as it requires the consumption of natural capital. Therefore, the plausible economic assumption that real capital and labour are substitutes does not mean that natural capital could be substituted by real capital or labour. Rather, the feature of complementarity is given. For instance, a house cannot be built with half the amount of wood, even if we have several power saws or carpenters to make up for it. Of course, we can replace wood by tiles, but that leads us to similar limits: we cannot replace tiles by masons and trowels (Costanza, 2001, p125).

Hence, certain resources are irreplaceable insofar as other goods can – at best – complement them. This is not reflected in the Cobb–Douglas functions used by most economists. They usually have the form $Y_t = f$ (capital, labour, resources) = $C^\alpha L^\beta R^\gamma$ with $\alpha+\beta+\gamma=1$. The input factor 'resources' can become infinitely small (though not zero) without keeping output from growing. This is unrealistic in many fields, for example the fishing industry or agriculture (Ott and Döring, 2004, p111 et seq.).

In summary, it can be said that a complete substitution of natural capital by real capital would extremely harm future generations. A generational balance based on the idea of 'weak sustainability' cannot yield any reasonable results. But that does not mean the 'strong sustainability' arguments were correct, as we shall now see.

'Strong sustainability'

Representatives of the 'strong sustainability' approach stress the complementary character of natural and artificial capital.[14] However, the counterthesis to the replaceability thesis examined above says that natural capital must not be substituted by other types of capital at all.[15] The counterthesis to substitutability is not complementarity, but non-substitutability. No matter how the quantity of the other types of capital develops, natural capital must remain undiminished, as an independent value for all future generations. The maxim of intergenerational justice could then be described as follows:

> *The capital available to mankind shall increase/stay equal/may decrease[16] over the course of time, but the natural capital must by all means be preserved.[17]*

Yet, this postulate has inappropriate consequences for intergenerational justice. Obviously, the first generations of mankind, much earlier than the Neolithic period, had the highest natural capital. If they had not been allowed to replace it, we would still be on the level of hunters and gatherers. The nature-philosopher Meyer-Abich recapitulates:

> *We humans are not here to leave the world as though we had never existed. As for all living beings, it is part of our nature and our life to change the world. Of course, that does not legitimise the destructive forms of life we have let ourselves in for. But only if we basically agree that man should change the world can we turn to the decisive question of which changes are appropriate for human existence and which are not. (Meyer-Abich, 1997, p247)*

We cannot live *without* nature. But the present global population of almost 7 billion cannot live on the interest of the natural capital that existed 100,000 years ago, either. 'Strong sustainability', taken seriously, means that our non-renewable resources should be preserved. These resources are limited, at least if we take only the next few millennia into consideration. Not using them at all would mean diminishing the welfare of present and future generations within that period – and that would not do generational justice to anyone (Knaus and Renn, 1998, p50; see also Hösle, 2002, p124). Therefore it makes sense to allow some consumption. But at which rate? We might be underestimating the degree to which future generations will need the resource. Or we might be overestimating it, as they might have a perfect substitute.

At first sight, a 'fund solution' appears to be an attractive alternative for future generations. It is the attempt not to distribute the *consumption*, but the *value* of the resource fairly among all future generations. On the surface, the logic seems convincing because a complete depletion of the resource is transformed into an endless series of financial income (El Serafy, 1988). From an economic point of view, the yield of the resource is divided into an income component that is consumed and a capital component that is saved or invested every year. In practice that could mean: if the state does not have a monopoly position regarding the depletion of the resource anyway, it shall cream off the profit of the mining companies by means of taxes and licence fees and invest it in a securities fund, thus transforming a non-interest-bearing asset into an interest-bearing one. The faster the resource is depleted, the faster the value of the fund will rise. The director of the Institut für Wachstum und Konjunktur (Institute for Growth and Economic Development) of Hamburg University, Bernd Lucke, recapitulates: 'The immediate and perhaps total depletion of a non-renewable resource is intergenerationally just, provided the value of the resource is made usable for all generations' (Lucke, 2002, p14).

However, experience with this strategy is less encouraging. The example of the Pacific island of Nauru shows that such a concept is not propitious (Gowdy and McDaniel, 1999).[18] Nauru has – or had – large phosphate deposits. After the island became independent in 1968, the resource was exploited almost to its limit and a fund was established that is now worth roughly US$1 billion and has been invested in the international capital markets. The generation in power justified this bold strategy with the necessity to plan ahead for future generations, but the depletion took its toll on the island's natural environment. Today, the islanders get their – relatively high, compared to the regional conditions – income from the proceeds of the fund. However, food and drinking water have to be imported, because the island can no longer provide for its population after approximately 80 per cent of its surface has been destroyed. The life expectancy of the men is only 49 years; alcoholism and diseases such as diabetes, heart complaints and high blood pressure are rampant. The extent to which the knowledge of having permanently destroyed their own environment and now being completely dependent on the proceeds of a fund (and thus on the development of the capital markets) affects their mental, spiritual and physical health remains to be further examined.

Moreover, one must ask how to protect the capital fund itself from being used up in democracies. In Norway, such a fund was established from oil proceeds, but a populist party promised to use the money for present-day purposes and was very successful in the next elections. There can be many and even normative justifications for dissolving such a fund: from the alleviation of the poverty of presently living people to the improvement of the overall economic situation or the warding off of dangers to national security. Although this option looks interesting at first sight, I believe it is bound up with more disadvantages than that of 'eking out' resources for as long as possible. In view of these doubts and the irreversibility of the process, it seems to make most sense to demand that present generations use resources as efficiently as possible. Resource productivity and recycling measures can slow down the depletion rate of non-renewable resources and extend their lifecycle as far as possible.[19]

Mediatory approaches as a solution?

All mediatory positions suppose that real and natural capital can partly be substituted and partly not. The rationale is that there are *some* (not *all*, like proponents of 'strong sustainability' say) elements and processes in nature that are so important to mankind that no generation is permitted to destroy them (Norton, 2003, p430). Substitution is admissible as long as the essential functions of natural capital are not touched. The essential substance to produce these functions is often called 'critical' natural capital (Lerch, 2001). This approach could be taken over for all types of capital; it would then be morally admissible to offset certain elements of cultural or social capital, as long as the critical elements are preserved. Would that solve the substitutability problem? Unfortunately not. It has only been shifted: if we say that some natural capital elements may be offset and others may not, we have now to determine which elements are critical. The normative notions vary, making it impossible to evaluate the elements objectively. What we consider a critical element in a certain type of capital depends on the 'options and preferences, power, and the context of the moment' (Kraemer et al, 2008). Thus, the debate will be endless.

As we can see, significant methodological difficulties arise if the term 'capital', which makes sense if used for real goods, is applied to nature. It is questionable if the language of capital is the right language to describe what natural values we should leave to future generations (Norton, 2003). Even the terms of 'investment' are fundamentally different: investments in real capital are always bound up with costs, whereas the idea of investing in natural capital seems unusual or even strange (Ott and Döring, 2004, p187). Nature often recovers by itself if it is left alone. Therefore, the 'investment' is often – though not always – idleness.[20]

Let us now take a closer look at the other forms of capital.

'Generational accounting' – a false label for a useful concept

Proper 'generational accounting' must include all types of capital. Unfortunately, however, this term is used for a method that only refers to explicit and implicit national debts. Let us take a brief look at this relatively young method. The indicators traditionally used in national budgeting, such as the net financing investment, national debts and the debt ratio, only refer to the current year or the results of past development. Future obligations of the state resulting from entitlements to benefit its citizens, so-called 'implicit national debts', are not taken into account. To rectify that, various approaches to measuring fiscal sustainability were developed in the early 1990s.

The most important ones were developed by the economists Alan Auerbach, Jagadeesh Gokhale and Laurence Kotlikoff in the US as well as by Olivier Blanchard of the Organisation for Economic Co-operation and Development (OECD).[21] Such forms of 'generational accounting' are based on intertemporal budget restrictions: over time, the state can only use up:

- the net assets it had in the initial year,
- plus the total future net payments of all present generations,
- plus the total net payments of all future generations.

The net payments are the difference between the payments individuals will make to the state and the transfers they will receive from the state in the future. It is determined how many taxes, social security contributions, levies and fees each average individual of today's cohorts will pay to the state in each year of its remaining lifetime. Then, the transfer payments (for example pension scheme, health insurance benefits, nursing care insurance benefits, children's benefits, welfare support, public education services, public goods) each individual will receive from the state in the years of his statistically remaining lifespan are deducted from the result. No sound comparison can be drawn between the age groups of present generations because a 70 year old will obviously receive more money from the state than he will pay in his remaining lifetime, because he is already a pensioner. Comparing today's newborn babies with those of future generations is interesting, however. In the first years of life, all of us start out as net receivers because we utilize the services of the educational system, then we pay more to the state than we receive as a transfer, until we finally become net receivers of state transfers again. All that is already taken into account in the net transfer payments to the zero year olds who must expect either to pay more to the state than they will get back, or vice versa, depending on the laws (for example pay-as-you-go pension system or funded system; tuition fees or free universities). The net transfer payments of a newborn child are compared to those of an average child that will be born in the future. If the future individual will pay more, the financial policy is considered intergenerationally unjust, and a sustainability gap (often referred to as fiscal gap) is ascertained. The sustainability gap shows by how much the state must lower its expenses to close the financing gap and be generationally just (Becker, 2003, p257).[22] The term 'sustainability gap' is then used as a synonym for a 'disadvantage of future generations', and far-reaching demands on politics are derived from it.

However, that conclusion is not well-founded. Justice issues are discussed in Chapter 6, but from an axiological point of view, the disadvantage of future generations cannot be derived from the development of national debts alone, but only from a total capital decrease. So-called generational accounting (which I will call from now on 'future-oriented measure for national debts') cannot provide any information on variations in capital because it compares only a few accumulated flow figures, but no stock figures. The method 'future-oriented measure for national debts' also assumes that the persons alive in the base year will enjoy the advantages of the current financial policy all their lives, despite the sustainability gap, while succeeding parallel generations will start closing that gap (intertemporal budget restriction of the state). The fact that the next generation can pass on its debts to the second next means that future generations can be just as well off as their predecessors, despite their high implicit debts.

There are more methodological issues of future-oriented measure for national debts.[23] First, financial policy and economic situation in the base year of the generational accounting process are treated as representational. That determines the result. Of course, a comparative analysis of generational balances of accounts in several consecutive base years can reduce the problem of economic fluctuations. Second, forecasts for a number of factors in several generations need to be made, such as the development of the economy, interest rates, life expectancy, birth rates and labour force participation. Depending on these forecasts, the generational accounting results will vary. Especially if demographic development prognoses are wrong, the results of what is wrongly called 'generational accounting' will change. These methodical problems limit the reliability of the 'future-oriented measure for national debts', but not to a degree that would make it worthless as an indicator for national debts. It makes sense to determine this measure in addition to the previous ones (for example debts/gross domestic product (GDP)) that have their own methodical problems.

The main point of criticism, however, is that the 'generational accounting' method does not do justice to the term. Debts – no matter how they are measured – are only a small fraction of the total capital account.

Approaches to measuring changes in total capital

Generational inheritance according to Hauser

The economist Richard Hauser has developed a more comprehensive approach that rather deserves the name 'generational accounting' (Hauser, 2004, 2007). Following the overall politico-economic calculation, Hauser works out the changes to real and financial capital between generations and at least mentions changes to other types of capital. Hauser starts from three temporal generations of 30 years each. Figure 5.1 shows the most important transfer flows between the three generations.

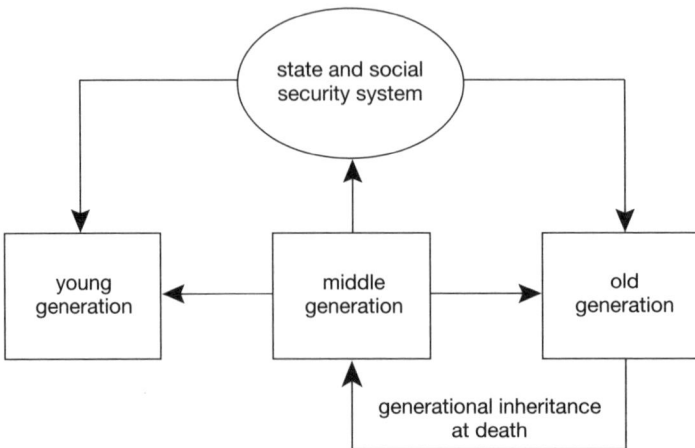

Source: Hauser (2004, p32)

Figure 5.1 *The most important transfer flows between three generations*

The generational inheritance is supposed to tell us what the older generation leaves behind for the middle generation when it dies. What did the generation that died around the year 2000 leave behind in Germany (see Table 5.2)?

Table 5.2 *Rough estimate of the generational inheritance left behind by the old generation that died around the year 2000 in Germany*

Elements of the generational inheritance	Amount at death
1) Tangible and real assets belonging to the individuals of the old generation (properties, houses, utility assets, jewellery, antiques, company shares or direct investments in companies, claims against the state or foreign countries)	1.25
2) Non-vested claims of the old generation against the middle generation on account of the pay-as-you-go system	zero
3) One-third share of the old generation in vested national debts (explicit national debts)	−0.2
4) One-third share of the old generation in the real capital held by the state (public infrastructure, environmental assets)	0.35–0.66
5) One-third share of the old generation in the assets of non-profit organizations	0.02–0.03
6) Human capital formed by the middle generation, but financed by the old generation, directly or indirectly (maintenance costs, education expenses for the young generation)	1.5
7) Contribution of the old generation to the given technological and organizational knowledge	memorandum item, unquantifiable
8) Contribution of the old generation to the constitutional state with its democratic institutions and to the development of the social security system	memorandum item, unquantifiable
Total	**2.92–3.24 more than GDP**

Source: Based on Hauser (2007, 2004, p41)

Hauser calculates the assets of the household sector. He does not list companies as an individual sector, because they either belong to the households, the state, foreign countries or non-profit organizations.[24] How does Hauser reach his values? He does not list the generational inheritance in euros or dollars, but in relation to the GDP. If item 1 (tangible assets) grows by 1.25, it grows by 25 per cent more than GDP.

Now to the individual items: from 1970 to 2003, i.e. in 33 years, the net assets of the German household sector, including non-profit organizations, climbed from €680.5 billion (thousand millions) to €8.1 trillion (a million millions) Deutsche Bundesbank, 1993, p31, 2001, p29; Hauser, 2007)[25] – nominally it increased eleven-fold. The net assets of the German household sector were twice as high as GDP in 1970, but 3.75 times higher in 2003. The household sector is made up of the young, the middle and the old generation. The households comprising the 30 cohorts of the older generation own almost 35 per cent of the total net assets recorded in this sampling (Stein, 2004). If this relation is applied to the above result – for lack of other information – we can assume that the net inheritable assets of the old generation were worth 1.25 times more than the GDP in the early 2000s (item 1).[26]

Now, the explicit debts of the public households (item 3) are juxtaposed against the considerable assets of the entire public (item 4), only a small part of which is included in the public financial reports. According to Hauser, they probably add up to one or two times the GDP, even if the evaluation problems cause uncertainty. A large share of the public debts is counterbalanced by the population's receivables, including those of the old generation. These claims are passed on to the middle generation in the form of bond issues, treasury notes, treasury bonds and such like. With regard to the state sector, there are three transfer flows from the old to the middle generation when the former dies: a legally formalized transfer of the old generation's government bonds, a fictitious transfer of the share of the total national debts previously allocated to the old generation, and a fictitious transfer of the share of the state's tangible assets previously allocated to the old generation. So, the next generation does not only inherit debts, but also claims and tangible assets. If the total claims of the old generation against the state equal its fictitious share in the total national debts, only its share in the state-owned tangible assets would be passed on, calculated net. The frequently discussed problem of children and grandchildren being burdened by national debts would no longer exist. Therefore, national debts are only a problem if they are largely owed to foreigners. If the claims against the state are mainly held by its own population, the interest payments only constitute an intragenerational redistribution from taxpayers to claim holders. Nevertheless, national debts are unacceptable if they are not used for financing investments in the public infrastructure, i.e. for increasing the state-owned tangible assets, and if the public household is unreasonably burdened by the interest payments.

Hauser allocates one third of the gross national assets and debts to each of the three generations. It would be wrong to allocate 100 per cent of the national debts to the old generation and 100 per cent of the GDP to the middle generation, as is often implicitly done in public debate, because a large share of the state-owned assets was financed by taxes paid by the old generation, and part of the national debts was spent on state-owned tangible assets that are used by all three generations (Hauser, 2007).

The human capital (item 6) of the middle generation was financed by today's old generation when both generations were in earlier phases of their lives. It is estimated that in 1990 the human capital of the overall population in Germany (old West German states) was worth €4.2 trillion, which is 3.4 times the West German GDP (Ewerhart, 2001, p134). Even if we take into account that the old generation makes up part of it and today's middle generation has also contributed to financing it, between 1.5 and 2 times the GDP can certainly be considered the accumulated transfer of today's old to today's middle generation. Plus the human capital formed in the former German Democratic Republic. These transfers already took place in the middle life phase of today's old generation, but they still have to be taken into account when we calculate the total intergenerational transfer or generational inheritance in a strict sense of the term.

Hauser regards natural, cultural and social capital as elements of the generational inheritance that cannot even be roughly estimated. But since their value is certainly not zero, he at least lists them as memorandum items.

If we add up the estimated results from Table 5.2, we reach the conclusion that the accumulated tangible and financial assets of the generation that died around the year 2000 were approximately worth three times more than the GDP. If item 6, the 'human capital accumulated with the succeeding generation', is not included in the total inheritance, it would only be worth roughly 1.5 times the GDP.

Is that more or less than that generation inherited itself? Has it achieved a positive savings rate? Hauser writes:

> *The previous generation received its generational inheritance between the late sixties and the late nineties from the generation that has now passed away. The inheritance also includes the payments made from 1940 to 1970 by the deceased generation to develop human capital in the generation that is now old. Assuming that one third of the national wealth directly or indirectly should have been allocated to the generation that has now deceased, and starting from an estimated national wealth of approximately 1.5 trillion Euros[27] in the year 1970, the generational inheritance already transferred would add up to 1.4 times the gross domestic product[28] at that time. Plus the accumulated expenses for the formation of human capital with the generation that is now old, which were presumably only a small fraction of those paid by later generations, because the participation in education was far lower and shorter then. If these accumulated education expenses are taken into account, the generational inheritance that will be passed on by today's old generation will probably be a larger multiple of the gross domestic product than the inheritance it has received. (Hauser, 2004, p42)*

Of course, that is only an estimate with many unknown quantities, because Hauser does not state a method for calculating the increase in human capital; he simply makes an assumption. Numbers on the other types of capital are not mentioned either. Hauser's calculations show that, during the last generation, the real capital probably increased by more than the GDP. That is all.

Generational inheritance according to the Economic Sustainability Indicator

A second approach for measuring the overall capital is the Economic Sustainability Indicator (ESI) by Peer Ederer, Philipp Schuller and Stephan Willms (Ederer et al, 2006). The authors present it as a measure that gives politicians and voters relevant information:

> *The simple information whether a political decision contributes or detracts from the long-term prosperity of society would allow much more effective and relevant communication on social, tax and budgetary policy or constitutional politics. The indicator makes long-term interests transparent for the citizens; it postulates the long-term goal of economic sustainability and shows the impact of any given policy on this goal; and finally it can differentiate between large and small steps towards economic sustainability. (Ederer et al, 2006, p131)*

The ESI is meant for measuring how much net capital will be handed down from current generations to future generations, compared to the net capital the current generations inherited themselves. For that purpose, the indicator defines and measures five types of positive or negative legacy: real capital, human capital, natural capital, structural capital and intergenerational debts:

1   Real capital comprises the costs of all production machinery and commercially used buildings in a society.
2   Human capital is defined as the number of all people employed in the workforce of a society, multiplied by the cost of their formal and informal education.
3   Natural capital comprises all natural resources used for the production process.
4   Structural capital is the total of all formal and informal rules and institutions a society has created to organize itself.
5   Intergenerational debts comprise all payments current generations expect from future generations, netted with the implicit cash flow embedded in private capital inheritance. In other words, the net debts or surplus of future generations towards the current generation.

If the ratio is above 100 per cent, the current generations have produced a positive savings rate; that means they have increased the stock of capital for future generations (Ederer et al, 2006, p132).

The abstract function of the ESI is:

(1) Capital inherited:
   Σ (real C + human C + natural C + structural C – debt C) per year alive

(2) Net capital created or destroyed per generation:
     Net capital handed down / net capital inherited = economic sustainability
     index in per cent

Real capital is not subdivided, as in Hauser's account. Instcad, it is calculated
with the standard formula:

(3) Cost of capital installed – depreciation + rate of expected reinvestment

and 'rate of expected reinvestment' is defined as:

(4) Domestic savings ratio × debt/equity ratio + foreign savings in/outflow

Hauser's method for measuring real capital is more detailed because Ederer et
al (2006) only mention the company sector. While Hauser does not mention
the company sector, he mentions its owners. Ederer et al do not take international transactions into account either. So, their economic system is either
closed or they refer to the whole world.

     Hauser only makes a global estimate of human capital, whereas Ederer et al
describe possible methods for measuring it in more detail. By now, there are
between 40 and 50 such methods (Scholz et al, 2004). According to Ederer et al,
these methods can be divided into the following categories: market-value measures, cost-based measures, indicator-based measures, value-added measures and
investment-return-based measures. The human-capital measuring method used
by Ederer et al for the ESI follows the logics of the real-capital measuring
method: it measures the cost of the entire human capital created, minus various
forms of depreciation, plus expected reinvestments under status-quo conditions
(Ederer et al, 2006, p132).[29] Thus the human capital stock is defined as:

(5) Human capital stock:
     Cost of human capital creation – depreciation + rate of expected human-
     capital reinvestment

Four types of human-capital expenditure are included in the above equation:

1   the cost of formal education received during schooling years,
2   the cost of formal education received through tertiary, professional or voca-
    tional training at universities, professional and vocational schools,
3   the cost of informal education received from parents (measured indirectly by
    their opportunity cost of time),
4   the cost of informal education generated during adulthood (again measured
    indirectly by the opportunity cost of time).

The depreciation of the human capital stock can be subdivided into three types:

1   education received but over time forgotten,
2   education received but over time rendered useless (for example, stenography
    courses for secretaries),

3   education received but not utilized at the workplace (a lawyer who works as a taxi driver).

Finally, according to Ederer et al (2006), the rate of reinvestment is determined by four factors:

1   the birth rate, which determines the number of people investments can be made for,
2   the education rate, which determines how much education each person receives,
3   the immigration rate, which determines the net inflow and outflow of human capital,
4   the cost of repairs invested in keeping human capital healthy and productive, in other words, health expenses aimed at increasing the amount of human capital available to the labour market (Ederer et al, 2006, p134).

This list reveals that human capital also depends on the size of the population. The larger a population is, the greater its human capital and ESI will be, *ceteris paribus*.

The third component of capital in Ederers et al's approach is natural capital. We have already discussed the difficulties bound up with weak vs. strong sustainability, and it will be interesting to find out how the authors deal with them. Unfortunately, they partly surrender right from the start:

> [O]nly to the degree that the natural resource consumption has a discernable and measurable economic impact, will it be incorporated in the calculations. It may very well be that depletion of such resources has cultural or moral implications that represent other types of losses to society, potentially even to a catastrophic extent, however, the measurement of these types of losses remain outside the scope of the Economic Sustainability Indicator. For instance, in recent years, questions have arisen in terms of whether the current level of CO_2 emissions is depleting the atmospheric resource of climate stability, on which in turn much economic activity depends. To the extent that this economic impact can be measured and calculated, such a resource depletion would have to be captured by the Economic Sustainability Indicator. In such a case, the depletion of the natural capital of 'climate stability' could be put in comparison to a potential built-up or depletion of other types of capital, human capital for instance, and thus the relative importance be established. The same applies as well to other such resources such as biodiversity or water supply. The depletion of these natural resources is only relevant to the Economic Sustainability Indicator if they have an economic impact. (Ederer et al, 2006, p136)

This defensive attitude shows that the authors do not agree with economic methods that consider the extinction of an animal species a very high loss in natural capital.

Instead of cultural or social capital, Ederer et al identify a further capital component which they call 'structural capital'. It comprises 'institutions that govern the interaction between real and human capital' (Ederer et al, 2006, p134), that is, laws, rules and regulations, cultural habits and social norms. But how can it be measured?

> *One way to measure long-term structural capital would be to apply the same logic as with real and human capital. Thus one would accumulate the costs of all public investments in building up institutions, which is mostly financed through taxes, add all the privately motivated institution building, and attempt to quantify the costs of cultural investments, both formal and informal (the latter to be measured by opportunity costs of time). From this total one would then deduct the depreciation of structural capital, measured as the rate at which institutions become inadequate over time, the degree to which they contradict and therefore neutralize each other, and the degree to which they are being ignored. However, there is to date little consensus on how to measure these aspects of structural capital. (Ederer et al, 2006, p135)*

Ederer et al suggest measuring structural capital indirectly: as the risk factor applied to expected returns on investment in human and real capital. The higher this risk factor, the lower the net structural capital available in that society. According to this method, 'failed states' have a low amount of structural capital, because nobody wants to invest money in them. This qualitative risk factor is then calibrated, so it does not subsume the differentiation of the other types of capital. According to Ederer et al, the values for structural capital turn out to be far lower than the real and human capital in the equation.

The most striking point is the denominator of the formula for calculating the ESI (1). In my methodical approach (see Table 5.1), I calculated the generational inheritance for each dying cohort, and Hauser calculated the inheritance for 30 dying cohorts together. Ederer et al, however, calculate the generational inheritance 'per year alive'. According to formula (1), the generational inheritance of a person who dies at the age of five would be 20 times higher than that of someone who lives to 100.[30] That does not make sense. The utilization of capital cannot be intensified. Apparently, Ederer et al assume that the capital is used up completely,[31] which is not the case. Their method may help accounting the situation within national security systems, but it fails when it comes to measuring the generational inheritance.

Is our present savings rate positive or negative according to the calculations of Ederer et al? In other words, is the ESI higher or lower than 100 per cent? During a presentation before members of the German Bundestag in autumn 2003, Schuller said the present generations would leave considerably less behind than they have received (Schuller, 2003). The ESI, he claims, is only 70 per cent, whereas it used to be 120 per cent in the past.[32]

So, Hauser calculated a positive generational inheritance, but Ederer et al come to the conclusion that each generation leaves less behind than it receives.

Both are only rough estimates. Our natural capital has probably decreased over the past decades, but none of the authors take that into account. After all, the quantifiable damages caused by the greenhouse effect add up to at least five per cent of GDP every year,[33] and the 27,000 animal species that become extinct each year are a grave loss of biodiversity.[34]

Besides, neither of the two approaches take cultural and social capital into account. We will now deal with these two types of capital. Why are they so difficult to record? As soon as these questions have been answered, we will know whether or not the capital approach will lead to quantitative results in the near future.

Cultural capital

Sociologists frequently use the definition of cultural capital by Pierre Bourdieu (Bourdieu, 1986, pp241–258). He distinguishes three subtypes: embodied, objectified and institutionalized cultural capital. Bourdieu considers goods (works of art, literature and culture, for example pictures, books) 'objectified cultural capital'. He calls the education, culture and articulatory powers a person obtains through socialization 'embodied cultural capital'. In Bourdieu's opinion, a well-educated person with fine manners is more cultured than others. 'Institutionalized cultural capital' is the institutional recognition of the cultural capital of an individual, mostly in the form of academic credentials or qualifications.

Bourdieu's definition cannot be used for generational accounting purposes. Cultural capital must not overlap with other types of capital in a generational balance of accounts. In the example given in Table 5.1, education is already included as 'human capital'. Books, expensive paintings, musical instruments and other objects Bourdieu refers to as 'cultural goods' are listed under 'real capital' by their market value in Table 5.1. Bourdieu's definition was not meant for generational accounting; therefore, he is not to blame for the fact that it includes too many other types of capital to be useful for generational accounting.

The definition of cultural capital I use in my generational accounting example is based on 'institutions' as defined by Rawls. They include political, legal and economic systems. The definition Ederer et al use for cultural capital (which they call 'structural capital') is similar. Institutions can be further subdivided into formal (for example all written laws) and informal ones (cultural habits and standards).

Investments in cultural capital are structural aids for institutions. For instance, complete Western European tax systems were exported to Eastern European countries after the collapse of the communist world in 1989/1990. In the balance of accounts in these countries, that would have shown as an increase in cultural capital.

Depreciations in cultural capital are entered in the balance of accounts if old institutions are deliberately destroyed or collapse by themselves. For instance, the elimination of the socialist social, economic and legal system was the most significant depreciation in cultural capital of our times.

As Adam Smith already knew, the *visible* hand of law is very useful in guiding the invisible hand of the market (Smith, 1991). But how should this hand be evaluated? The indirect measuring method suggested by Ederer et al is not satisfactory because it can lead to completely incorrect results. A country may be interesting for investors on account of its human capital, even if its institutions are in need of improvement. It is worthwhile for companies to invest in low-wage countries because labour is cheap and there are fewer rules and regulations.

In principle, I consider it impossible to quantify the value of cultural capital (defined as institutions). This difficulty is even greater if we use wider definitions of cultural capital that include languages, customs, regional and national cuisine, traditional costumes, dances, music, etc. No one would deny that all these cultural manifestations can be valuable, but their value cannot be expressed in euros or dollars. We could conduct surveys on the people's willingness to pay for a certain cultural good that has no market price, as is done to evaluate biodiversity. However, most people will find it difficult to give a clear answer to the question 'How much is the constitution of your country worth to you?'.

Cultural capital has an important property that has not been mentioned yet: much of it has to be preserved from one generation to the next, but some of it has to be destroyed. The succeeding generation sometimes needs to create new institutions and cultural forms, just as old, ramshackle buildings have to be destroyed and new ones built. Each new generation decides which knowledge of its predecessors to preserve and which to forget. And each generation must decide whether a certain law or standard shall be considered an asset.

The American journalist and politician Thomas Paine wrote: 'Every age, every generation is and should be as free to act for itself in all cases as were previous ages and generations' (Paine, 1996, p261). This sentence, originally written in 1795, also defended the right to a revolution, which was even anchored in the French Constitution of 1793. Article 28 says: '*Un peuple a toujours le droit de revoir, de réformer et de changer sa Constitution. Une génération ne peut pas assujettir a ses lois les générations futures*' ('The people of a nation always have the right to examine, review and amend their constitution. No generation can force the forthcoming ones to follow its rules') (Godechot, 1979). Thomas Jefferson, in a letter to James Madison in 1789, had even proposed a time span for the rewriting of a constitution: every 19 years.

Generations continuously intertwine over the whole length of human history. 'They do so like the strands that wind round one another to create a piece of thread, each strand being shorter than the piece of thread itself' (Laslett, 1992, p46). In a few decades of overlapping lifetime, cultural goods must be handed down from one generation to the next.[35] This process guarantees the preservation of culture, but it is also a motor of progress. Each generation has a new approach to the accumulated culture and makes a new selection, while some goods are lost when their bearers die.

Social capital

In recent years, social scientists, political scientists, organization researchers and economists have framed a new type of capital: 'social capital'. An analysis of international literature revealed that there were only 20 contributions on social capital prior to 1981, 109 between 1991 and 1995, and 1003 between 1996 and March 1999 (Putnam and Goss, 2001, p18). There are many competing definitions, and the only thing they have in common is that social capital is seen as a metaphor for the value social structures, i.e. relationships and networks, can have for individuals and groups (Riemer, 2005, p58). At this point, already, an important distinction must be made. Most definitions regard the relationships that are useful for individuals *and* their groups as social capital. One type of social capital is thus defined as a zero-sum game – one player wins what another loses[36] – and another is defined as a positive-sum game – everyone can win. An example for social capital of the first type would be a private directory full of phone numbers. Its owner is more likely to get a job, not because he is better qualified than other applicants, but because he has more connections. Other applicants will go away empty-handed. Social capital of the second type could be a toddlers' group, for instance, that brings lonely and isolated mothers together and encourages them to undertake joint activities. Their leisure time becomes more enjoyable because they can communicate while their children play with each other. Of course, that is beneficial for each individual, but only because they share a collective good. The capital is 'in between' the individuals, so to speak, not with certain ones of them.

In other words: actor and system-oriented variants of the term 'social capital' must be distinguished. The definition by Pierre Bourdieu, for example, according to which social capital is an individual resource derived from social relationships to other individuals, is actor-oriented (Bourdieu, 1983). The resource that Bourdieu calls 'social capital' is certainly an important source of social standing. The careers of elite university graduates and members of exclusive networks are steeper, they have a higher income and are more successful in life than others. However, what is an advantage for them is a disadvantage for others.

System-oriented definitions, by contrast, see social capital as the sum of factors that promote the co-existence and development of a society. In that case, only win–win situations are defined as 'social capital', whereas win–lose situations are excluded from the start. These two meanings of the term 'social capital' are distinguished in Table 5.3.

In the following, I concentrate on type A because type B is not relevant for a study on generational inheritance.[37] It is easy to decide whether a certain form of social capital belongs to type A or type B: only forms that offer an added social value alongside the personal value belong to type A. Richard Putnam, who contributed a lot to the popularity of the term with his book *Bowling Alone*, describes:

> *Whereas physical capital refers to physical objects and human capital refers to properties of individuals, social capital refers to connections among individuals – social networks and the norms of reciprocity and trustworthiness that arise from them. In that sense social capital is closely related to what some have called 'civic virtue.' The difference is that 'social*

Table 5.3 *Social capital and its relevance for generational accounting*

	Type A: collective goods	Type B: individual or particularistic goods
Relevant for generational accounting?	Yes	No
Increase possible in an accounting period?	Yes, positive-sum game for the overall society	No, zero-sum game for the overall society
Properties	Basically open to everybody	Basically closed, exclusive, so non-group members are ruled out
Examples	Cooperation between two schools, beneficial for both	Separation of elite and standard schools
	Active social life, high participation in democracy and civil society	Networkers aiming at promoting their own career, e.g. access to certain positions
Associated terms	Public spirit, public-welfare orientation, social network, social coherence, participation, democracy, solidarity, empathy, trust, civil commitment networks	Connections, 'who you know', access to positions thanks to networking, career promotion, individual success
Such a definition of social capital tends to be used by:	Putnam, Hanifan, Fukuyama, Ostrom, Halpern, World Bank	Bourdieu, Coleman, Portes and Landolt, Baker, Granovetter, Adler and Kwon, Brehm and Rahn

capital' calls attention to the fact that civic virtue is most powerful when embedded in a dense network of reciprocal social relations. A society of many virtuous but isolated individuals is not necessarily rich in social capital.[38]

According to the social capital theory, the more we are connected – family, friends, neighbours and our democratic structures – the better. If the fabric of our connections with each other unravels, our lives will be impoverished and we will be less happy (Layard, 2005, p68). Putnam collected many empirical facts (concerning the US) that prove that people sign fewer petitions, belong to fewer organisations, know their neighbours less well, meet with friends less frequently, and even socialize with their families less often than 30 years ago.

Literature on social capital makes the following distinctions:

1   Formal vs. informal social capital: formal types of capital, for example trade unions, parties or churches, are strictly organized. They have office-bearers, contributions, regular meetings. Informal types of social capital do not. They include spontaneous football matches between boys who live in the same neighbourhood, regular meetings of friends at a city café or joint sports activities at a bowling studio.

2   Weak ties vs. strong ties (Granovetter, 1973; Offe and Fuchs, 2001, p420): some networks are close-knit, e.g. between families or friends. Others are loose, e.g. persons who greet each other on the bus every morning on their way to work. Even these loose contacts are reciprocal in a certain sense, as experiments have proven: a person whom I greet warmly every morning will be more willing to help me in case of an emergency (Putnam and Goss, 2001, p26).

3   Bridging vs. bonding social capital: bridging social capital refers to social networks that unite completely different kinds of people. Bonding social capital refers to relationships between people who are similar in some respects (ethnicity, gender, age, social class, etc.). Normally, bridging social capital is considered more valuable than bonding social capital, but both can be type A social capital.

Social capital is closely connected to 'trust' (Putnam and Goss, 2001, p21). This trust is based on reciprocity, but in a wide sense. The balance of giving and taking does not have to be established at once. Nor is the exchange limited to two actors, but can be borne by an entire system of relationships. In many countries, for instance, it is customary not to split bills when groups go out together; instead, one person pays for all. Based on many years of experience, the paying person knows that, according to the principle of reciprocity, he will be invited in return next time. On a micro-level, trust develops by face-to-face interactions. It is then transferred to all members of a network (meso-level) and eventually generalized as trust in the overall society, its institutions and its laws (Schechler, 2002, p69). Such social trust also keeps the economy running smoothly. If we know we can trust someone, no lawyers are required, and deals can be made by shaking hands, so transaction costs are saved (Fukuyama, 1999, p4).

But can social capital be quantified? Putnam clearly says 'no' (Putnam and Goss, 2001, pp23 and 28). First of all, social capital is very heterogeneous. An extended family is a form of social capital, but so are Sunday school students, skat-playing commuters on a suburban train, club members, neighbours in a two-bed room of a dormitory. How shall they all be brought down to a common denominator? Listing all possible kinds of *formal* groups, as Putnam does, is certainly not a sensible approach to quantifying social capital, because not all groups have the same social capital accounting value. In many countries, the number of informal types of social capital is gradually rising, while that of formal types is decreasing. Literary societies are being replaced by online discussion groups, for instance. Yet, unlike clubs, informal groups do not record their activities, so informal types of social capital are even more difficult to measure than formal ones. Fukuyama goes to the trouble of quantifying social capital and reaches the following conclusion: 'As this exercise indicates, producing anything like a believable census of a society's stock of social capital is a nearly impossible task, since it involves multiplying numbers that are either subjectively estimated or simply not existent' (Fukuyama, 1999, pp6–9).

Real capital requires investments in order not to diminish, and social capital requires continuous care and renewal. If networks are not active and contacts are lost, social capital will erode. In many respects, however, social capital is the exact opposite of real capital. Real capital, first, is owned by someone, and second, decreases when used. But social capital (type A) is, first, not owned by anyone, and second, can even increase when used.

Is social capital (type A) always good? Imagine a world without friendship and with an absolute minimum of interaction between people. Would it be a worse world?[39] Social capital theorists believe so, and so do communitarians. To start with, let us forget about the overall society and concentrate on particular networks instead. Here, strong ties within bonding social capital definitely cut off the network from the outside world. That applies to ethnical gangs in large cities or networks such as the Mafia. Antisocial standards often develop in such networks. This problem has been discussed under catchwords such as 'the dark side of social capital', 'civil society vs. community' or 'inclusion vs. exclusion'. In this context, some authors speak of 'social and unsocial capital' (Levi, 1996; Field, 2003, p71).

The principle of reciprocity is also critical, even if used in a wider sense. An individual who donates a large amount of money to an orphanage does not increase the social capital in the generational balance of accounts. Putnam is very clear about this: 'Social capital refers to networks of social connection – doing *with*. Doing good *for* other people, however laudable, is not part of the *definition* of social capital' (Putnam, 2000, p117, emphasis original).

Alternatively, the generational inheritance *can* be increased by negative forms of social capital. Mafia networks may not increase the social capital value in the generational balance, because the close ties between the Mafia members (profit in the balance) are more than compensated by a general loss of trust among the rest of the society (loss in the balance). But how about the increase in social capital on account of closer ties in the overall society, or large parts of it? Especially in times of crisis, people often move together and strengthen their relationships. Putnam and Goss (2001, p38) even praise the value of wars in this respect. But can that be desirable? In Nazi Germany, most people stuck together, but they distanced themselves from minorities within their own nation and from most other nations. Since generational accounting is conducted on a national level, Nazi Germany would have had a high social capital value, which is obviously absurd. In present day South Africa, some hundreds of white racists have established a whites-only community. They have purchased land, erected a fence and revived apartheid. The mayor boasts that he never locks his doors because he trusts his neighbours (N.N., 2006).

These shocking examples of high social capital may be worrying. But the point of criticism of the social capital concept is more fundamental and also refers to examples that look good at first sight (such as toddlers' groups, clubs, conversations on a bus). The social capital concept always rates being alone as bad and socializing as good. But some people prefer being alone to having company, and there is not necessarily something wrong about that. People even pay to have access to the first class of an airplane or train to have less company. Obviously, the rule 'the more interaction, the better' does not always hold true. Even for time reasons: the more interaction there is, the less time will be left for inspiring private activities.

That brings us to the conclusion that, at the moment, it is not clear whether type A social capital is positive or not (type B certainly is not). At any rate, further research is required. That means that, for the time being, social capital should not be incorporated in a generational balance of accounts at all.

Independent of whether we consider a multitude of social relationships good or not – is our social capital (type A) presently increasing or decreasing? In a number of studies on the US, Putnam shows that the social capital, especially social, political and religious commitment (the last of these represents a large share of the total social capital of the US) as well as social trust[40] have been eroding since the 1960s (Putnam, 1995, 1996, 2000). He believes the reasons are a lack of time and money, the separation of home and workplace, the increased exposure of Americans to television, and the fact that the long civic generation born between 1910 and 1940 is being replaced by new generations with different behavioural patterns (Putnam, 2000, p283). No such decrease in social capital has been measured in other industrialized countries, yet (Kern, 2004, p125). And by the way, agnostics or atheists might even welcome the fact that religious communities are becoming less important.

Summary

The generational accounting concept is an attempt to sum up all relevant generational inheritance components. Although we can gain some valuable insights from the capital approach, there are three reasons for the fact that the capital approach cannot tell us what will be important for future individuals.

First, we do not know in which types of capital to divide generational inheritance. It is not simply a matter of adding up various types of capital; they have to be clearly defined and must not overlap. At the moment, for instance, the concept of social capital is very popular. But a closer examination makes it doubtful whether it should be included in generational accounting at all. In the end, we must admit that there is no sound generational accounting concept, yet.

Second, even if we succeed in subdividing the world into the proper types of capital, we will still not know how to measure or quantify each of them. Most of our natural, social and cultural capital is not tradable. Even human capital is only tradable on the labour market. Only real capital is readily tradable (with a few limitations). It has been balanced and quantified by statistical offices, although questions regarding the usefulness of weapons and cigarettes, which are considered a profit in the generational balance of accounts, remain unanswered.

The term 'capital' implies quantifiability. But actually, the reasons mentioned make it particularly difficult to quantify social and virtually impossible to quantify cultural capital. Hauser tells us what follows from the evaluation problem:

> *It often leads to the fact that only individual elements, that are easier to quantify, are selected and compared with regard to consecutive generations. Based on such partial comparisons, publicity-grabbing and politically influential judgements are then made concerning the violation of generational justice, although such judgements ought to be based on the total generational inheritance. (Hauser, 2007, p157)*

If our conclusions are based on incomplete balances, they are wrong. Some disciplines prefer to develop precise concepts from incorrect basic information, instead of developing vague concepts from correct information, which is like looking for one's car keys underneath a streetlight because it is brighter there. Every serious researcher and every good scientist ought to start looking, however difficult this may be, where it makes sense to look.

Third, even if we could solve the problem of quantification, it remains unclear whether one type of capital can be substituted against another in the annual balance of accounts. From a methodological point of view, it would not be convincing to offset the increases and decreases of all types of capital against each other. But if we do not accept the principle of substitution, we have to decide which elements of each type of capital are indispensable for our offspring and label them 'critical'. That would be a never-ending story.

The well-being approach

The result of our axiological reasoning so far is that 'capital' is not the societal objective that each generation should have in view. What about 'well-being'?

If well-being were the appropriate social end, the intergenerational justice maxim could then be described as follows: 'A society can be called intergenerationally just if the well-being of future generations is higher than/is as high as/ is lower than that of today's generation.'

Before we take a closer look at the terms 'higher', 'as high as' and 'lower' – in the chapter on justice (Chapter 6) – we will continue the axiological discussion and find out whether 'well-being' is a better objective than 'capital' or whether it ought to be replaced by something else. I believe 'well-being' is the most suitable generic term for specific states in which an individual's needs, wants, preferences and/or interests are at least partly fulfilled. This state can also be outlined by the terms 'welfare', 'quality of life', 'happiness', 'felicity', 'satisfaction', 'utility', 'pleasure' etc. However, all these terms are vague and partly overlap. Some concepts, particularly 'major league' concepts such as well-being, justice, gender or race, while generally understood, are characterized by a multitude of terminological conceptions (cf. Chekola, 2007, p53). Even Jeremy Bentham, the founder of utilitarianism, encountered this problem:

> *By utility is meant that property in any object, whereby it tends to produce*
> *benefit, advantage, pleasure, good, or happiness, (all this in the present case*
> *comes to the same thing) or (what comes again to the same thing) to*
> *prevent the happening of mischief, pain, evil, or unhappiness to the party*
> *whose interest is considered. (Bentham, 1907, p2)*

Social sciences have made great progress in the field of 'well-being research' over
the past years, and statistics concerning the terms 'well-being', 'happiness' and
'satisfaction' have now been developed for people of various countries, profes-
sions, religions, social and economic groups. However, the field is now a domain
of economists, psychologists and sociologists rather than philosophers
(Haybron, 2000, p208). What can philosophers contribute? First of all, they
should clarify the terms that have hitherto been used quite arbitrarily by well-
being researchers.[41] Second, they should take an outside view of all the empirical studies and find out whether the right questions have been dealt with. As we
will see, that is not the case when it comes to measuring the well-being level of
a series of generations. So we will start by defining the terms.[42] Later on, they
will be replaced by the indicators by which states of well-being can be measured.
That will lead to a lot more accuracy.

All the subterms of 'well-being' are placed in one circle (see Figure 5.2). There
are two alternatives for the social end: 'asceticism' (Bentham, 1907, p8) and
'virtue', which have their own subterms. Terms within each circle refer to various
aspects of a conception. In the words of Amartya Sen: the position of the circles
in relation to each other is marked by competitive plurality, whereas the relation of
the terms within a circle is marked by constitutive plurality (see Sen, 2000, p18).

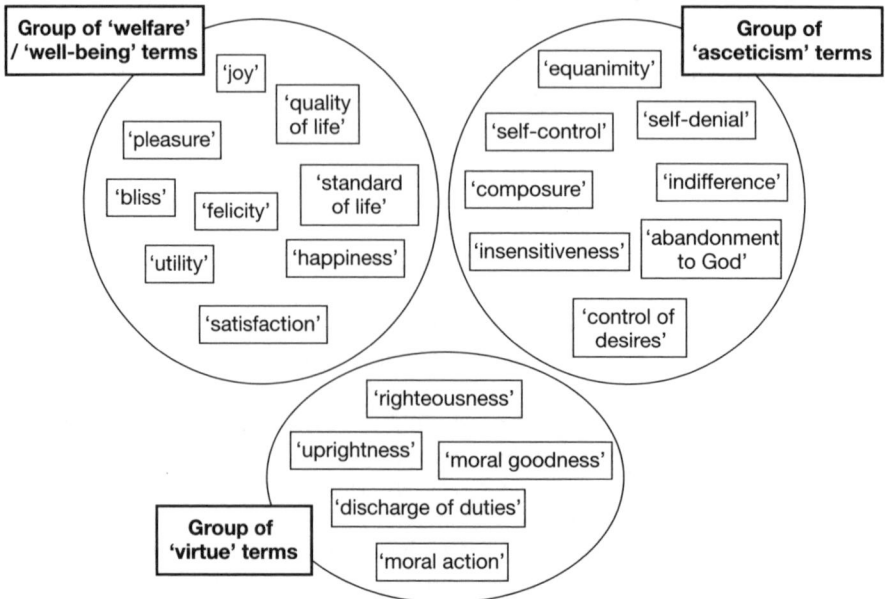

Figure 5.2 *Possible societal objectives and clarifying terms*

Defining the 'well-being' terms

Well-being and welfare

'Well-being' and 'welfare' have the same radical and are listed in most English dictionaries as synonyms. Collins' *Cobuild Dictionary* defines: 'If you refer to someone's well-being, you are referring to whether they are healthy, happy, etc, so that life is enjoyable and worth living'.[43] Note that 'well-being' thus can encompass both objective living conditions and subjective states of mind and be measured by objective and subjective indicators.[44] According to the same dictionary, 'welfare' has three distinguishable meanings:

> 1. *The welfare of a person, group, or organisation is their general state of well-being, for example the good health and comfort of the person or group, or the stability or prosperity of the organisation.*[45]
>
> 2. *Welfare is used to describe the activities of an organisation, especially the government, which are concerned with the health, education, living conditions, and financial problems of the people in society.*[46]
>
> 3. *Welfare is money which is paid by the government to people who are unemployed, have poorly paid jobs, or cannot work because of illness or disability, used in American English.*[47]

The last two meanings are obviously not identical with 'well-being'. If I use 'welfare' in the next two chapters, I refer to the first meaning of the term. Unless otherwise indicated, 'welfare' is thus used as a synonym to 'well-being'.

Happiness

Happiness, the central term of eudaimonism, designates a specific state of an individual whose wants and preferences are fulfilled. In the relatively young 'science of happiness', the term is largely used synonymously with *subjectively* asserted states of well-being.[48] It is undisputed that happiness has a cognitive ('being happy') and an affective dimension ('feeling happy') in the sense of sensations and moods. The former dimension falls primarily in the research field of social scientists, the latter in that of psychologists and psychiatrists. In part connected with the two dimensions of happiness are two concepts of happiness: either as life satisfaction or as an episodical state. Ruut Veenhoven, the editor-in-chief of the *Journal of Happiness Studies* and a sociologist, writes: 'Happiness is defined as the degree to which people evaluate their overall quality of present life as a whole positively. In other words, how much they like the life they live' (Veenhoven, 2007, p244). Although Veenhoven acknowledges that 'happiness' has a cognitive and an affective dimension, his definition does not fully reflect the latter. The competing definition would be to define 'happiness' as a brief, short-lived feeling of elation.[49] Csikszentmihalyi asked hundreds of test persons what they take 'happiness' to be and how happiness feels for them. The test persons referred to 'a flow' or to having 'butterflies in one's stomach' and the like (Csik-szentmihalyi, 1990). If that is what we consider happiness, then the statement:

> *The best society is the one in which the happiness (i.e. 'flow') of the citizens is greatest.*

takes on a meaning that is completely different from the statement:

> *The best society is the one in which the well-being of the citizens is highest.*[50]

John Stuart Mill has already discussed this ambiguity of the term 'happiness':

> *When, however, it is thus positively asserted to be impossible that human life should be happy, the assertion, if not something like a verbal quibble, is at least an exaggeration. If by happiness be meant a continuity of highly pleasurable excitement, it is evident enough that this is impossible. A state of exalted pleasure lasts only moments or in some cases, and with some intermissions, hours or days, and is the occasional brilliant flash of enjoy-ment, not its permanent and steady flame. (Mill, 1979, p12)*

There is a certain truth about a remark that is usually attributed to George Bernard Shaw: 'But a lifetime of happiness! No man alive could bear it: it would be hell on earth.' Happiness is based on contrast. Hardly anything is as foolish as dreaming of everlasting *Cockaigne* (Schneider, 2007, p71). According to Schopenhauer, frustration is even a condition for enjoyment (Schopenhauer, 2007, p57). And Sigmund Freud says:

> *What we call happiness in the strictest sense stems from the rather sudden satisfaction of pent-up needs and can, by nature, only be an episodical phenomenon. Any continuation of a situation longed for by the pleasure principle will merely lead to a feeling of lukewarm contentment; we are so constituted that we can derive intense enjoyment only from contrast – but very little enjoyment from a state of affairs. (Freud, 2007, p72)*

'Happiness,' thus defined, cannot replace the term 'well-being' as the heading of the upper left circle. Even for the most privileged members of the most privi-leged generation, it would remain episodical. And with respect to the definition criteria 'common use', the episodical dimension of 'happiness' cannot simply be ignored. This meaning of the word is well-entrenched in contemporary English and has its partisans (Haybron, 2000, p213).

Moreover, the philosophical purpose of eudaimonism was completely differ-ent for the authors of antiquity than, say, that of utilitarian ethics. Eudaimonism deals with happiness in life for individual practical purposes, but as an axiological matter in the intergenerational context, 'happiness' would need to become a social, ethically and politically relevant social end. To sum up so far, 'well-being' is a better concept than 'happiness' in order to grant information on how to properly shape a society.

Satisfaction

Many researchers use the terms 'happiness' and 'satisfaction' interchangeably (Brülde, 2007b, p19). Yet, in everyday language, 'satisfaction' has a less positive connotation than 'happiness'. For instance, one might say: 'He was satisfied all his life, but never truly happy.' The negative condition for well-being is the absence of worries, fear and suffering; the positive condition is happiness and the satisfaction of wants. 'Satisfaction' as a societal objective means the pursuit of security, self-preservation and survival in a Hobbesian world of continuous danger. The term describes a state in which the negative conditions are absent, but the positive conditions for a good life are not present. Nobody who suffers physical or mental pain is in a state of well-being. Yet, the absence of such pain is a necessary but not sufficient condition for a fulfilled life. Positive factors such as recognition, a meaningful occupation and being able to exercise one's abilities are also required.

Pleasure

Pleasure is the 'ultimate goal' in all hedonistic theories. But 'pleasure' only refers to a few positive conditions for well-being, especially to sexual and other sensual experiences. While 'satisfaction' only covers the absence of the negative dimension of well-being, 'pleasure' only covers certain elements of its positive dimension.

Utility

Even if the term 'utility' has been very successful in economics and is often used synonymously with the satisfaction of human wants and needs, it is not equivalent to them. Bentham himself defined 'utility' by referring to other, more general terms. For him, this superordinate term was 'happiness' (Bentham, 1907, p2). Since the neoclassical movement, standard economic theory has employed an 'objectivist' position based on observable choices made by individuals. This view is summarized by Frey and Stutzer:

> *Individual utility only depends on tangible factors (goods and services), is inferred from revealed behavior (or preferences), and is in turn used to explain the choices made... Subjectivist experience (e.g. captured by surveys) is rejected as being 'unscientific', because it is not objectively observable and is not necessary for economic theory. (Frey and Stutzer, 2001, p2)*

But they suggest focusing more on happiness than on utility:

> *Happiness is not identical to utility, but it well captures people's satisfaction with life. For many purposes, it can be considered a useful approximation to utility which economists have evaded to measure (with the exception of benefit-cost analysis). This allows us to empirically study problems which so far could only be analyzed on an abstract theoretical level. (Frey and Stutzer, 2001, p21)*[51]

Quality of life

The term 'quality of life' also designates a state of satisfaction of certain wants and preferences. One of the founding fathers of welfare and environmental economics, the British economist A. C. Pigou, defined 'quality of life' as 'non-economic welfare' in the 1920s (Pigou, 1932). We use this term in contexts in which 'happiness' or 'satisfaction' are not appropriate; for instance, when we say that the quality of life is higher in one city than in another. Also, the term is not only used in social philosophy when discussing societal development objectives, but takes on a different focus in medicine and psychology where it is used to describe a patient's state of health after a certain treatment (Hörnquist, 1982; Rupprecht, 1993, p17; Brock, 1993). The concept is therefore ambiguous.

For the reasons set forth, 'well-being', the state of being well, seems most appropriate as an umbrella term for the group of partly overlapping terms mentioned. In the following, I assume that 'well-being' (and not 'happiness' etc.) is the most desirable societal goal.

Fulfillment of what?

The terms examined so far describe certain states and provide possible answers to the question: 'What to strive for?'. We will now also ask the related but slightly different question: 'What to fulfil?'. Figure 5.3 shows a number of terms that describe human dispositions.

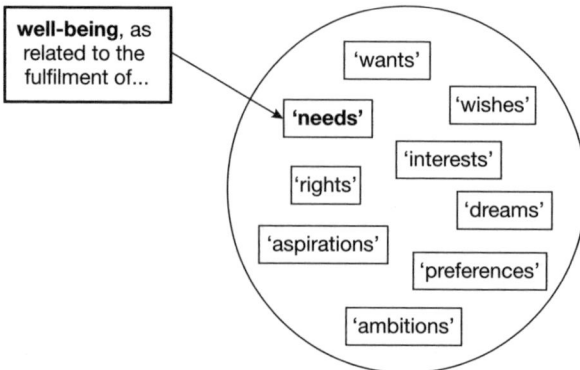

Figure 5.3 *Human dispositions*

As mentioned, the term 'well-being' designates states in which an individual's needs, wants, preferences and/or interests are at least partly fulfilled. Now, there are theories of well-being that focus more on the fulfilment of one or another of these dispositions.[52] In an intergenerational context, 'well-being' must refer to what people might *need* rather to what they might want, wish or dream of. Why? Since the beginning of mankind, about 5000 intertemporal generations have inhabited the earth (see Chapter 6 for details of this calculation). The overwhelming majority of them were very much like today's world's poorest poor. There is a broad consensus in development policy that in such a setting, the highest priority lies on satisfying basic or minimum human needs (Morris, 1979, p2). Their fulfilment is the primary objective; the fulfilment of preferences comes second. As far as that is concerned, comparisons of various previous generations are most informative if they focus on the question of the degree to which their needs were fulfilled.

If 'needs' are made central, then 'well-being' is understood as the 'the degree of need-fulfilment' (Drewnowski, 1974, p7; Erikson, 1993, p73).[53] The question of the rights of future generations, be they moral or legal individual rights or even group rights, becomes secondary. The primary question of need-based well-being theories in the intergenerational context is how the need-fulfilment of present and future individuals can be balanced. According to Doyal and Gough (1991), human beings have three basic needs: the need for food, physical health and personal autonomy.[54] The pursuit of any wants, interests, preferences and dreams requires, at the very least, a body that is alive and the mental competence to deliberate and to choose (Doyal and Gough, 1991, p52). Instead of ad hoc adding other items to the list of *basic* needs, Doyal and Gough point out 11 broad categories of 'intermediate needs' that define how the need for food, physical health and personal autonomy are fulfilled: adequate nutritional food and water, adequate protective housing, a safe environment for working, a safe physical environment, appropriate health care, security in childhood, significant primary relationships with others, physical security, economic security, safe birth control and child-bearing, and appropriate basic and cross-cultural education (Doyal and Gough, 1991, p158 et seq.).

In contrast, if we use 'needs' in a broad sense, like Abraham Maslow, encompassing basic *and* higher needs, we will end up with a hierarchy of needs and, what is more important, a temporal sequence according to which the lowest needs must be fulfilled before one can think of satisfying higher ones (Maslow, 1943, 1954). However, with Maslow's definition, it becomes difficult to distinguish 'needs' from 'wants'. In our everyday language, there are many situations in which we clearly talk about 'needing' and not 'wanting', for example, 'we *need* so and so many calories per day', but not 'we *want* so and so many calories' (cf. Birnbacher, 1979, p33). Alternatively, we say 'I want self-actualization', but not 'I need self-actualization' (self-actualization forms the peak of Maslow's hierarchy of needs). Thus, there are many reasons to use Doyal and Gough's definition of 'needs,' rather than that of Maslow.

Martha Nussbaum (1992), in an insightful article, puts forward a capabilities approach.[55] She lists ten 'Basic Human Functional Capabilities', as she calls them. These are 'being able to live to the end of a complete human life', 'being able to have good health', 'being able to avoid unnecessary and nonbeneficial pain and to have pleasurable experiences', 'being able to use the five senses; being able to imagine, to think and to reason', 'being able to have attachments to things and persons outside ourselves', 'being able to form a conception of the good and to engage in critical reflection about the planning of one's own life', 'being able to live for and with others', 'being able to live with concern for and in relation to animals, plants, and the world of nature', 'being able to laugh, to play, to enjoy recreational activities', and last but not least, 'being able to live one's life and nobody else's' (Nussbaum, 1992, p222).

So how are needs related to capabilities? Given that there are features that pertain to all humans, say, to have a body that needs a certain calorie intake to survive, the need is 'enough food' whereas the capability is 'being able to get enough food'. Basically the same questions apply to both the needs and the capabilities approach: How many? Are they really universal? How can their degree of fulfilment be measured? That is why Nussbaum's list is important in our context.

According to Nussbaum, *all* items on her list are of central importance (Nussbaum, 1992, p222), so her account differs from Maslow's in this regard. Compared to Doyal and Gough's short list of basic needs, Nussbaum's is much more extensive. But this is due to overlaps, for instance, 'ability to think' and 'ability to form a conception of the good'. The latter would be called an 'intermediate need' in Doyal and Gough's terminology, which I find more convincing and therefore I will stick to this concept in the following.

Basic needs are limited, objective and universal, part of the condition of being human. Our desires and dreams, by contrast, are unlimited and infinite. And, of course, the modes of fulfilling 'needs' are also innumerable and vary across cultures. For example, the need for food and shelter applies to all people of all nations, but there is an almost endless variety of cuisines and forms of dwelling (Doyal and Gough, 1991, p155). 'Needs' (either basic or intermediate) must not be confused with 'satisfiers of needs'. Relativist accounts only make sense if they are applied to the different ways to satisfy needs, not to the need themselves.

Does each generation have different needs?

Wants and preferences vary from culture to culture and from individual to individual. Fashionable subjectivist and cultural relativist approaches thus relate to wishes, wants or aspirations rather than needs. The needs of every member of every generation are identical, no matter which age or culture he lived (lives, will live) in. Most probably, future individuals will also need air to breathe and water to drink (Feinberg, 1973). Therefore, the so-called 'uncertainty argument' that we have no obligations towards future generations because we cannot know all their higher preferences loses ground.[56] Partridge writes:

> *The very enormity of the changes that are projected, or imminent, may render a finely tuned science of forecasting somewhat irrelevant. For what-*

ever their tastes in music or poetry, or whatever their preferences in sports and other amusements, our descendants will need croplands and watersheds to supply their food and water. (Partridge, 1980a, p2; see also Kavka, 1978, p189 et seq.)

If we use well-being in the sense of need-fulfilment as a societal objective, we are not particularly obliged to consider the idiosyncrasies or even 'expensive tastes' of future generations, from a moral point of view. The limited nature of our needs also qualifies the objection by John Stuart Mill – aimed against his intellectual father Bentham – who demanded that not only the *quantity*, but also the *quality* of pleasures be taken into consideration (Mill, 1979, pp7–11). Mill gave an example that became very popular:

> *It is better to be a human being dissatisfied than a pig satisfied; better to be Socrates dissatisfied than a fool satisfied. And if the fool, or the pig, are of a different opinion, it is because they only know their own side of the question. The other party to the comparison knows both sides. (Mill, 1979, p10)*

Now, this is a complicated example that can point to a valid argument but also an unfounded one. Let us examine the example in detail. A pig is a being that – like any other animal – has less cognitive and intellectual abilities than man. Yet swine are considered filthy, be this justified or not.[57] The example thereby designates two different arguments:

- Mill's argument, version one: some people are easy to please. As long as their basic needs are met, they will be fairly content. Others are more demanding and more resources are required to satisfy their desires. However, it is better to satisfy the more demanding (in this sense: higher) pleasures of this second type of people.
- Mill's argument, version two: the preferences of human beings can be divided into three categories, based on their effect on others – preferences that increase the well-being of others, preferences that do not affect the well-being of others, and preferences that diminish the well-being of others (Tremmel, 2003c, pp20–23). It is better to satisfy the preferences that increase the well-being of others, because they have a greater moral value (in this sense: they are higher).

Let us deal with version 1 of Mill's argument first.[58] For all we know, all higher animals are capable of experiencing pleasant *and* unpleasant sensations. The example indicates that the animal's level of satisfaction depends only on a few things such as food, sleep, etc. But this is an unproved assumption, because we do not know if zoo animals (who are always well fed) are happier than wild animals. Humans and animals are difficult to compare, we can rather compare adults with infants. To refine Mill's argument, Nagel writes: 'Suppose an intelligent person receives a brain injury that reduces him to the mental condition of a contented infant, and that such desires as remain to him can be satisfied by a custodian, so that he is free from care' (Nagel, 1979, p5). Infants cry many hours of the day, and not out of pleasure! To justify version 1, this is an utterly bad example.

Granted that Mill's argument applies only to people with more or less the same mental and cognitive powers and the same level of moral standards, it is not at all clear why the fulfilment of the needs of the 'simple mind' – maybe someone who prefers to sleep in a hut instead of a palace – should count more that the fulfilment of the wants of the more spoiled character. Even if we define 'higher pleasures' as 'pleasures of the mind' and 'lower pleasures' as 'pleasures of the body', it is unclear why an evening at the opera or a debating club should be considered better than sports achievements or consensual sex.[59]

Let us consider version 2. The fact that some people enjoy sadistic pursuits is a problem for all theories that are based solely on the quantity of pleasures (narrow hedonism), but in particular for preference-based well-being theories, not for need-based ones. There are antisocial '*desires*' or '*wants*'. There may be even evil '*preferences*'. But there are no such things as antisocial or evil human '*needs*'. The characteristics of human needs versus human wants are summarized in Table 5.4.

Table 5.4 *The characteristics of human needs vs. human wants*

Needs	Wants
Universal (for all humans identical)	Different for humans depending on culture, epoch and context
Limited	Unlimited
Objective	Subjective
Directed towards survival	Sometimes self-destructive (smoking, suicide) or anti-social

Source: Based on Doyal and Gough (1991)

But even the higher wants and preferences (that admittedly vary more than the needs) are less tricky when it comes to whole generations rather than the individuals within a generation. When we compare generations, we combine the wants of all individuals belonging to them to form an average. No matter how different the wants and preferences of the individuals may be, those of generations are not. Each generation has its clever and simple-minded people, egoists and altruists, law-abiding citizens and criminals. All their different preference structures boil down to an average. It is very unlikely that the average or median[60] individual that represents its generation should have abnormal or particularly extravagant preferences. Focusing on generations instead of individuals also makes it less problematic that the wants of some individuals oppose their needs – the wish to commit suicide being the most prominent example.

Ultimate justification of 'well-being' as a societal objective

A non-cognitivist might call it impossible to ultimately justify the intrinsic value of a societal objective. He might refer to the logicist argument that it would lead to an infinite regress if every statement required a justifying meta-norm. This attitude is called Agrippan Scepticism, because it goes back to the Pyrrhonian sceptic Agrippa.[61] According to his 'tropes', it is impossible to give adequate reasons for a proposition. If I claim A (A standing for any proposition), I have to prove it by referring to something other than A, because nothing is proof of itself. So, for example, I would prove A by B. But now I need C to support B, etc. Ultimately, the non-cognitivist sees three possibilities: (1) Infinite regress – an infinite regress cannot be completed, so I can never adequately support my original proposition; (2) Circularity – my justification leads me back to a proposition made earlier (e.g. C is supported by A). This vicious circle will also make my justification attempt fail; (3) Dogmatism – at some point, I simply abort my justification attempt. Such an unjustified abort is dogmatic. My original proposition remains unjustified.

When I began studying philosophy, this trilemma seemed very important to me. At times, I was sadly convinced that it is ultimately impossible to adequately justify a statement such as 'All human beings have needs.' However, this changed when I met someone who actually did question all my explanations of the world by asking 'why?'. I mean my two-and-a-half year old son Finn. As a response to all the serious answers of his PhD-awarded Dad, he stubbornly kept asking 'why?'. The point is not that it was annoying but that it was not intellectually stimulating and thought-provoking.[62] That was when I gradually came to understand that why-questions might be less meaningful and competent than the answers. In other words: there are unjustified 'why' questions. And why should the burden of proof for meaningful statements always lie with the answering person and not with the one asking the question? The sceptic must be able to adequately answer why he is still in doubt. If he cannot do so, it is not dogmatic to abort the justification of the original proposition A.

A similar rejoinder used by Konrad Ott against the logicist argument reinforces the plea for choosing 'well-being' as a societal objective. Ott argues that the non-cognitivist uses 'justification' in a certain sense, but the cognitivist is free to use a different definition (Ott, 1997, p193).[63] What can be 'justified' at all? Obviously, no one can 'justify' the stoniness of a stone. Using the verb in this context would be a classic category mistake.[64] A stone has certain qualities, and only on account of these qualities is it defined as a stone. The same applies to human beings. The fact that a human being has typically human needs cannot be justified. If we ask a person why he does sports, he might answer: 'Because I want to stay healthy and fit.' If we ask him why he wants to stay healthy and fit, he will reply: 'Because illnesses are painful and make life shorter.' If we keep on asking why he wants to avoid pain or an early death, he will shrug his shoulders and no longer be able to give an answer, because justifying life itself does not make sense (at least not for non-believers, but even for most believers it does not).

Asked why he wants to stay healthy and fit, he could also have answered: 'Because otherwise I would lose my job.' If we ask him why he does not want to lose his job, he will probably respond that he has to earn money. If we continue asking, he will say: 'I need at least a small income to fulfil my needs.' At this point, it would be absurd to continue asking for reasons. We have reached the end of all why-questions (Höffe, 2007b, p80).

In the social–philosophical context, the situation is similar. The conceptual opposite of a social structure that concentrates on the well-being of its population would be one that tries to make its population suffer and to prevent the fulfilment of their needs as best possible. No moral philosopher I know would approve of such a society, and I dare say no philosopher has ever seriously advocated 'suffering' as a societal objective.[65]

To strive for the fulfilment of one's needs is the common denominator, the *conditio humana*, of all human beings, present and future. Marx famously defines human beings as 'creatures of need' (Marx, 1959). And Bert Brecht writes: 'Human beings do not like the boot in their face, for the very reason that they are human beings' (cited in Ott, 1997, p219). Human beings have human needs, simply because they are human – no further justification is possible or required.[66]

Alternative 'social ends'

Asceticism

'Asceticism' and 'virtue' are two further groups of terms that compete with 'well-being'. Bentham already considered asceticism the most important counter-concept to the concept of welfare (Bentham, 1907, pp8–23).[67] 'Self-denial', 'equanimity', 'self-control', 'composure', 'indifference', 'insensitiveness', 'control of desires' or 'abandonment to God' are related terms.[68] The objective 'well-being' is about fulfilling needs and wants to create a positive sensation, whereas an ascetic will try to suppress this positive sensation. All passion, all desire shall be discarded. Neither does he feel joy if he experiences something good, nor pain if something bad happens, for example if a beloved person dies. The Stoic Epictetus, for instance, says:

> *With all things you enjoy, find useful, or like, keep telling yourself what they actually are. Start with insignificant things. If, for example, you are attached to a pot, then tell yourself: 'it is a plain pot I am attached to.' Then you will not get upset if it breaks. When you kiss your child or your wife, then tell yourself: 'it is a human being I am kissing.' Then you will not lose your composure if they die. (Epictetus, 2007, p35)*

The ascetic attitude is normally justified by powerlessness in the face of overwhelming forces, therefore it is mostly adopted by religious persons. The Christian mystics who belonged to the circle of Meister Eckhart (1260–1327) strove to unite with God by meditation and inward contemplation. In Zen Buddhism, forgetting one's ego and one's own needs is a high objective. The 'empty mirror' is a goal that is diametrically opposed to being self-centred. This attitude culminates in the ars moriendi in which the mature, purified consciousness leaves the body quietly and consciously. Since death is not considered the end, but only the crossing of a border, one can die calmly (von Brück, 2007, p126). One's own fate is regarded as insignificant and is placed in the hands of God. The theologian Dorothee Sölle explains: 'There is no need for me to hold on to myself, because I am being held; there is no need for me to bear the burden, because I am being borne; I can leave and surrender myself' (Sölle, 1975, p25). All ascetic views have in common that human needs are not important. Life is a preparation for the after-life. Instead of wasting energy on satisfying one's physical or mental needs, one should rather concentrate on the hereafter.

This concept, however, is not convincing for secular societies. If we were only willing to create conditions that allow the next generation to live according to ascetic standards, that generation would rightly reproach us and maintain that asceticism was no societal objective for today's generation either, but at best for a tiny minority.

In fact, even if the ascetic decides to die because of a higher good, he wants to have all his survival needs fulfilled until the day he chose to die. So, he does not generally opposes need-fulfilment. Nussbaum states:

> *Moreover, all human beings have an aversion to death. Although in many circumstances death will be preferred to the available alternatives, the death of a loved one or the prospect of one's own death is an occasion for grief and/or fear. If we encountered an immortal anthropomorphic being or a mortal being that showed no aversion to death and no tendency to avoid it, we would judge, in both these cases, that the form of life was so different from our own that the being could not be acknowledged as human. (Nussbaum, 1992, p216 et seq., emphasis original)*

Virtue

The axiological aim 'asceticism' does not only reject the fulfilment of wants, but even the fulfilment of needs (even if it may mean accepting death). In contrast, the axiological aim 'virtue' does not go that far. It acknowledges that basic human needs first have to be satisfied. Feuerbach, for instance, writes:

> *Wherever there is a lack of the necessities of life, there will also be a lack of moral necessity. The basis of life is also the basis of morals. If you are so hungry and miserable that you have nothing to cover your body with, you will have no reason or substance of morals in your mind, your senses, and your heart. (Feuerbach, 2007, p112)*

And Feuerbach does not mean that in a negative sense, like Brecht who writes: 'A full stomach comes first, then morals' (Brecht, 2004, p67). Rather, Feuerbach describes the plain fact that someone starved to death is no longer in a position to help others.

But what about our wants and aspirations? Should virtue be our ultimate objective, even if that means rejecting what we desire? This question only makes sense if virtue and well-being (or happiness, satisfaction, quality of life, utility, etc.) are not considered identical in the end. Economics, sociology or psychology never equated morals and well-being. Philosophy did. In ancient Greek philosophy, virtue and happiness were originally thought to be intertwined. But already in the 5th century BC, Greek sophists raise the outrageous question of whether a happy life must necessarily be virtuous. And, the other way around, whether a virtuous life always leads to happiness. And if not, what reason would an individual have to live by morals?[69] Socrates (469–399 BC) tries to re-establish the unity of happiness and virtue. For him, it is unthinkable that an individual should actualize himself at the expense of the community. He teaches that the supposed difference between happiness and morals is mere illusion. Plato (427–347 BC) develops this idea further and tries to prove that only a moral life can be happy and a truly happy life is always moral. In his dialogue *Gorgias*, the characters discuss whether it would be advantageous for a powerful person to be guided by virtues (Plato, 1971, pp468e–469c). The platonic Socrates makes his sophistic opponents believe they did not actually want happiness, wealth or power, but virtue. For that purpose, however, he uses misleading arguments and reaches false conclusions (Birnbacher, 1979, p35). Last not least Aristotle (364–322 BC) regards happiness and virtue as two sides of the same coin. In his *Nicomachean Ethics*, he points out that neither happiness nor virtue are means to an end, but an end in themselves (Aristotle, 2005, p222). But they are not competing ends because one cannot be achieved without the other. 'Human flourishing' according to Aristotle is both the development of desirable, (morally) good qualities as well as the achievement of a life that is subjectively good (in a non-moral sense).

One of the first philosophers after Aristotle to dissolve the unity of happiness and virtue is Epicurus around 300 BC. For him, the objective 'virtue' and the objective 'happiness' are not necessarily identical. He propagates the path to happiness. Virtue is at best instrumental.[70] His contemporaries criticize him heavily for that.

Equating virtue and welfare *by definition* is not fruitful because it limits our possibilities to build up scientific theories. The equation that virtuous conduct always leads to happiness and a life that is subjectively considered happy must necessarily be virtuous is wrong both ways. Kant makes that clear: 'It is unfortunate that these men applied their acumen… to thinking up an identity between such extremely unequal terms, that of happiness and that of virtue' (Kant, 1968a, p240 [A 201]). And: 'The venerableness of duty has nothing to do with enjoyment of life.' On the contrary, Kant says, duties are marked by the absence of joy.[71] Now, that is taking it too far. A life dedicated to virtue and discharge of duties can certainly be considered happy from a subjective point of view. But not necessarily so. If what makes a person happy automatically coincided with what makes all other persons happy, moral action would not be needed anymore (Baurmann and Kliemt, 1987, p5).

For many, virtue is a worthwhile objective. But it is not the end of all why-questions. Mill is right in saying:

> *It is noble to be capable of resigning entirely one's own portion of happiness, or chances of it; but, after all, this self-sacrifice must be for some end; it is not its own end; and if we are told that its end is not happiness but virtue, which is better than happiness, I ask, would the sacrifice be made if the hero or martyr did not believe that it would earn for others immunity from similar sacrifices? Would it be made if he thought that his renunciation of happiness for himself would produce no fruit for any of his fellow creatures, but to make their lot like his and place them also in the condition of persons who have renounced happiness? All honor to those who can abnegate for themselves the personal enjoyment of life when by such renunciation they contribute worthily to increase the amount of happiness in the world; but he who does it or professes to do it for any other purpose is no more deserving of admiration than the ascetic mounted on his pillar. He may be an inspiriting proof of what men can do, but assuredly not an example of what they should. (Mill, 1979, p15 et seq., emphasis original)*

Whoever gives up his seat in a lifeboat to someone else or goes to a concentration camp in someone else's place, does so for the well-being of that other person. If it were not possible to increase the welfare of others, no virtuous deed would make sense – to answer Mill's rhetorical question.

Future generations would not like it if we left behind a world in which they could not satisfy their needs, but could be virtuous and conscientious instead. Suppose, one representative each of the intertemporal generation A (all persons alive in 2008) and B (all persons alive in 2300) would meet and hold the following dialogue:

> A: *I want to be virtuous, so I can respect myself. I consider it my duty and responsibility to leave behind a world in which the people you represent can be moral and conscientious.*

> B: *On a personal level, you are free to strive for virtue, and I welcome that. But as a social planner, you cannot force others to do the same. Otherwise you will create a tyranny.*

> A: *But if I am not supposed to exert force on others, wouldn't it be wrong to force well-being on them?*

> B: *Around the world, the majority of the individuals you represent try to satisfy their needs and strive for happiness. The people I represent will decide for themselves whether they want to be virtuous. But it is your duty to leave behind a world in which need-fulfilment remains possible.*

A: *But won't the pursuit of happiness alone necessarily lead to immoral action?*

B: *No. The men and women alive in 2300 will be able to fulfil their basic needs without thereby being immoral. Stipulating well-being as the objective of mankind on an axiological level does not mean promoting egoism on a normative level.*

Axiological considerations and utilitarianism

Every theory on generational justice gives rise to axiological questions: which good (in the widest sense of the word) will be important to the members of future generations? Since future individuals will also be *human beings*, the question can also be formulated as: what has an intrinsic value for *all* human beings and should therefore be the objective of intergenerational arrangements?

Utilitarians also intensively discuss the question of the ultimate objective and the suitable measures to achieve it. The propagation of human welfare or happiness is a core element of all utilitarian theories. Does that mean that whoever agrees with my above theoretical expositions on value is necessarily a utilitarian? Are my theoretical considerations on value 'utilitarian'? This question becomes particularly urgent if we consider the following statement. Peter Singer writes:

> *While it is common for writers in ethics to deny that utilitarian considerations are the only valid moral considerations, it is quite rare for them to deny utilitarian considerations any place at all in their moral systems. For instance, intuitionists... are strong critics of utilitarianism; but they include duties of beneficence – promoting happiness and relieving suffering – in their list of prima facie duties. This, I suggest, is evidence that utilitarianism has a kind of appeal unique in moral theory. (Singer, 1976b, p85)[72]*

In my opinion, replacing the word 'utilitarianism' in Singer's quotes with 'axiological considerations' would make the terminology clearer. Every moral theory must contain axiological elements, but not necessarily utilitarian ones. Axiological and utilitarian debates can benefit from each other, but should nevertheless be analytically distinguished.

The two key questions in moral philosophy are those of the good (the axiological question) and the right (the justice question). Utilitarianism defines the good independently from the right; and then the right is defined as that which maximizes the good (Frankena, 1963, p13; Cf. Mill, 1979, section V). The utilitarian thus takes a double step (Birnbacher, 2002, p95 et seq.; see also Narveson, 1976, p67; Sen and Williams, 1982, p3; Leist, 1991, p338). Let us take a closer look at this double step in the account of John Stuart Mill, one of the best-known classical utilitarians. He first discusses the good, pointing at the characteristics of happiness.[73] This is the first part of the double step. According to Mill, however, an acceptance of the utilitarian norm (the second step) would not have required this clarification (Mill, 1979, p11). Mill's utilitarian norm is: 'The creed which accepts as the foundation of morals "utility" or the "greatest happiness principle" holds that actions are right in proportion as they tend to promote happiness; wrong as they tend to produce the reverse of happiness' (Mill, 1979, p7).

An objective is not a norm. The *objective* is human 'welfare' (according to many, but not all utilitarian theories). The norm is the promotion of the highest possible level of welfare through *actions*. Normative utilitarianism concentrates on how to deal with conflicts: '[I]f the principle of utility is good for anything, it must be good for weighing these conflicting utilities against one another, and marking out the region within which one or the other preponderates', says Mill (1979, p23). According to him, that is even how to decide what is 'just' (Mill, 1979, section V).

Opponents of utilitarianism criticize that the utilitarian norm of action accepts 'harm' to some if it increases the 'welfare' of many and the overall balance is positive. Thus, for instance, it would be justified to torture a suspected terrorist in order to prevent hundreds of children from being harmed. But this point of criticism is aimed against the normative category, and it does not deny that the 'welfare' of the tortured person and that of the many children (and not their 'asceticism' or 'virtue') is of intrinsic value on an axiological level. I might consider it inadmissible to *offset* the welfare of certain individuals against that of others in this example, but that does not deny the notion that the welfare of all persons mentioned in the example is a good with an intrinsic value.

When philosophers theorize on axiology, they are interested in the objective; when they theorize on justice, they are interested in norms. My explorations above solely treated axiological issues, it would thus be misleading to call them 'normative-utilitarian'. On an axiological level, many deontological theories also implicitly or explicitly justify 'duties' by a reduction of unnecessary suffering. Every *reasonable* deontological theory must be oriented by human well-being. Even Rawls, whose justice theory is meant as a counter-concept to utilitarianism, cannot manage without axiological considerations. He mentions 'welfare', 'sum of satisfactions', 'prevention of suffering and rigours' and other terms quite arbitrarily throughout the book (Rawls, 1971). Of course, Rawls emphasizes that in his theory of justice the concept of the right is prior to that of the good (Rawls, 1971, p31). But he forgets to develop an own theory of the good altogether – and this is a major weakness of his account.

Often, normative utilitarians are not very strict about axiological questions themselves. And this is fatal. If it should turn out that an objective cannot be achieved by certain actions, this has repercussions on the utilitarian principle of action. Mill uses 'utility', 'happiness', 'pleasure' and even the 'satisfaction of interests' as synonymous axiological objectives. But for an axiologist, it makes a big difference whether one wants to measure 'happiness' or 'pleasure'. Probably Mill even introduced the artificial coinage 'utilitarianism' (orientation by 'utility') in order to avoid such problems (cf. Mill, 1979, p7 (footnote 1)). Unlike in everyday usage, 'utility' in Mill's terminology is not a relative value (in the sense of 'usefulness' with regard to something), but an absolute value and a synonym for welfare, pleasure, happiness, etc. (Birnbacher, 2002, p95).

Every theory on justice, and thus every theory on generational justice, must deal with axiological questions. But that does not make the theory normative utilitarian; it can do without normative utilitarian statements, if it wants to. Many of the usual normative utilitarian debates about the 'offsetability' of welfare between contemporaries can hardly be applied to the intergenerational context anyway.

First, it is difficult to offset welfare between generations, because time is one-directional. 'The temporal direction of causation generates problems of asymmetry of power as well as restrictions to the possibility of giving back to the past', as Gosseries puts it (Gosseries, 2008, p447). Second, comparisons between generations are not based on real individuals, but only on masses of people and their average welfare. In fact, theories of intergenerational justice often deal not only with a large number of people, but with a large number of generations and therefore with basic characteristics that must have an intrinsic value for *all* human beings. And that is, above all, needs. Utilitarian thinkers, by contrast, focused on interests (for example John S. Mill or Peter Singer), preferences (for example John C. Harsanyi, 1982) or even desires (Richard M. Hare, 1982) in the *intra*generational context. The question of which axiological objective there should be for consequentialist theories in an *intra*generational context, is not part of my subject. But for long-term *inter*generational comparisons, only a *needs*-focused consequentialism makes sense. Distinguishing between quantitative and qualitative forms of fulfilment, as discussed by Mill, may make sense with regard to wants or interests, but not with regard to needs. And, as will be shown later, my approach demands of each generation to consider future generations' well-being, using the ambitious Human Development Index instead of utilitarian subjective happiness. That is why I would not call my theory of intergenerational justice a utilitarian one.

I shall leave it with these few remarks. For reasons of space, I have only clarified the intersection between my own expositions on axiology and utilitarian theories, without examining utilitarianism in more detail.[74]

Measuring well-being

Objective vs. subjective indicators

Many philosophers believe that happiness cannot be measured (for example Pieper, 2003, p31). Most happiness researchers outside philosophy would strongly disagree. In fact, the very progress that has been made in research of 'happiness', 'quality of life' (and whatever else belongs to the generic term 'well-being') is in the area of measuring. The development of indicators for 'well-being' started in the 1960s – as a counter-concept to purely economic approaches such as GDP (Doyal and Gough, 1991, p152; Birnbacher, 1999;

Glatzer, 2006, p170). Von Wright was the first to distinguish between two different methods of measuring well-being: objective living conditions and subjective perceptions (von Wright, 1963).[75] Numerous indicators were developed for both approaches. Objective (descriptive) approaches describe observable living circumstances and resources of individuals that are usually monitored by experts in social sciences, economics and medicine. These objective conditions exist independently of whether the individuals concerned are aware of them (Glatzer, 2006, p171). They might range from personal conditions to the situation in the community and global environmental conditions. Some approaches focus on social problems such as poverty or social exclusion.

Subjective (evaluative) approaches are based on the perceptions and evaluations of individuals. Well-being is here in the eye of the beholder. Hereinafter, this method will be referred to as 'asking people', because research on whether people are satisfied with their present circumstances and whether they allow them to lead a good life is carried out by means of interviews, questionnaires or common surveys (Buhlmann, 2000; Veenhoven, 2007, p245).

Subjective indicators for well-being

Methods and indicators

Subjectively measured well-being is usually examined under the assumption that it is cardinally measurable and interpersonally comparable (Frey and Stutzer, 2001, p4). Another assumption is that well-being[76] is a single dimension, measurable on a continuous scale from low to high, like temperature.[77] If well-being is a single item, we would be at a certain level at all times. That can be illustrated by describing a random day of my life (see Figure 5.4).

The day starts when my alarm clock goes off at 6 am and I wake up from dreamless sleep. I prepare breakfast and as soon as I drink my latte macchiato, I start to see some meaning in my life. But when I read the morning paper, I am reminded of all the wars and famines in the world, which makes me feel worse. My mood deteriorates even more as soon as I hit a traffic jam on my commute to work. After arrival in my office at the university, I delve into my current research projects. That makes me happy. At 11 am, I bang my head against a shelf, and my head hurts for a few minutes. I continue my work but my concentration is interrupted at smaller and smaller intervals by hunger. After a delayed lunch, I continue my work albeit with a little drowsiness. At 5 pm, I give my lecture and feel inspired by my great students. After dinner, I discuss interesting philosophical questions and the latest rumours with my colleagues; that makes me feel great. The day ends with a romantic hour with my wife.

Such subjective evaluations of well-being are quite common in psychiatric and psychological treatment, for instance with depression patients. They can also be used in empirical well-being research (Kahneman et al, 2004). Most people have no problems in making such charts for their own days in life. The single days can be added up to charts that represent well-being levels in weeks, months or years.

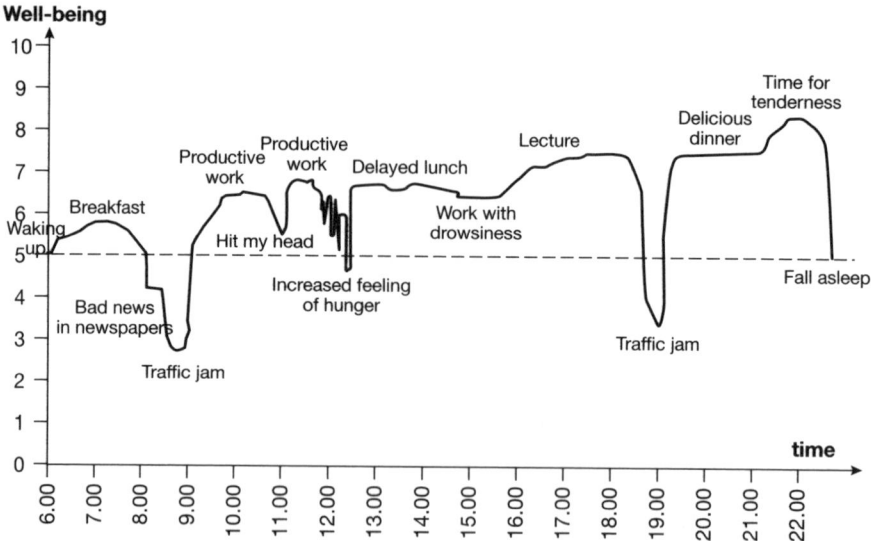

Source: Adapted from Tännsjö (2007, p82)

Figure 5.4 *Well-being at different times of a day (subjective evaluation)*

Tännsjö – who described a similar day and inspired my above example – believes it is very unlikely for two completely different types of feelings to exist *at the same time* (Tännsjö, 2007, p82). For him, all thoughts and perceptions add up to either highs or lows, as illustrated in Figure 5.4. This means that it is impossible to be 'happy' and 'sad' at the same time (single dimension hypothesis).

Information on people's assessment of their own well-being can be obtained by asking one or several questions. Two types of indicators can thus be distinguished: first, one-item indicators such as the 'overall satisfaction of life' (OSL), which describe the inner state of a person in a single number (Figure 5.4 shows an example of a 'one-item indicator'). Second, multi-domain indicators, which ask for a number of items that represent a big share of the variance of perceived well-being. The 'personal well-being index' (PWI), for instance, represents seven items based on the question: How satisfied are you with (1) your standard of living, (2) your health, (3) your achievements so far, (4) your personal relationships, (5) how safe you feel, (6) feeling part of your community, and (7) your future security? (Cummins at al, 2006, p4). Both indicators, the OSL and the PWI, are obtained by 'asking people'.

Subjective measuring methods have the advantage that, ultimately, only an individual himself can know how happy or satisfied he really is (Glatzer, 2006, p178). And only subjective assessments are largely independent of changing social and cultural values, as Birnbacher points out:

> *The more the concept of quality of life is analysed by objective character-*
> *istics, the less likely it will be applicable independently of specific cultural*

norms and ideals. If, however, quality of life is to function as a culture-independent standard, it must focus on subjective well-being rather than on the nature of the objective conditions on which subjective well-being depends. In other words, it should make no difference to the quality of life ascribed to a person whether subjective well-being is derived from true or false pleasures (Plato), from experiencing higher or lower pleasures (Mill), or from the exercise of capacities and functionings (Sen). (Birnbacher, 1999, p30)

However, the results of studies based on questionnaires are highly inconsistent and lead to 'happiness paradoxes' or 'unhappiness dilemmas'. Respondents under objectively bad circumstances sometimes claim they are satisfied and happy, whereas respondents under objectively good circumstances and with few worries might subjectively assess their situation as bad (Diener and Suh, 1997, pp200–209). Already the first well-being measuring projects surprisingly revealed that the relation between objective circumstances and subjective perception is not as strong as one might expect (Zapf, 1984; Glatzer, 2006, p172).

Do wage increases make people happier?

A striking result of happiness measurements is that increased wages do not lead to more happiness, once a certain threshold is passed.[78] Beyond that threshold, the principle of habituation applies (also called 'hedonic adaptation'): an increased income is a new situation for an individual. It differs from the previous condition for a while, but then soon becomes normal (Frederick and Loewenstein, 1999). A 'hedonic treadmill' develops in which objective improvements of the standard of living do not lead to a higher level of subjective satisfaction (see Figure 5.5).[79]

The happiness on the basis of a given aspiration level curve, for example along the points a, b and c on aspiration level curve A_1, is not permanently increased. At first, people's aspirations are as low as A_1, so income Y_1 leads to happiness H_1. If the income rises from Y_1 to Y_2, the happiness will rise from H_1 to H'_2. The curves A_1, A_2 and A_3 depict a decreasing marginal utility of income as usually assumed by economists. In addition to the decreasing marginal utility, we get the habituation effect. Together with the increasing income, aspirations also rise. After a short period during which people are happy about the higher income, their aspiration level curve A_1 moves to the right and becomes A_2. Although their standard of living is higher, their subjective happiness drops from level H'_2 to H_2 after the habituation process is completed. If their wages are increased once more (from Y_2 to Y_3), the process is repeated: after a short while, their level drops from H'_3 to H_3.

The same process can take place the other way around if the standard of living drops. It's all a matter of habit. In the fairytale, Lucky Jack swaps his gold for a horse, the horse for a cow, the cow for a pig, the pig for a goose, and the goose for a whetstone. When the whetstone finally falls into a well and Jack no longer has to carry it, he rejoices: 'I am the happiest person under the sun'

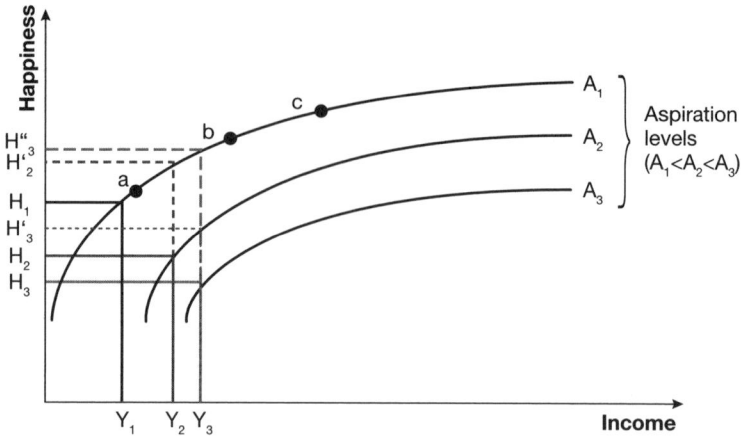

Source: Based on Frey and Stutzer (2001, p35)

Figure 5.5 *Happiness, income and the role of aspiration levels*

(Grimm's Fairytales). Even the worst situation can have its sunny side, especially if it cannot be changed. Figure 5.5 also shows how the reverse process functions: the aspiration level moves to the left several times. The habit formation thesis stresses that the satisfaction one derives from goods (or income) is influenced by comparisons with one's past. If a man who is now rich forgets that he was once poor (or vice versa), his satisfaction will move back to its original level. Only as long as he is aware of the contrast, his satisfaction values will temporarily stay high (or low). According to the findings of some scientists, people always return to their baseline level sooner or later (Kahneman et al, 2004; Easterlin, 2005).

The broader concept that explains why wage increases do not make people permanently happier can be called 'goal attainment' – and it even takes place on Robinson Crusoe's island, when Crusoe tries to improve his own standards, for example, in matters of cultivation, fishing, etc. (Bruni and Porto, 2007, p12 et seq.). Imagine a mountaineer who has reached his first 3000 metre peak after one year of preparation. According to the goal attainment thesis, he will most probably not lean back and be happy for the rest of his life. Instead he will rather become restless after a few days and will start training to climb a 4000 metre high mountain. The same effect can be observed with virtually all goals in life, be they material, educational or even romantic.[80] Emptiness starts to spread as soon as a goal has been reached. A new goal is needed. And it has to be even higher, even more, even better. We thus have to distinguish between 'hedonic treadmills', which also take place after sheer luck and 'satisfaction treadmills' based on goal attainment (Kahneman, 1999, p14).

However, an important finding in empirical happiness research is that these treadmill effects do not take place equally throughout all domains. Less habituation arises with regard to family circumstances and health than to material goods (Easterlin, 2007, p53). Likewise, 'cultural goods' such as music, literature and art are less subject to habituation than 'comfort goods' such as homes and cars. Assuming people *want* to be happy, they should want to avoid treadmill effects. If they were aware of their self-deception, they would buy fewer conspicuous goods and spend more time on their family life and health, which, in turn, would increase their subjectively measured well-being and make them happier (Easterlin, 2007, p54). In the economic sphere, they would buy more cultural goods and less 'positional' goods, and thereby reach the same effect: more happiness.

But are habituation and the endless pursuit of ever more ambitious goals everyone's destiny, a law of (human) nature? Both anecdotal evidence and empirical studies prove that individuals differ greatly. One person might quickly get used to a new situation while another enjoys his higher income level for a long time. Suppose someone becomes rich by a surprise event, such as a lottery jackpot.[81] Is it impossible for him to experience his entire life thereafter as more fulfilled and better? Certainly not. The fact that many people raise their demand level after a short while is almost a form of ingratitude or a lack of moderation. Neither the habituation treadmill nor the satisfaction treadmill are inherent aspects of human nature. Some people avoid these treadmills – and become happy.[82]

Social comparison and the aggregate well-being of nations

Social comparisons – Layard calls them 'rivalries'[83] – take place in society. 'Social comparison' means that the satisfaction one derives is affected by comparisons with others. A study focused on the US found that a rise in the average income of the state a person lives in reduces his happiness by one third of the degree but that a rise in his own income increases it (Blanchflower and Oswald, 2000).[84] It is the old 'keeping up with the Joneses' scenario, where one's happiness is influenced by the difference between our level of income and the level of income of others, instead of the absolute level (Bruni and Porta, 2007, p13).[85] Many significant acts of consumption are carried out under the eyes of others. For these conspicuous or 'positional' goods, for example cars or homes, the results 'tend to be mutually offsetting, just as when all nations spend more on armaments' (Frank, 2007, p84). These are the 'consumption traps' already described by Scitovsky in his *Joyless Economy* (1976). If the relative gains and losses of different individuals cancel each other out, the happiness values of a society as a whole cannot increase or decrease.

Intercultural comparisons

The happiest people in the world live in Nigeria, according to the World Values Survey. When asked how happy they presently were, almost 70 per cent of the Nigerian interviewees said 'very happy' (followed by Mexico, Venezuela and El Salvador – see Figure 5.6) (Bond, 2003).[86] But every year, thousands of people risk their lives to flee from Nigeria and reach Europe. Should Nigeria be a model for other countries? Nigerians probably compare themselves mainly with other

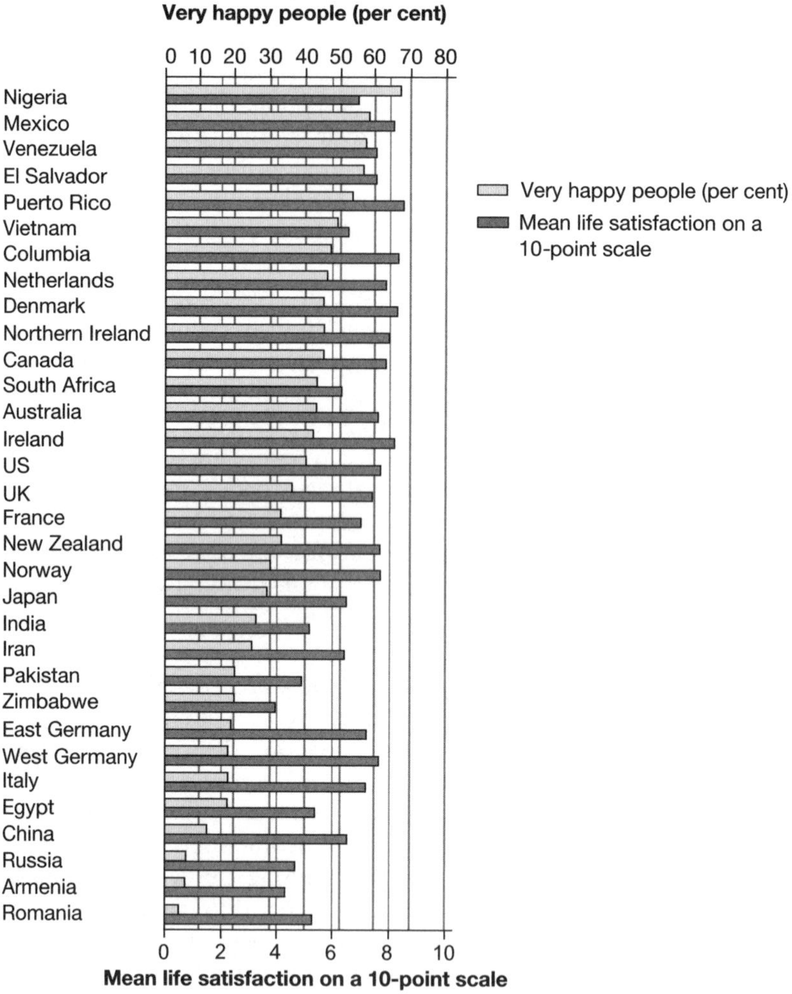
Very happy people (per cent)
0 10 20 30 40 50 60 70 80
Nigeria
Mexico
Venezuela
El Salvador
Puerto Rico
Vietnam
Columbia
Netherlands
Denmark
Northern Ireland
Canada
South Africa
Australia
Ireland
US
UK
France
New Zealand
Norway
Japan
India
Iran
Pakistan
Zimbabwe
East Germany
West Germany
Italy
Egypt
China
Russia
Armenia
Romania
0 2 4 6 8 10
Mean life satisfaction on a 10-point scale
Very happy people (per cent)
Mean life satisfaction on a 10-point scale

Source: Bond (2003) and data from the World Values Survey, www.worldvaluessurvey.org/

Figure 5.6 *Global distribution of happiness and life satisfaction*

Nigerians and not with, say, Britons. Therefore, someone who belongs to the top 10 per cent of the Nigerian society might be as happy as someone who belongs to the top 10 per cent in a Western country.

Also, the underprivileged tend to adjust their desires to their means. They forsake the exclusive desires of people in rich countries in order not to be disappointed. Sen writes:

> *Our reading of what is feasible in our situation and station may be crucial to the intensities of our desires, and may even affect what we dare*

> *to desire. Desires reflect compromises with reality, and reality is harsher*
> *to some than to others... In some lives small mercies have to count big.*
> *(Sen, 1985, p190)*

Many researchers who originally come from LDCs, as well as those who advocate the third generation of human rights, are therefore against subjective well-being indicators and favour objective ones (see Sen, 2000, pp26 and 29).

Nussbaum gives a good example for a 'happiness paradox' (and how it could be solved):

> *A poll of widowers and widows in India showed that the widowers were*
> *in full complaint about their health status; the widows, on the other hand,*
> *in most cases ranked their health status as 'good'. On the other hand, a*
> *medical examination showed that the widows were actually suffering far*
> *more than the males from diseases associated with nutritional deficiency.*
> *The point was that they had lived all their lives expecting that women will*
> *eat less, and the weakened health status produced in this way was second*
> *nature to them. Some years later, after a period of 'consciousness raising',*
> *the study was repeated. The utility of the women had gone down, in the*
> *sense that they expressed far more dissatisfaction with their health. (Their*
> *objective medical situation was pretty much unchanged.) (Nussbaum,*
> *1992, p230)*

In this example, the discrepancy between objectively bad circumstances and positive subjective assessment of one's situation was abolished.

Statements on happiness in generational comparisons

The most important question for our context is: Can changes in well-being across generations be measured by subjective indicators? In global or nationwide surveys, interviewers usually ask respondents to indicate how happy or satisfied they are.[87] Substantial time-series data for longitudinal analyses are available from national opinion research institutes (for instance Gallup in the US; Allensbach (2002) in Germany).[88] The 'happiness question' is only one from an extensive catalogue of questions regarding all life spheres. To reflect about the 'happiness question', interviewees have only a few seconds time before they answer. The result: in high-income countries, the percentage of happy or very happy people stays more or less the same, as shown in Figure 5.7.

Can the chart be interpreted that US-Americans were as happy in 2002 as they were in 1957? This interpretation neglects that *different* people were interviewed now and than. Different 'cohorts' (or 'generations' as more than 30 years have passed) were asked. Obviously, the respondents in each given year compared themselves with contemporaries, but not with members of past or future generations. People living in 1957 did not compare their actual lives with what it would be like if they could live their lives in the year 2002. And people

Source: Myers (2003) and data from Gallup

Figure 5.7 *Happiness in the US, 1957–2002*

who were asked to fill out the questionnaire in 2002 compared not their actual lives with the hypothetical lives they would have lived in the year 1957. There-fore, the chart does not tell whether today's generation is happier or unhappier than earlier ones. Interpreting the chart this way is misleading.

The time-related Figures 5.8a and 5.8b illustrate the fictitious happiness distribution in the years 1850 and 2005. They show two equal shares of very happy people. Both charts, as well as for all intermediary years, may be methodologically correct, but it would be wrong to derive Figure 5.8c from Figures 5.8a and 5.8b and then claim that happiness did not increase between 1850 and 2005. [89]

But what was everyday life like, a few generations ago? In the year 1850, the average life expectancy worldwide was between 30 and 40 years. Most people were not free, there were enormous gaps between social classes, frequent wars and numerous epidemics. Doing the laundry took days, and travelling took weeks. Surgeries were done without anaesthesia, which means that even kings had to endure the excruciating pain, whereas today, no health-insured day labourer would. The basic needs of most people were not met as well as they are today. Even in the most developed countries the lives of much of the population was marked by bitter poverty, a fight for survival and lack of protection against sickness.[90]

When we take all generations that have ever lived into account, most of them were hunters and gatherers. For quite some time now the myth has been debunked that pre-agricultural people were better off because they led a natural and stress-free life.[91] On average, the life of hunters and gatherers was in no way agreeable. Schneider (2007, p275) emphasizes: 'Most alternated between fear and need, were hunted by predators, plagued by vermin, with worms in their gut and fly larvae in their eyes. And what nature didn't make them suffer, they did themselves: they were continuously at war with neighbouring tribes, enslaved

a

1850: Taking all things together, would you say you are very happy, quite happy, not very happy, not at all happy?

b

2005: Taking all things together, would you say you are very happy, quite happy, not very happy, not at all happy?

c

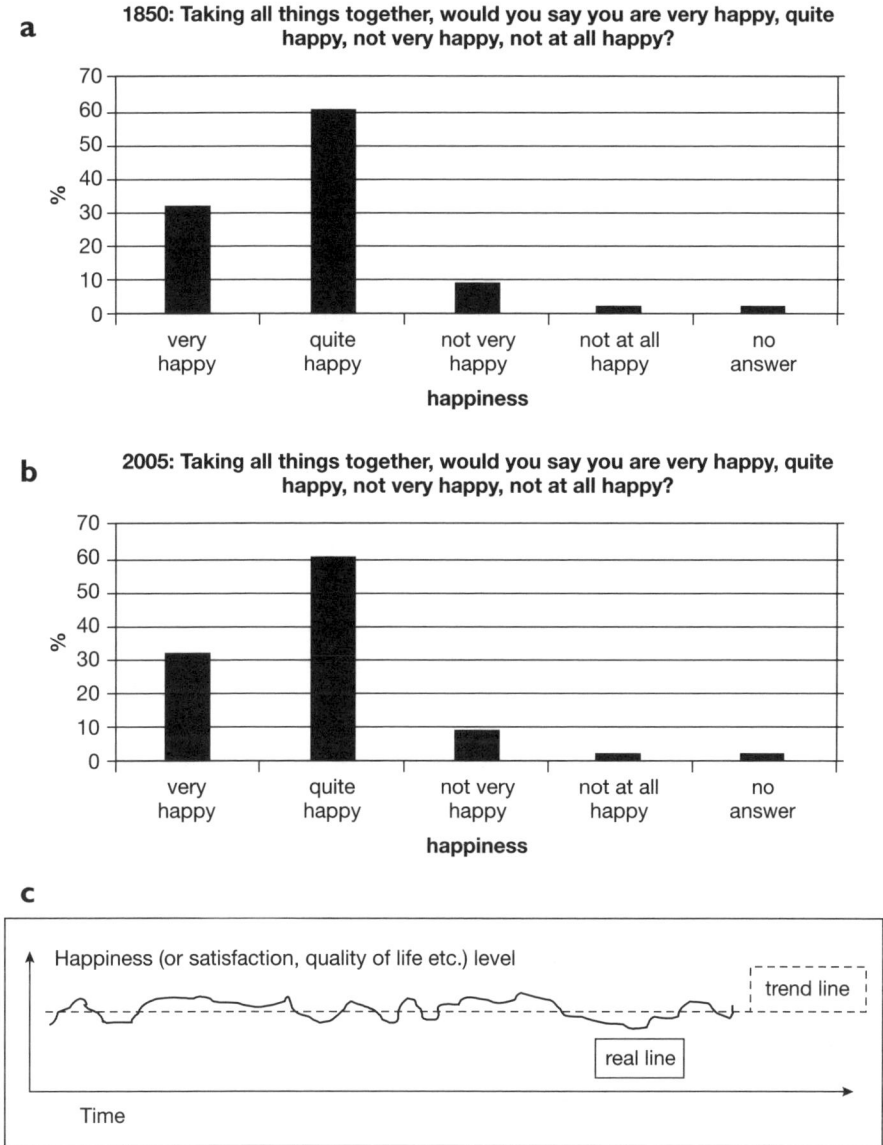

Figure 5.8 *Levels of happiness 1850 and 2005 and the wrong conclusion*

their women, maimed each other in gruesome rituals and waded through a quagmire of superstition that threatened them with even worse calamity for the future.' Still, had sociologists asked them how happy they were, they would probably have answered much like people today.

Research on the preferred year of birth

The right questions to ask in order to compare the subjectively evaluated well-being of different generations are: If you could choose when to be born, which year/era would you choose? And how much would your well-being decrease if your chosen birthday were to be placed back 100 years in history? Such a study was carried out with students as respondents (Tremmel, 2007a, 2009). The respondents had one hour time to think, no spontaneous answers were demanded (see Figure 5.9).[92]

The rationale was to apply some elements of an intergenerational 'veil of ignorance'. If a person prefers another year of birth than his own, he implicitly assumes that the other year is somehow better. If the majority prefers to be born in the future, they obviously believe the general well-being in the future will be at least as high as it is today. If, however, most people would prefer to have been born in the past, they are likely to believe that the average well-being in the past was at least as high as it is today. The results of the study can be seen in Figure 5.9. Only few people chose a year that was not included in their own intertemporal generation. No one wanted to be born prior to 1895. The reasons stated included inferior medication and technology, fewer chances and opportunities, more wars, conflicts and suffering, superstition and a lack of education. By contrast, surprisingly many wanted to be born in the future, and roughly 15 per cent even chose the distant future. They believed that welfare will continue to increase, medical conditions will improve and there will be more opportunities in life in the future (Tremmel, 2007a, p7 et seq.).

Since few people want to have been born at an earlier point in time, we can draw the conclusion that they would have been far less happy if they had belonged to an earlier generation. The earlier the year, the worse it is considered. Further empirical studies should determine the degree to which a person born in 1976 or later, for instance, would be less happy if he had been born earlier, say in 1975, 1950, 1900, 1800, 1700, etc. Such studies will probably show that the subjectively reported level of happiness (or satisfaction, quality of life, etc.)

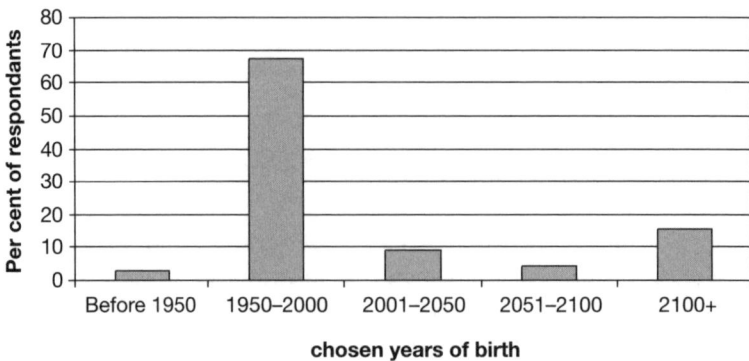

Source: Tremmel (2007a)

Figure 5.9 *The most preferred years of birth*

has increased over time (cf. Easterlin, 2002). The upward trend will vary from country to country but the longer the periods of time referred to, the closer it will get to Figure 5.10.

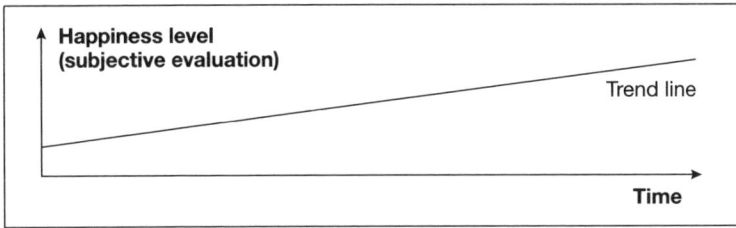

Figure 5.10 *Happiness over time, based on the 'preferred years of birth' method*

To sum up, the structure of the questionnaires strongly influence the results of studies on happiness over time. When asked how happy they are, people tend to compare themselves with their contemporaries, so today's results will be the same as those 50, 100, 500 or 10,000 years ago. But if people are asked to choose their preferred year of birth and how much less satisfied they would be if they had been born earlier, we learn that the degree of happiness has increased over time. If we determine the distribution of happiness over time, based on the preferred year of birth, the results are completely different from those shown in Figure 5.7, which are based on the usual questionnaires.

Far-reaching and systematic measuring problems bound up with subjective approaches

Let us turn to the measuring problems of the common happiness surveys, their major drawbacks. The reliability and validity of survey answers on well-being are questionable. That applies to intrapersonal comparisons, comparisons between individuals within a society, between countries, and above all between generations. The validity is claimed by arguments such as: happy people are, for example, more often smiling during social interactions (Fernández-Dols and Ruiz-Belda, 1990) and are rated as happy by friends and family members (Sandvik et al, 1993), especially by spouses (Costa and McCrae, 1988). The arguments *against* validity are far more convincing. The first problem relates to words, and it is not easy to settle. Everyone has his own understanding of the terms listed in the well-being/welfare circle (see Figure 5.2), and it makes a big difference whether we refer to well-being, happiness, quality of life or satisfaction. The results differ, as Figure 5.6 shows. If researchers use these terms interchangeably, their results are flawed.

Even the same word, for example 'happiness', causes a lot of misunderstanding. The World Database of Happiness in Rotterdam is a central archive that contains subjective indicators and statistics from all over the world (Veenhoven, 2005). Its director, Ruut Veenhoven, explains that the word 'happiness' has no precise equivalent in some languages. Even in English, there are more than 15 separate academic definitions (Bond, 2003). Obviously, the same word means different things to different people.

But even if these language problems did not exist, still no one *could* give correct answers to the question of how happy, satisfied, etc. he is. The indicators for well-being determined through interviews are systematically distorted. Misrepresentations reach from lapses of memory, cognitive dissonance, social desirability, and even the weather (if the weather is good, more people say they are happy). These effects have comprehensively been studied and described (Strack et al, 1991; Schwarz and Strack, 1991; Bertrand and Mullainathan, 2001; Thomä, 2003, pp153–161). Let us take a closer look at some of the reasons that keep interviewees from subjectively assessing their well-being accurately. First of all, there are distortions caused by intra-individual comparisons. Every respondent bases his answers on information he has best access to at the time he is interviewed (Schwarz and Strack, 1999, p63). Usually, more importance is attached to recent events than to events that took place long ago. We cannot expect people to ignore the circumstances, evaluations and moods of *today* when looking back at the last 30, 60 or even 90 years. None of us can weigh joyous memories against painful ones, money against health, private life against professional success, the mood of one's spouse against the life quality of a region or the tensions in the world within a few minutes.

Also, the structure of questionnaires can lead to distortions, since events called to mind by previous questions suddenly stand in the foreground although they otherwise might not even have been considered (Schwarz and Strack, 1999, p63). In an interesting study, respondents were asked two happiness questions: 'How happy are you with your life in general?' and 'How often do you normally go out on a date?'. If the dating question was asked first, the answers to both were highly correlated, but if it was asked second, they were basically uncorrelated. The dating question apparently made people focus on one particular aspect of their life (Bertrand and Mullainathan, 2001, p68).

Mental constructs also cause distortions. Respondents sometimes take a particularly positive or negative event as a reference point (Schwarz and Strack, 1999, pp65–69). That can make positive or negative current events or situations appear better or worse than they actually are. They also tend to forget the duration of a situation and concentrate on its beginning or end instead. Thus, the same importance is attached to two weeks of suffering as to six months.

In addition, people might answer differently, depending on their level of reflection. If an interviewee is asked: 'What makes you happy?', he might say: 'more income', 'a bigger house', etc., but if he had read an article on happiness research, happiness paradoxes and treadmills, he would certainly answer differently.

So far, we have concentrated on an intra-individual level. Things become even trickier if we compare different people. Schwarz and Strack repeat the 'social comparison hypothesis': 'In fact, the more people assume that their own living conditions are better than those of others, the more satisfaction they report', but we are never quite sure about the circumstances of others, and that can lead to invalid measuring results (Schwarz and Strack, 1999, p71). There is a tendency to overestimate the happiness of our neighbours and, according to the 'social comparison' thesis, this makes us underestimate our own. But correct measuring can also cause difficult questions as the following example illustrates.

Let us assume a dandy has booked a very expensive hotel at the beach for a day. Although the weather is fine, the dandy is quite grumpy, bemoaning the wind. The breakfast is excellent but the dandy wants something extraordinary: a grapefruit juice. Even if it is not available. After a long discussion, the waiter runs to the village to buy a grapefruit and gets Mr Dandy his grapefruit delight. Being the only one in the breakfast hall with a grapefruit juice

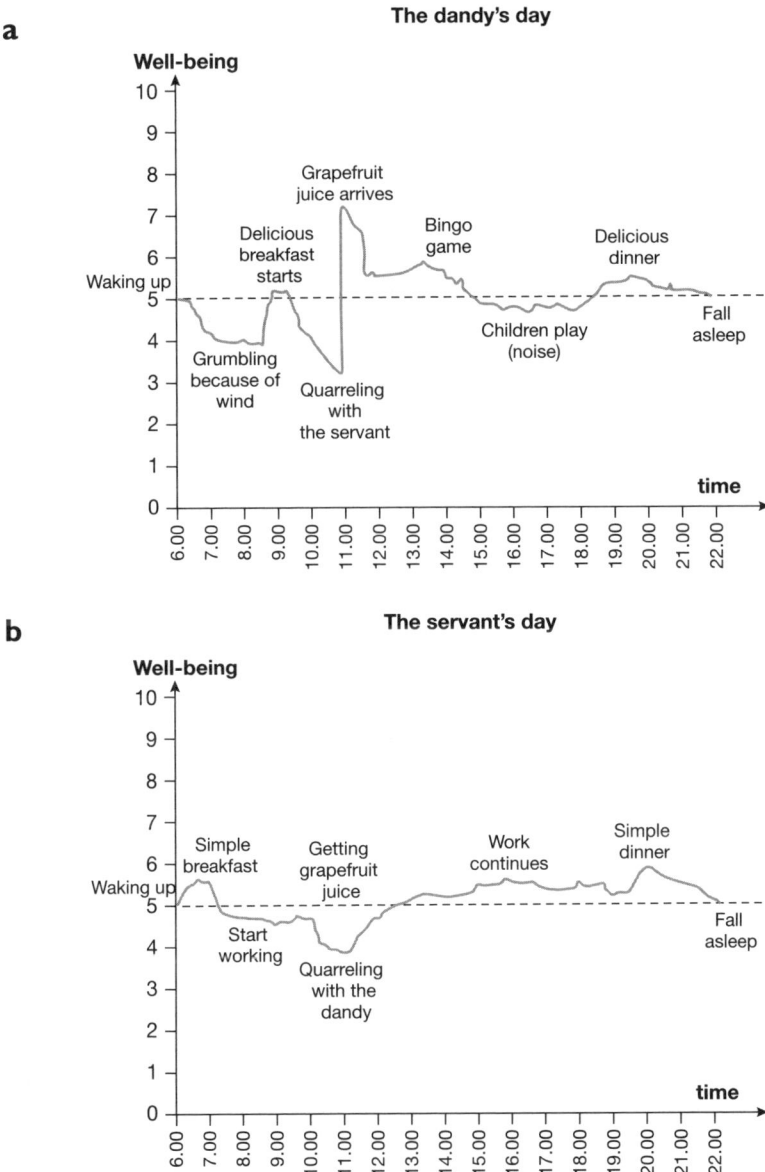

a The dandy's day

b The servant's day

Figure 5.11 *Interpersonal comparison of well-being levels (dandy and servant)*

makes the dandy extremely happy. Now, when we look at the well-being charts of both parties, we see that this incident caused loss in the well-being of the waiter, but this is more than outweighed by the well-being gains of the dandy. From a utilitarian point of view, that takes subjective well-being instead of objective well-being in consideration, one must approve the action because the total good was increased. It seems unfair to pay so much attention to the 'expensive tastes' and 'idiosyncrasies' of some people. This is a strong argument for measuring well-being with objective indicators (see Figure 5.11).

Usually, researchers do not let people fill out daily charts of their well-being, instead they ask the question: 'How happy are you?'. We have seen that the results are distorted by selective recall effects. But even if people *could* give correct answers in questionnaires, they still would not *want* to tell a stranger what makes them happy. In the philosophical debate, sensual pleasures are often described as a source of happiness (de La Mettrie, 1985). But who would be willing to talk about them with an unknown interviewer? According to studies that ask for the item 'sex', it makes people happier than any other activity (Layard, 2005, p15).[93] Unfortunately, however, very few studies include such a question. Instead, some try to examine the correlation between happiness and 'price stability' (Di Tella et al, 1999).

Another problem with socially desirable answering behaviour is that people adapt to the optimism or pessimism of others around them. Latin American countries that report high happiness levels have a similarly high regard for people with an upbeat attitude. In the US, too, success or failure is typically seen as one's own responsibility, and that might keep people from admitting they are unhappy. Answering an interviewer is much the same as answering your neighbour when he asks you how you are. Eckersley mentions that the public appearance (or 'mask' as he calls it) of individuals who want to look happy and successful may conceal the private person behind (Eckersley, 2000, p276).

To sum it up, asking people about their present happiness or satisfaction does not lead to sound results. That does not mean the subjectively perceived degree of well-being or need satisfaction is the wrong social objective. The problem with 'reported subjective well-being' is not so much the 'subjective', but the 'reported'.

Measuring brainwaves

There might soon be an alternative to doubtful questionnaires and dishonest answers. According to Richard Davidson from the University of Wisconsin, we can already pretty accurately measure the brain processes that take place when a person is happy or unhappy (Davidson, 2000). These measurements are made by means of magnetic resonance imaging (MRI) and positron emission tomography (PET). In modern brain physiology, electrodes are placed on the scalp. When the test person experiences a positive feeling, the front left part of his brain becomes more active. When he experiences a negative feeling, this activity subsides and there is more activity in the front right part of the brain. In the future, experiments could be carried out while people are living their regular lives.[94] They could answer two of the most important questions in the science of happiness, namely:

1 Is happiness a single dimension that merely changes from low to high, or is it made up of different incommensurable dimensions?
2 To what degree do certain activities and experiences influence our happiness?

Remember Figure 5.4 that described well-being at different times during a random day of life. Until now, it is just an unproven assumption that one can draw such a graph. The 'single-dimension' view of well-being is not the only one that is possible. Parfit assumes the opposite. He writes: 'Compare the pleasure of satisfying an intensive thirst or lust, listening to music, solving an intellectual problem, reading a tragedy, and knowing that one's child is happy. These various experiences do not contain any distinctive common quality' (Parfit, 1987, p493).[95] This dispute cannot be solved by means of sociological or economic methods, but only by measuring brainwaves. If certain pleasures would activate completely different brain areas than other pleasures, it would make sense to use different terms. Perhaps we would then have to strictly distinguish between pleasant conditions triggered by physical activities and those triggered by mental activities, and we would need two (or several) curves instead of one, as in Figure 5.4.

The second question, to which degree certain activities and experiences trigger happiness or unhappiness, can also be answered far better by measuring brainwaves than by asking people as distortions due to selective memory, cognitive dissonance or social desirability could be avoided.

Measuring brainwaves is not a purely subjective (evaluative) method, but partly objective (descriptive). Unlike with objective indicators (see Chapter 6), the subjective emotional differences are taken into consideration. The same experiences or activities can be perceived quite differently inter-subjectively, as is proven by measuring brainwaves. But in contrast to 'asking-people' methods, experts can measure the happiness or well-being of the test persons directly. Their 'self-report' is no longer based on their statements, but on their brain activity.

The consumption of glucose is usually measured in millimetres. So it might be possible to compare a person's well-being in the front left part of his brain by millimetres in the future. In principle, the indicator 'Personal Well-being Index, measured by the glucose consumption in mm' is more valid and reliable than the 'Personal Well-being Index, based on a questionnaire'. In 1780, Bentham did not have such methods available, but he assumed that pleasure or pain depended on the intensity of an event, its duration, the certainty or uncertainty and its propinquity or remoteness (Bentham, 1907, p29; see also Lumer, 2002, pp163–188, 2003, p106). If brainwaves can one day be measured and compared, Bentham's dream will have come true. Should neuroscience make such progress, this method could make valid and reliable intra-personal, intra-country and inter-country comparisons possible. In the long run, we could even compare different generations. If a person who is hungry or thirsty has a high millimetre value in the front right part of his brain, we would measure less suffering in the brain of an average person of today's generation than in that of an average citizen in the year 1850. For instance, an annual consumption of more than 50 millimetres would be measured five instead of ten times per year, because there was less food and there were more illnesses in the 19th century than now.

Escaping from reality

If the spots on the MRI become an ever more important indicator for subjectively measured well-being in the future, why not enlarge them by virtual reality or drugs? Robert Nozick asks us to imagine an 'experience machine' that could make people believe all their needs were satisfied (Nozick, 1974, p44, 1989, pp104–107). With electrodes attached to one's brain, one could believe one was riding a roller coaster, reading a great novel, visiting a club, enjoying a delicious dinner, or whatever else one's preferences are.[96] Nozick says that we would not use such a machine. But as long as it was not permanent, he is surely wrong, as far as the majority of people is concerned. People pay a lot to use the virtual reality devices we have developed so far.[97] Most people would refuse to live in virtual reality if it were forever, but even then, some philosophers state that they personally would (Tännsjö, 2007, p95).

Positive brainwaves can also be triggered by drugs. Can, or should, people therefore use more drugs? That is a theoretical question. There are still no drugs that could cause permanent well-being. Each high is followed by a low that is all the worse. Until now, there are no drugs that are a fast and easy way to satisfy needs. In his book *Happiness*, Layard advocates using psychiatric drugs more often, but only for ill people, not for healthy ones (Layard, 2005, pp205–222). If drugs without side effects should ever be developed, philosophers will have to seriously discuss whether they are a legitimate means of increasing one's well-being. Until then, it is a waste of time.

To sum things up, there are three methods of measuring the well-being of different generations: questionnaires, social indicators and brainwaves. Questionnaires are least suitable. Measuring brain activity might yield the best results one day, but this method is still in its infancy. It will be long before it will enable us to compare the well-being of generations A and B. That is why we now turn to social indicators of human, economic, political and social progress, which are currently the best way to track human well-being across generations.

Objective measurement of well-being

Researchers who rely on objective indicators to measure well-being use observable living conditions that can be measured according to scientific standards. That takes for granted that our well-being depends on the satisfaction of identifiable needs and interests. This approach is more politically oriented, because – more than the subjective approach – it assumes that a society can influence the well-being of its members, or an earlier generation can influence the well-being of later ones. But not only policy makers, theorists of intergenerational justice also need a clear answer to the question of whether society has progressed over time. We will now examine three indices, the Human Development Index, the Human Well-being Index and the Weighted Index of Social Progress.[98]

Human Development Index

In 1990, the United Nations Development Programme (UNDP), the responsible sub-organization of the United Nations Organization (UNO), presented a new measuring standard, the Human Development Index (HDI). The HDI is calculated and used all around the world. It was developed by the Pakistani economist Mahbub ul Haq, who explicitly calls it the best standard for measuring human welfare (Ul Haq, 1995, p4)[99] and introduces it into the philosophical debate by declaring it the answer to the question of the ultimate societal objective: 'The idea that social arrangements must be judged by the extent that they promote "human good" dates at least back to Aristotle' (Ul Haq, 1995, p13). The basic idea of the HDI is that human development must not be limited to economic growth, but should also include a widening of choices and the creation of an environment that allows man to live a long, healthy and productive life. Two thirds of the HDI are based on non-economic objectives. Unlike a number of post-materialistic approaches, one third of the HDI acknowledges that material wealth is an important factor in an overall concept of well-being. We must not forget that many previous intertemporal generations had difficulties in fulfilling their basic needs. An index that does not include a material component would not enable us to measure whether and to which degree *poverty* has decreased over several generations and how far generations' opportunity sets to consume goods and services have been extended.

The three goal areas of the HDI are operationalized in the following way:

- a long and healthy life, as measured by health expectancy at birth;
- knowledge, as measured by the adult literacy rate (with two-thirds weight) and the combined primary, secondary and tertiary gross enrolment ratio (with one-third weight);
- a decent standard of living, as measured by GDP per capita.

Until the Human Development Report (HDR) of the year 1994, *the highest or lowest observable* values were taken as reference points for the minimum or maximum values of the respective dimension in order to calculate the HDI. Later HDR reports used *fixed* minimum and maximum values for life expectancy (25/85 years), the literacy rate (0 per cent/100 per cent), the average number of school years (0/15 years), and income (100/40,000 true GDP per capita, measured in the dollar purchasing power parity) (Berger-Schmitt, 1999, p15). The calculation of the HDI is based on a principle of relation. The minimum value is deducted from the value observed in a country (for example life expectancy of 83 years in Japan), and the difference is divided by the difference between the maximum and the minimum value:

$$\text{Index} = \frac{83 \; (Japan) - 25 \; (fixed\_lower\_value)}{85 \; (fixed\_upper\_value) - 25 \; (fixed\_lower\_value)}$$

The standardization made it possible to draw reliable comparisons over time. On this basis, country ranking lists in ascending HDI order have been developed every year since the HDR was introduced. As this study is focused on intergenerational, not intragenerational justice, only a generational comparison of the aggregated HDI is depicted here. However, UNO also calculates disaggregated forms of the HDI. In a disaggregated form, the index displays differences between social strata, ethnic groups or regions that can supply data for the debate on justice between contemporaries. For instance, gender questions can be taken into account by calculating a separate HDI for men and women in each country. In the following, however, we will concentrate on the historic development of the aggregated HDI.

Ultimately, we are interested in progress of mankind as a whole on a global level. However, it is necessary to look at certain countries as examples or because others may lack the required data. But as of 1975, HDI data are available for all countries. The global HDI value then was about 0.6, but it has continuously increased ever since (see Figure 5.12).

The positive trend does not only apply to industrialized countries, but also to developing continents, as can be seen in Figure 5.13 for Africa, Latin America and Asia (without Russia and Japan).

To compare generations, however, we need statistical series that go back much further in the past. Such data only exist for very few countries, such as the US, Germany, France, UK, Japan and The Netherlands (see Figure 5.14).[100]

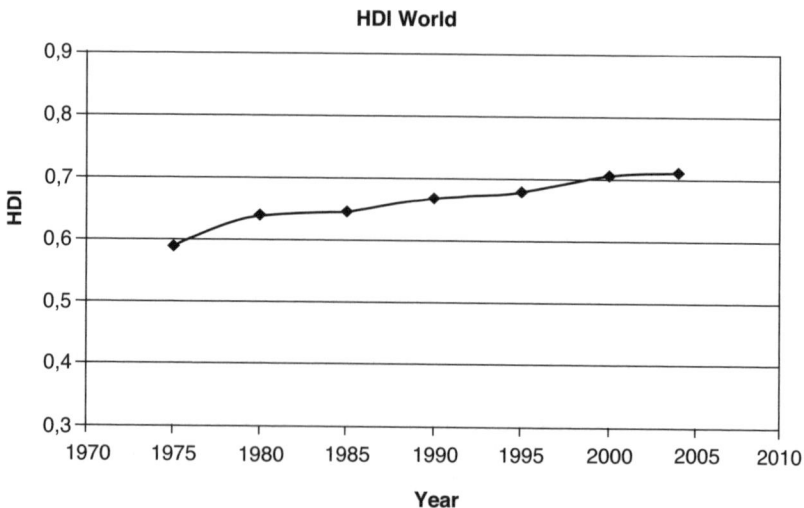

Source: Based on data from http://hdr.undp.org/hdr2006/statistics/data/HDR06_excel.zip

Figure 5.12 *Global HDI development, 1975–2004*

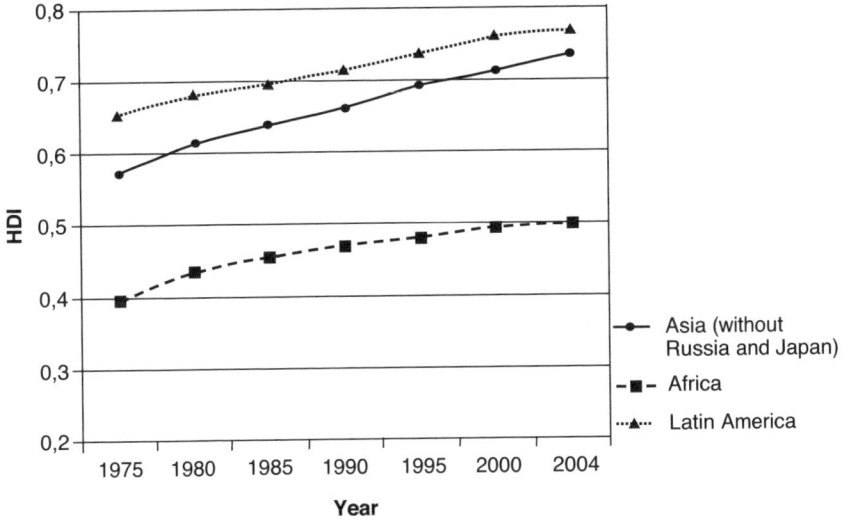

Source: Based on data from http://hdr.undp.org/hdr2006/statistics/data/HDR06_excel.zip

Figure 5.13 *HDI values in the developing continents, 1975–2004*

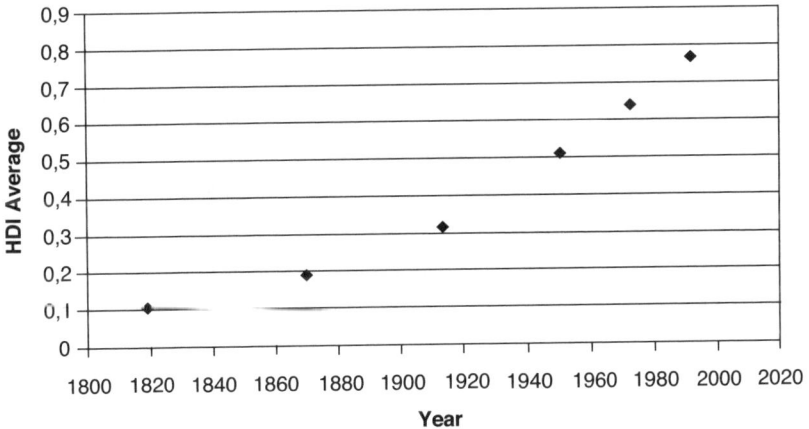

Source: Based on data taken from http://thecommunityguide.org/nchs/data/nvsr/nvsr54/
nvsr54_14.pdf; Maddison (1995); Goklany (2007); www.destatis.de/jetspeed/portal/
cms/Sites/destatis/Internet/DE/Content/Statistiken/Zeitreihen/LangeReihen/Volk
swirtschaftlicheGesamtrechnungen/Content100/lrvgr04a,templateId=renderPrint.psml;
www.destatis.de/jetspeed/portal/cms/Sites/destatis/Internet/DE/Presse/pm/2006/04/PD0
6__167__12621.psml; http://hdr.undp.org/hdr2006/statistics/countries/data_sheets/
cty_ds_DEU.html

Figure 5.14 *Development of the average HDI in the US, Germany, France, UK,
Japan and The Netherlands, 1820–1992*

The above graph shows the average HDI values in the five countries Germany, France, UK, Japan, The Netherlands and US in the years 1820, 1870, 1913, 1950, 1973 and 1992. It reveals that, in the examined period, the HDI averages for the ensemble have increased, on average as well as in each of the countries. In all cases, this growth was not only caused by an increase in individual factors (for example GDP) alone, but by an increase in each of them. That means that the quality of life has improved in all dimensions included in the HDI. That can be seen in Table 5.5.

In the countries for which we have data, the objectively measured well-being has constantly and rapidly improved. For instance, in 1820 the HDI value in Germany was roughly 0.092. It increased by more than ten times by the year 2004 to 0.932 (for comparison, the lowest value in 2004 was reached in the Republic of Niger with 0.311, the highest in Norway with 0.965) (UNDP, 2006).

It is controversial how far the life expectancy can still increase. Figure 5.15 shows the increase in the last 160 years, depicting the countries that held the record at a given time. National life expectancy has steadily risen about 2.5 years per decade and there is no deceleration of this trend so far.

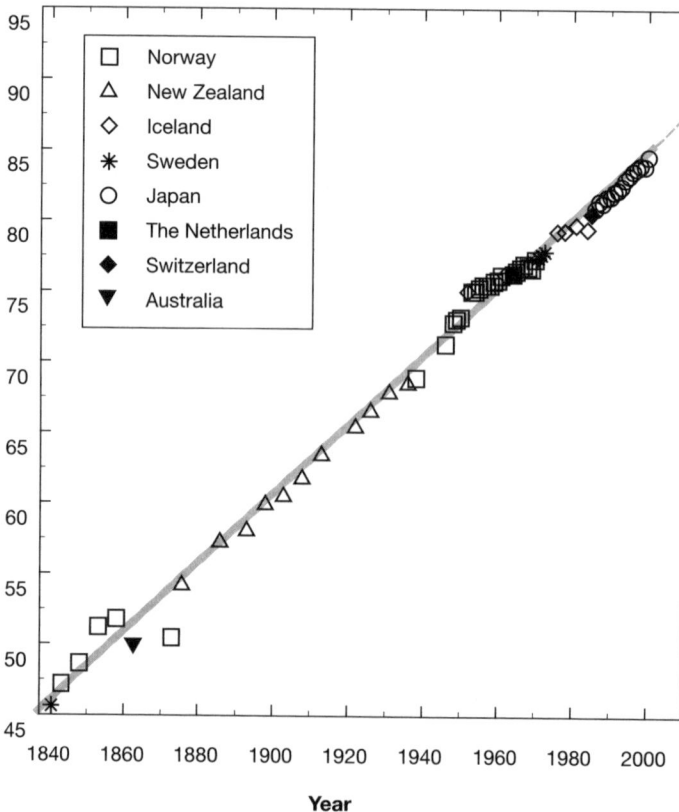

Source: Oeppen and Vaupel (2002)

Figure 5.15 *International record life expectancy and trend for Germany*

Table 5.5 *Development of the HDI values in Germany, France, UK, Japan, The Netherlands and US, 1820–1992*

Year Country	1820 Life Expectancy	GDP/ capita	Education	HDI	1870 Life Expectancy	GDP/ capita	Education	HDI	1913 Life Expectancy	GDP/ capita	Education	HDI
USA	39	1287	1.75	0.13	42	2457	3.92	0.20	47	5307	7.86	0.34
Germany	33.1	1112	1.75	0.09	40.6	1913	3.9	0.19	47	3833	8.37	0.34
France	40	1218	1.75	0.13	41.6	1858	3.9	0.19	47	3452	6.99	0.31
Great Britain	39	1756	2	0.14	45	3263	4.44	0.24	51	5032	8.82	0.38
Japan	35	704	1.5	0.09	38	741	1.5	0.11	44	1334	5.36	0.23
Netherlands	32	1561	1.75	0.09	40	2640	3.9	0.19	52	3950	6.42	0.32
Total				**0.11**				**0.19**				**0.32**

Year Country	1950 Life Expectancy	GDP/ capita	Education	HDI	1973 Life Expectancy	GDP/ capita	Education	HDI	1992 Life Expectancy	GDP/ capita	Education	HDI
USA	68.07	9573	11.27	0.57	73.88	16607	14.58	0.73	77	21558	18.04	0.87
Germany	68.7	4281	10.4	0.51	73	13152	11.55	0.63	76	19351	12.17	0.71
France	69.2	5221	9.58	0.50	72.8	12940	11.69	0.63	77	17959	15.96	0.79
Great Britain	69	6847	10.6	0.54	73.2	11992	11.66	0.63	76	15738	14.09	0.73
Japan	70	1873	9.11	0.47	74	11017	12.09	0.63	79	19425	14.87	0.79
Netherlands	69	5850	8.12	0.47	73	12763	10.27	0.60	77	16898	13.24	0.72
Total				**0.51**				**0.64**				**0.77**

Source: Based on data taken from http://thecommunityguide.org/nchs/data/nvsr/nvsr54_14.pdf; Maddison (1995); Goklany (2007); www.destatis.de/jetspeed/portal/cms/ Sites/destatis/Internet/DE/Content/Statistiken/Zeitreihen/LangeReihen/Volkswirtschaftliche Gesamtrechnungen/Content100/lrvgr04a,templateId=renderPrint.psml; www.destatis.de/jetspeed/portal/cms/Sites/destatis/Internet/DE/Presse/pm/2006/04/PD06_167_12621.psml; http://hdr. undp.org/hdr2006/statistics/countries/data_sheets/cty_ds_DEU.html

To compare generations on a global scale over several centuries or even millennia, we can only use the GDP, because no data are available on the other two partial indicators of the HDI for such long periods of time. Table 5.6 shows the GDP per capita in important economic regions as well as worldwide, since the birth of Christ.

Table 5.6 *GDP per capita since the year 1 AD*

Area/Year	1	1000	1500	1700	1820	1913	1950	1989	1996	2001	2003
Western Europe	450	400	771	998	1,204	3,458	4,579	15,856	17,097	19,256	
USA	400	400	400	527	1,257	5,301	9,561	23,059	25,0566	27,948	28,797
USSR/ former USSR	400	400	499	610	688	1,488	2,841	7,098	3,854	4,626	5,267
Latin America	400	400	413	441	692	1,481	2,506	5,123	5,556	5,811	
China	450	450	600	600	600	552	439	1,827	2,82	3,583	4,185
India	450	450	550	550	533	673	619	1,27	1,630	1,957	2,194
Japan	400	425	500	570	669	1,387	1,921	17,942	20,494	20,683	21,104
Africa	430	425	414	421	420	637	894	1,463	1,403	1,489	
World	445	436	566	615	667	1,525	2,111	5,140	5,517	6,049	

Source: Based on Goklany (2007, p42)

As explained above, the possibility of satisfying needs is an important criterion for the well-being of all generations that have ever lived. Objections have been raised against measuring well-being by the GDP, for instance, the distribution of income and wealth is not taken into account, nor are goods and services that are not marketed (in particular housework). Politico-economic losses and social expenses are not considered, and changes in capital (for instance resources, property and human capital) are not evaluated. 'Services' rendered by nature are considered cost-free (see Morris, 1979, pp7–14; Daly and Cobb, 1989, pp62–85; van Dieren, 1995). However, these distortions affect each epoch, so a relative comparison is still possible and useful.

It shows that in the year 1 AD the GDP per capita in all regions listed was just above the poverty line of $365 dollars per year. Only as of 1913 most regions, and as of 1989 all regions listed, had a four-digit GDP per capita. But the GDP per capita increased over the centuries in all regions examined.

If wealth increases, poverty should decrease. Figure 5.16 shows the development of poverty on a global scale. Figure 5.16a focuses on the years 1820 to 1992, Figure 5.16b on 1980 to 2001. The continuous black line shows the percentage of people living in absolute poverty compared to the total number of people on earth. Absolute poverty is defined as a maximum income of $1 per day or $365 per year (Goklany, 2007, p58). The continuous lines are clearly moving downwards on both graphs. That means the global percentage of people living in absolute poverty is decreasing. However, if we concentrate on the jotted

a

Global Poverty, 1820–1992

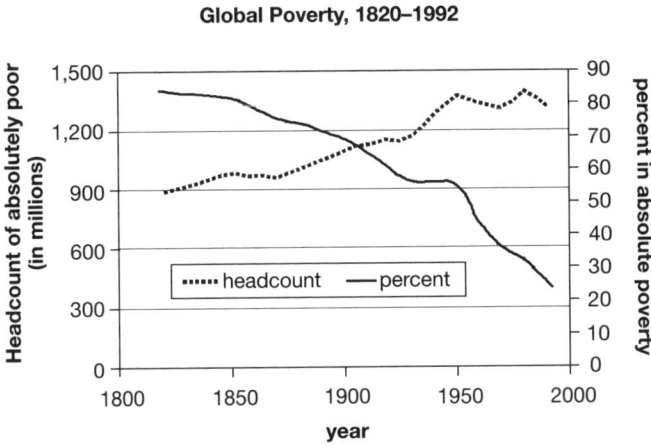

b

Global Poverty, 1982–2001

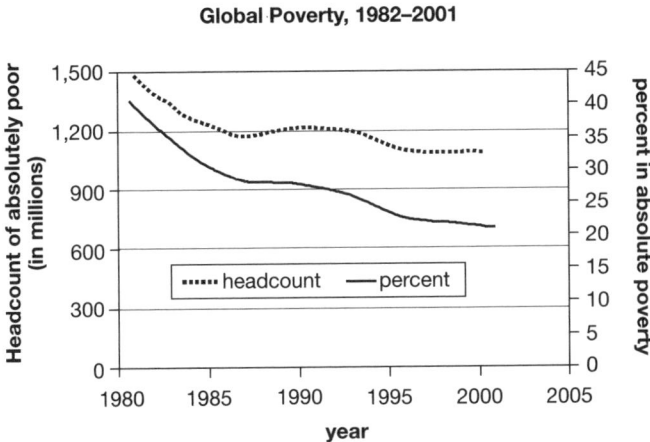

Source: Goklany (2007, p59 et seq.)

Figure 5.16 *Development of global poverty, 1820–2001*

line, things look different. The number of poor people continuously climbed from about 900 million in 1820 to roughly 1.35 billion in 1950 and has remained at that level for three decades. From 1980 to 2001, both the actual number of people living in poverty as well as their global percentage dropped (see Figure 5.16b). Based on the global population, these graphs suggest that the share of people living in absolute poverty has decreased, and as of 1980, the actual number of people living in absolute poverty has also dropped.

Human Well-being Index

The Human Well-being Index (HWI) was developed by Robert Prescott-Allen as an alternative to the HDI. The HWI acknowledges the definition of human development and quality of life underlying the HDR: 'Human well-being is a condition in which all members of society are able to determine and meet their needs and have a large range of choices and opportunities to fulfill their potential' (Prescott-Allen, 2001, p13). However, the HWI is not limited to the three variables of the HDI (income, education, life expectancy), but is meant to include the variables of self-respect, opportunities for being creative and productive, security against crime and violence, guaranteed human rights, and political, economic and social freedom (Prescott-Allen, 2001, p13). For that purpose, Prescott-Allen divides his index into five main categories that are again divided into two subcategories, so we end up with ten subcategories. The main categories are 'health and population' with the subcategories by the same names, 'wealth' with the subcategories 'household wealth' and 'national wealth', 'knowledge and culture' with the subcategories by the same names, 'community' with the subcategories 'freedom and governance' and 'peace and order', and finally 'equity' with the subcategories 'household equity' and 'gender equity' (Prescott-Allen, 2001, p14) (see Figure 5.17).

Prescott-Allen operationalizes each of these subcategories by means of various indicators, but he admits that he was unable to find a suitable indicator for the field of culture (Prescott-Allen, 2001, pp14 and 36). The result Prescott-Allen reaches in his examination of the global conditions based on the HWI is far more negative than that of the UNDP based on the HDI. Figure 5.18 shows the global distribution of the various HWI values in the individual countries. Only three countries (Denmark, Norway and Finland) were rated 'good', that means they achieved more than 80 points in *each* individual category. Most of the 180 countries that were evaluated in the year 2001 ended up in the 'medium' category (52 countries), closely followed by the category 'poor' (51 countries). The next largest were the categories 'bad' (40 countries) and 'fair' (34 countries) (Prescott-Allen, 2001, p15). Most countries in Africa and Southeast Asia, but none in Europe or America ended up in the 'bad' or 'poor' category. Most European countries belong to the category 'fair' (except for Eastern European

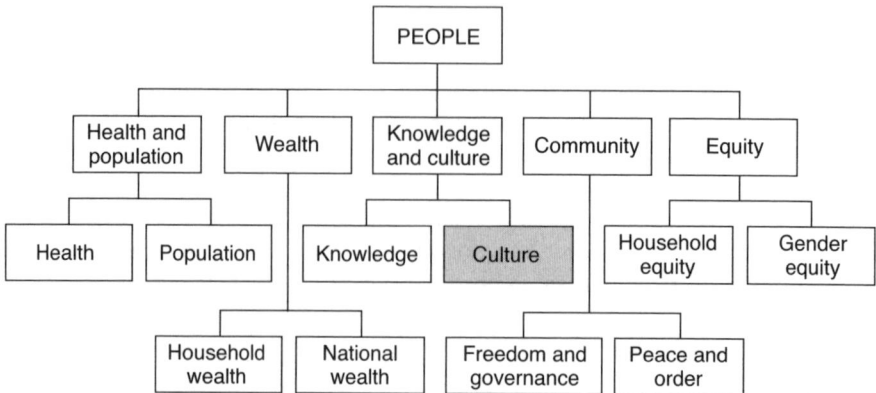

Source: Prescott-Allen (2001, p7).

Figure 5.17 *Structure of the HWI*

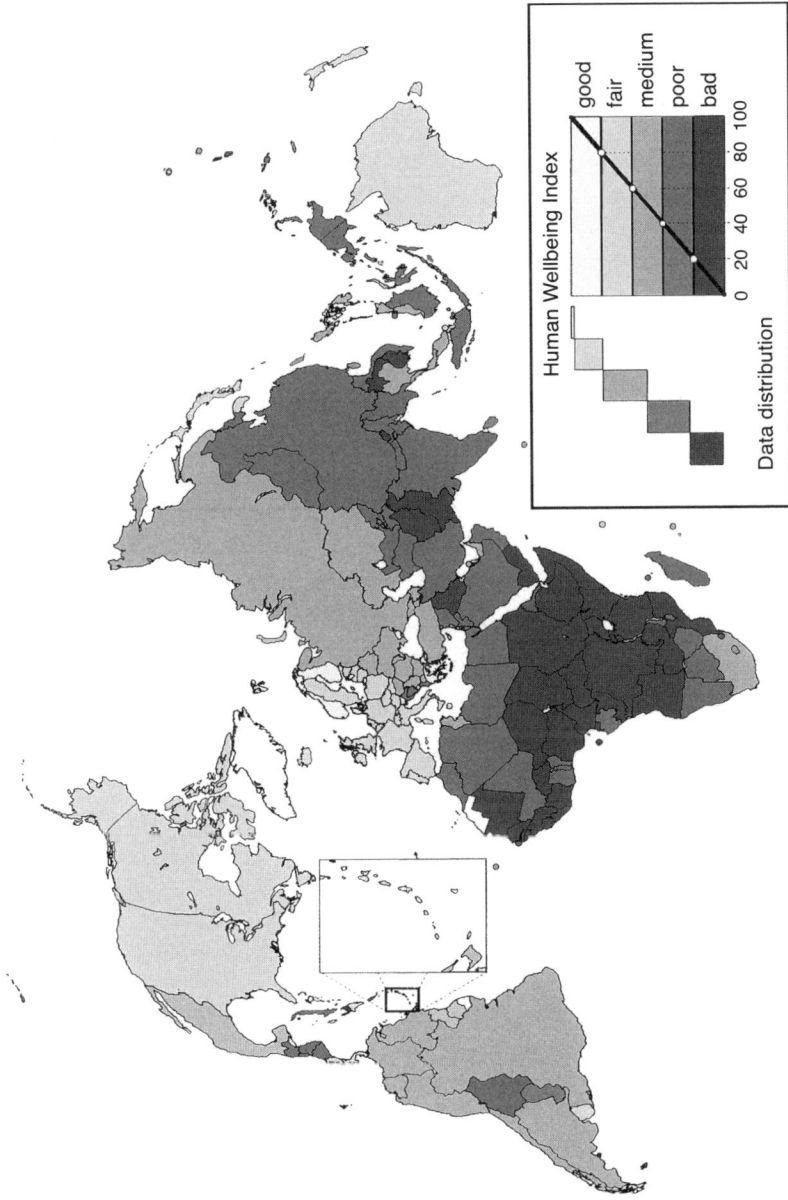

Source: Prescott-Allen (2001, p15)

Figure 5.18 *Global distribution of HWI values*

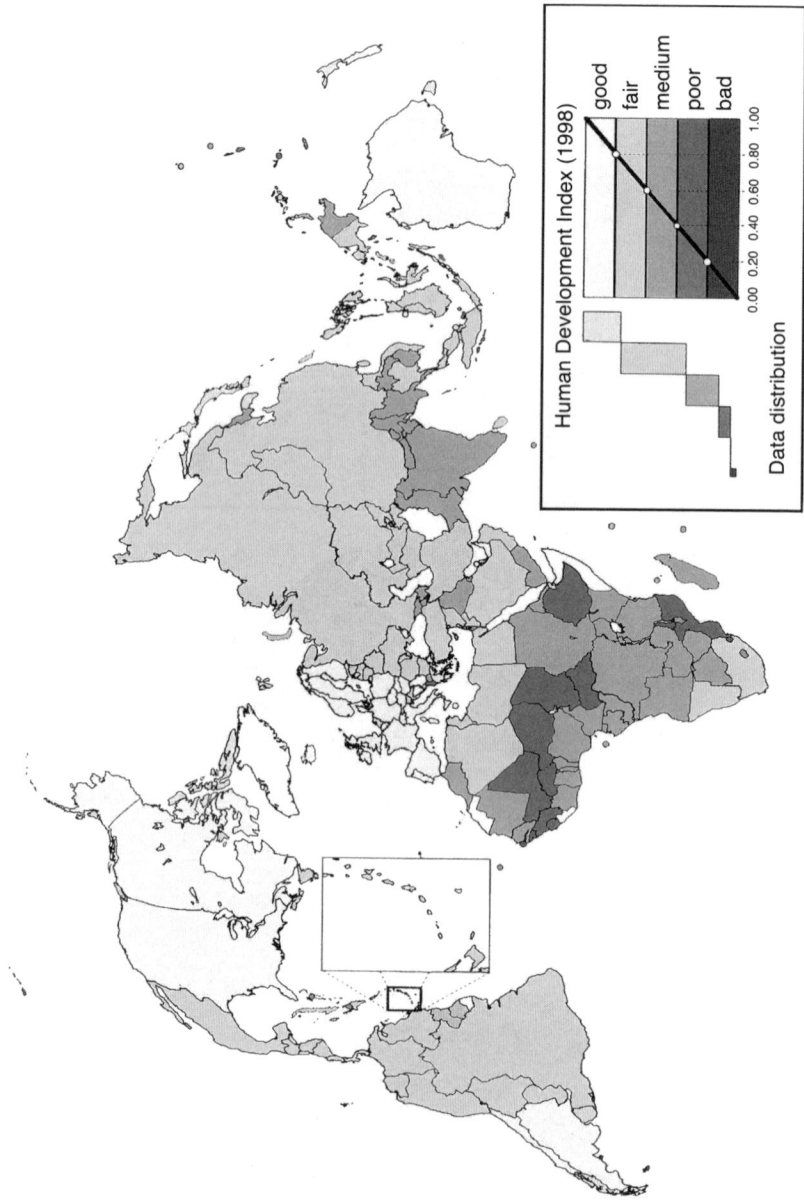

Source: Prescott-Allen (2001, p18)

Figure 5.19 *Global distribution of HDI values*

countries, most of which belong to the 'medium' category). The global result is that 16 per cent of all people on earth live in countries with a 'fair' HWI, 17 per cent live in countries that belong to the 'medium' HWI category, 54 per cent live in countries that belong to the category 'poor', and 12.5 per cent live in countries rated 'bad' (Prescott-Allen, 2001, p15). Thus, according to Prescott-Allen, two thirds of the global population live under precarious conditions.

Prescott-Allen also applies his good-bad-scale to the HDI; the results are illustrated in Figure 5.19. We immediately notice that none of the examined countries are rated 'bad' according to the HDI, but most of them are considered 'good' or at least 'fair'.

In numbers, the result of the comparison between the HDI and the HWI is shown in Table 5.7.

Table 5.7 *Comparison between HWI and HDI in 2001*

Category	Good	Fair	Medium	Poor	Bad	Total
HWI	3	34	52	51	40	*180*
HDI	44	76	38	15	0	*173*

Source: Prescott-Allen (2001, p18)

The differences between the two different indicators are massive, especially with the two extreme categories 'good' and 'bad'. Prescott-Allen puts that down to the different objectives and approaches of the indices. According to him, the HDI is mainly aimed at showing how far we are from living in scarcity. The HWI, by contrast, is aimed at showing how far we are from satisfying all our desires (Prescott-Allen, 2001, p18).

As mentioned, to achieve a 'good' HWI grade, each individual category must be rated 'good'. Since it is easier to reach only three 'good' categories instead of nine, more countries are rated 'good' on the basis of the HDI than on that of the HWI. Prescott-Allen considers the greater number of categories an advantage of the HWI: 'Because the HWI measures progress toward a high level of human well-being, it cannot omit such major concerns as freedom, violence or equity' (Prescott-Allen, 2001, p18).

Weighted Index of Social Progress

The Weighted Index of Social Progress (WISP), developed by Richard J. Estes, also includes more indicators than the HDI. It is made up of 40 social indicators that are again divided into ten sub-indicators: education, health, status of women, defence effort, economy, demography, environment, social chaos, cultural diversity and welfare spending (Estes, 2004, p128). In his study published in 2004, Estes examines 36 European countries for which reliable and intelligible data were available (Estes, 2004, pp129–131). Based on previous studies, Estes uses data of countries in other continents. He divides them into six economic regions: North America (N Am) with the US and Canada, Australia

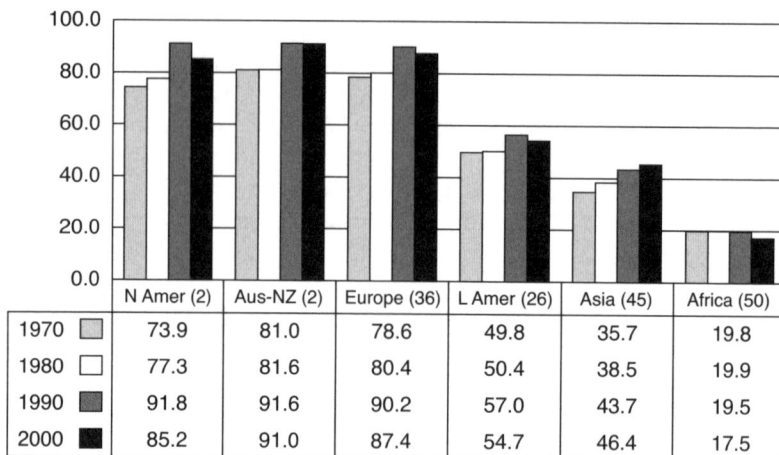

	N Amer (2)	Aus-NZ (2)	Europe (36)	L Amer (26)	Asia (45)	Africa (50)
1970	73.9	81.0	78.6	49.8	35.7	19.8
1980	77.3	81.6	80.4	50.4	38.5	19.9
1990	91.8	91.6	90.2	57.0	43.7	19.5
2000	85.2	91.0	87.4	54.7	46.4	17.5

Source: Estes (2004, p135)

Figure 5.20 *WISP values, 1970–2000*

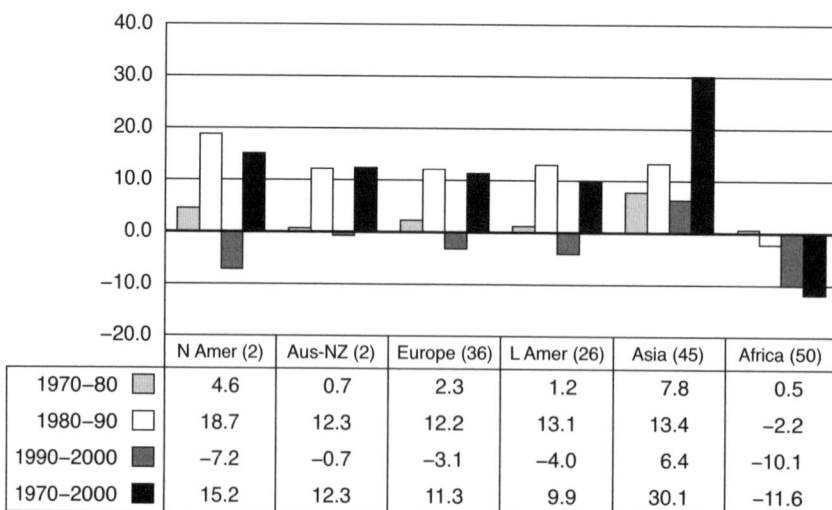

	N Amer (2)	Aus-NZ (2)	Europe (36)	L Amer (26)	Asia (45)	Africa (50)
1970–80	4.6	0.7	2.3	1.2	7.8	0.5
1980–90	18.7	12.3	12.2	13.1	13.4	−2.2
1990–2000	−7.2	−0.7	−3.1	−4.0	6.4	−10.1
1970–2000	15.2	12.3	11.3	9.9	30.1	−11.6

Source: Estes (2004, p139)

Figure 5.21 *Development of WISP values in selected periods*

and New Zealand (Au-NZ), Europe (Eur), Latin America (L Am), Asia and Africa (see Figure 5.20). In Figure 5.20, the number of countries included is stated in brackets; the values show the arithmetic mean of the examined data.

This study concentrates on the years 1970 to 2000. Apart from Africa, all examined regions had a higher WISP value in the year 2000 than they did in 1970. From 1990 to 2000, however, the value declined in all regions except Asia.

Asia is thus the only examined region in which the WISP value has continuously been increasing since 1970. The WISP value in Africa, by contrast, has even dropped from 19.8 points in 1970 to 17.5 points in 2000.

This development is even more evident in Figure 5.21. It shows the WISP growth rates in per cent in the six economic regions in the examined decades. From 1970 to 2000, the total WISP increase was 15.2 per cent in North America, 12.3 per cent in Australia and New Zealand, 11.3 per cent in Europe, 9.9 per cent in Latin America, 30.1 per cent in Asia, and Africa had a WISP decrease of 11.6 per cent. Worldwide, the WISP improved by an average of 11.2 from 1970 to 2000. For the period (30 years) under examination, the WISP confirms the result of the HDI: the situation of mankind is improving every decade.[101] Yet a comparison between generations is not possible, because the available data are insufficient.

Which index is best for measuring changes in the well-being of generations?

Which one of the three discussed indices is best for objectively measuring well-being across generations?[102] To measure the well-being of several successive generations, we need an index that is not ethnocentric.[103] As mentioned earlier, the index should rather measure the fulfilment of needs, so as to avoid misery, instead of the fulfilment of wants, because the overwhelming majority of former generations was very much in the same situation as today's poorest poor. The needs of mankind are limited, and so should the values determining the index also be limited. That clearly weighs in favour of the HDI. The HWI and the WISP with their nine or even 40 measured categories provide more information. However, certain measured values and evaluations might be culture-specific instead of universal.

Another problem that becomes more significant along with the growing number of indicators is the quality of the data. In general, the quality of data on GDP per capita, life expectancy and education (literacy and school enrolment) is very good, but that cannot be said for all nine HWI or even all 40 WISP indicators. Let us take the category 'security' as an example: it is known that rape incidents are greatly under-reported, and therefore rape statistics are doubtful (Diener and Suh, 1997, p195). Furthermore, the degree of under-reporting may vary across cultures and eras.

Another important question is whether the individual factors that determine an objective index are positively correlated with the subjective self-reports of happiness. That is certainly the case with the three HDI values: the healthier, the better educated and the wealthier (with the limitations described) we are, the happier we will be.[104] However, not all categories of the HWI or WISP are positively correlated with subjective self-reports of happiness.

What about the technicality of the indices? All three are composite indices. Weighing their individual parts is a technical problem. With the HDI, that has been solved by attaching the same importance to each of them. That is the most convincing approach. Still, it can be criticized that the HDI results of the more developed countries are very similar, so their differences are not captured to a sufficient degree. Yet this could be changed if the technical make-up of the HDI was reformed (as it was done in 1994). But the two most important arguments in favour of the HDI have not even been mentioned: long-term data availability and international acceptance.

For the HDI, values of almost two centuries are available. Moreover, its calculation formula is not complicated, so it is easy to calculate the HDI for certain periods oneself. The HWI data are only available for the year 2001, and the WISP values are only available for three decades. Therefore neither the WISP nor HWI can be used for long-term generational comparisons because we do not have the required data.

And as far as acceptance is concerned, an intercultural agreement on the definition of well-being has been reached by the UN. The HDI is thus the only international instrument for measuring well-being that has been accepted by the community of states. This gives it a legitimacy that the other well-being indices lack, as they are often only used by individual institutes or even individual researchers. The HDI has been developed by a large group of researchers from all cultures. The participation of a great number of researchers, as in the comparable case of the Intergovernmental Panel on Climate Change (an international group of more than 500 scientists), makes it possible to discuss technical questions in detail on a UN level, and it is the declared objective of UNDP to incorporate external criticism and continuously improve the HDI (Ul Haq, 1995, pp67–76). Perhaps the committee will soon replace 'life expectancy' by the 'number of quality adjusted life years',[105] which I would welcome because it would emphasize the importance of health. But such possibilities for improvement do not discredit the HDI, which is by far the best of all indices we have. This is a widely held belief among well-being researchers. Heylighen and Bernheim write: 'Although the number of included factors is quite limited, the HDI is at present the most reliable overall indicator of progress' (Heylighen and Bernheim, 2000, p337). And according to Sen (1999), the HDI represents the most important example of putting into operation his capabilities approach that measures individual well-being on the basis of what a person is capable of doing.

The HDI can be considered the best way of operationalizing the well-being of the members of societies *so far*. Perhaps UNO, in accordance with the scientific community, will one day replace the HDI by a better index, but until then, it is the only index that is measured in every country by means of comprehensive statistics.

As mentioned, when we compare two birth cohorts, we should always look at their total lifetime. This is the indirect comparison that is usually the most meaningful. Provided the HDI enables us to operationalize well-being consistently, the above study shows that quality of life has been improving from generation to generation. Despite a 'bad news' bias of the media, empirical data show that global well-being has progressed. This does not only hold for the HDI as a composite index, but also for its individual categories wealth, health and education.

Will the global HDI continue to grow?

How likely is a further global increase of the HDI? According to Karl Popper, we are not able to make (long-term) predictions (Popper, 1945, 1960).[106] And indeed, no reliable statement can be made on the future development of the HDI. However, there are indicators that the living conditions of future generations will be worse than those of today. For instance, the greenhouse effect is forecast to cause additional deaths and enormous costs in the future. Climate change threatens the basic elements of life for people around the world – access to water, food, health, and use of land and the environment (Stern, 2007, pp65–68).[107]

Furthermore, the nuclear waste we produce will endanger the welfare of future generations for a long time to come. However, the perhaps greatest danger for future generations comes from nuclear proliferation.

In the 1960s, five states had nuclear weapons (US, Soviet Union, China, UK and France). In 2009, nine states (in addition, India, Pakistan, Israel and North Korea) had already developed and successfully tested nuclear weapons, and another country may be about to do the same (Iran). One does not need Cassandra's clairvoyant abilities to fear that even more countries could have joined the nuclear club 30 years from now. The more nations that have nuclear weapons of mass destruction, the more likely they will be used. Already today, the nuclear weapon states 'have more than 23,000 nuclear weapons, many of which are programmed to launch in minutes'.[108] A nuclear conflict – or accident – could cause millions to die in a flash and adversely affect the living conditions on earth for thousands of years. A fully fledged nuclear war still poses the risk of human self-annihilation, which would wipe out all future generations. Whatever stabilizing impact nuclear weapons may have had during the Cold War, in the new security environment of the 21st century any residual benefits of these arsenals are outweighed by the growing risks of proliferation and terrorism. In the days of the Cold War, there was a 'red telephone' between Moscow and Washington DC. But there is no such hotline between Theran and Jerusalem today. 'Global Zero' is the only state of the world that can guarantee the survival of mankind for the next centuries. Since nuclear proliferation is so important for the future of our descendents, it will be dealt with in more detail.

First of all, we should ask why so *few* states have nuclear weapons.[109] After all, 26 states that have toyed with the idea of obtaining them have given up such plans, some by force, but most voluntarily. In alphabetic order, these were Algeria, Argentina, Australia, Belarus, Brazil, Canada, Chile, Egypt, Germany, Indonesia, Iraq, Italy, Japan, Kazakhstan, Libya, Nigeria, Norway, Romania, South Africa, South Korea, Spain, Sweden, Switzerland, Taiwan, Ukraine and. Yugoslavia. Since the end of the Second World War, these states have either initiated feasibility studies, installed multi-purpose plants, conducted weapons research and development, or even manufactured nuclear weapons (or, in three cases, 'inherited' them). They have all given it up. That is most surprising and calls for explanation.

If states always act selfishly,[110] why have so many refrained from nuclear weapons? To some extent, the Nuclear Non-Proliferation Treaty (NPT) that was signed in 1970 after lengthy and difficult negotiations explains why most Central Powers have refrained from nuclear weapons: the vast majority of these states started their nuclear activities prior to 1970. Only Algeria, Libya, Iraq, Iran and Nigeria developed their ambitions after 1970, and none of them had a democratic structure then. Most of the states that refrained from nuclear weapons did so during or after the NPT negotiations. Prior to these negotiations, only Canada, Norway and Indonesia had renounced their nuclear weapons programme. For most states, striving for the bomb lost its legitimacy with the NPT.

According to the deal of the NTP, the signatories without nuclear weapons undertook not to obtain any, whereas the five official nuclear powers promised to agree on complete nuclear disarmament under international supervision. While the 1980s were marked by disarmament, the 2000s were marked by rearmament, especially in the US, which had a military budget that was as high as those of the ten next states put together. At the last NPT Review Conference in 2005, the block-free movement was confronted with a phalanx of states with nuclear weapons that ignored previous disarmament agreements. In the year 2000, the five official nuclear powers had still accepted the 'Thirteen Steps' – a modest, yet progressive disarmament programme – but now the US ('that was a different government') has disregarded these political obligations and even announced its intention to develop new weapons and carrier systems, for example, high-precision mini-nukes. The UK itself had no problem with the 'Thirteen Steps', but still demonstrated the usual unconditional solidarity with the US. To justify their own breach of the treaties from the year 2000, Russia and China referred to the fact that the US had terminated the Anti-Ballistic Missile Treaty and planned to base weapons in outer space. For states without nuclear weapons, the disputes among the nuclear powers were irrelevant. What counted was the unilateral defiance of a consensus previously considered reliable. The permanent violation of the NPT deal by the nuclear powers, if not rectified soon, is likely to initiate a trend towards ever more nuclear powers.

The refusal of the nuclear powers to disarm is a breach of the principle of justice incorporated in the regime and thus undermines its legitimacy. If the regime is considered fundamentally unfair, it will ultimately fail.[111] The NPT can be described as a 'Kantian project', according to which the member states have seemingly acted against their immediate will to power by placing their security in the hands of a joint legal instrument. As long as the some heads of state try to convince the rest of the world that we live in a Hobbesian world, our future looks gloomy.

If, 100 years from now, people look back at our present-day generation and take stock of its achievements and failures, our failure to disarm might very well be considered the worst of all.

Advantages and disadvantages of the capital approach and the well-being approach

In this chapter, we have discussed whether capital or well-being in the sense of fulfilment of needs is a better societal objective in generational comparisons. Table 5.8 shows the main differences between these two approaches.

Table 5.8 *The well-being approach vs. the capital approach*

	Well-being	Capital
Arguments in favour of an intrinsic/ instrumental value	Well-being is what all generations at all times have strived for, still strive for today and will strive for in the future	The value of capital is purely instrumental. From a human point of view, it is only valuable if it increases human welfare
Measurability	Objective (descriptive) measuring methods have made great progress since the 1960s. The concepts are theoretically sound and internationally established. A large amount of data is collected with great effort.	Real capital and financial capital are easy to measure; natural, cultural, human and social capital are not
Implications of changing population numbers	Indicators such as the HDI are calculated per capita. An increase or decrease of the population does not affect the HDI value	The numerical value of some types of capital (human capital or social capital) mathematically depends on the size of the population. A decrease in population will decrease the social and human capital and thus the overall capital. That will lead to distortions because it will therefore appear that the next (smaller) generation is worse off than its predecessors, which is actually not the case

Source: Influenced by Dworkin (1981a, 1981b)

Obviously, the well-being approach is better suited to measure well-being than the capital approach. Capital is only an auxiliary value. It does not meet the criterion of being the *ultimate* axiological goal. Of course, changes in the capital balance of various generations can supply important information.[112] But if generation B has a higher HDI than generation A, although generation A has more capital, generation B is still better off. At the end of the day, it is well-being that matters, not capital.

Ott and Döring (2004, p58) point out that it is not possible to actively distribute well-being among different generations. That is true; only goods that add up to the GDP per capita or resources that influence the education level and life expectancy can be distributed. However, it cannot be denied that the HDI of the different generations that together compose mankind *has been* unevenly distributed in the past and *will remain to be* in the future. That is an empirical observation. To *allow* an uneven distribution of well-being in the future, measured by the HDI, is not the same as to *initiate* the distribution of well-being in the way Ott and Döring have in mind. In the remainder of this study, 'to distribute well-being' refers to processes that result in empirically observable distributions of well-being. We return to this point when we deal with 'distributive justice' and 'justice of opportunities'.

Let us now take a closer look at the last item in Table 5.8, the effect of changes in the population. It shows a basic difference between the two possible societal objectives 'well-being' and 'capital', which is known as 'average utilitarianism' (or 'person-affecting utilitarianism') and 'total utilitarianism' (or 'impersonal utilitarianism').

Average utilitarianism vs. total utilitarianism: A repugnant conclusion?

It is fundamental for the question of generational justice to distinguish between 'average utilitarianism' (AU) and 'total utilitarianism' (TU).[113] Let me first summarize how these two options are described in standard philosophical literature. In 'total utilitarianism', the utility values of all members of a society are added up. The social order with the highest total utility is best. Of the many possible conditions of the world, the following one would be most preferable:

$$\max \sum_{i=1}^{n} U_i, \forall i = 1,.....,n.$$

In 'average utilitarianism', the total happiness of a society is divided by the number of its members. According to this approach, the formula for the best possible condition of the world is:

$$\max \frac{1}{n} \sum_{i=1}^{n} U_i, \forall i = 1,.....,n.$$

The 'greatest possible average utility of the members of a society' would then be the objective.[114]

If two successive generations have the same number of members, the TU and AU will yield the same results. In two 'same number' scenarios, an increase or decrease in utility cannot change the ranking of two alternative states. In reality, however, the number of individuals varies in each generation. The two approaches especially lead to radically different conclusions with regard to possible population policies.[115] In 'total utilitarianism', the preferred moral strategy is quite simple: as long as each additional individual contributes to the total utility, the global population should continue to grow. Even if there were already 500 billion people on earth, 'total utilitarianism' would promote further growth as long as each additional person considers his life worth living. It would only be immoral to give birth to people who do not consider their life worth living (Bayles, 1976, pxix). That leads to the so-called 'repugnant conclusion' (Parfit, 1987, p388).[116]

In Figure 5.22, the height of the rectangles illustrates the happiness level of an individual, and the width of the rectangles illustrates the number of individuals living on earth in various scenarios. B is double as wide as A. But B is *more* than half as high as A (for example B is two-thirds as high as A). According to 'total utilitarianism', B is better than A, C is better than B, and Z is the best condition of all.[117] This conclusion is 'repugnant', because we intuitively believe it would be better if there were less people but on a higher level of happiness (Leist, 1991, p339). According to the TU conclusion, however, the opposite is true: the more people, the better, as long as they just barely consider their lives worth living. From a mathematical point of view, the number of people can grow almost infinitely, whereas the happiness or utility of each individual moves asymptotically towards a very small number (but not zero), which symbolizes the survival minimum. As Narveson, a fierce advocate of 'average utilitarianism', points out, that reduces man to a container for the maximandum 'happiness' (or 'utility' or 'well-being', etc.) (Narveson, 1976, pp66–68). According to this opinion, not happiness itself but happy people

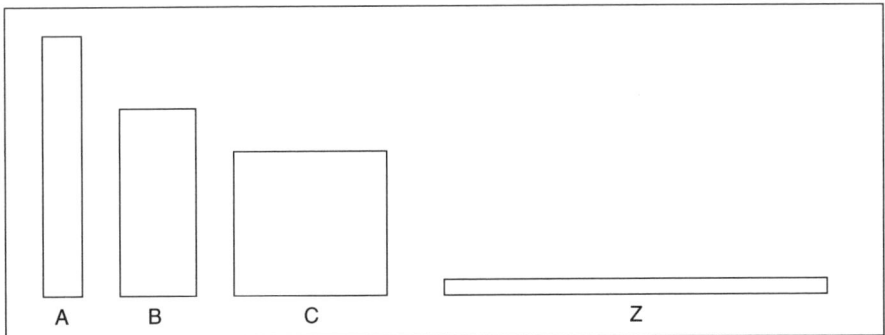

Source: Parfit (1987, p388)

Figure 5.22 *The so-called 'repugnant conclusion'*

are the societal objective. Parfit summarizes Narveson's point of view: 'Of the two ways of increasing the sum of happiness – making people happy, and making happy people – only the first is good for people' (Parfit, 1987, p394).[118] Thus there is much on the distinction between AU and TU and the presentation of the 'repugnant conclusion' in literature.

My point of view is that the so-called 'repugnant conclusion' is not a valid or at least debatable conclusion. This is due to the fact that, for a long time, abstract terms such as well-being, happiness or utility were not operationalized. Operationalizing them sheds new light on the old philosophical problem of AU and TU. As shown, well-being can largely be regarded as a superordinate concept that includes utility, happiness, satisfaction, etc. Let us take another look at Figure 5.4 with the title 'Well-being at different times of a day'. Well-being is the integral of the well-being curve over time. The well-being figures of each day are added up to calculate lifetime well-being. Sleep cannot be not be counted as positive or negative (or even as zero), but must simply be ignored. The same applies to the first years in life, because they are not experienced consciously. Because of the possibility of rational suicide, the values cannot permanently be negative, except in very few cases, for instance if a person is tortured and would immediately commit suicide if only he could. Or if someone (subjectively) does not consider his life worth living and thinks it is even worse than death, but does not commit suicide for religious or other reasons. The analogue in Figure 5.4 to square Z in Figure 5.22 would be a line that continuously runs just above the zero line (x axis). Such a low parallel line would symbolize a life that just barely seems worth living. But that can certainly not be called well-being, happiness or utility. On the y axis, this value stands for unpleasant thoughts or feelings, for instance when I feel physical pain because I bumped into a lamp post or when a report on a starvation disaster makes me sad. Tännsjö (2007, p82) lists another example: one could witness an accident, and a little girl could die in one's arms. All these are cognitive evaluations or affective experiences that make us unhappy, even if we still consider our life worth living.

Until now, the problem has been described as follows: 'There are two ways of increasing the sum of happiness – making people happy, or making happy people' (cf. Parfit, 1987, p394). But this is wrong. Instead it should read: 'There are two options – making people happy, or making people who are unhappy but not unhappy enough to commit suicide.' Or: 'There are two options – making people happy, or making people who constantly experience unpleasant or painful things, but not enough to judge their own lives not worth living.' This point is illustrated in Figure 5.23, which combines my Figure 5.4 (Well-being at different times of a day) and Figure 5.22 (The so-called 'repugnant conclusion').

Obviously, in correct terms, there are no longer two moral options. No philosopher I know would approve of the societal objective of 'light suffering' just as no one would advocate 'severe suffering' as a societal objective.

'Utility' is a rather technical term, but it belongs to the same group of positively connotated terms as 'well-being', 'happiness' or 'quality of life'. Therefore, it misleads people to believe that 'total utilitarianism' is about calculating some-

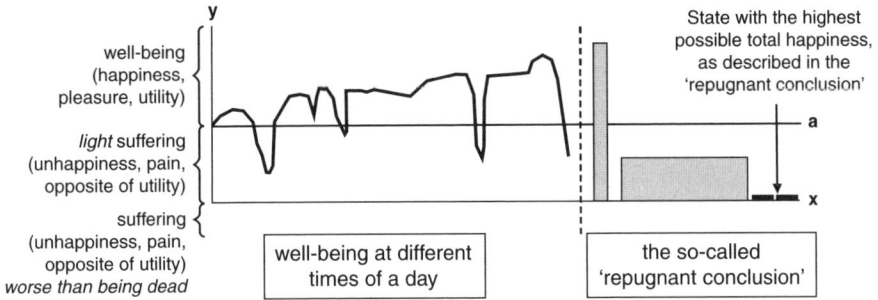

Figure 5.23 *Light suffering cannot be an axiological goal*

thing positive: the more, the better. The term itself does not imply that this concept encapsulates pleasure *and* pain (happiness *and* unhappiness, well-being *and* suffering). If this would be reflected in the name of the concept, no one would consider the 'repugnant conclusion' a debatable conclusion. If a threshold representing a decent level of life was introduced, say in the middle of the y axis of Figure 5.4, then the 'repugnant conclusion' would be debatable, but it would no longer be 'repugnant'.

Neither should my argument be confused with a plea for the position usually called 'sufficientism',[119] nor does it discredit all forms of total utilitarianism. My intention here is solely to point out the misleading terminology in the so-called 'repugnant conclusion'.

6

How Much to Sustain?
The Demands of Justice in the
Intergenerational Context

A compass for the no-man's-land?

The last chapter examined what constitutes 'well-being' and how it is measured for present and future generations. This chapter is dedicated to the question of how well-being can be distributed between generations in a just way.

As mentioned in the Introduction, *intra*generational relations differ enormously from *inter*generational relations. If Hans Jonas is right and the intergenerational sphere is a no-man's-land for traditional ethics, it is unlikely that any theory of intergenerational justice could be derived from traditional theories of justice. Instead, a novel kind of theory would be needed. To test this assumption, I will take a brief look at established theories of intragenerational justice.

The applicability of intragenerational justice theories in the intergenerational context

Many people fundamentally doubt that consensus on 'justice' can be reached. A newspaper commentator claims:

> *Whoever wants to join in a summer discourse has to repeat the watchword as often as possible – a mantra rather than a taboo. Retirement pension from the age of 67? How unfair! More money for childcare for lower-income earners? Fair, absolutely. Tax breaks for SUVs who pollute the air? Unfair, for sure! But the opposite can always be justified, too, and even in the case that seems clearest, there was a direct contradiction in the debate on justice... We are indeed at the beginning of a never-ending exchange of blows. (Kissler, 2003)*

Philosophy is not that pessimistic. Although many philosophers consider justice indefinable (for example Kelsen, 2000), there still are plenty of scientific papers that accept the challenge to analyse concepts of justice and define the term. Obviously, the task is not easy. If one compares all the contexts in which justice is used, one can easily conclude that the term is hopelessly ambiguous. The words 'just' and 'unjust' are applied to:

- people and groups of people;
- their actions, attitudes, behaviour and characters;
- ensuing judgements, assessments and evaluations;
- procedures, norms and laws;
- social institutions, social and economic systems, political and societal situations;
- methods and procedures of distribution (for example contests, application procedures or competitions by lot);
- results of these procedures of distribution;
- gift–barter ratio, offence–penalty ratio, effort–reward ratio;
- natural situations (such as the global distribution of oil fields) or nature and destiny itself (cf. Horn and Scarano, 2002, p10 et seq.).

To approach the term of justice, four points should first be noted. First, justice should not be equated with morality. Morality involves more than justice, for instance benevolence, mercy, generosity, compassion, empathy and charity. Justice is only a part of morality, albeit a very important one. Whoever is not empathetic, generous and charitable will disappoint others, but whoever is unjust will outrage them. Public opinion can only demand what we owe each other, and that is justice. Meritorious conduct that goes beyond that is up to each individual (Höffe, 2007a, p4). Justice is sometimes referred to as the 'totality of enforceable standards', whereas morality is called 'the totality of recommended standards' (Steinvorth, 2007, p12). But that is not correct as such: enforceability is not a constitutive property of justice. For instance, the slavery in the US of the 18th century was certainly unjust, but the laws of those days allowed it, so its abolishment was not enforceable.

Second, there are circumstances of justice. One precondition is that humans – in relation to each other – desire scarce goods.[1] Robinson Crusoe cannot have a justice problem, as the smallest scale on which such a problem can arise is with at least two people.[2] Two men want to marry the same woman, two generations want to use the same fossil resource. Principles of justice are only necessary where people have diverging – and potentially conflicting – interests, and goods are not abundant enough to fulfil them all.[3]

Third, the question of a just social order is a problem of secular-liberal societies. Religious societies have a preset order. Everyone has his predefined place in the world. Whatever has been decided by God, or the Gods, is just. In the Middle Ages, Europe was characterized by such a static order. Only when this order was abolished during the Enlightenment, justice had to be determined by man himself. All of a sudden, the world was seen as the product of human action. Hence, moral principles (including those of justice) had to be defined and established by man (Kersting, 2002a, p164; Veith, 2006, p137).

Fourth, the above mentioned plurality of contexts in which the words 'just' and 'unjust' are applied looks more frightening than it is. The Austrian philosopher Peter Koller writes:

> *If we call a* person *just, we mean that he or she uses to act justly...* *However, if an* action *is referred to as just, this implies that it complies with certain rules governing interpersonal behaviour.* Social rules *are considered just if they regulate social relations between people in a way generally considered acceptable from an impartial point of view. The same applies to social* institutions, *which are nothing but stable systems of social rules that focus on certain partial areas of social life. And the justice of* social conditions, *the actual results of social action, again depends on the rules and outcomes of these actions. These few observations alone point to the fact that among the various application objects of justice there are two of central importance because all the others can be traced back to them: on the one hand* actions *and on the other hand* social rules. *(Koller, 2007, p7, emphasis original)*

The term 'justice' is therefore mainly used in *personal* and *institutional* contexts. While many early discourses on justice[4] based on Plato tend to refer to a personal context, modern debates focus on institutional approaches. This is even more so in an intergenerational context. Although it is theoretically possible to call a *generation* 'just' or 'unjust', the debate on intergenerational justice usually revolves around procedures and institutions that are considered 'intergenerationally just' (or 'unjust'). That shall also be the focus of this study.

This is not meant to be a book on *intra*generational justice. To avoid it unintentionally becoming one, I will not delve too deeply into the 'oldest problem of political philosophy' (Barry, 1989, pxiii) but only examine three main justice theories:

- justice as impartiality;
- justice as the equal treatment of equal cases and the unequal treatment of unequal cases;
- justice as reciprocity.[5]

These three theories (they are in fact families of theories, and each of them yields different results, depending on the definition of its components) are first introduced. Then they are analysed *only* with regard to their applicability to the intergenerational context. A taxonomy of justice theories is not intended, neither of justice principles nor of justice procedures.

The following section first summarizes Rawls' considerations on intergenerational justice. Rawls tries to apply his 'veil of ignorance' thought model to the intergenerational context, but his corresponding expositions are largely assessed critically in the literature. Nevertheless, the 'veil of ignorance' is a fruitful model for reconstructing unbiased decisions on justice. Subsequently, I continue the

considerations Rawls himself does not further pursue and I discuss the principles of generational justice representatives of all generations under the 'veil of
ignorance' could define.

Justice as impartiality: Rawls' 'original position' theory

A decisive feature of justice, impartiality, is often symbolized by the covered eyes
of the Roman goddess Justitia; statues of her adorn many court buildings and
public places. The basic assumption of 'justice as impartiality' theories is, in
Brian Barry's words, that:

> *justice should be the content of an agreement that would be reached by*
> *rational people under conditions that do not allow for bargaining power to*
> *be translated into advantage... The motive for behaving justly is, on this*
> *view, the desire to act in accordance with principles that could not reason-*
> *ably be rejected by people seeking an agreement with others under condi-*
> *tions free from morally irrelevant bargaining advantages and*
> *disadvantages... The significance of speaking of 'justice as impartiality' is*
> *that this approach, however it is worked out in detail, entails that people*
> *should not look at things from their own point of view alone, but seek to*
> *find a basis of agreement that is acceptable from all points of views.*
> *(Barry, 1989, p7 et seq.)*

'Justice as impartiality' theories arose in the Age of Enlightenment. Kant is
considered their most significant representative. Since then, the thought experiment of an 'original position' has often been used in theory-building to fulfil
conditions of impartiality.[6] This can be called a procedural approach to justice:
if a method is just, the outcome – whatever it might be – should also be just. The
most monumental of these theories is Rawls' 'veil of ignorance' theory; it shall
be used for further discussing 'justice as impartiality' theories.

The 'veil of ignorance'

John Rawls' *A Theory of Justice* contains one of the earliest modern debates on
the question of intergenerational justice.[7] Rawls' famous paragraph 44 included
in his chapter 'Distributive Shares' (Rawls, 1971, pp284–293) and called 'The
Problem of Justice between Generations' caused a broad echo among experts.
Laslett and Fishkin (1992, p20) claim that in the 1970s and 1980s most of the
works on intergenerational justice were a reaction to Rawls.

Rawls proposes the concept of a 'veil of ignorance' from behind which a
group of participants would be required to decide how to construct a just
society:

> *First of all, no one knows his place in society, his class position or social*
> *status; nor does he know his fortune in the distribution of natural assets*
> *and abilities, his intelligence and strength, and the like. Nor, again, does*
> *anyone know his conception of the good, the particulars of his rational*
> *plan of life, or even the special features of his psychology such as his aver-*
> *sion to risk or liability to optimism or pessimism. (Rawls, 1971, p137).*

In such a setting, we can assume that 'no-one is in the position to tailor principles to his advantage' (Rawls 1971, p139). Rawls rightly believes the participants would reach an unanimous decision. It is important that the 'veil of
ignorance' creates a situation of *choice*, not of *negotiation* (D'Agostino, 2003, p1).
By identifying with others, a universalizable standpoint would be chosen. For
example, if someone is wealthy in reality and knows it during the assembly, he
could propose lower tax rates. If he knows he is poor, he could be inclined to
suggest the opposite. But if he does not know whether he is rich or poor, black
or white, healthy or disabled, intelligent or dull, he will decide impartially which
principles of justice the assembly should pass and should be applied to society.[8]
   The underlying idea – deliberating in ignorance – is simple but ingenious.
However, it should be noted that the participants cannot be without any knowledge at all while they are behind the 'veil of ignorance'. There are a number of
things they must not know in order for the experiment to work, but there are
many other things they have to know. Rawls allows the participants to know the
following: 'They [the participants] understand political affairs and the principles
of economic theory; they know the basis of social organization and the laws of
human psychology' (Rawls, 1971, p137). And:

> *Finally, there is the condition of moderate scarcity understood to cover a*
> *wide range of situations. Natural and other resources are not so abundant*
> *that schemes of cooperation become superfluous, nor are conditions so*
> *harsh that fruitful ventures must inevitably break down. While mutually*
> *advantageous arrangements are feasible, the benefits they yield fall short*
> *of the demands men put forward. (Rawls, 1971, p127)[9]*

To make the thought experiment work, Rawls makes another important assumption: there is no altruism. The people in the 'original position' must act as if 'the
parties take no interest in one another's interest' (Rawls, 1971, p127). This position must not be called 'egoistic' or 'selfish' because it does not exclude 'win/win'
situations. Rather, it should be called 'self-interested' (for a detailed explanation
of this terminology, see the section on 'Self-interest and egoism). Rawls has been
criticized for assuming self-interested individuals instead of ones with at least
certain altruistic traits (for example Dierksmeier, 2006, p78). However, I agree
with Jane English that the technique of the 'veil of ignorance' only generates a
fair distribution if self-interest is assumed. Consider the example of a fair division of a pie by asking one person to cut it so that each gets a fair share under
constraint that the others can choose their pieces first. If the decider exercises

altruistic principles by intentionally cutting a smaller piece for himself, the division is distorted.[10]

Is everybody suitable for the assembly in the 'original position'? In his earlier text 'outline of a decision procedure for ethics' (1951), Rawls elaborates on the characteristics of 'capable ethical judges' (Rawls, 1951). They should at least be averagely intelligent and capable of logical conclusions. They should also be prepared to revise their own opinion if new findings and arguments make it necessary. Apparently, Rawls intentionally avoids some of these comments in his later work *A Theory of Justice* (1971), probably because he regards them as misleading. This shows that each parameter of the imagined 'original position' is important and the omission or addition of parameters can change the result of the choice of the participants. Parameters can be set regarding objective basic conditions and assumptions on human nature (and knowledge about it). These objective conditions include, for example, the scarcity of goods and the self-interest of man. A second group of parameters includes the subjective properties of the participants (such as their class, their gender, their generation or their personal risk affinity). Changing the objective or subjective parameters will alter the result of the choice in the 'original position'. Therefore, 'veil of ignorance' theories always have to fulfil two conditions: first, they must be based on reasonable and plausible parameters concerning the participants' knowledge and ignorance behind the 'veil of ignorance'; second, they must logically and precisely deduce the results of the discussion the participants would reach under the respective parameter constellation.

Rawls states that the participants in the 'original position' would follow some kind of maximin principle because each participant is at risk of ending up at the bottom of society once the 'veil of ignorance' has been lifted (Rawls, 1971, pp153–156). But is this correct? The participants might consider two possible models of society, an egalitarian and a non-egalitarian model. The number of positions is equal to the number of participants in the 'original position'. The probability of ending up in either of these positions, once the 'veil of ignorance' has been lifted, is the same. If, for instance, 100 positions need to be filled and there are 100 participants in the 'original position', the probability of each of them ending up in a certain position is 1 in 100 (see Harsanyi, 1982, p45, for a more formal account).

To exemplify the maximin principle, let us assume that every position in the egalitarian society provides an income of €1000, whereas in the non-egalitarian society, half of the positions are paid €500 and the other half €1500 (see Table 6.1).

Table 6.1 *Alternative models of society 1*

	Position 1	Position 2	Position...	Position 99	Position 100
Egalitarian	1000	1000	1000	1000	1000
Non-egalitarian	1500	500	...	1500	500

According to the maximin principle (*max*imize the *min*imal, i.e. the worst possible distributional situation in which one might find oneself), the participants would choose the egalitarian society because it is the only alternative that will definitely leave them with an income of €1000, once the 'veil of ignorance' has been lifted. However, it is a mistake to believe that the 'veil of ignorance' model will necessarily and under all circumstances prompt the participants to apply the maximin principle. It would, if one's position in society were to be determined by one's greatest enemy. But under the 'veil of ignorance', positions are distributed by chance. The 'expected value' is therefore a better decision basis for an individual who (a) has well-ordered and consistent preferences and is (b) is neither risk-seeking nor risk-averse. When faced with a number of action options, the procedure is to identify all possible outcomes, determine their values and the probabilities that will result from each course of action, and multiply the two. The action that leads to the highest total expected value should be chosen. This is shown by Table 6.2 in which, again, a hundred positions need to be filled in a hypothetical society.

Table 6.2 *Alternative models of society 2*

	Position 1	Position 2	Position ...	Position 99	Position 100	Expected value
Egalitarian	1000	1000	1000	1000	1000	**100,000**
Non-egalitarian	1500	1500	1500	1500	999	**149,499**

According to the maximin principle, the egalitarian society still ought to be chosen. But according to the expected value – and common sense – the other society is more attractive. For a risk-adverse person, it might, however, still be rational to choose the egalitarian society. According to the parameters set by Rawls, the participants do not know their risk affinity. They can therefore not assume that they are risk adverse. Rather, they have the same chances of being either extremely willing or unwilling to take risks, or somewhere in between (Laplaceian principle). As a result, risk affinity has no influence on the selection of a society model.

I agree with Rawls that the parameter 'risk affinity' should be 'unknown', but I disagree with his conclusion that the participants will then adopt the maximin principle. Rather, rational deciders will adopt the principle of expected value under the given circumstances.[11]

Rawls' presumption in favour of maximin leads him to his final justice principles, which are moderately egalitarian. According to Rawls, the parties would first grant everyone in society equal civil and political rights. Second, a consensus would be reached that social and economic inequalities should be shaped according to 'the difference principle' (Rawls, 1971, p303), which indicates that injustices are only acceptable if there is no way to improve the situation of the least privileged members of society. The main implication of this and of the maximin principle is that a society should be constructed in a way that an adequate social minimum is assigned to everyone. In his book *Justice as Fairness: A Restatement*, published in 2001, Rawls reformulates his views. He now assumes that his selected 'original position' parameters would lead to the following revised two principles of justice:

> *1.) Each person has the same indefeasible claim to a fully adequate scheme of equal basic liberties, which scheme is compatible with the same scheme of liberties for all;*
>
> *2.) Social and economic inqualities are to satisfy two conditions: first, they are to be attached to offices and positions open to all under conditions of fair equality of opportunity, and second, they are to be to the greatest benefit of the least-advantaged members of society (difference principle). (Rawls, 2001, p42 et seq.)*

To justify the second part of the latter principle (the difference principle), Rawls is forced to face the question of accumulation between generations. Otherwise, the participants in the 'original position' could easily support the least-advantaged members of their generation by failing to save for the next generation. For Rawls, the obligation to save for future poor people limits the leeway for redistribution in the present. Therefore, Rawls is forced to first address the question of intergenerational justice before he can formulate his theory of justice.[12]

Criticisms of Rawls' theorizing on intergenerational problems

Rawls ingenious 'veil of ignorance' thought experiment is admired worldwide. The Argentinean philosopher Gabriel Stillman even describes the derived principles for the intragenerational context as the 'Justice of Justices',[13] meaning that this theory of justice is convincing to everybody and therefore fundamentally different from subjective theories of justice. Rawls' thought experiment is equally promising in the intergenerational context because the 'veil of ignorance' demands to treat the viewpoint of each generation equally.[14] Discounting the future would go against this demand. However, Rawls' application of the 'veil of ignorance' in the intergenerational context has been criticized by most commentators.[15] Even Rawls himself concedes that the problem of justice between generations exhausts him: 'it submits any ethical theory to severe if not impossible tests' (Rawls, 1971, p284).

Core weaknesses of Rawls' concept

Rawls ignores environmental aspects

The question of intergenerational justice only became a key issue in academic and public discourse when evidence was increasing that the ruling generation would pass on considerably diminished natural resources to future generations. It is surprising that questions of environment and natural resources are not addressed at all in Rawls' explanation. Birnbacher explains:

> *Rawls takes for granted that later generations will be better off than rela-*
> *tively earlier ones, because of technological advances and further accumu-*
> *lation of capital. This view conforms to standard models of economic*
> *growth which do not take into account non-renewable resources and*
> *environmental damage. Given the limited availability of natural*
> *resources and the ecological risks associated with the continued exploita-*
> *tion of nature, this model can in no way be regarded as realistic... By*
> *assuming a positive growth rate without discussing it, Rawls reduces his*
> *theory by exactly the dimension which has been the prime motivation*
> *behind the questions regarding intergenerational justice in the last few*
> *years, the dimension that created awareness among the public. (Birn-*
> *bacher, 1977, pp386–387)[16]*

Birnbacher's critique hits the mark. How meaningful is a theory of intergenerational justice if it does not take into account a possible loss in well-being due to
ecological destruction?[17]

Rawls disregards axiological questions

Of the two questions of 'How much to sustain?' and 'What to sustain?', Rawls
gives priority to the former and neglects the latter. He therefore fails to exten-
sively discuss one of the key questions of intergenerational justice theories. The
question of 'What to sustain?' can be paraphrased as: 'What should we leave to
future generations?', 'What constitutes their well-being?', 'What are the needs
and preferences of future generations?'.

Rawls sees the most important duty of each generation in creating just institutions and realizing fundamental freedoms (Rawls, 1971, p290). 'Just institutions' and 'fundamental freedoms' are part of our cultural capital. But what
about natural, real or human capital? What about the debate on weak and strong
sustainability? Would it be just to leave to future generations fairer institutions
(respectively an increasing cultural capital), but far less natural capital and infrastructure? Neither does Rawls adress these questions and nor does he deal with
the different approaches to measuring well-being, need fulfilment and quality of
life. The most important such measuring standards, i.e. the HDI, HWI and
WISP, were developed in the 30 years following the publication of the *Theory of
Justice*.[18] Looking back from today's position, Rawls' response to axiological
question seems vague and unsatisfactory. The (unsatisfactory) answer to this
question must indirectly lead to an equally unsatisfactory answer to the question
of 'How much to sustain?'. Rawls' axiology can only lead to one conclusion:
'Once just institutions are firmly established, the net accumulation required falls
to zero. At this point a society meets its duty of justice by maintaining just institutions and preserving their material base' (Rawls, 1971, p287 et seq.).
Gosseries calls this a 'two-phase model' and explains:

> *First, there is an accumulation phase where generations are required to*
> *adopt a positive savings rate – that is, to leave more than they received...*

> *Then comes a steady-state stage where each generation is required only to leave at least as much as it received from its predecessors. (Gosseries, 2002, p467)*

Rawls himself puts it like this: 'Once just institutions are firmly established, the net accumulation required falls to zero. At this point a society meets its duty of justice by maintaining just institutions and preserving their material base' (Rawls, 1971, p287 et seq.). He adds: 'all generations are to do their part in reaching the just state of things *beyond which no further net saving is required*' (Rawls, 1971, p289, my emphasis).

An end of the accumulation period can only be defined in advance in Rawls' work because he considers just institutions the ultimate goal. (Rawls, 1971, p289). This would not be possible if the answer to the axiological question were, for example: well-being as measured by the HDI. There is no limit to increasing the HDI, but 'just institutions' cannot continuously be made 'more just'.

Rawls' various 'veil of ignorance' models

The main criticism in literature concerning Rawls' arguments on intergenerational justice is that he switches between three different models of the 'veil of ignorance'. The exact *inter*generational analogy to the *intra*generational 'original position' is as follows:

> *Model 1: Representatives of all past, present, and future generations meet in the 'original position'. Because of the 'veil of ignorance', they do not know which generations they belong to and will later live as. Each representative is only guided by self-interest. (Rawls, 1971, pp287–289)*

This model was replaced by Rawls' second model described below. The only vague explanation given is that the first one would 'stretch fantasy too far' (Rawls, 1971, p139):

> *Model 2: Only people from one generation come together in the 'original position' behind the 'veil of ignorance'. They do not know which generation in the history of mankind they belong to and will later live as. Each representative is only guided by self-interest. (Rawls, 1971, pp287–289, pp139–140)*

Rawls then dismisses this model, too, and replaces it by a third one in which the individual representatives do not act out of pure self-interest, but also keep in mind the well-being of their offspring. Now, the 'original position' contains a gathering of *parents* who do not know which generation they will later live as (Rawls, 1971, p289).[19] Rawls states: 'For example, we may think of the parties as heads of families, and therefore as having a desire to further the welfare of their nearest descendants' (Rawls, 1971, p128). This model forsakes one of the central premises of the whole Rawlsian theory of justice: the self-interest of the actors. Birnbacher rightly condemns this sharply: 'By allowing an altruistic interest in the "original position", the whole theoretical contract with its program of deduction is disavowed' (Birnbacher, 1977, p393).

Barry criticizes that this can no longer be called a discussion about justice *between* past, present and future generations, as Rawls continues to do. Instead, it becomes a matter of 'justice *with respect to* future generations' (Barry, 1989, p192, emphasis original). English points out that Rawls' modified parameter in his 'veil of ignorance' model would change the result even on the *intra*generational level, because it leads to a concept of justice focused on families, not on individuals (English, 1977, pp93–96). So far, it has been ignored that Rawls' definition of the term 'generation' changes when he switches from model 2 to model 3. At first, he usually addresses all people living at one moment in time and therefore uses 'generation' in the intertemporal sense.[20] But when he refers to the parent-child model, he starts using the family-related meaning of the term 'generation'.

By switching to model 3, Rawls wants to avoid that 'no-one has a duty to save for posterity' (Rawls, 1971, p140). However, the self-interest of actors is a central assumption of the whole Rawlsian theory of justice. It is illegitimate to ignore it, simply because it leads to an undesirable result in the intergenerational context.

Rawls' response to his critics

Rawls later rectifies what he calls 'the more serious' (Rawls, 2001, pxv) faults of his theory of justice in response to the wide criticism it received. In his book *Political Liberalism* (1993), Rawls already rejects his disputed assumption of parental altruism in a footnote (Rawls, 1993, p274, footnote 12). In *Justice as Fairness: A Restatement* (2001), his most recent book, Rawls reinforces his renunciation of the problematic assumption of parental affection, and he reformulates the 'just saving principle' as follows:

> *the one the members of any generation (and so all generations) would adopt as the principle they would want preceding generations to have followed, no matter how far back in time. Since no generation knows its place among the generations, this implies that all later generations, including the present one, are to follow it. In this way we arrive at a savings principle that grounds our duties to other generations: it supports legitimate complaints against our predecessors and legitimate expectations about our successors. (Rawls, 2001, p160)[21]*

This is an attempt to circumnavigate the outcome that no one would save for posterity without inducing love for the offspring as a premise, as in model 3. But does this entirely new principle offer a satisfying solution? Prima facie, the participants would introduce a positive savings rate, because otherwise they would risk inheriting nothing at all and having to start from scratch. But this new principle creates new problems.[22] It only applies to model 2, in which the convention solely consists of coevals. Only here, there are 'past generations' from the participants' point of view. In model 1, all generations take part in the convention. As there are no 'past generations' here – from the participants' point of view – Rawls' new principle cannot be applied.

In 2001 – unlike in 1971 – Rawls does not state what decision would taken by the participants regarding the savings rate: high, low or not at all. So, which savings rate would the participants choose? Rawls' new principle is a variation of the Golden Rule: 'Do unto others as you would have them do unto you.' But in our case, this rule cannot be justified by the principle of reciprocity. The previous generation has either saved or not – in any case is it gone. Let us assume the previous generation has chosen a very low savings rate. The situation of the participants is then comparable to a group of campers who reach a campsite with the sign 'Please leave this place in the state that you want to find it', but in fact it is filthy. Should the participants nevertheless select a high savings rate? If so, how does this go together with the assumption of self-interest?

Rawls' new principle is an intergenerational categorical imperative, i.e. ultimately deontological, and not intended as a contract theory. Why should the parties in the 'original position' adopt it without further deontological assumptions? Rawls does not address this question. In the relevant paragraphs of his later works, he only briefly touches on the question of intergenerational justice. He leaves us a principle without any explanations.

In 1971, Rawls illustratively describes the danger that the participants take for granted the savings by earlier generations - and nevertheless decide not to save. As shown, this danger is not averted by using his principle of 2001.

The original model 1 was dismissed much too hastily by Rawls. It is a sound starting point for further deliberations even if Rawls himself did not build on it.

What would really be discussed in the 'original position'?

Let us therefore take a step back. To apply the prolific thought experiment of the 'veil of ignorance' to the intergenerational context, we first have to clarify how many generations are to be taken into consideration: an infinite number of generations starting with generation G_0, or a finite number of generations starting with generation G_0 and ending with generation G_n? (Birnbacher, 1977, p395). It is worthwhile contemplating both scenarios for model 1, because only model 1 is indeed the intergenerational parallel to the intragenerational 'original position'. As we are dealing with a thought experiment, one cannot argue that model 1 is unrealistic. Whether a thought experiment is 'far-fetched' or 'very far-fetched' is irrelevant, as long as it is a guideline for deriving principles for justice as impartiality. This guideline is that rational and self-interested[23] actors have to be in a situation that does not allow an individual to translate his bargaining power into personal advantage. As long as this is so, the parameters of a 'veil of ignorance' model can be changed (see Barry, 1989, p321).

Model 1, infinite n

An infinite number of participants in the 'original position' would mean that an assembly will become impossible to imagine. It seems far more fruitful to assume a finite n.

Model 1, finite n

Let us concentrate on a variant of a finite number of generations and assume a few things that are close to historical facts. The first modern man (homo sapiens)[24] appeared around 130,000 BC. Back then, life expectancy was limited to 25 to 30 years. It only increased in the mid-18th century and again rose significantly in the 20th century on a global scale. If we assume further increases, life expectancy will soon reach 120 years. We do not know the future but let us further assume that man will continue to exist for another 130,000 years. We then reach the figure of approximately 6000 non-overlapping generations of homo sapiens.[25]

No matter whether the participants are members of generation 878, 1739, 2345, 3009, 4574 or 5234, we will keep the assumption that they must know how societies work and be aware of human evolution and history to some extent. It would be rather absurd to change this parameter. One of our central premises is that the participants under the 'veil of ignorance' are human beings. Unlike animals, humans are not limited to genetically inherited or experience-based information, but have access to knowledge and information generated by the many generations before them. They are far more capable than even the most developed ape of causally linking the past, present and future. Man can compare and plan his actions or form his future, thanks to knowledge passed on orally or in writing. Therefore, each generation has some knowledge about the level of civilization and the average well-being of past generations. Each has a fundamental understanding of evolutionary processes and knows that higher states evolve from lower ones. Generation 4574, for instance, knows that its HDI is far higher than that of generations 878, 1739, 2345 or 3009.

The basic idea of the 'veil of ignorance' as described above was: first, the participants do not know which generation they had belonged to before they came under the 'veil of ignorance'; nor, second, do they know which one they will belong to, once it is lifted. The second aspect is the more important one.[26] It is a *conditio sine qua non* because 'justice as impartiality' theories presume that the participants are unable to translate their bargaining power into personal advantage. Participants in an *intra*generational 'veil of ignorance' scenario know that in every society 'there are those who give orders and those who obey them, those who receive deference and those who give it, those who have more than they can use and those who have less than they need' (Barry, 1989, p3). It does not influence 'justice as impartiality' models if we assume that the participants under the 'veil' know what they were *before* the 'veil of ignorance' was installed. But it is crucial that they do not know what their role in society will be *after* the 'veil of ignorance' has been lifted. The same is true in the *inter*generational context. Even under the 'veil', a representative of generation 4574 knows that a series of generations with a lower HDI has preceded his generation. This is not an infringement of the fundamental condition of 'justice as impartiality' theories. The decisive fact is that the representatives of generation 4574 do not know in which generation they will grow up *after* the 'veil of ignorance' has been lifted. Just as to us, the history of humankind is an open book to each of the participants (see the area to the left of the dashed line in Figure 6.1). We know the medical advances that have increased the number of years spent in full health, the economic and technological achievements that have increased the availability of consumer goods and lowered working hours, as well as the political and social developments that have spread human and civil rights and led to democracy (cf. Lumer, 2003, p114). The rise of the HDI is a global trend. Despite regional disparities, it is not limited to the 'more developed countries'. However, the future (the area to the right of the dashed line in Figure 6.1) is unknown. We do not know whether the human race has reached its limits, i.e. whether our HDI will continue to grow, or whether factors such as the climate change will lead to a regression.

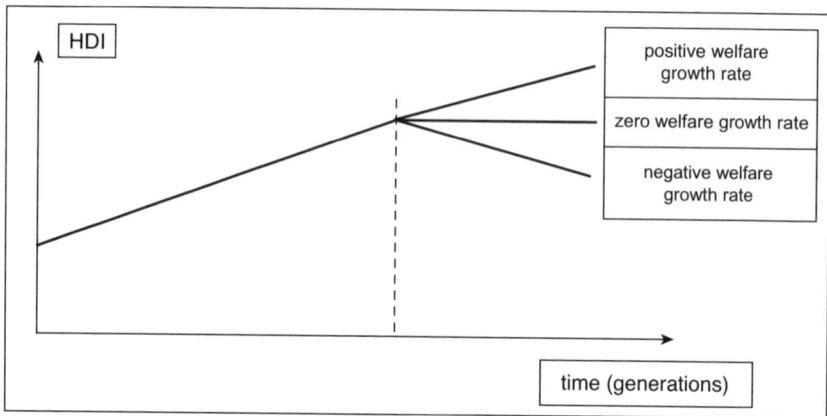

Figure 6.1 *HDI development (past and future scenarios)*

Model 1, finite n, unalterable history

In model 1 with a finite n, another parameter is crucial: can the past be changed or not? Let us first look at the model assuming an unchangeable past. To simplify matters we will group the 6000 generations into six generations of 1000 each. We will attribute historical names to these generations of 1000 ('Neanderthal Man', 'Early Nomad', 'Late Nomad', 'Tiller', 'Modern Man', 'Man of the Future'). The first 1000 generations that lived between the first 25,000–30,000 years after the advent of mankind ('Neanderthal' generations) are represented by the 'Neanderthal Man'; the next 1000 generations are represented by the 'Early Nomad', etc. Hence, we can envision a meeting of only six persons, each representing a certain level of well-being or human development (measured by the HDI). The size of the generations may vary. This does not affect the decision-making process, as long as we assume that each representative of a generation in model 1 has the same speaking and voting rights. Hence, the 'Neanderthal' has the same say as the others, although the 1000 generations he represents include fewer individuals than the 1000 generations of 'Modern Man'. The model refers to the number of generations and not to the number of people (see Table 6.3).

Table 6.3 *6000 generations and their average well-being*

Generations	1–1000	1001–2000	2001–3000	3001–4000	4001–4573	4574	4575–5000	5001–6000
	Neanderthal	Early Nomad	Late Nomad	Tiller	Modern Man	Present Generation (belongs to Modern Man)	Modern Man	Man of the Future
Average HDI	100	200	300	400	450	500	?	?

Note: As shown in Chapter 5, real HDI values are tiny and odd. To simplify calculations in this chapter, real HDI numbers are transformed into fictional ones, which are easier to calculate. Note that in column 1 row 3, the number 100 is the average, not the cumulated HDI of the members of generations 1–1000.

Let us assume that $G_{present}$ (the generation alive today, i.e. you and me) is G_{4574} in the line of all 6000 generations and has an HDI of 500. To us, the future is unknown. We, the external thinkers of this thought experiment, only know history until today. The participants in the 'original position', however, also have knowledge about the future: the 'Man of the Future' is among them and he knows exactly what will happen between G_{5000} and G_{6000}. What matters for the outcome of the thought experiment is the participants' knowledge, not our own. Therefore, we must consider various possible scenarios: if all goes well, the HDI of the 'Man of the Future' might have increased to 600. If things stay the same, it will have stagnated at 500 (like that of the 'Modern Man'), and in case of a catastrophe, it will have dropped to, say, 50.[27]

The six participants will analyse their position as follows:

- 'Man of the Future': if the HDI continues to rise, he will have the most to lose. His chances are five out of six to end up in an earlier, less-developed generation. He also knows that someone else would then belong to the sixth generation (of thousand) and enjoy its benefits. In case of a catastrophe, he has the most to win. His chances are five out of six to wake up as a member of an earlier generation with a higher HDI. Like for everyone else, his chances are one out of six to stay on the same HDI level.
- 'Neanderthal Man': he has a lot to win. If mankind will develop further, his chances are five out of six to improve his fate. Even if a catastrophe should take place in $G > G_{present}$, reducing the 'Man of the Future's' HDI to 50, the 'Neanderthal Man's' chance to be better off than before he came under the 'veil' would still be four out of six.
- The 'Early Nomad' will have a good chance of improving his fate if mankind makes further progress (four out of six). In case of a catastrophe, chances are three out of six to achieve a higher HDI.
- The chances of the 'Late Nomad' to improve his fate if mankind makes further progress are three out of six; his chances to improve his living conditions would be two out of six in case of a catastrophe.

- The chances of the 'Tiller' to improve his fate if mankind makes further progress are two out of six; his chances to improve his existence in case of a catastrophe would be one out of six.

We have chosen the parameter 'unalterable history', which means that the participants can hope not to wake up in an unfavourable generation, but they cannot influence anything. All the plagues, all the wars and all the other events described in history books do take place. On an intragenerational level, it is possible to improve the well-being of the least-advantaged members of society by worsening the situation of the most-advantaged ones. This is not possible on an intergenerational level: generation 1 would not benefit from worsening the situation of generation 4574. No matter what will happen later when the 'veil of ignorance' is lifted, generation 1 will always wake up in a cold cave, plagued by vermin and infectious deseases, in the year 130,000 BC. The participants cannot change anything about that, because they cannot influence the past. An equal distribution of well-being, as shown in Table 6.4, is certainly not an option.

Table 6.4 *Equal distribution of well-being among 6000 generations*

Generations	1–1000	1001–2000	2001–3000	3001–4000	4001–5000	5001–6000	Average
Average HDI	300	300	300	300	300	300	**300**

Model 1, finite n, alterable history

Obviously, our parameter constellation is not wise as long as we assume that history is unalterable. The main attraction of the 'veil of ignorance' in the *intra*generational context is that the participants could harm themselves. If they imprudently introduce a slave-holding society, they might end up as slaves themselves, once the 'veil of ignorance' is lifted. Tough luck, one might say.

This mechanism can be maintained in the intergenerational context by exchanging the parameter 'unalterable history' for 'alterable history'. Let us assume the 'Neanderthal Man', the 'Early' and 'Late Nomads', the 'Tiller', the 'Modern Man' and the 'Man of the Future' were supposed to design rules for a parallel world that still has the entire history of mankind ahead of it. If this were simply a world for others, there would be no risk involved for the participants, so their self-interest would be irrelevant. Therefore, we must assume that the participants – respectively the 6000 generations represented by them – will populate the new world themselves. However, they do not know which generation they will belong to once the 'veil of ignorance' has been lifted. Randomly, a position between 1 and 6000 will be assigned to them, and they will have to bear the fate of that generation, whether they like it or not. How would their decision-making process work? They could, for example, want well-being to be divided as shown in Table 6.5.

Table 6.5 *Well-being distribution (wishful thinking)*

Generations	1–1000	1001–2000	2001–3000	3001–4000	4001–5000	5001–6000	Average
Average HDI	800	800	800	800	800	800	**800**

However, we must take into account that, according to our assumption, they have knowledge of the fundamental principles of evolutionary processes. They are no illusionists. They know that it took millions of years for man to evolve and that the development of civilization and of all the amenities that prolong life and make it comfortable also took time. Later generations will inevitably benefit from the inventions, experiences and innovations of their predecessors. Alternatively, there is no way earlier generations could benefit from future technology and medicine, as time is one-directional and irreversible. Justice as 'equality' is still not an option, unless the participants behind the 'veil of ignorance' ordered each generation to burn down all its libraries and destroy all innovations and inventions before it dies. But then all generations would vegetate on the lowest possible level of civilization. Abiding by the idea of equality, they could consider a distribution such as that in Table 6.6.

Table 6.6 *Well-being distribution (smallest denominator)*

Generations	1–1000	1001–2000	2001–3000	3001–4000	4001–5000	5001–6000	Average
Average HDI	50	50	50	50	50	50	**50**

But such an equal treatment in a bad sense is very unattractive and will surely not be chosen by the participants. But which well-being distribution will they prefer? We should not forget that the 'Man of the Future' knows the course of history, even if we do not. How will the participants decide if he shares his knowledge with them?[28] Let us assume 'Modern Man' will trigger a nuclear or ecological catastrophe in the real world, leading to diseases and misery for all future generations. The few survivors would have an HDI of only 50, and the well-being of all generations would be distributed as shown in Table 6.7.

Table 6.7 *Well-being distribution (decline after a catastrophe)*

Generations	1–1000	1001–2000	2001–3000	3001–4000	4001–5000	5001–6000	Average
Average HDI	100	200	300	400	500	50	**258.33**

Obviously, the participants will do their best to avoid the decline between generations five and six. This principle can be generalized: they will do their best to avoid any disturbance in the path of human development. That will lead to a distribution of well-being as shown in Table 6.8.

Table 6.8 *Well-being distribution (steady HDI growth)*

Generations	1–1000	1001–2000	2001–3000	3001–4000	4001–5000	5001–6000	Average
Average HDI	100	200	300	400	500	600	350

But that is not the end of the discussion. The participants know the history of the real world, so when they develop principles of justice for the parallel world, they will take into account that the HDI growth has not been steady, even if the trend line suggests so (see Figure 6.2).

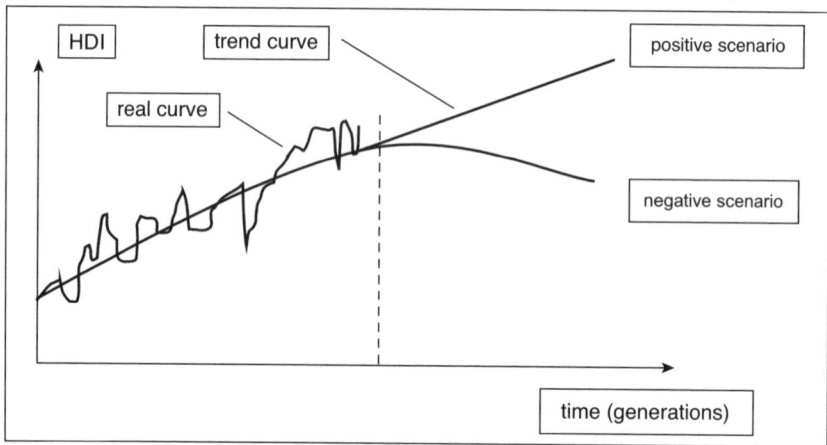

Figure 6.2 *Real HDI increase and trend line*

The participants will try to eliminate the erratic movements of the actual HDI curve as far as possible. In the real world, generation 4566 may have started the Hundred Years' War and thereby made the HDI of generation 4567 drop considerably. In the parallel world, the war could be avoided because history can be changed in this model. Such a rectification of mistakes of individual generations does not go against the underlying long-term development trend.[29] The prevention of wars and man-made ecological, social or technical disintegration means that the values of Table 6.8 have to be adjusted upwards, as in Table 6.9.

Table 6.9 *Well-being distribution (prevention of mistakes)*

Generations	1–1000	1001–2000	2001–3000	3001–4000	4001–5000	5001–6000	Average
Average HDI	100	200	300	400	518	630	358

The distribution in Table 6.9 is preferable to the distribution in Table 6.8.

Savings are not decisive for the welfare of the next generation

Traditionally, the accumulation problem was formulated as follows: 'Each generation needs to balance investment against consumption. If a generation consumes everything, then subsequent generations will be left with nothing and will starve' (Mulgan, 2002, p12). The challenge for political philosophers has been to show that intergenerational saving in the sense of making sacrifices is morally desirable. This task has driven many of them into despair. Empirical research on human development has shown that the assumption itself was wrong. First, it ignores that the growth in human development and human well-being is largely triggered by autonomous factors. Second, the shocks and deflections of the actual HDI curve, i.e. the deviations from the trend line, are not a result of the consumption or saving decisions (= investment decisions, as in economic theory, saving = investing) of individual generations like, for example, G_{4258} or G_{4566}. Rather, they are caused by wars, epidemics and other catastrophes. Therefore, it is wrong to ask how high the intergenerational savings rate should be to secure the well-being of the next generation. Dealing exclusively with that question will rather obscure the obligations we have to future generations. It is therefore important to distinguish three rates:

- r_{aut}: the well-being growth rate triggered by inventions, innovations and improvements. This rate is autonomous. It results as a by-product of mankind's inventive talent. It is part of human nature to try, to invent and to improve.[30] This accumulation of theoretical knowledge and its practical implementation continuously and cumulatively benefits later generations. In this sense, each generation stands on the shoulders of its parents and forebears. The well-being growth rate caused by inventions is *not* the result of a sacrifice of some kind by earlier generations and the term 'saving' does not apply as the generation that produces r_{aut} does not have to abstain from consumption. On the contrary, it would enact a generation effort and money to prevent r_{aut}. Assuming G_{4125} invented the wheel,[31] would it be a sacrifice to pass it on to G_{4126}? No, it would rather be arduous to destroy all existing wheels. And it would be impossible to eliminate all knowledge concerning wheels anyway. Later generations benefit from the unconscious, but fortunate conservation of the works previous generations created for their own purposes (Baier, 1980, p173). Our model divides mankind into a long procession of 6000 non-overlapping generations. In reality, generations overlap, which makes it even more difficult to eliminate knowledge.
- r_{care}: the well-being growth rate triggered by a prevention of wars and man-made ecological, social or technical collapses.[32] Apart from epidemics and crop failures, the largest HDI decreases in human history occurred due to wars, enslavement and oppression. In the future, ecological disasters and accidents with large-scale technologies might play a more prominent role. The participants would compel each generation to avoid such disasters. An important aspect here is that such man-made disasters do not only harm future generations but also the generation causing them.

● s: the savings rate triggered by sacrifices. This rate s results from a generation's restraint. The savings rate is defined as one generation accepting a
smaller HDI increase or even an HDI decrease for the sake of its succeeding
generation. The rate s is similar to the economic savings rate, i.e. the share of
the GDP that is not consumed, but put aside for the future, except that s
refers here to the HDI instead of the GDP.

The lower curve in Figure 6.3 shows the HDI growth based exclusively on r_{aut},
whereas the upper curve shows the additional effect of the prevention of man-
made catastrophes (r_{care}).

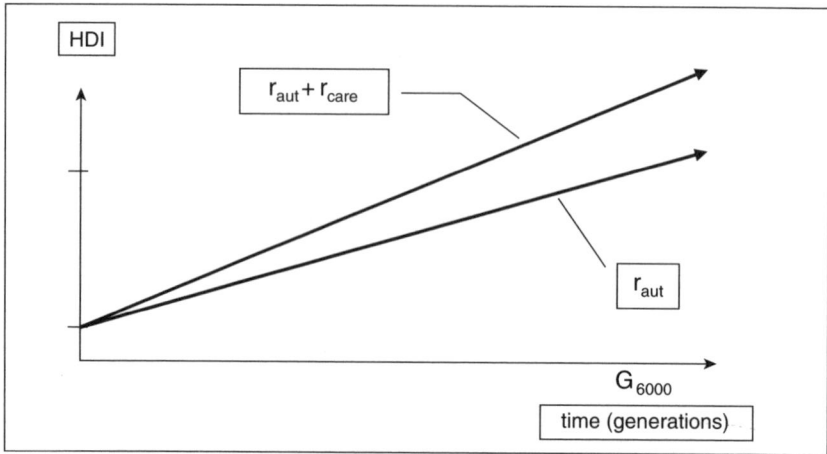

Figure 6.3 *Well-being growth rates r_{aut} and $r_{aut} + r_{care}$*

The question of whether a savings rate s should be adopted will surely be
debated by the participants. If a savings rate is introduced, human well-being
would be distributed as shown in Figure 6.4.

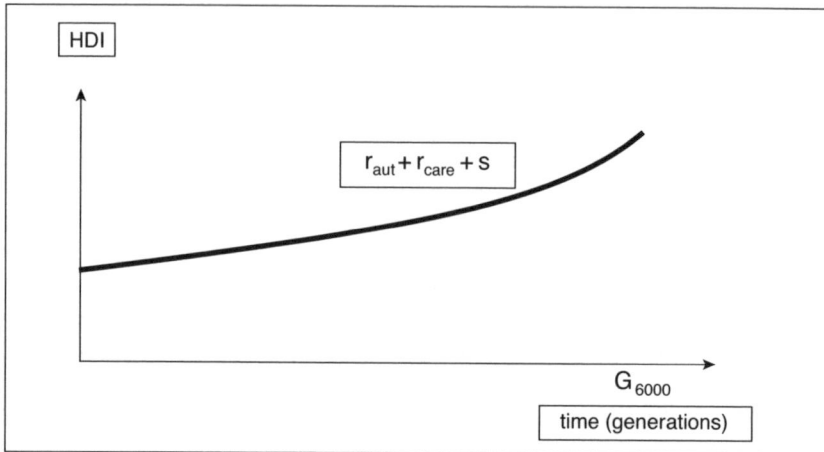

Figure 6.4 *Well-being growth rate in case of savings*

The maximization of the average well-being might reach a higher level if each generation is obligated to save – that depends on the individual values assigned to different well-being distributions. Table 6.9 showed the well-being distribution without s, whereas Tables 6.10 and 6.11 both show two possible well-being distributions with s.

Table 6.10 *Well-being distribution ($r_{aut} + r_{care}$ + s) with high average*

Generations	1–1000	1001–2000	2001–3000	3001–4000	4001–5000	5001–6000	Average
Average HDI	80	190	295	405	528	662	**360**

Table 6.11 *Well-being distribution ($r_{aut} + r_{care}$ + s) with low average*

Generations	1–1000	1001–2000	2001–3000	3001–4000	4001–5000	5001–6000	Average
Average HDI	80	190	295	405	526	640	**356**

Still, the gathering would not instill any obligation for net savings, no matter whether Table 6.10 or 6.11 applies. The principle of well-being maximization is limited by the principle that new savings are not morally required.[33]

Why is this? Since time is one-directional only earlier generations can save for later ones but not vice versa. Due to r_{aut} earlier generations are worse off than later generations anyway.[34] It thus would be an unfair burden for earlier generations to save (sacrifice) for future generations. Since each participant might belong to one of the earlier generations, he will not make their situation even worse.

No generation is obliged to save for new investments. But what about reinvestments? Does a generation have the right to dissave if the previous generation saved? Or must the savings level be maintained on all accounts? Here, it should be kept in mind that s must always refer to human well-being (measured on the basis of the HDI). If generation 1 creates a higher HDI for generation 2, for whatever reason, generation 2 is obliged to pass it on to generation 3. No generation has the right to dissave. However, generation 2 is not obliged to do the same as generation 1 by realizing an additional s.

The principles of intergenerational justice – derived from the 'original position'

Finally, representatives of all generations under the Rawlsian 'veil of ignorance' would agree on the following prnciples of intergenerational justice:

1   Maximize the average individual well-being of all members of all generations. This principle primarily obliges every generation to avoid wars as well

as ecological, social and technical collapses that might significantly reduce human welfare.

2   No generation is obligated to save more than the previous generation.

In comparison to former models,[35] my theory has three innovations:

1   Instead of using utilitarian subjective happiness, subjective well-being, subjective preferences, etc. it uses an objective indicator, the HDI.
2   The role of saving (in the economic sense) for the well-being for future generations is not overrated as it is in earlier theories. It would be worthwhile for social scientists, historians and statisticians to correctly calculate the exact HDI decrease caused by specific disasters or catastrophes. Among all individual calamities, the Second World War would probably break the record.[36]
3   No generation is obliged to generate new savings, even if this leads to a smaller average well-being for all generations than without this principle.

The asymmetrical information background

The six participants' asymmetrical information background in model 1 has been mentioned several times. We have already contemplated the possibility that 'Modern Man' might trigger a nuclear or ecological catastrophe and thereby lower the HDI of the 'Man of the Future' (see Table 6.7). But what if the 'Man of the Future' actually has an HDI of 600 but deceives the others by *claiming* to have an HDI of 50? First, we have to clarify whether the assumed self-interest of the participants reaches as far as to betrayal and delusion. Self-interest (or orientation towards one's own life plan) is not the same as selfishness. For the sake of the argument, let us nevertheless assume that each of the six participants is prepared to lie and deceive for his own advantage. The 'Man of the Future' knows most about the course of history. He could make up stories about catastrophes that allegedly took place after t_{5000}. Due to backward induction, the same applies to 'Modern Man' who could also lie to the generations before him, etc. In the end, the 'Neanderthal Man' could be faced with a series of lamentations from the other participants. But why should that happen? The 'Man of the Future' knows that he, too, could wake up in the role of the 'Neanderthal Man', once the 'veil of ignorance' is lifted, so there is no point in lying. As mentioned, the most important parameter of the 'justice as impartiality' situation is that the participants do not know what their role in society will be *after* the 'veil of ignorance' has been lifted.

Let us now turn to the variants of Rawls' model 2.

Model 2, finite n, alterable history

Only representatives of a single generation meet in the 'original position' behind the 'veil of ignorance'. They do not know which generation they previously belonged to or will belong to later. No matter which generation it is, mankind's past, however extended it may be, is clearly visible to them. There are three possibilities. Let us first assume that G_{meet} (the generation that meets) is $G_{present}$

(the generation alive today, i.e. you and me), which is G_{4574} in the series of all 6000 generations. We, $G_{present}$ or G_{4574}, are aware of past, that is, of the course of history on the left side of Figure 6.1, whereas the right side remains unknown to *us*. If, second, the generation represented by the participants in the 'original position' has a lower number than 4575 ($G_{meet} < G_{present}$, for instance $G_{meet} = G_{3009}$), the dashed line will simply move further to the left. Even then, the area left of the dashed line would be known to G_{meet}. In that case, progress will not have led to today's HDI level yet, but the HDI per person will still be higher than that of G_{1000}. The third option is to move the dashed line to the right if $G_{meet} > G_{present}$. Of course, the participating generation ($G_{meet} > G_{present}$, for example $G_{meet} = G_{5111}$) is still aware of *its own* history, whereas *its* future is still unclear.

The first option, $G_{meet} = G_{present}$, must not be confused with the Rawlsian 'present time of entry interpretation', which only states that the participants in model 2 are contemporaries. Rawls does not say that the generation to which the participants belong to is the one that presently lives. Rawls correctly surmises the following deliberations of the participants:

> *Since the persons in the original position know that they are contemporaries (taking the present time of entry interpretation), they can favor their generation by refusing to make any sacrifices at all for their successors; they simply acknowledge the principle that no one has a duty to save for posterity. Previous generations have either saved or they have not; there is nothing the parties can now do to affect that. (Rawls, 1971, p140)[37]*

According to the assumption of self-interest, G_{meet} will indeed not save anything. The savings rate s is zero. But what about r_{aut} and r_{care}? G_{meet} will not bother to destroy all its inventions and innovations, so r_{aut} will definitely be realised. r_{care} would not be realized. Since we are only considering non-overlapping generations, G_{meet} could become careless towards the end of its life. It might therefore hardly care about catastrophes it causes. For instance, G_{meet} could trigger a nuclear disaster in the last days of its life. However, that would require G_{meet} to be a technically advanced generation, because the first few thousands of generations did not have the technical potential to irreversibly impair the future fate of mankind and nature by actions or omissions. Anyway, a careless attitude of G_{4575} or a later generation could indeed leave posterity with less than what G_{meet} had. That would break a long tradition of increasing prosperity and be a tragedy for all generations $G > G_{meet}$, because they will have a lower HDI or even a zero HDI if the catastrophe extinguishes mankind.

Some authors argue that the contemporaries gathered in the 'original position' as defined in model 2 could even prevent future generations from being born (Unnerstall, 1999, p420). Another option is that they could simply neglect their children in their self-interest instead of preventing reproduction altogether.

Model 2, infinite n

An infinite number of participants in the 'original position' means that reaching a consensus would be, literally, impossible. Apart from that, a careless conduct of G_{meet} would have even further-reaching consequences: in the previous situation, it harmed an unknown, but limited number of generations, but in this case it would harm an infinite number.

These prospects are dire. But let us keep in mind that model 2 is *not* the intergenerational analogy to the intragenerational 'veil of ignorance'. Originally, model 2 was introduced by Rawls to facilitate things, whereas in fact it rather seems to be an unnecessary complication we may safely omit.

Summary

If justice is conceived as impartiality, 'veil of ignorance' theories are helpful tools for deducing principles of justice. In an intragenerational context, principles of justice were chosen by rational and self-interested individuals who have no knowledge of their role in society, their talents, their genetic endowment, their personal identities, or their natural or social advantages as long as they are under the 'veil of ignorance'. In the analogous intergenerational situation, representatives from all generations come together under the 'veil of ignorance'. They do not know which generation they will belong to, once the 'veil' has been lifted. Nevertheless, they know the basic rules of societies and evolution. Each participant knows the course of history – not in detail, but in general – up to the point of his existence. The participants know that later generations usually have a higher HDI than earlier ones. This is at least true by and large from the advent of mankind until the present. This autonomous rate is owed to the one-directionality of history and the fact that each generation invents, innovates and researches, and thereby makes progress, for example in medicine and technology. Within these bounds, the participants will agree on the following principles:

1 Maximize the average individual well-being of all members of all generations. This principle primarily obliges every generation to avoid wars as well as ecological, societal and technological collapses that might significantly impair human welfare.
2 No generation is obliged to save more than the previous generation.

The two principles of justice developed under the 'veil of ignorance' are on the top level, then comes the constitution, then follow the laws and political programmes, and finally their application in individual cases. Here, only the top level is discussed.

If a procedure is just, its outcome – whatever it might be – will also be just. Now, we have seen that intergenerational justice is certainly not the equality of all generations. The members of later generations will necessarily be better off than the members of earlier generations, or, put differently, mankind will progress in a normal state of affairs.

Another point worth mentioning is that well-being in an intergenerational comparison and from an empirical point of view is not decisively influenced by economic consumption and savings rates. History teaches us that the major factors influencing the ups and downs of human well-being are wars and catastrophes. The question of how high the intergenerational *economic* savings rate has to be is thus wrongly posed, and an exclusive pursuit of this question will rather obscure which duties we have to future generations.

Justice as the equal treatment of equal cases, and the unequal treatment of unequal cases

What does 'justice as equality' actually mean?

As we have seen, the procedural concept of 'justice as impartiality' can be transferred from the intragenerational context to the intergenerational context. But what about the principle 'justice as equality', which is also often used in the intragenerational context? 'The notion of justice inevitably evokes the idea of a certain degree of equality. From Plato and Aristotle to contemporary lawyers, moral philosophers, and other philosophers, all have agreed on this point. Formal or abstract justice can be defined as a principle of action according to which equal cases must be treated in the same way (Perelman, 1967, p307 et seq.). But this statement is only half of the truth, because it automatically leads to the question of how to treat unequal cases. And the only answer can be: whoever treats unequal cases equally acts unjustly! Therefore, 'justice as equality' is an inadmissible abbreviation for a concept that should actually be: 'justice as the equal treatment of equal cases and the unequal treatment of unequal cases'. This inadmissible abbreviation is widespread. Koller is right in saying that there is a principle that expresses the largely undisputed core of the concept of distributive justice:

> *The members of a society must be treated alike, and their goods and burdens must be distributed equally among them, unless there are sound reasons that justify unequal treatment or distribution, i.e. reasons that are generally acceptable from an impartial point of view. (Koller, 2007, p9)*[38]

It is all the more surprising when Koller continues: 'This principle – let us call it the principle of equal treatment' (Koller, 2007, p9). Why should we? Rather, it should be called 'equal cases equally, unequal cases unequally'. Which arguments could prove that the first half of the sentence is more important than the second one? An egalitarian could reply that there is a presumption in favour of equality. The theorist Ernst Tugendhat believes equality and inequality are not equal options. In case of doubt, he says, matters should be treated equally (Tugendhat, 1993, p374).[39] This is correct in the intragenerational context. But it is of less help to the egalitarian than he thinks. After all, a 'presumption' is not a 'conclusion'. A presumption can (and must) be made if something has to be distributed although we have little information on the situation.

Imagine the following task: You have two apples to give to two children who wait outside. How will you distribute them? We would all probably decide that each of them gets one apple. However, one of the two children might be full, and the other might be starving. If we knew that, of course we would not give each of them an apple.[40] The presumption in favour of equality refers to distribution under unknown conditions. As soon as we have more knowledge, we are no longer forced to make presumptions. In real life, we rarely have to distribute goods with such a lack of information. In most disputes on distribution that are brought before court, there is so much information that there is no need to implicitly give equal treatment priority to unequal treatment. The highest court in Germany, for instance, adopted the formal principle of justice as a standard for its decisions as follows: 'Neither may equal cases arbitrarily be treated unequally, nor may unequal cases arbitrarily be treated equally.'[41] If expressed like this, the formal principle of justice can certainly no longer be called 'justice as equality', as Koller suggests.

The formal justice principle inevitably includes a tension between equal and unequal treatment. If justice aims at equality, it should be in a general form applicable for as many people as possible – so it incorporates the attempt to treat each individual according to his incomparable unique nature, by means of specific treatment. This requirement to treat unequal cases differently weakens the position of all egalitarian concepts of justice. The egalitarian Stefan Gosepath tries to avoid the problem by reinterpreting the second half of the formal definition of justice, so in his account it reads: 'Treat equal cases equally and unequal cases proportionally.' (Gosepath, 2004, p127). He explains: 'On the other hand, a treatment is *proportional* [emphasis original] or *relatively* [emphasis original] *equal* [emphasis added] if all persons concerned are treated as or granted what they deserve' (Gosepath, 2004, p125). So, equality is reintroduced through the backdoor; no wonder that Gosepath's chapter is entitled 'Proportional Equality'. Unfortunately, things do not always work that way. As we will see, there are many just distributions in which persons who work one third more do not receive one third more, or in which persons who need double as much of something do not receive double as much of it. Even if a certain degree of proportionality is a suitable guideline, there can rarely be *equal* proportionality.

According to Aristotle, the common goods and burdens of a community should be distributed among its members in accordance with their 'merit' or 'worthiness' (Aristotle, 2005, p103 et seq., 1130b–1131a). This is the understanding of justice in the saying 'to each his own' or in the Latin proverb: '*suum cuique*'.[42] 'To each his own' is exactly to say 'not the same for all', but 'something else for each individual'. Even Aristotle points out that the standards of worthiness are controversial and vary from one society to another. That is why there are several ancillary concepts of justice: 'justice according to performance', 'justice according to effort' and 'justice according to needs' (cf. Lumer, 2003, p105).

Justice according to performance

Advocates of desert-based principles argue that some deserve a higher level of benefits or goods even if their rewards generate or increase inequalities within a society. The basic idea of justice according to performance is that people perform differently because of unequally distributed talent and motivation. That is why the principle of equality ('equal pay for equal work') is often converted to a principle of unequal payment. Consider as an example two serious runners A and B who earn their living on sports. In a 100m race at an international sports event, the winner gets €10,000 and the second-fastest gets €5000. A wins. It would generally be considered unjust if B were to demand the same pay as A after the race, even if he put more effort into it or needed the money more than A. Proportional prize money would also be unjust: then B could demand €9987 Euros, because he ended up only a few thousandths of a second slower than A. Most people would think A deserves at least double as much as B, even if A did not run double as fast as B.[43]

Justice according to effort

Most cases are less clear. Let us look at the following example of a conflict between remuneration according to justice or according to effort:

> *In a co-operative industrial association, is it just or not that talent or skill should give a title to superior remuneration? On the negative side of the question it is argued that whoever does the best he can deserves equally well, and ought not in justice to be put in a position of inferiority for no fault of his own; that superior abilities have already advantages more than enough, in the admiration they excite, the personal influence they command, and the internal sources of satisfaction attending them, without adding to these a superior share of the world's goods; and that society is bound in justice rather to make compensation for the less favored for this unmerited inequality of advantages than to aggravate it. On the contrary side it is contended that society receives more from the more efficient laborer; that, his services being more useful, society owes him a larger return for them; that a greater share of the joint result is actually his work, and not to allow his claim to it is a kind of robbery; that, if he is only to receive as much as others, he can only be justly required to produce as much, and to give a smaller amount of time and exertion, proportioned to his superior efficiency. (Mill, 1979, p56)*

Until today, there is no answer to this well formulated example of the basic conflict by John Stuart Mill[44] and there is not likely to be one in the near future in the intragenerational context.

Justice according to needs

Needs-based theories of justice are founded on the idea that goods, especially basic goods such as food, shelter and medical care, should be distributed according to the individuals' basic needs. And not only basic needs are concerned, but all kinds of necessities. If, for example, three mountaineers would reach their bivouac for the night, but there was only one blanket, they would try to find out who needs it most urgently. Perhaps one of them does not feel cold, the second one is ill, the third one exhausted. In this case, there cannot be proportional treatment – one of them gets the blanket, the others don't. So three patterns of distribution can be derived from the formal justice formula 'equal cases equally, unequal cases unequally': parity (equality), proportionality or priority. According to Young, priority means 'that the person with the greatest claim to the good gets it' (Young, 1994, p7).

Needs-based concepts of justice are based on the idea that existing inequalities should be levelled or compensated to achieve *equality* or at least balance things out as far as possible. Perhaps the question of which of the three mountain climbers needs the blanket most is easy to answer: the one who has a cold and is coughing. If he gets the blanket and is thus able to sleep well, he might feel better the next day, but the others will probably feel a little worse because they did not sleep as well, so the final situation is more balanced. If the ill person did not get the blanket, there would be even more inequality the next day, because his condition would become even worse, compared to the climber who had the blanket.

Of course it is important to know if the initial situation was self-imposed or not. If the ill mountaineer was not dressed warmly enough although his comrades told him so, and if that is the reason why he is now coughing, they will be less willing to give him the blanket. They probably still would, basically because every individual is entitled to the same dignity. The presumption of the same dignity for every human being is one of the strongest justifications for needs-based concepts of justice.[45]

In reality, the criteria performance, effort and needs are often intertwined. Normally, a strong and efficient person needs less in a specific situation. So, even needs-based concepts implicitly deal with efficiency.

Let us look at a question of justice that is not about the distribution of goods or rights, but of burdens: military service for men and women. Since each country has its own rules, this problem seems like a counterexample to the formal justice principle 'equal cases equally, unequal cases unequally'. But that is not the case. Rather, the question of how the specific burdens of military service affect women (or how equal men and women are in this context) requires an empirical answer, and until now the research is not complete. Consider the fact that nobody would think of excluding red-haired men, for instance, from military service. Here, it is empirically proven that a different hair colour does not make a man unequal enough to justify unequal treatment. That proves that the formal principle of justice is not affected by this objection (Sidgwick, 1981, p284). Often we do not know yet what is equal and what is not (Kelsen, 2000, p34). But this is not an objection against the formal justice principle, as Kelsen contends. Rather, the reason why the question of justice will remain disputed in individual cases is because it sometimes takes time to figure out whether a different performance, different efforts or different needs are given.

Justice according to performance, effort or need in the intergenerational context

Are these reasons for unequal treatment relevant in the intergenerational context? Theoretically, yes. In theory, one could construe examples in which one generation was more ambitious, industrious and hard-working than another. However, I know of no historical case in which such an assumption could be proven. The whole well-known debate on protecting the industrious from the lazy is far less relevant in the intergenerational context. At least on a global level, industriousness and ambition are equally distributed, prima facie. Of course, the number of working hours has varied in different epochs, as it still does in different countries. However, it should not be forgotten that the axiological objective is well-being, and it is not increased by maximizing the number of working hours at the cost of education and health.

All human beings have the same basic needs, as we have seen. Throughout history, the degree of need fulfilment of the average members of each generation has tended to increase. Need fulfilment has been chosen as an axiological objective. But does that mean everyone should get what and as much as he needs? Can the initial inequality that generations suffer through no fault of their own be eliminated, so the needs of all members of a generation will be fulfilled to the same degree in the end?

Elimination of inequality?

In the section 'Justice as impartiality', above, the conclusion was reached that the initial situation of different generations cannot be made equal because of the autonomous innovation rate. In the past, the initial situation of later generations was usually better than that of earlier ones. The initial situation of today's generation is better than that of all previous generations. Since time is one-directional, the level of need-fulfilment of *previous* generations cannot be lifted to the level of today's generation. Therefore, even harsh differences that annoy us in the intragenerational context must not be considered unjust in the intergenerational context.

Life and health – basic needs of every human being – are threatened by diseases. Let us compare two examples – HIV/AIDS in the 20th century with smallpox in earlier centuries – with reference to a needs-based concept of justice.

The scourge HIV/AIDS

Acquired Immune Deficiency Syndrome (AIDS) is a specific combination of symptoms that occur with people whose immune system has been destroyed because they have been infected with the HI virus. AIDS was recognized as an individual disease on 1 December 1981 and is spreading pandemically at present.

To which degree is AIDS plaguing the present generation? According to the World Health Organization (WHO), an estimated roughly 2.9 million persons died of AIDS in 2006, 39.5 million persons are presently infected, and another 4.3 million get infected every year. Worldwide, an average of approximately 1 per cent of 15–49-year-olds is infected with HIV, but in some African countries, that number has reached roughly 20 per cent. Normally, a disease is considered a misfortune. How come AIDS has become a question of justice?

Until recently, help for low-income countries focused on the provision of food and water supplies. But in recent years, people have started to become aware of the fact that HIV/AIDS is a problem of at least the same gravity. Eventually, when discussion started about HIV issues in the late 1990s, people started to ask why there were so many deaths occurring when the drugs existed that could prevent them, and why these drugs, known as antiretrovirals, were so very expensive. People in resource-poor countries began demanding access to the medication that could save their lives.

Pilot projects had demonstrated that people in the poorest parts of the world were able to adhere to the antiretroviral treatment and the benefits were similar to those seen for people in Western countries. There, the death rate had dropped dramatically after 1997, thanks to the new combination therapies.

But AIDS treatment is also a question of patent law. There are two basic forms of modern-day drugs – proprietary (or 'brand-named') drugs that are developed and produced by large multinational pharmaceutical companies, and generic drugs that are either copies or the basic form of a proprietary drug. Normally patent protection rules under TRIPS (Trade-Related Aspects of Intellectual Property Rights), a World Trade Organization agreement, would make it illegal to copy any proprietary drug that was still under a patent. Generic antiretroviral drugs cost about $350 per patient per year. By contrast, brand name drugs fetch between $10,000 and $15,000. Developing countries argue that the Western world would harm their economies in the long run by selling huge amounts of expensive brand-name drugs. Therefore, they consider themselves morally entitled to produce generica of these drugs themselves.

Major pharmaceutical companies argue that the prices of brand-name drugs reflect the amount of research and development required to manufacture the drug. However, though it is not always easy to tell exactly how much money is spent by large pharmaceutical companies in different

*areas, much of their profits are thought to go on executive salaries, public-
ity, advertising, promotion, corporate sponsorship and branding, rather
than research and development (R&D).*

*In 2001, 39 major pharmaceutical companies, citing TRIPS regula-
tions, sued the South African government for passing a law that allowed
the production of far cheaper drugs with the same effect. Following
immense pressure from the South African government, the European
Parliament and 300,000 people from over 130 countries who signed a
petition against the action, however, they were forced to back down. Self-
help organizations such as TAC (Treatment Action Campaign) demonstrated against the pharmaceutical companies in Pretoria during this
process. 'Give people living with HIV/Aids equal treatment' was their
battle cry.*

A misfortune became a justice issue. Representatives of poor countries want the
companies in the more developed countries to grant them the licences they need
to produce the required drugs themselves. So, there are people who do not have
access to the drugs that could relieve their suffering. There are other people that
can provide what the poor people need. The poor individuals thus demand these
drugs, distributive justice and redistribution from the other individuals.

Let us now take a look at smallpox with regard to justice issues.

The scourge smallpox

*Smallpox has been known for millennia. The mummy of Pharaoh Ramses
II from Egypt clearly has pockmarks. For very many members of previous
generations, this illness was a scourge that caused much suffering and
significantly reduced their HDI. Smallpox had been spreading around the
world since the 15th and 16th centuries. As of the 18th century, the
number of smallpox cases rose and took the place of the plague as the worst
disease in the world. An estimated 400,000 people died of smallpox every
year, including every tenth child. From 1871 to 1873, 175,000 cases of
smallpox were still registered in Germany, and more than 100,000 of
them were lethal.*

*There is no cure for smallpox, only a preventive vaccination. Edward
Jenner was the first to test a safe vaccination method in 1796 in England.
He used vaccinia viruses, and the word 'vaccination' was actually derived
from this method. The mandatory smallpox vaccination was enforced
against the resistance of the Church (in 1824 Pope Leo XII even prohib-
ited the vaccination), and Bavaria was the first province worldwide to
introduce it in 1807. As of 1967, WHO made smallpox vaccination
mandatory worldwide. A worldwide vaccination campaign was initiated
to eradicate smallpox. The last known case of smallpox occurred in the
Merca district of Somalia in 1977. On 8 May 1980, WHO announced
that smallpox had been eradicated.*

> *Earlier generations could have suffered far less, because smallpox could have been wiped out much earlier. The means had always existed, but the method was only discovered in the 18th century. In 1770, Jenner had observed that people who caught cowpox while working with cows were known not to catch smallpox. Twenty-six years later, Jenner took the opportunity to test his theory and inoculated eight-year-old James Phipps, the son of his gardener, with cowpox. After only a weak bout of cowpox, James recovered. Jenner then tried to infect James with smallpox, but nothing happened because the boy proved to be immune to smallpox.*
>
> *The discovery of the fact that an infection with less dangerous variants of the virus make people immune against the illness led to mass vaccinations and, ultimately, to its eradication.*

People could easily have been protected from smallpox in the 17th or 18th centuries, but the required knowledge was not distributed equally among generations. Again a justice issue? With smallpox as well as with AIDS, there were people who knew how to fight or relieve the disease and others who did not and who suffered from it. Those who suffered from smallpox had the same dignity as those who suffer from AIDS, but in their case, the people holding the solution were members of another generation. That means, none of the members of those early generations could have called it unjust that those who were to live after them would suffer less. AIDS is a justice issue; smallpox is not. Understanding why, means understanding the core of the concept of generational justice. 'Ought implies can', and we cannot travel to the past and impart our knowledge to earlier generations to increase their HDI. In the intragenerational context, equality of opportunity is a leading justice principle.[46] Applicants for positions or goods are winnowed by fair competition independently of their sex, race or religion. It is irrelevant whether or not their parents are of noble blood, for instance. But equal opportunities require the possibilities of a 'level playing field'.[47] The playing field of different generations is not level. No generation has exactly the same initial opportunities as another, because the past cannot be changed. Civilization has developed since the time when men were hunters and gatherers. Past actions are irreversible, and justice can only be implemented in one direction. We present individuals are 'dwarves on the shoulders of a giant who is again made up of many thousands of dwarves' (Radermacher, 2002, p103) because our standard of living would be much lower without the accumulated capital of earlier generations.

We can, however, influence the HDI of *future* generations. If mankind continues to develop as it has in the past, our intertemporal successor generations will be better off than we are today, provided they utilize their potential. Should we try to destroy their potential in the name of justice? Should we try to reduce their HDI, for the sake of equality? Let us take a look at another example, this time from the intragenerational context:

The talented and the untalented pupil

Imagine two young pupils,[48] both work equally hard, but one of them is highly gifted, the other is completely untalented. In both cases, these inborn abilities are matters of fate. The difference in talent becomes obvious after only a few days at school, so the class teacher starts to coach the untalented pupil. This slightly balances the difference between the two girls, but does not eliminate it. To make them equal, the teacher would have to fully concentrate on the untalented child and neglect the other. Then the talents of the better pupil would not be trained, and she would not reach her full potential as an adult. I think almost everyone would agree that for justice reasons, the gifted pupil should also be given the possibility to develop her native talents, even if it means that she will be more successful than the untalented pupil later in life.

Can we ask the less talented pupil to make some kind of extra sacrifice for the highly gifted one, for example a donation for a training course that is offered only for very talented pupils? Surely not, because that would even increase the difference between them. But even a reasonable egalitarian would not ask the talented pupil to stop her development at the level the untalented pupil reaches by means of coaching. For justice reasons, whoever has an inborn talent should be allowed to develop it.

But the next question is whether it would be just to ask the talented pupil to make a sacrifice in a different field to balance the situation. If fate gave her talent, an egalitarian might want to put her at a disadvantage in a field that does not immediately affect that talent to balance the living conditions during the whole life course between her and her classmate.

Suppose both families paid school fees for their children, and both families earned the same money. Since one of the pupils is more talented and will probably be better off later in life, the parents of the other pupil might want her family to pay a higher tuition fee. The talented pupil would then have to pay off her family's debts when she starts working, so there would be less difference between the overall lifetime income of the two pupils. But that does not seem just, either. School fees can be based on the parents' income, but in this case, both families earn the same money. Hard-working and talented pupils can be given a scholarship. But in this case, the question is whether the less talented pupil should be subsidized, precisely because she is less talented. Obviously, that would not be just.

Different opportunities must be acknowledged and incorporated into an intra-generational theory of justice. The same applies to generations. Their initial situations do not differ on account of their hereditary dispositions, but on account of the time when they come into existence. For the sake of justice, whoever is lucky enough to be born late in the course of history should not be punished for it, but be allowed to fully develop *his specific* potential. *Suum cuique.* In the inter-generational context, there is no such thing as a presumption in favour of equality, as there is in the intragenerational context. We all know that mankind has made progress since the Neanderthals, and that later generations are usually better off (have a higher HDI) than relatively earlier ones. It would be dishonest to make a presumption despite this knowledge. As we have seen, presumptions are only admissible if there is a lack of the information needed for evaluating the pertinent case in a differentiated manner. But we do have the required historical information. As mentioned, history is probably the most important science that is needed in addition to philosophy for a theory of generational justice.

The here described concept of 'justice as enabling advancement' is compatible with the formal principle of justice. But there is a crucial precondition: an unlimited flow of human inventions and innovations. Otherwise, the presumption in favour of equality would also be applicable in the intergenerational context. So, should the innovative powers of man ever fail in the future, a new theory of generational justice would be required. But that is not to be expected. More knowledge is an advantage that later generations have on account of the time of their birth, and it cannot be taken away from them. Should we therefore put them at a disadvantage wherever we can? That would be unjust, as the school-fee example shows. Each generation should have the right to fully exploit its potential. Nobody may be kept from developing his abilities for reasons of equality. Even in the intragenerational context, we do not give fast runners paralysing drugs to slow them down or implant beepers in the ears of intelligent persons to keep them from thinking.[49] The present generation could put future generations at a disadvantage by means of national debts or an exploitation of the social security system, for instance. But that would be as unjust as the paralysing drug or the ear beeper. No generation may deprive the successor generation of its scope of action by burdening it more than it was burdened itself or would be willing to bear.[50] However, we cannot ask earlier generations to save in the sense of making a sacrifice like a reinvestment rate that is much higher than those of earlier generations (which would mean sacrificing consumption to an undue high degree).

No generation needs to feel guilty because it has a better initial position than a prior one and thus will probably be – if it fulfils its potential – better off in a life course comparison than its predecessors. There is nothing unjust about it. That goes for intertemporal as well as temporal generations. For the latter, this principle can be formulated as follows: 'No young generation is required to justify that it is better off than the young generation prior to it.' Or: 'No old generation is required to justify that it is better off than the old generation prior to it.' Comparisons of overall life courses, however, are more convincing because, as was mentioned above, the HDI includes the factor 'life expectancy'.

Distributive justice and justice of opportunities

Is the maxim 'each generation shall be able to fully exploit its potential' still a maxim of distributive justice? Allowing the exploitation of potential is not the same as distributing goods. Real capital and human capital, for instance, must continuously be renewed. Each generation must compensate for the depreciation of building, roads, etc. by reinvestments and must make new investments to increase the real capital. The same applies to the knowledge and abilities that each generation must acquire. The talented pupil will probably exploit her potential, and generations do the same. But theoretically, the talented pupil as well as the successor generation could waste their potential by being lazy, so their standard of living could be worse than that of the untalented pupil or the previous generation, despite their better opportunities. We have already seen that this normally does not happen in generations because each generation has its industrious as well as its lazy members. From a historical point of view, the HDI is distributed unequally among individual generations. Obviously, this form of distribution is different from the examples that are usually discussed in the context of distributive justice (see Figure 6.5).

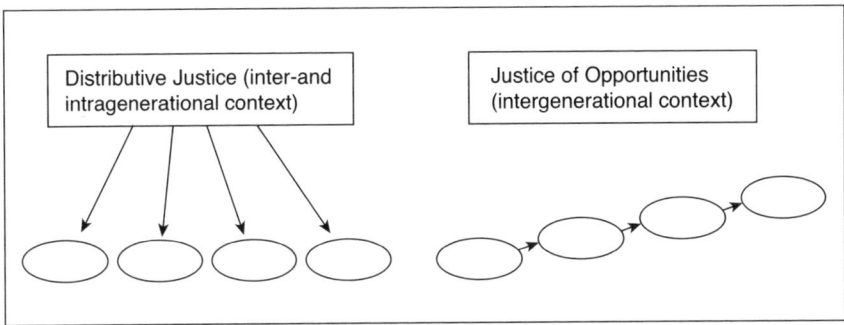

Figure 6.5 *Distributive justice and 'justice of opportunities'*

Distributive justice is about the distribution of a certain good or burden among various entities. Concepts of the pure distribution of a good among various parties are less important in the intergenerational than in the intragenerational context. But theories of distributive justice are still important in *partial* areas in which a certain good must be distributed, for example a non-renewable resource among various intertemporal generations, or the national income among various temporal generations (e.g. the young, the active generation and the pensioners).

To sum it up, in our attempt to transfer the formal justice principle 'equal cases equally, unequal cases unequally' from the intragenerational context, where it is very important, to the intergenerational context, we have reached the conclusion that the second half of this principle can be transferred more easily. Generations are unequal, but not with regard to their achievements or needs, but with regard to the time of their existence. As the smallpox and AIDS examples show, the present generation cannot raise the material or health level of previous generations to its own, nor can it benefit from drugs that will be developed in the future. We have to live with AIDS and cancer, and we do not consider it unjust that the second-next intertemporal generation might have an effective cure for these diseases. So, in the intergenerational context, *suum cuique* means accepting this improvement in the living conditions of generations, just as we accept that the most talented musician, runner or artist will have more success in his field than his less talented colleagues, provided he makes use of his abilities.

Justice towards past generations?

This study is mainly focused on the relationship between present, succeeding and future generations. The relationship with earlier generations and responsibilities towards them are of secondary importance for a theory of intergenerational justice. Already in 1978, Kavka explained why that is so:

> *Now, of course, temporal location does make a difference to morality – when the location is in the past. For surely, it would be absurd to give equal weight to the desires of living and dead persons. This, however, may be admitted without affecting the claim of equal status of future people. There are two main reasons for favoring the desires of the living over those of the dead. First, nearly all of the desires of the dead concerned matters in their own lifetimes that are now past and cannot be changed. Second, consider those desires of persons now dead that were directed toward future states of affaires that living people might still bring about. Since the persons having had those desires will not be present to experience satisfaction in their fulfullment or disappointment in their non-fulfillment, it is reasonable to downgrade the importance of these desires (and perhaps ignore them altogether) in our moral decision making. (Kavka, 1978, p188)*

The present intertemporal generation can only do justice to future generations, not to past ones. We can (and should) nevertheless pay honour and respect to the dead. Normally, that means remembering their hitherto almost forgotten achievements and personality, or continuing their work. But these are obligations of benevolence, not of justice. Past generations cannot subsequently be helped or harmed in any material way. It is not possible to change the level of well-being of a dead person. [51]

It goes without saying that the question how much attention we should pay towards the interests of deceased people is not the only relevant question that is treated by the subfield of ethics that many name 'historical justice' though the definition of the term and the relevance of the field is still disputed (Vernon, 2003, 2009; Schefezyk, 2009). 'Historical justice' also treats questions such as how can we deal with past wrongdoings if they have lasting effects on the well-being of currently living people, especially those grave immoral acts that were committed in the name of an unlawful state or political entity?[52] Can current members of a nation be said to have obligations (for example to pay compensation or to give back land) to either the victims or the descendants of victims of a past injustice that was committed by previous members of this nation? And, how far back in time should we go (Waldron, 1992; Sher, 1992)? All these questions are left out of account here for reasons of space.[53]

Justice as reciprocity

Justice as reciprocity in the intragenerational context

Reciprocity as a balance of deterrence between egoistic individuals

Thomas Hobbes (1588–1679) can be considered the father of the concept of 'justice as reciprocity as a balance of deterrence'. According to Hobbes, man has three characteristics that can lead to conflicts: rivalry, mistrust and the thirst for glory (cf. Hobbes, 1985, p185, part 1, ch. 13). Hobbes elaborates what that means for our coexistence:

> *And from this diffidence of one another, there is no way for any man to secure himself, so reasonable, as Anticipation; that is, by force, or wiles, to master the persons of all men he can, so long, till he see no other power great enough to endanger him: And this is no more than his own conservation requireth, and is generally* allowed. *Also because there be some, that taking pleasure in contemplating their own power in the acts of conquest, which they pursue farther than their security requires; if others, that otherwise would be glad to be at ease within modest bounds, should not by invasion increase their power, they would not be able, long time, by standing only on their defence, to subsist. And by consequence, such augmentation of dominion over men, being necessary to a man's conservation, it ought to be allowed him. (Hobbes, 1985, p184 et seq., part 1, ch. 13, emphasis added).*

The physical strength of an individual is not what matters. Even a physically weak person can defeat a strong person by forming an alliance with others. Hobbes continues his line of thought: 'Hereby it is manifest, that during the time men live without a common Power to keep them all in awe, they are in that condition which is called Warre; and such a warre, as is of every man, against every man' (Hobbes, 1985, p185, part 1, ch. 13). Hobbes's image of man is summed up in the expression '*homo homini lupus*' ('man is a wolf to man'), which he coined himself.[54] Man can only control his negative impulses if he is forced to do so by the state, the Leviathan. If this authority is inexistent or collapses,[55] there will be blood and thunder, rape and theft. According to Hobbes, man is not by nature a moral being. Rather, he is even immoral in the sense of seeking his own advantage at the expense of others.[56] Hobbes conception is called 'contractarian' because man protects himself from attacks by concluding contracts with others who have the potential to harm him.

Is such a setting 'justice as mutual advantage', as Barry calls it (Barry, 1989, p8)? It can be but it can also become 'justice as mutual disadvantage' as we will see later when we discuss prisoner's dilemmas and iterated games. The contractarian conception between egoistic individuals should therefore rather be called 'justice as reciprocity'. Obviously, this is a special form of reciprocity with rather disgusting implications. Everyone is only obliged to fulfil contracts he has concluded, and no one is under obligation to consider the well-being of parties with which one has no agreement. The fatal inner logic of a calculus that establishes rights and obligations based upon the sole notion of a symmetrical exchange, or barter, of measurable advantages is that those who cannot return benefits or detriments are not taken into consideration. Wherever there is need for unconditional commitments and duties, all that reciprocal justifications can offer are merely conditional agreements of people who give only under the condition that they receive, who contribute only insofar as they benefit, who help only as long as it furthers their interests (Dierksmeier, 2006, pp76 and 80). If the world were as described by Hobbes, woe to those who do not have the potential to threaten others, for instance persons who do not want to become aggressors for one reason or the other, or weak persons who cannot (for example disabled persons or children). According to Hobbes's concept, there is no reason to conclude a contract with them. We do not owe them anything for reasons of justice.[57]

But is this a form of justice at all? Can't it simply be called 'immoral behaviour'? Justice as well as benevolence, mercy, generosity, etc. belongs to the realm of moral behaviour. If Hobbes's concept refers to an immoral way of thinking and acting, it obviously cannot be a concept of justice. Brian Barry, who is plagued by this question, puts it this way:

> *Is the theory of justice as mutual advantage really a theory of justice at all? It is surely normally regarded as a paradigm of injustice to kill some innocent person simply because that person is in the way of your getting something you want, or to take what you want from someone under threat of death. To say that this killing or taking is rendered just by the inability of the victims to organize an effective resistance would surely be a hollow mockery of the idea of justice – adding insult to injury. Justice is normally thought of not as ceasing to be relevant in conditions of extreme inequality in power but, rather, as being especially relevant to such conditions. (Barry, 1989, p63)*

But already Aristotle identified *retributive justice* as the second important field of justice, next to *distributive justice* (Aristotle, 2005, p103, 1130b). Here, the principle of reciprocity is an important criterion for finding out what the proper response to wrongdoing is. For instance, the bible mentions the *lex talionis* (law of retaliation), which is a theory of retributive justice. It says that proper punishment should be equal to the wrong suffered: 'life for life, eye for eye, tooth for tooth, hand for hand, foot for foot, wound for wound, stripe for stripe'.[58] We are familiar with the 'mutuality principle' or 'reciprocity principle' from a number of contexts: it is used for work performance and payment just as for gift and gift in return, visit and 'visit in return', from market exchange or from modern civil law. According to Binmore (2005, 2006), the principle of reciprocity has become mankind's second nature by the forces of biological and social evolution.

Whether inherent or acquired, the reciprocity principle is a moral basic principle of every society.[59] 'Treat others as you want to be treated by them' is one of the famous maxims derived from the reciprocity principle.[60] There is thus a great number of examples that show that we follow the principle of reciprocity without this being connected to an egoistic mind. But where to draw the line between legitimate concepts of 'justice as reciprocity' and illegitimate ones? What is the basis to place 'reciprocity as a balance of mutual deterrence' outside the realm of morality? The solution to this problem lies in the terms 'self-interest' and 'egoism'.

'Self-interest' and 'egoism'

If the two terms 'self-interest' and 'egoism' are distinguished from each other, this will have a great effect on wide areas of contemporary philosophy and economy. Let us first draw up a scheme of possible actions that may influence the distribution of well-being (or utility) between two people (see Table 6.12):[61]

1 Actions/omissions that increase individual A's and at the same time individual B's well-being (or utility). For example, if a host has prepared a meal and is now happy because her guest feels at ease during her stay (win/win).
2 Actions/omissions that increase individual A's well-being (or utility), but decrease that of individual B. For example, if a private person sells her old car while cunningly hiding defects (win/lose).
3 Actions/omissions that increase individual A's well-being (or utility) and have no effect on the well-being (or utility) of other people. For example, if somebody goes shopping at a supermarket where there is enough of everything (win/no effect).
4 Actions/omissions that decrease individual A's well-being (or utility), but increase that of individual B. For example, if under a dictatorship it is suggested to a university teacher that she becomes a government spy and informs the secret service about rebellious students. She knows that her beautiful life will come to a sudden end if she rejects this. Nevertheless she refuses (lose/win).
5 Actions/omissions that decrease the well-being (or utility) both of individuals A and B. For example, if a frustrated pupil kills an innocent teacher at a highschool rampage before he kills himself (lose/lose).[62]
6 Actions/omissions that decrease individual A's well-being (or utility), but have no influence on other people's well-being (or utility). For example, if a hermit commits suicide (lose/no effect).
7 Actions/omissions that do not decrease individual A's well-being (or utility), but increase the well-being (or utility) of B. For example, if A throws away something that has no value for her. B, for whom it is very useful, finds it on the street (no effect/win).
8 Actions/omissions that do not influence individual A's well-being (or utility), but decrease that of at least one other individual. For example, if a pedestrian

accidentally destroys the pattern of pebbles made by a child, without the pedestrian becoming aware of this at all (no effect/lose).

Table 6.12 *Effects of several human actions/omissions on the well-being of others*

		Individual B's well-being or utility		
		+	**–**	**0**
Individual A's well-being or utility	+	Example 1: good host *(self-interest)*	Example 2: cheating when selling a car *(egoism)*	Example 3: shopping at a supermarket *(self-interest)*
	–	Example 4: resisting a secret service *(altruism)*	Example 5: rampage with suicide	Example 6: lonely suicide
	0	Example 7: useful waste	Example 8: carelessness	[irrelevant]

For moral philosophers, it goes without saying that actions that increase my own well-being at somebody else's expense (case 2) must be conceptually closed off from other self-interested actions (case 1 or 3). Using the same term for so very different actions like '+/–', '+/+' and '+/0' would be a grave loss of information and blur matters. According to the 'adequacy' definition criterion, we must not define the term 'self-interest' too broadly. Thus, the following definitions meet the definition criteria:

> *Definition of 'egoism' ('selfishness'):*
> *An egoistic or selfish action/omission is one that increases the agent's well-being and at the same time reduces the well-being of at least one other human*[63] *(+/–).*

> *Definition of 'self-interest':*
> *A self-interested action/omission is one that increases the agent's well-being without reducing the well-being of at least one other agent (+/+ and +/0).*

> *Definition of 'altruism':*
> *An altruistic action/omission is one that reduces the agent's well-being and at the same time increases the well-being of at least one other agent (–/+).*

Now, which actions belong to the field of moral behaviour, which ones to the field of immoral behaviour? All actions that increase or at least leave equal the well-being of other people can be counted as moral behaviour (+/+, +/0, 0/+ and –/+). In contrast, all actions that negatively affect the well-being of other people belong to the realm of immoral behaviour ($+/-$ and $-/-$). Other actions, the remaining cases ($-/0$ and $0/0$), are neither moral nor immoral behaviour. Thus, egoistic actions do not belong to the field of moral behaviour. Accordingly, an 'egoistic morality' is a contradiction in itself.

The premise of utility-maximizing individuals in economics

One of the most essential premises of mainstream economics is that people act like a homo oeconomicus, a person who always tries to maximize his own utility. Wording is important, and usually the formulation is like this:

Economic premise: 'People always try to maximize their own utility.'

A lot could be said about this premise, but here, the question if this homo oeconomicus is actually an 'egoistic' or 'only' a self-interested agent, and which implications result from this, are only to be discussed at the terminological level.[64] Sometimes, homo oeconomicus is undoubtedly described as an egoist in literature (for example Elster, 1989, p263 et seq.), but usually it is not explicitly said that the premise also holds in win/lose situations.

The principle of striving for maximum utility is necessary already for the simplest model of neoclassical economics, which is the distribution of a given budget among two different goods. Two goods, A and B, respectively create a certain utility, so that by way of combining these goods alternatively different utility levels can be calculated. Figure 6.6 shows an indifference curve if those combinations of goods as creating the same utility level are combined. In this case, the consumer does not care about his buying decision – three pairs of trousers and two shirts are as good as five pairs of trousers and one shirt. Due to Gossen's First Law (diminishing marginal utility), these indifference curves are convex. Now, in case of a given budget, a rational consumer will choose the highest utility level that he is just able to realize.

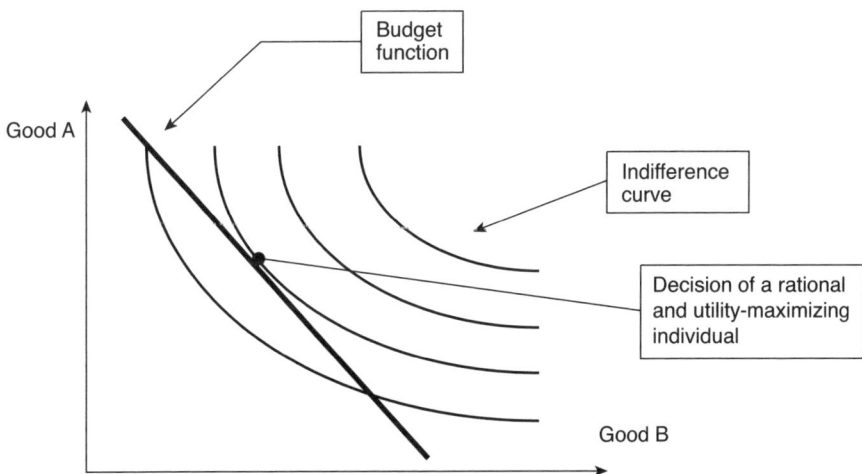

Figure 6.6 *Budget function and indifference curves*

This example is given to young economics students, the author himself having once been one, as giving evidence to the premise that humans always try to maximize their own utility. But it obviously concerns a 'win/no effect' action, and no philosopher would count it as belonging to the field of immoral behaviour. Before we continue the discussion of egoistic vs. self-interested behaviour, let us take a quick look at another implication of the 'economic premise': that altruistic behaviour, which has by definition the aspect that a rational individual voluntarily and deliberately reduces his own well-being, is impossible.

This is decisive particularly because economists increasingly claim that also in non-economic areas of our lives, such as keeping up a relationship or reproductive behaviour, we act as a homo oeconomicus. Small wonder that many empirical objections are raised against such a model. As a matter of fact, humans who never do anything altruistic are rather an exception than the rule. The sociologist Michael Baurmann states:

> There is doubt whether the model of homo oeconomicus as the only foundation of a general social scientific research programme still meets the minimum demands of empirical adequateness which must be raised even for the hard core of any empirical theory. (Baurmann, 2000, p132)

If confronted with this, economists like to argue that in cases that look like lose/win actions (case 4) the individual *still* always maximizes his self-interest, even if he acts in a seemingly altruistic way. They simply integrate, as the explanation goes, other people's utility functions into their own ones. This would mean that, for example, Mother Teresa did her life-threatening job of nursing lepers only because she was publicly adored for this; that Dietrich Bonhoeffer sacrificed his life in the concentration camp because he was hoping for paradise; that an anonymous donation was not given out of charity but first of all because the donator's utility was after all increased. Under the assumption of complete information, as the neoclassical argument goes, they did what they did out of self-interest.

Let us take the example of the university teacher under a dictatorship (case 4) and try to understand what she might think about during a long night, when planning what to tell the secret service officer the next morning. As she is a rational person, she will compile her own, subjective, cardinal utility balance (see Table 6.13).

Table 6.13 *Utility balance with explicit breakdown*

	Positive effects on me	Negative effects on me	
+10	Being proud of my courage	Loss of many privileges (car, summer cottage)	−50
+81	Utility for *others* whom I have prevented from suffering damage		
		Career stopped, maybe loss of university position	−40
Sum	+91		−90
Balance		**+1**	

Note: Numbers chosen randomly.

A neo classical economist would not topically object, but suggest a different illustration of the utility balance of our professor (see Table 6.14).

Table 6.14 *Utility balance with implicit breakdown*

	Positive effects on me	Negative effects on me	
+91	*Own* utility for reasons of being proud and having prevented others from suffering damage	Loss of many privileges (car, summer cottage)	−50
		Career stopped, maybe loss of university position	−40
Sum	+91		−90
Balance		**+1**	

Indeed, if illustrated this way, there cannot be any lose/win actions. Thus, in the end the neoclassical position comes down to a suggestion to define the term 'self-interest' in an unconventional way, namely in such a way as to include not only my own, but at the same time also other people's utility.

Is that a good idea? There can be no doubt that the lower illustration suffers from a grave loss of information, as there is no distinction anymore between one's own original utility and that kind of one's own utility resulting only from taking other people's utility into account. Thus, there are strong arguments in favour of taking account of the utility functions of others separately. Then, for the kind of action as described by example 4 (lose/win), an independent term becomes necessary, for example 'altruism'. If economics, the 'dismal science', gave up the widespread practice of implicitly integrating the utility functions of others into that of the agent, this would be a revolution. If the slogan 'people always try to maximize their own utility' was differentiated according to egoistic and self-interested behaviour, economists would not be misunderstood so often by philosophers.

Market and society

From an empirical point of view, probably most people are self-interested, but neither predominantly egoistic nor altruistic. They demand reciprocity in many areas of life, but they do not tend towards a kind of win/lose behaviour, if they have the chance, for example in situations without repeat and without fear of punishment. Here, the context matters. First, the distinction between the economic sphere and other areas of life is important. Second, to put it game theoretically, the distinction between repeated and non-repeated games is essential.

On the first aspect: the deeply rooted animosity of economists and philosophers is partly due to the fact that many economists, consciously or maybe due to a lack of terminological clarity, support the idea that even egoistic behaviour of the individual will result in public good.[65] Let us at first look at this thesis in respect of the purely economic sphere, using the distinction between egoism and self-interest. The pursuit of self-interest results in society being provided with necessary goods and services. This is the market's 'invisible hand', which has so impressively been worked out by Adam Smith (1991). A rational merchant recognizes that, in the long run, honesty and cooperation with other economic players will bring him more profit than a quick bargain. Thus he will try to identify win/win situations or at least win/no effect situations. In other words: he behaves in a self-interested but not in an egoistic way (and in so far not immorally). Of course, there is egoistic behaviour also in the realm of economic players: fraud, embezzlement, illegal price agreements, the formation of monopolies, etc. Much of this is listed in the penal law under economic crime. But especially where trade is accompanied by a long chain of exchange, liberal thinkers considered 'the market' a suitable field for bringing positive characteristics such as righteousness, reliability and readiness to compromise to light.[66] They even hoped for spill-over effects for society at large. In the Age of Enlightenment, the thesis of '*doux* commerce', that is that trade and exchange alone create enough stimulation for moral behaviour, was transferred from the sphere of the market to the sphere of the entire society. But already Adam Smith refuted these exaggerations: the invisible hand works only on the market, not in society. And even on the market it works only if it is defied by the clearly visible hand of law, as his credo was. With the industrial revolution, the critics' voices became louder and louder, and they stated that the attitude created by trade and commerce was just the opposite of a genuinely moral attitude towards our fellow men. To sum up so far, the thesis:

> *that the egoistic behaviour of an individual in the economic field results in an abundance of goods and services, and thus positive effects for the common good*

is a lot more questionable than the thesis:

> *that the self-interested behaviour of an individual in the economic field results in an abundance of goods and services, and thus positive effects for the common good.*

During the 1960s and 1970s, the problem of collective rationality was newly discussed in the context of external effects.[67] Since the 1980s, game theory has enlarged the economic debate as an important new tool.[68]

Single and repeated games

That brings us to the second aspect: single vs. repeated games. As indicated, cooperative behaviour has a greater effect if agents meet repeatedly. This is as true in market relations as in respect of other areas of life. Essential is an 'open time horizon' (Baurmann, 2000, p151). According to standard economic textbooks, single games, such as the famous prisoner's dilemma, result in non-cooperation. Also in the case of iterated, but not infinitely often played games, the outcome is non-cooperation (if the number of rounds is known in advance by the players). This is attributed to the so-called 'backward induction', which claims that it is possible to roll back the game from back to front. Indeed, the last round of a series of ten rounds is always a one-level game; this way we would *then* be back again at the original prisoner's dilemma. As during the tenth round the result is 'non-cooperation', this is said to be the same during the ninth round, etc. (Feess, 1997, p364 et seq.). However, Robert Axelrod in his book *The Evolution of Cooperation* (1984) reports on a tournament he organized in which participants had to choose their mutual strategy again and again, and remembered their previous encounters. If a distinction is made between self-interest and egoism, an egoistic player might be inclined to start with the choice 'defect' instead of 'cooperate' when he meets a new and unknown player. The self-interested player, by contrast, would start with cooperation on the first iteration of the game; after that, the player does what his opponent did on the previous move ('tit-for-tat'). Unlike an egoistic player, a self-interested player is also able to play 'tit-for-tat with forgiveness': when the opponent defects, the player sometimes cooperates anyway in the next round to prevent both players from getting trapped in a cycle of defections. To sum up, egoistic strategies tend to do very poorly in the long run, while self-interested strategies do much better. Here, these few examples must be enough to make clear that a systematic *terminological* distinction between self-interested, egoistic and altruistic behaviour would be useful for economic theory. According to the definition criterion 'fruitfulness', it would make new and fruitful theories possible.

Reciprocal contracts with Hobbes and Rawls

Let us go back to reciprocity models in philosophy: if we make a terminological distinction between egoistic, self-interested and altruistic behaviour, we will become aware of the grave differences found in different concepts of reciprocity, for example in those of Rawls and Hobbes. With Hobbes, agents are assumed who would do harm to others if there were no contract. They are egoistic in principle. With Rawls, however, the agents are self-interested but not egoistic. All individuals act in a mutually disinterested manner, Rawls says (1971, p127). Unfortunately, both concepts are often put together under the collective term 'contractualism'. This term indicates the view that morality is based on a contract or agreement. But, as we have seen, 'justice as mutual agreement' encompasses very different concepts: a) justice is derived from the mutual agreement between selfish individuals; or b) justice is derived from what self-interested (but not selfish) people would agree to under *hypothetical* conditions including equality and the absence of bias. In model a), the contract establishes a balance of deterrence. In the contractual ethics of egoistic parties, real contracts that are sometimes derived from history are assumed. Justice – if it were justice – is understood as 'doing justice to that what has been agreed on'. After all, this interpretation reduces 'justice' to '*pacta sunt servanda*'. This has nothing to do with impartiality, i.e. with 'putting oneself in the other person's shoes'. In model b), whose godfather is Kant, people voluntarily forego benefits if they are deemed unfair. 'The liberal, Kantian social contract theory understands moral reciprocity to be motivated by a desire for rational integrity and to consist of a commitment to impartiality, that is, to consider the interests of self and others equally', the philosopher Daniel Vokey explains (2001, p1). Here, a favour in return for another is not given out of calculated selfish motives, but out of an intrinsic sense of fair play (Page, 2007, p102).

The most prominent exponents of model b) are Rawls (1971, 1993, 2001) and Scanlon (1998, 2003). The most prominent supporters of the model of egoistic parties in Hobbes's tradition are Nozick (1974) and Buchanan (1975).

To sum up so far, concepts of reciprocity that legitimize egoism are simply immoral and thus excluded from the realm of justice. But a concept of reciprocity that rules out egoistic behaviour would belong to the field of morality and, in so far, it would be worthy of consideration as a concept of justice at least in the intragenerational field. As a matter of fact, this is true for many concepts and applications of reciprocity.

Justice as reciprocity in the intergenerational context

The notion of 'reciprocity as a balance of deterrence' seems inapplicable to intergenerational justice.[69] As future generations do not yet exist, they do not have any potential to threaten us and thus cannot be contract partners. Humans who will live 200 years from now are not able to impose sanctions for damage we do to them today. We are affected by our contemporaries and by past generations, but not by future intertemporal generations. It therefore seems impossible to construct reciprocal agreements between non-overlapping generations. Page puts it this way:

Members of earlier generations seem, in this sense, to be in a similar situation to those living in an upstream community who have just realised that their industrial and agricultural sectors are polluting the environment of many distant communities living downstream without having to bear any costs themselves. (Page, 2007, p105)[70]

Contractarian theories (type a) fail to provide adequate justifications of our obligations to future generations. From this, the French philosopher Olivier Godard concludes 'that the idea of justice is not suitable for determining our relationship to future generations' (Godard, 2006, p19). This judgement is consequential if 'justice' is understood only or primarily as 'justice as reciprocity between egoistic individuals'. However, such notions of 'justice as reciprocity' do not belong to the realm of justice at all, as I have argued. Some philosophers turn the tables. They consider the new efforts of developing a cross-generational concept of justice a challenge for 'justice as reciprocity' concepts that might result in the latter losing their reputation. The fact that 'justice as reciprocity' is not applicable in the intergenerational context, they say, is not a problem for intergenerational justice but for 'justice as reciprocity' as such. Hösle points out 'that a certain model of justification of moral standards, namely that of a reciprocal consideration of interests for egoistic reasons, has been impeached by the idea of the rights of future generations' (Hösle, 2003, p132 et seq.) Leist draws a negative conclusion in respect of the explanatory power of contract theory: 'As a conclusion of this going through several ethical positions, the result is all but satisfying. As far as contract theory is concerned, the ambiguous impression remains that it fails where justifying duties are most needed' (Leist, 1991, p352).

Reciprocity between temporal and family generations

Many theories of intergenerational justice do not distinguish temporal from intertemporal generations. In respect of the applicability of reciprocity norms, however, one comes to different conclusions if doing so. The fact that future generations will not be able to affect contemporary ones is true for non-overlapping intertemporal generations (English, 1977).[71] It is not true for temporal generations. There can be no doubt that a young generation has the possibility to 'pay back' on its previous generation or, alternatively, to be grateful as soon as they have become the middle generation and the middle generation has become the old one. 'Tit-for-tat' happens among the *same* agents, only at different times.

It is obvious that the reciprocity principle can be directly applied to family generations.[72] If children are cared for and nourished by their parents while they are young, according to the reciprocity principle they are obliged to care for their parents when the latter have become old and bedridden and need care. If, by contrast, children are neglected by their parents, the reciprocity principle would state that they may also neglect their parents when the latter need nursing. Höffe reconstructs an exchange with shifted phases among temporal generations. In his model with egoistic agents, the starting point is the different potential to threat on the part of the young, middle and old generations (Höffe, 1994a,

	Direct reciprocity between temporal generations		Direct reciprocity between family generations	
	Period 1	Period 2	Period 1	Period 2
1st generation	G_1 61–90 years		G_1 grandparents	
2nd generation	G_2 31–60 years	G_2 61–90 years	G_2 parents	G_2 grandparents
3rd generation	G_3 0–30 years	G_3 31–60 years	G_3 children	G_3 parents
4th generation (=new)		$G_{4=new}$ 0–30 years		$G_{4=new}$ children

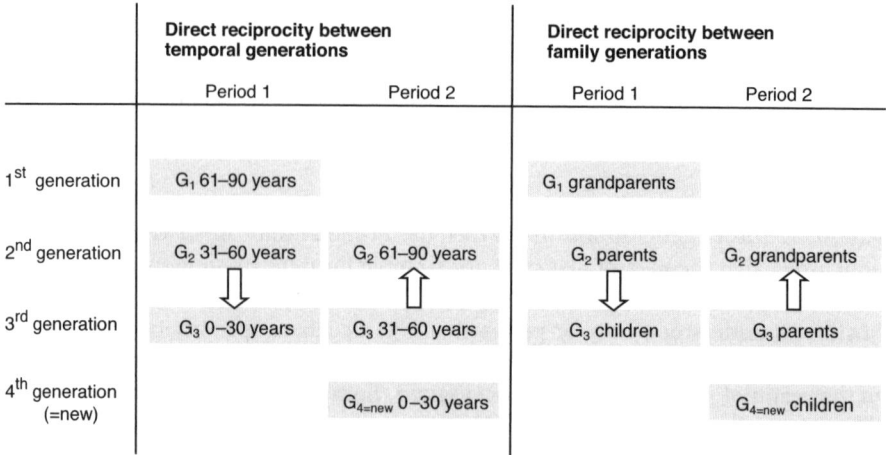

Figure 6.7 *Direct reciprocity between temporal and family generations*

p729 et seq.). In a Hobbesian sense, children and old-aged persons are weak and helpless. The middle generation is powerful and strong, but it knows that it will also be the older generation one day. As it does not want its 'weakness' to be exploited then, it treats the following generation well. This is true both within family relations and in the overall society. Höffe writes: 'In short, the intergenerational view shows that it is not at all arguments of solidarity, more exactly: of a just exchange, that include the aforementioned groups in the generally favourable exchange of freedom' (1994a, p730).

However, in Höffe's account we must at least assume contractual fidelity. The exchange he describes is not a step-by-step business where none is able to betray the other. As soon as we assume egoistic agents, this argument will not explain why the older generation is treated well, for it has no possibility to retaliate against the middle generation.

Indirect reciprocity with family and temporal generations

As soon as we assume agents that are not selfish, a new form of reciprocity becomes possible: indirect reciprocity. The holy script of the Jews, the Talmud, tells a powerful parable: 'An old man is asked why he is planting a carob tree, as after all he will not live to see this tree bloom. He answers: "When I was born the world was full of blooming carob trees"' (Talmud, Ta'anit, p23). The principle of *indirect* reciprocity is valid both for family generations, temporal generations and intertemporal generations.[73] Applied to family generations, an example for this is a family in which the parents pay for expensive university education for their children because in the past their own education was also paid for by their parents (cf. Gosseries, 2005, p41).

In countries where university education is paid for by the state, there is also indirect reciprocity, however not directly within families, but among temporal generations: the middle generation pays university education for the younger generation, because their education was paid for by the then active generation (see Figure 6.8).

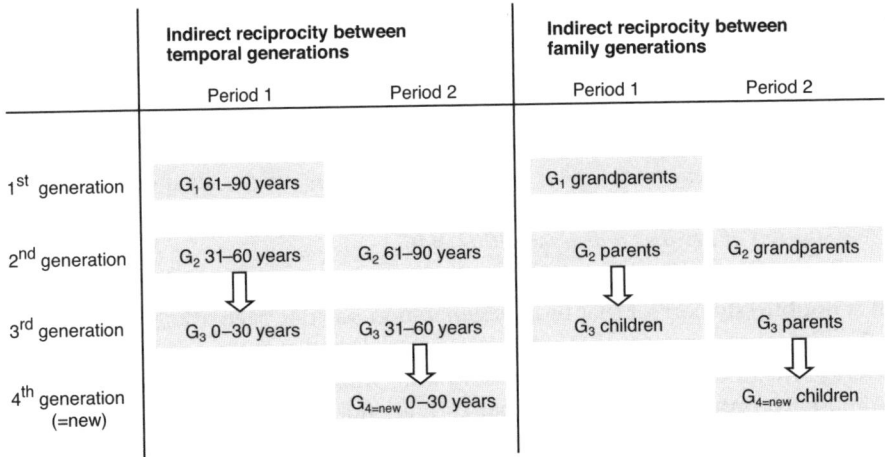

Figure 6.8 *Indirect reciprocity between temporal and family generations*

Indirect reciprocity between intertemporal generations

What is the situation like with intertemporal, non-overlapping generations? The creditor generation cannot be paid back. But does that render the obligation invalid? Only if there were no debtor generation (Gosseries, 2002, p465). But that is not the case. Instead, the principle of indirect reciprocity is also valid in this context. Just as temporal generations, intertemporal ones also have obligations towards their successor generations because they have received something from their predecessor generations. This way, within the chain of generations develops a cascade-like obligation (Hösle, 1997, p809).[74] Every generation gives back something, not to the generation from which it has received something (their ancestors), but to a generation that has not yet done anything for it (their descendants). This idea was also formulated by John Rawls:

> Each [generation] passes on to the next a fair equivalent in real capital as defined by a just savings principle... This equivalent is in return for what is received from previous generations that enables the later ones to enjoy a better life in a more just society. (Rawls, 1971, p288)

And also Edith Brown-Weiss emphasizes the 'dual role' of each generation as beneficiary of the planetary legacy and as trustee of the planet (Brown-Weiss, 1989, p45). Prima facie, the exchange is fair if it equally burdens or benefits each generation.

Thus the fact that we shall leave something for future generations is also demanded by the third concept of justice under analysis. Whether, however, 'justice as indirect reciprocity' offers a basis for a theory of generational justice that is as able to take weight as 'justice as impartiality' or 'justice as unequal treatment of unequal cases' must be doubted. Gosseries names one objection:

> The 'gift-obligation' objection asks whether any gift should give rise to corresponding obligations. Either it is a gift for which nothing is expected in return, in which case we would not be bound to anything. Or, if something is expected in return, the person who accepts the gift should be able at least to understand what it entails as well as to refuse such a gift. Can you expect a newborn to refuse 'gifts' for which she will be bound over for the rest of her life? (Gosseries, 2002, p466)

It is doubtlessly correct that today's generation has not been asked if it wants to take the entire heritage of mankind as a gift. But if it were possible to ask an average member of the next generation, what would his answer be? Surely 'yes'. Almost everything seems to be better than not to – exist. This might be a common-sense view that overlooks that no relation is possible without a relatum. According to this argument, we cannot make comparisons between a certain condition of live and 'never existing' (as distinguished from 'dead', meaning 'formerly existing') (Partridge, 2007, p14, footnote 16).[75]

Anyway, mankind has now reached a level of civilization that provides every average newborn child with a rather high HDI expectation.[76] Once the generation takes this 'gift', it cannot deny the ensuing obligations towards the next generation. Now, there might be the objection that an average representative of the next generation, when asked whether he likes the 'gift', could answer that he would like to enjoy modern democracy, anaesthesia when he is ill, also supermarkets well-provided with everything in winter, and satellite TV, but would happily give up AIDS, motorway traffic jams and other unpleasant things. This clever representative wants to accept not the entire inheritance of mankind, but only parts of it, so to speak. But this kind of cherry-picking is rightly considered unfair in private law, if a person makes an inheritance (Tremmel, 2004a). It is not possible to appropriate everything valuable from an inheritance, but to reject taking over the debts. One can only completely reject a private inheritance. This principle should be transferred to the social sphere. At least according to the commonsense view, a representative of the next generation would then not reject mankind's complete, mixed-structured inheritance, even if he could.

Intergenerational justice as enabling advancement

'Why should I do anything for posterity? What has posterity done for me?' Narveson once asked (1978, p38).[77] We have seen that established concepts of justice provide more or less satisfying answers. Testing intragenerational justice concepts might have produced the result that they hardly offer any help in the intergenerational context, as the two contexts are fundamentally different (Jonas, 1980, pp29–33). Another possible upshot might have been that intergenerational ethics are only a special case of general ethical principles.[78] The truth lies in between: intergenerational ethic problems are very different from those about which ethic researchers were thinking before the 20th century ('neighbour ethics'). Nevertheless, general knowledge of traditional concepts of justice is helpful for the intergenerational debate, if only to see for which reasons they cannot be applied.

Of the three concepts of justice under consideration, 'justice as impartiality' can best be transferred to the intergenerational context. The original position, consisting of representatives of all generations, shows a clear result. The two other concepts, 'treating equal cases equally, and unequal cases unequally' and 'justice as reciprocity', cannot be directly transferred, but even they provide starting points for intergenerational ethics. As for the formal principle of justice, it is rather the second half-sentence, as generations are always unequal due to the one-directionality of time and progress. As for 'justice as reciprocity', at least indirect reciprocity can be proclaimed.[79]

What conclusions can be drawn for a concept of intergenerational justice now? Because of the 'autonomous factors of progress', each generation has a different initial situation. The initial situation of later generations is normally better than that of earlier ones. So, opportunities are never equal. Ultimately, the participants in the 'original position' will decide that it is nevertheless just for each generation to fully exploit its potential. No generation has the right to spoil the initial advantage of its successors by appealing to an ideal of equality. Instead of a net savings rate in the sense of sacrificing consumption, a 'preventive measures rate' will be imposed on each generation, i.e. an obligation to avoid ecological, societal or technical collapses.

Just like the great majority of philosophers, I do not support an absolute standard with regard to generational justice, but a comparative one; that is a standard that determines the well-being of future generations by comparing it to that of today or of earlier generations. One of the few proponents of a non-comparative view, Angelika Krebs, argues that we are obligated to leave to future generations (and future sentient animals) the conditions for a life worth living – regardless of our own level of well-being (Krebs, 2000b, p314). But Krebs does not explicitly formulate what we owe future generations for reasons of *justice*. She would probably not dispute that there are circumstances of justice, one of them being that sentient beings – in relation to each other – desire scarce goods. Poverty in itself is an ill, but not an injustice. It can only become an injustice if there are others that are not poor. Thus, a non-comparative standard of intergenerational *justice* is untenable.

Within comparative standards, a considerable number of scholars postulate principles of strict equality between generations ('as good as').[80] An even greater number of texts in literature on generational justice use the formulation 'at least as good', and sometimes the word 'better' is used. See some examples: just like John Locke, 300 years ago ('at least as much and as good'[81]), the philosopher Otfried Höffe suggests: 'Responsible parents leave their children an inheritance that is *preferably larger* than what they have received from their parents' (2007a, p6, emphasis added). Using the languages of resources, Eric Rakowski, Dieter

Birnbacher and Gregory Kavka express the same thought. Rakowski puts it this way: 'Everyone born into a society is entitled, *as a minimum,* to the same quantity of resources that all who participated in the original division of the community's goods and land received' (1991, p150, emphasis added). Likewise, Dieter Birnbacher argues: 'Everyone should leave *at least* as many natural resources as it was left to him. What someone has inherited, he should pass on undiminished ('to sustain'), and *possibly* increased ('to cultivate'), to future people, be it as a private citizen or as a representative of a collective' (1988, p220, emphasis added). Kavka's intuition is quite similar: 'I interpret this to mean that, in this context, the generation in question leaves the next generation *at least* as well off, with respect to usable resources, as it was left by its ancestors' (1978, p200, emphasis added). James Woodward adds 'opportunities', but he sings the same tune: 'Each generation ought to leave for succeeding generations a total range of resources and opportunities which are *at least equal* to its own range of resources and opportunities' (1986, p819, emphasis added). Among economists, a non-declining welfare principle is popular. According to it, generational justice is achieved if a once achieved level of welfare will, at a minimum, not decline in the future (cf. Bayer, 2004, p144). The economist Robert Solow writes: 'The duty imposed by sustainability is... to endow [posterity] with whatever it takes to achieve a standard of living *at least as good* as our own' (1992, p15, emphasis added).

But the idea of an obligation to *improve* the quality of life for future generations is also expressed sometimes, and this by very different parties. The economist Richard Hauser formulates:

> *One must follow the principle that each generation should leave a larger total inheritance than it received. This means that each generation should have a positive net transfer that is* higher *than the one it received from the previous generation. (Hauser, 2004, p36, emphasis added)*

A representative of the extreme left, Karl Marx, wrote something very similar in the third volume of *The Capital*:

> *Even a whole society, a nation, or indeed all concurrent societies taken together are not the owners of the earth. They are only its possessors, its beneficiaries, and like* boni patres familias *[emphasis original], they must hand it down to succeeding generations in an* improved *condition [emphasis added]. (Marx, 1975, p784)*

Depending on whether we use 'at least as good' or 'better', different implications will result. After all, the first variant is still an egalitarian standard of generational justice, the second one is not. Which wording is more appropriate for the concept of intergenerational justice? This book has produced the upshot that the objective must be improvement rather than equality. The theory of intergenerational justice devised here suggests that our duties to posterity are more extensive than is often supposed. In the past, I used 'at least as good' myself,[82] but I would like to correct myself. In order to judge whether a society is generationally just, 'at least as good' must be replaced by 'better', so it reads:

> *Intergenerational justice has been achieved if the opportunities of the average member of the next generation to fulfill his needs are better than those of the average member of the preceding generation.*[83]

This concept of intergenerational justice does *not* imply that today's generation must sacrifice itself for the next one. As for family generations, generational justice does not mean that parents should restrict their own well-being *in order to* improve the well-being of their sons and daughters beyond their own level. We have seen that all concepts of generational justice must include both elements of justice of opportunities and of distributive justice. Indeed, where it is about pure distribution, the maxim of equal treatment is valid. If a good has to be distributed among two generations with the same number of members, it is just for each one to receive one half.[84] But is this not a paradox? How could such an equal distribution lead to a higher degree of well-being for the next generation? This paradox is solved by the autonomous progress factors. The empirical part of this study played a crucial part in illustrating that, under ordinary circumstances, the second generation has a better initial position. It should be able to generate a higher degree of well-being (measured by the HDI) from its half of the aforementioned good than the previous one. The members of today's generation A need not give more than they have received to the members of the next generation B, but if they give them as much of it, they will provide their descendants with the possibility to satisfy their own needs to a higher extent than A. Thus, I call my concept 'intergenerational justice as enabling advancement'. It is just to make improvement possible for future generations. The present generation should prevent everything that might disturb or even reverse the historical trend that has existed since ancient times and has improved the HDI until now.

The above concept of generational justice refers to 'needs' (instead of 'wants', 'interests', 'preferences', 'aspirations', etc.) as an axiological goal and emphasizes 'opportunities' (instead of 'distributions'). The reasons for this have already been discussed (see Chapter 5 and 'Distributive justice and justice of opportunities'). However, it has two more features that shall briefly be explained.[85] First, in contrast to, for example, Woodward's formulation that uses generations in the plural form, only *two* subsequent generations are compared. If every 'next generation' receives and hands over its inheritance in the sense of indirect reciprocity, this will create a chain of obligations that ultimately affect *all* future generations. However, the formulation of a concept of generational justice should compare comparable things, that is: generation A to the following generation B – and not to generations B, C, D, E... Z. The aggregated well-being of the members of *all* future generations inevitably exceeds the well-being of the members of the just *one* (the present) generation; that makes comparisons impracticable. If we weigh the well-being of 6.5 billion people against that of trillions of people, the concern for the latter group will always prevail. Such an overdue concern for the well-being of future generations may demand too great a sacrifice from today's generation. By comparing two succeeding generations, we solved this problem. But what about the conceivable implication that generation A fulfils its duties to generation B but at the expense of generation C, which is worse off than both A and B? The rejoinder is that A has not properly fulfilled its obligations to B in such a scenario. When A has passed away, B is still obligated to C. Because of A's negligence to the further future, B must now strive harder to secure C's opportunities for a good life than A has striven with regard to B. Reconsidering its former deal with A, generation B will justifiably feel cheated if it is forced now to make up for the shortcomings of A. Implicitly, A has thus not met its obligations to B. If *each* generation acts according to the above mentioned concept, *all* future generations will benefit. Thus, the question of the right comparison (either A to the following generation B, or A with the generations B, C, D, E... Z) should not be confused with the question of determining how far into the future our obligations reach (only to the next generation, or to all future generations).[86] Upholding the view that we have obligations to all future generations[87] and favouring comparisons between only two generations is not contradictory.

Second, unlike for example Hauser's formulation, my wording refers to the 'average member of a generation' instead of a 'generation'. It is an important question whether a formulation of a concept of generational justice refers to the next generation as an *entity* or to its individual *members*. Implications are far-reaching. To give a rather simple example, let us imagine that today's generation A, consisting of only 20 individuals, wants to justly share the existing 100 units of a non-renewable resource with the only succeeding generation B. If we regard generations as entities, it seems to be just for A to use up 50 units and save another 50 units for B. However, due to population growth, B will consist of 30 individuals (which A knows from a prognosis). Therefore, today's generation A – if the formulation of a concept of generational justice refers to the members of future generations – should save not 50 but 60 units of the resource and would therefore be able to consume less itself, in order to make the same per-capita consumption rate possible for future individuals. I think a definition of generational justice should be person-affecting (in the sense of average utilitarianism) and thus refer to the *members* of future generations, to 'average future individuals'.[88]

7

Conclusion

Where did we start and where have we gone to so far? We started with the aim of research. Ever since Greek antiquity, the notion of justice has been in the centre of intense philosophical debates. Nevertheless, systematic concepts and theories of justice between non-overlapping generations have only been developed in the last few decades. This delay can be explained by the fact that the impact of man's scope of action has increased. Only since the 20th century has modern technology given us the potential to irreversibly jeopardize the fate of mankind and nature for centuries to come. In Plato's or Kant's days, people did not have the same problems with regard to the environment, pension schemes and national debts as we have today. Therefore, there was no objective need for theories of justice that were unlimited in space and time. According to Hans Jonas, the new territory man has conquered by high technology is still no-man's-land for ethical theory. As mentioned in Chapter 1, this book is meant to contribute to exploring that no-man's-land.

There followed a brief epistemological section on scientific criteria for definitions; I repeatedly referred to it whenever controversial terms required clarification. The study was then divided into four main chapters: (1) comparisons between 'generations'; (2) arguments against theories of generational justice; (3) what to sustain and whether capital or well-being should be an axiological goal?; and (4) how much to sustain and the demands of justice in the intergenerational context.

Chapter 3 dealt with the fact that statements on generational justice require comparisons between generations. Yet, the term 'generation' is ambiguous. Distinctions were drawn between 'societal', 'family-related' and 'chronological' meanings of the term 'generation'. Statements on generational justice normally refer to the chronological meaning of 'generation'. They can also refer to the family-related meaning of 'generation', but not to its societal meaning. Then, various comparisons between chronological generations were distinguished: vertical, diagonal, horizontal and overall life courses. As a result, it was shown that diagonal comparisons as well as comparisons of overall life courses are decisive. Other comparisons are of only limited use for statements on generational justice.

Chapter 4 dealt with the most important arguments against all theories of generational justice. In this context, the non-identity paradox was discussed, as well as the claim that, for logical reasons, future generations cannot be granted rights. The non-identity problem coined by Schwartz, Kavka and Parfit says that we cannot harm potential individuals if our (harmful) action is a precondition for their existence. According to this argument, we would not harm future people by using up all resources because these particular people would not exist if we would preserve the resources. Several arguments were discussed that, in their totality, show that the non-identity paradox is irrelevant for the kind of problems that are usually discussed in the context of intergenerational justice such as wars, environmental pollution or national debts, and that it can only be applied to a very limited field of reproductive medicine. The argument of 'your neighbour's children' distinguishes between individual actions and the collective actions of entire generations. By focusing on the former, the limitations of the non-identity argument become obvious. It can be used only with regard to a person's own children but not to other members of future generations. Second, the 'butterfly-effect argument' questions the validity of the non-identity problem altogether. A monocausal relationship cannot be construed on the basis of a weak multicausal connection. The causality between actions that are hostile to posterity and the generic identity of the next generation, is not greater than the famous butterfly effect, according to which the beat of a butterfly's wing in Asia can set off a tornado in the Caribbean. A phrase such as 'because of a war or a certain environmental policy, x per cent of all children were conceived at a different time' is contestable because of the 'because of' in it. Other arguments such as the 'quasi-harm argument' and the 'catching-up argument' were mentioned.

Subsequently, the objection was dealt with that future generations cannot have rights. The theory of generational justice elaborated in this book is based on the well-being and not on the rights of future generations. Therefore, the question as to whether potential future individuals can have rights and, if so, which ones, is not a major challenge for such a theory. We should distinguish the concept of justice, which has been discussed for more than 2000 years, from the concept of rights, which was only developed a few centuries ago. Nevertheless, the objection that future generations cannot have rights was dealt with in this book, and my answer was:

> *No logical or conceptual error is involved in speaking about rights of members of future generations. Whom we declare a rights-bearer with regard to a moral right is a question of convention. Whom we declare a rights-bearer with regard to a legal right is an empirical question.*

Chapters 5 and 6 dealt with the questions of what and how much should be sustained. Chapter 5 examined the axiological question of what is ultimately the valuable good that should be preserved and passed on to the next generation. 'Capital' and 'well-being' (in the sense of need-fulfilment) were examined as two alternatives. Capital was divided into natural, real, financial, cultural, social and knowledge capital. The many facets of 'well-being' were also discussed, and subjective methods of measuring it were compared with objective ones. It was concluded that the axiological objective 'well-being' is superior to 'capital', because capital is only a means of increasing well-being. But *real* generational accounting also provides valuable information.

Many utilitarian accounts have only a weak conception of the axiological good and refrain from operationalizing it. A closer look at such concepts as well-being, happiness and utility revealed that the so-called 'repugnant conclusion' is a misled concept, based on misleading terms.

In Chapter 6, answers were sought as to how much we owe future generations for reasons of justice. The section focused on three concepts of generational justice that are established in the intragenerational context and asked whether they can also be applied to the intergenerational context: 'justice as impartiality', 'justice as the equal treatment of equal cases and the unequal treatment of unequal cases', and 'justice as reciprocity'. The core of this study was the use of Rawls' 'veil of ignorance' for determining principles of justice between generations. Rawls himself did not complete this train of thought. It was concluded that the individuals in the 'original position' would not opt for all generations to be equal, as it would mean that late generations would have to remain on the low level of early generations. In this context, the 'autonomous savings rate' is of particular importance:

> *Later generations will inevitably benefit from the experiences, innovations, and inventions of earlier ones. But there is no way earlier generations could benefit from future technology and medicine, because time is one-directional. Justice as 'equality' is not an option, unless the participants behind the veil of ignorance ordered each generation to burn down all its libraries and destroy all innovations and inventions before its death. But then, all generations of mankind would vegetate on the lowest possible level of civilization.*

On account of the inequality of all generations, only the second part of the justice maxim 'treat the equal equally and the unequal unequally' can be transferred to the intergenerational context. The maxim 'treat the unequal unequally' requires treating different generations in a differentiated manner. Each generation should have the right to fully exploit its potential and reach the highest well-being attainable for *it* (and only it).

Whenever the principle 'justice as reciprocity' legitimizes egoism, its consequences are purely and simply immoral, be it in the intergenerational or in the intragenerational context. In such cases, the well-being of the acting person is increased at the cost of another person (win/lose situation). But not every principle of reciprocity requires the assumption of an egoistic nature of man, thus many versions still can be applied as a moral concept. A variation of 'justice as reciprocity', namely the 'principle of indirect reciprocity', can even be applied to the intergenerational context and sensibly justify our actions affecting posterity.

The core element of a convincing theory of generational justice, however, is the demand for making improvement possible for the next generation. Our duties to posterity are stronger than is often supposed. Intergenerational justice has only been achieved if the opportunities of the average member of the next generation to fulfil his needs are better than those of the average member of the preceding generation. This does *not* imply that today's intertemporal generation must sacrifice itself for the next one. If a good has to be distributed among two generations with the same number of members, it is just for each generation to receive one half. How can equal distribution produce an improved standard of living? This is not a paradox because we have to take into account the autonomous progress factors. The members of today's generation A need not give more than they have received to the members of the next generation B. But if they give them as much of it, they will provide their descendants with the possibility to satisfy their own needs to a higher extent than A. Thus, I called my concept 'intergenerational justice as enabling advancement'.

The normative setting of our ethical obligations must not be confused with the empirical prognosis of whether future generations will have an equal or even higher HDI. The normative and empirical level must be strictly distinguished. To cut a long story short: while our normative obligations to future generations are greater than we commonly assume, the empirical probability that we will leave behind a world with better or at least equal opportunities for future generations has dropped over the past decades.

The following sentence is attributed to the poet Heinrich Heine: 'Every age has its specific task, and by solving it, mankind moves on.' Today's generation, generation 4574, as I have called it, lives in a particularly decisive age. Just now, more and more states have nuclear weapons, there is man-made global warming and we have huge amounts of toxic waste. So today's generation has the potential to irreversibly reduce the well-being of numerous future generations. It bears a great responsibility.

Normative theories are not an end in themselves. They are supposed to guide our actions in the material world. If they are well-reasoned, they may be able to make a difference regarding our willingness to take on responsibility for the well-being of future generations.

Notes

I Introduction

1 Written information provided by Frauke Stamer, press spokesperson of the German Federal Ministry for the Environment, Nature Conservation and Nuclear Safety (BMU), dated 2 August 2006, in response to my inquiry.

2 The calculation is as follows: $q(t) = q_o \times e^{\wedge}(t/T \times \ln 0.5)$, whereas $T = 24,110$ years, the initial quantity is 118 tonnes, and 1g of it is left at an unknown point in time $t \times 1g/118000000g = e^{\wedge}(t/(24110 \text{ years}) \times \ln 0.5)$ has to be solved for t, and the result is: $\ln(1/118,000,000) / \ln 0.5 = t/(24,110 \text{ years})$ or $12.882969 = t/(24,110 \text{ years})$. So, 1g will still be left after 12.882969 half-time periods; in other words: $t = 12.882969 \ 24,110 \text{ years} = 310,608 \text{ years}$.

3 For a profound risk assessment of nuclear energy and other modern technologies, see Perrow (1984).

4 The terms 'intergenerational justice' and 'generational justice' are used synonymously. Just like 'gender justice' means justice between the genders (and not within one gender group), 'generational justice', of course, means justice between generations and not within one generation. Hence, the prefix 'inter' is dispensable.

5 A similar statement is made by Ott (2001, p130).

6 Thomas Jefferson in a letter to John Taylor (28 May 1816): 'Funding I consider as limited, rightfully, to a redemption of the debt within the lives of a majority of the generation contracting it; every generation coming equally, by the laws of the creator of the world, to the free possession of the earth he made for their subsistence, unincumbered by their predecessors, who, like them, were but tenants for life... And I sincerely believe ... that the principle of spending money to be paid by posterity, under the name of funding, is but swindling futurity on a large scale.'

7 UNO speaks of 'more developed countries'. This terminology is used here because I consider it more appropriate than the alternative terms 'industrial countries', 'wealthy countries', 'First world' or 'Western countries'. In the same way, 'less developed countries' is used instead of 'Third World' or similar terms.

8 Only English-written publications have been taken into account. The results of several search processes in the catalogues of the British Library (and the Library of Congress, www.loc.gov) have been evaluated. First, a search process with the parameters 'any word' (instead of 'word from title') and 'not exact phrase' was carried out at the British Library, for instance, and then the results were consolidated by excluding double entries and entries that are not suitable for our context. An example for such an unsuitable entry would be 'future generations of computer systems'. The search was conducted on 8 January 2009.

9 Only German-written publications were taken into account, www.ddb.de accessed 8 January 2009.

10 For comparison, the term 'social justice' was found roughly 5000 times.

11 For example Kavka (1982) and Parfit (1987). An early approach that is often referred to in today's discourse was developed by Schwartz (1978). An up-to-date summary can be found in Gosseries (2002).

12 This is a variation of the well-known sustainability definition issued by the Brundtland Commission (cf. World Commission on Environment and Development, 1987, p43). 'Sustainable development' was replaced by 'generationally just society', and 'development' was replaced by 'society'.

2 Criteria-based Definitions of Scientific Terms

1 Pawlowski (1980) deals with criteria for definitions in social sciences. In a less elaborate form, criteria collections can also be found with Prim and Tilmann (1977, pp31–80); von Savigny (1980); Tremmel (2003c, 2004c), . Criteria collections for definitions in natural sciences and treatises on defining in general can be found with Essler (1970).

2 There are more criteria, such as 'necessity' or 'meaning used by the inventor' (cf. Tremmel, 2003c, p62 et seq.), but these four are the most important ones.

3 A more sophisticated example is 'a mammal is a viviparous vertebrate'. This definition is also too narrow. Approximately 200 years ago, animals were discovered that hatch from eggs but were nevertheless considered mammals after a long scientific debate (the so-called monotremes) (see Pawlowski, 1980, p40).

4 Numerous further examples for too narrow and too broad definitions can be found in Pawlowski (1980).

5 An example is the debate in the administration of George W. Bush on whether certain interrogation methods should be regarded as 'torture'.

6 The word was invented by the French thinker Auguste Comte in 1838.

7 Popper (1995) has described in detail how theories can be falsified.

8 Other accounts attribute this act of naming to the Greek philosopher Leucippus.

9 The term 'generation' is also used in technology (for example 'the latest generation of nuclear weapons', 'a computer with a third-generation processor'). However, this book focuses on the meaning that refers to groups of individuals.

3 Comparisons between Generations

1 For the different meanings of the term 'generation', see also Gukenbiehl (1995, p89 et seq.); Schüttemeyer (1998, p211); Kilian (2000, pp177–179); Solum (2001, pp169–171); Lepsius (2002, pp162–165); Tremmel (2005a, pp87–92).

2 Synonyms are 'social generations', 'sociological generations' or 'historic generations'.

3 Societal generations are sometimes divided into 'political', 'cultural' and 'economic' generations (cf. Kohli and Szydlik, 2000, pp8–10). See also Kohli (2006).

4 Although some societal generations might have had an international impact, each country has still predominantly own denominations for their generations. For the US, see Strauss and Howe (1991, 1993). For Germany, see Jureit and Wildt (2005).

5 This term was coined by Martínez Ruiz in 1913. It refers to a group of Spanish authors that aimed for a mental renovation of their country, including its development in line with the other European countries (especially as the last overseas colonies had been lost during the Cuban War in 1898).

6 A term supposedly coined by Gertrude Stein during the 1920s, referring to a group of American authors (such as Ernest Hemmingway or F. S. Fitzgerald). Having experienced the First World War, they were disillusioned and alienated from current moral concepts.

7 Synonyms are 'demographic generation' and 'genetic generation'.

8 Further differentiations are often made, for example 'young senior citizens' or 'old senior citizens'. To simplify matters, only three generations (young, middle-aged, old) shall be referred to hereinafter.

9 Birnbacher (1988, p23), also distinguishes these two types of chronological generations. Moreover, he lists the family-related generations as a third meaning of the equivocal term 'generation'.

10 'Intergenerational equity' and 'intergenerational justice' are used as synonyms in this study.

11 Motel-Klingebiel and Tesch-Römer (2004, p9) do not even want to use the term 'generation' for the designates I have referred to as 'chronological–intertemporal generations'. They think the term 'generation' should only be used for societal and family generations.

12 Actually, milliseconds or even nanoseconds would have to be stated here as well, but my wristwatch is not precise enough.

13 This definition is also used by De-Shalit (1995, p138, note 1); Unnerstall (1999, p33); and Solum (2001, p171). Solum states that by the phrase 'unborn future generations... we shall refer to all future persons who will not be born until the last person now alive has died'.

14 www.grg.org/Adams/E.HTM accessed 22 April 2009.

15 Own calculations based on Vaupel et al (2006, pp51–53). These demographers state: 'The assumption of a lower increase of life expectancy in the future goes against all empirical evidence from the past.'

16 Golding's definition is also criticized by Birnbacher (1988, p25 et seq.) with the same arguments. However, Birnbacher's terminology is not identical with mine as he names existing children 'future generations', which I count together with unborn generations as 'succeeding generations'. Muñiz-Fraticelli (2002, p4) defines, like me, 'future generations' as those people who have not yet been born.

17 The German demographer Wilhelm Lexis developed the diagram named after him in 1875.

18 These comparisons are also called 'inter-cohort comparisons'.

19 This is partly due to the use of indicators in each field. However, an extensive discussion of different possible indicators is beyond the scope of this chapter. Some indicators are discussed later. The results also differ for different regions (the following examples are taken from Germany).

20 The relevant number of species is the global one, not the endemic (national) number, because the aesthetic value of biodiversity includes species beyond one's own country. For instance, many Europeans would deplore the extinction of tigers or polar bears, even if there are no wild ones in Europe anyway. Species are not the property of one country but are a common heritage of mankind.

21 The following example is taken from Tremmel (2003a, pp40–42).

22 Assuming a maximum life expectancy of 130 years, they will be born roughly between 2170 and 2300.

23 That is those who were born between the years 1600 and 1700, assuming the maximum life expectancy was then 100 years.

24 In a life-course analysis, the cohort or generation effects can be distorted by age effects and period effects. Here, however, we shall assume that no such distortion takes place and shall therefore only examine the generation effects.

25 On the yield of different cohorts in public pension systems, see also Tremmel (1997, 2003d, 2007b); Rürup (2002); Bäcker and Koch (2003); Schmähl (2004).

26 A comprehensive anthology of generational justice in pension schemes is VDR (2004).

4 Objections to Theories of Generational Justice

1 First mentioned by Schwartz (1978) and Adams (1979), then discussed in more detail by Kavka (1982), and most famously by Parfit (1987). Until today, most authors who discuss this topic refer to his section 'Future Generations' (pp351–438). A summary of the debate can be found with Gosseries (2002) and Page (2007, pp132–159).

2 In fact, the Anglo-American discussion on responsibility to future generations reached its first peak in the 1970s when the remarkable anthologies by Bayles (1976), Sikora and Barry (1978) and Partridge (1980c), as well as other studies, appeared.

3 Parfit himself puts forward the 'no-difference view', that non-identity does not make a moral difference. I deal with this argument later in detail.

4 Cf. Morreim (1988); Heyd (1992); Jackson (1996); Shapira (1998); Roberts (1998); Strasser (1999); Unnerstall (1999, pp110–115); Shiffrin (1999); Nelson and Robertson (2001, pp102–105); Gosseries (2004a).

5 Parfit (1987, p358) thinks there is such a thing as a life not worth living, and I agree. For a discussion of this question, see the Chapter 5 section 'Measuring well-being'.

6 More precisely, we usually distinguish between two interpretations of harm: 1) an action (or inaction) at time t_1 harms someone only if the agent causes (allows) this person to be worse off at some later point in time t_2 than he was before t_1; and 2) an action (or inaction) at time t_1 harms someone only if the agent causes (allows) this person to be worse off at some later point in time t_2 than he would have been at t_2, had the agent not interacted with (or acted with respect to) this person at all (Meyer, 2003, p7).

7 'Very many of our choices will in fact have some effect on both the identities and the number of future people' (Parfit, 1987, p356).

8 Example taken from Page (2007, p133).

9 If 60 million of a total of 80 million Germans are not affected at first, the chances of every non-affected person to meet a non-affected partner are six out of eight in a first mating round. So, after the first generation, there will be 6/8 60 million non-affected persons. In mathematical terms: if we call the total population V and the number of persons who are, at first, not affected (generation 0) B_0, one generation later, the number of remaining non-affected persons would be $B_1 = (B_0/V) \times B_0 = (B_0)^2/V$. In the second round, the same principle would apply, so two generations later, the number of remaining non-affected persons would then be $B_2 = (B_1/V) \times B_1 = (B_0)^4/V^3$. After generation n, the number of remaining non-affected persons would be $B_n = (B_0)^{(2n)} / [V^{(2n-1)}]$. If we resolve this equation with respect to n (number of generations), we get:

$$n = \ln [\ln(B_n/V) / \ln(B_0/V)] / \ln 2$$

In this example, it would be

$$n = \ln [\ln(1/80000000) / \ln(60000000/80000000)] / \ln 2$$
$$n = 5.983124$$

Since one generation lasts 30 years, only one non-affected person would be left after 5.983124×30 years = 179.49 years. And, of course, one microsecond later, no 'full' non-affected person would be left at all.

10 In the July 1986 edition of the magazine *Ethics*, which dealt solely with Parfit's *Reasons and Persons*, further objections were raised against the 'non-identity problem'. But Parfit (1986) convincingly answered them in the same magazine, so they will no longer be elaborated here.

11 The same applies to Parfit's example that says that either a resource conservation or a resource depletion policy is chosen (Parfit, 1987, p361 et seq.).

12 In 1963, the meteorologist Edward N. Lorenz was computing a weather forecast and he examined the behaviour of heated liquids or gases. He characterized their behaviour by means of three differential equations. Then he projected the numerical result to the phase space and received the strange attractor that later became known as the 'Lorenz attractor': an endlessly long trajectory in a three-dimensional space that does not cross itself and is shaped like the two wings of a butterfly. Interestingly, Lorenz stumbled on the chaotic behaviour of his model rather coincidentally: to save time when working out the numerical solution of the equations, he fell back on intermediate results of previous calculations, but only took three decimal places into account, although the computer supported six decimal places. That led to increasing deviations over the course of time between the old and the new calculations. Starting from almost the same point, with a difference so small that it could be caused by the flapping of a butterfly's wings, the weather curves diverged until they had almost nothing left in common. In a study of 1963, Lorenz used different expressions, finally he called this the 'butterfly effect' (Lorenz, 1963).

13 For the differences in Eastern religions and philosophical traditions, see O'Flaherty (1980); Pappu (1987); Kim and Harrison (1999); Halbfass (2000); and von Brück (2007).

14 For more details see Gosseries (2004a). Gosseries' argument is not applicable in 'wrongful-life' cases.

15 Woodward (1986) for instance argued that 'harming a person' and 'making him worse off' are not identical actions.

16 Page also considers 'group rights' as an antidote to the 'non-identity problem'.

17 This objection against the 'non-identity thesis' was raised by Mulgan (2002) and Tremmel (2006c) independently.

18 Perhaps it would be demanding too much if all (mutually incompatible) notions of death and after life were to be considered in ethical issues.

19 Some writers discuss the question of rights of future generations on the basis of the 'non-identity claim', for instance Parfit (1987, p124). The argument usually goes like this: 'Future persons have no rights because they are contingent on our decisions.' The contingency argument can be rephrased like this: 'We cannot harm future generations because they are contingent on our decisions.' This claim has already been discussed. As the 'non-identity claim' does not hold in my opinion with regard to questions of intergenerational justice, I will hereinafter only discuss arguments against rights of future generations that bracket the 'non-identity argument'.

20 I will first discuss the question whether future individuals, not future generations, can have rights. Afterwards, I deal with the question whether entities such as generations can have rights as groups.

21 Ahrens (1983, p4) also contends that the issue of the rights of future generations is a crucial one.

22 Hardly any philosopher explicitly claims that future people will not only have rights in the future, but already have them today. Exceptions are Elliot (1989,

p161) and Partridge (1990, p54). But I agree with Gosseries (2008, p453) that their present-rights-of-future-people view is completely untenable. Even the language of 'conditional rights' (Birnbacher, 1988, p120) is unfortunate. Rights are not something that float around in the air waiting for a bearer to come into existence. Future persons do not have rights (of whatever type) now.

23 I assume Baier has 'members of generations' in mind.

24 It referred to the 'ancient rights and liberties' established by English law and derived from English history, but it did not declare the universality of rights (Hunt, 2007, p20 et seq.).

25 According to Hunt, they were grounded in the rejection of torture as a means of finding the truth; the changing idea of human relationship displayed by novelists, playwrights and artists, and the spread of empathy beyond insular communities. Before human rights were codified in corresponding declarations, enlighteners had intensively debated their existence. Thus, the proclamation of 'moral rights' preceded the creation of legal rights.

26 Cf. also Bentham who favours utilitarian theory over rights talk. He writes: 'The strength of this argument is in proportion to the strength of lungs in those who use it. The principle of utility, with the united powers of Bacon, Locke, Hume, Smith, [and] Paley to develop it, would be nothing against one Danton bawling out natural rights' (cited in Stark, 1952, p336). See also Paley (1826).

27 In this very insightful and thorough article, Partridge *accepts* the 'non-identity-paradox' in the formulation, 'We have no obligation to any individuals who will be our distant descendants to adopt policies designed to improve future conditions or avoid future harms.' However, he *denies* that from this conclusion follows that 'we have no moral obligations to improve the living conditions of persons who will live in the remote future' (Partridge, 2007, p11). See also Partridge (2008).

28 For this analysis, the terms 'obligation' and 'duty' are used as synonyms.

29 Party A can be a particular person or a state administration.

30 Among others, Narveson (1976, p65), Kavka (1978), Pletcher (1980), Waldron (1984, p12) and Birnbacher (1988) select option 1. Among others, Macklin (1980, p151), Bandman (1982, p98) and Beckerman (2004) cling to option 2. Hart (1984, p80) opts for option 3. Brown-Weiss (1989, p99) chooses option 1 with regard to planetary rights, but option 2 with regard to individual rights.

31 See also Partridge (1990, p42) and Waldron (1984, p6).

32 I have changed this example by replacing tigers for dodoes and talking about a species becoming extinct today instead of in the past. Among others, De George (1980, p161) and Bandman (1982, p96) also think we do not have the right to any goods if there is no provision to effectively claim this right.

33 This has been done by Brown-Weiss (1989, pp297–328). The task was repeated by Tremmel (2006b) and Haeberle (2006). For the case of France, see in detail Bourg (2006).

34 An empirical study that indicates this growing sense of responsibility for posterity is Russell et al (2003).

35 For details, see Tremmel (2006b, pp192–197). Other countries such as Israel, Hungary or Finland have already set up or are currently discussing new institutions for the protection of future generations instead of including clauses for the protection of future generations in their constitutions. The new institutions are called 'Ombudsman for Future Generations', 'Committee for Future Generations', 'Ecological Council', 'Future Council' or 'Third Chamber'; see the articles of Posner (1990b); Shoham and Lamay (2006); Jávor (2006); and Agius (2006).

36 For the background of minister Däubler-Gmelin's statement, see Tremmel et al (1999).

37 The precise age when a young person becomes more powerful is admittedly hard to pin down. A crucial criterion is the voting age.

38 The Philippines Supreme Court, Minors Oposa v. Secretary of the Department of Environment and Natural Resources (DENR), 30 July 1993, 33 ILM 175 (1994). For comments see Rest, 1994; Allen, 1994; Oposa, 2002; Westra, 2006, p135; and Gosseries, 2008, p466.

39 Westra (2006, p152) criticizes that it is allowed to use resources instead of preserving them for future generations. However, if nobody was ever allowed to use non-renewable resources, all generations would lose. Therefore, a sustainable use should be aimed at, for the benefit of all generations. Such a regulation could require each generation to create renewable resources to the same extent as it uses up non-renewable resources (cf. Pearce and Turner, 1990; Daly, 1991; Enquete Commission of the German Bundestag, 1994).

40 Published as UN document A/AC.256/16, www.unicef.org/ceecis/Final_ Berlin_Report.pdf accessed 8 August 2001.

41 The declaration can be ordered through www.cousteau.org accessed 1 September 2004.

42 www.cousteau.org/en/cousteau_world/our_programs/future_generations.php.

43 One of the mentioned critics is Macklin who contents: 'It is common practice to ascribe rights to a class of persons in the legal traditions of some countries and to file class action suits. But the class of persons involved in such a suit is comprised of identifiable individuals' (Macklin, 1980, p152).

5 What to Sustain? Capital or Well-being as an Axiological Goal?

1 Also Ott and Döring (2004, p100) see a fair bequest package, imagined as a set of capitals, as the answer to the question 'What to sustain?'.

2 'Services' should not be mentioned here as it is a flow figure, not a stock figure.

3 Domestic receivables and domestic debts must not be mentioned in this balance sheet. The domestic financial receivables of (members of) each generation are the domestic financial debts of (other members of) the *same* generation. Variations of *domestic* receivables and debts may change the welfare distribution *within* a generation, but not between generations. By

contrast, variations of *foreign* claims and debts do change the financial capital of a country's generations. In the balance sheet of the world as a whole, the position 'Financial capital' vanishes.

4 And those who count it in did not develop methods to measure its value.

5 Cf. Costanza (2001, p126); Rat von Sachverständigen für Umweltfragen (2002, p64).

6 For this extensive debate, see Rolston (1974, 1988); Goodpaster (1978); Birnbacher (1980, 1982, 1997); Taylor (1981, 1986); Attfield (1983); Regan (1983); Hare (1987); Norton (1987, 1991, 1992, 1995); Scherer (1990); Wolf (1990); Fox (1990); Johnson (1991); Goodin (1996); Nutzinger (1996); Krebs (1997); and Attfield (1999). If an intrinsic value is attributed to nature, then nature conservation is justified, independently of any inter-generational obligations. Whether or not my theory of intergenerational justice supports protectionism for other than anthropocentric reasons is the subject of a forthcoming paper that is too long to be included in this study.

7 This opinion is, for example, held by Atkinson et al (1997); Pezzey (1997); and Simon (1998).

8 The question of how to *distribute* the axiological good (for example the capital) among the generations is discussed in Chapter 6. In this chapter, the question of whether the 'societal end' shall increase from generation to generation, whether it shall remain equal, or whether it may even sink shall remain unanswered.

9 For a critical view, see for example Rat von Sachverständigen für Umwelt-fragen (2002, p59); and Norton (2003, pp425–428).

10 Most definitions refer to the totality of nature as 'natural capital', cf. Neumayer (1999). The definition issues are comprehensively outlined by Ott and Döring (2004, p211): 'We can offer two definitions: 1) Everything natural belongs to the natural capital. 2.) Everything that is somehow useful for humankind, that is the sum of functions of the natural resources, belongs to the natural capital.' Ott and Döring advocate the second definition. This may imply that some parts of biodiversity (for example viruses) do not belong to the natural capital if one believes that they are not – and will never be – useful for humans (Ott and Döring, 2004, p213). It remains to be seen if this new definition gains acceptance in the scientific community.

11 For an overview, see Garrod and Willis (1999) and Sukhdev (2008, pp9–46).

12 The rationality and ethical legitimacy of discounting is controversial. For most economists, discounting is simply axiomatic. From the viewpoint of philosophy and ecological economy, it is immoral to discount not one's own benefit or damage, but that of others (Ott, 2003; Ott and Döring 2004, p124). I hold the same opinion (cf. Tremmel, 2003e). On the discounting debate, see also Birnbacher (1988, pp28–91, 2003b); Cowen and Parfit (1992); Hampicke (2001); Schwarze (2003); and Bayer (2004). A good account of the legal–political, economical and mathematical considerations that speak against discounting is Ederer et al (2006).

13 The famous study by Costanza et al (1998), who calculate the value of nature's functions, aggregates marginal values to total values in an objection-

able way. It also is an intractable problem to calculate the share of such goods in a *national* capital accounting system (instead of a global one). Even if we could calculate the value of the ozone layer, we would not know what its value was for an individual country.

14 Examples can be found with Dobson (2000); Haber (2001); Costanza (2001, p121); Held and Nutzinger (2001, p7); and Rat von Sachverständigen für Umweltfragen (2002, pp64–66).

15 Ott and Döring speak of 'constant natural capital rule' (2004, p140). Barrett and Grizzle (1999, p25) contend: 'Current generations cannot expend so much natural capital as to leave future generations predictably worse off than contemporary folks.' Also see Knaus and Renn (1998, p48 et seq.).

16 As mentioned, the question of the fair distribution among the generations of *what* to sustain (for example the capital) among the generations is discussed in Chapter 6.

17 Normally, no statements are made regarding other types of capital such as social or cultural capital. It remains unclear if the proponents of strong sustainability regard a condition only as acceptable if at least one type of capital is increased, but none is decreased.

18 Also see Scherhorn and Wilts (2001) and Ott and Döring (2004, pp134–136).

19 The alternative maxim that an equivalent of renewable resources shall be created for each consumed unit of non-renewable resources is not realistic, as I have discussed elsewhere (Tremmel, 2003a).

20 Of course, there are cases in which investments in natural capital cost money, for example replanting a forest.

21 See Blanchard (1990); Auerbach et al (1991, 1999); Raffelhüschen (1999, 2002); Deutsche Bundesbank (2001).

22 For the year 2000, for instance, the German Central Bank ascertained a fiscal gap of 2.8 per cent of the German GDP (Deutsche Bundesbank, 2001, p36).

23 Cf. Grütz (1999) and Wissenschaftlicher Beirat beim Bundesministerium der Finanzen (2001).

24 Thus, the generational accounting exemplified in Table 5.1 is aggregated higher than that of Hauser because it was set up for an entire country, whereas Hauser breaks down the individual sectors.

25 Amounts converted at a rate of €1 = DM1.95583.

26 Thus, each individual cohort owns an average of one thirtieth of this value.

27 Cf. Engels et al (1974, p93).

28 GDP was €345.3 billion in 1970.

29 For more details, see OECD (2007, p28) and Ederer et al (2002).

30 Example calculation: 1000/5 = 200; 1000/100=10.

31 Upon inquiry, the authors emailed to me: 'Someone who lived only for five years has indeed inherited a lot without being able to take advantage of it, and without being able to pass it on to the next generation. This is of course not his fault but nevertheless an enormous burden, just look at the developing countries.'

32 The time period of 'past' was not specified.

33 The best-known calculation of the damages caused by the greenhouse effect is the report of the former chief economist of the World Bank, Nicolas Stern, who speaks of damages ranging between 5 and 20 per cent of the global GDP over the next decades (Stern, 2007).

34 The biologist Edward Wilson assumes that between 0.1 and 1 per cent of all animal species become extinct every year, or at least 27,000 species (Wilson, 1992, p280).

35 Cf. Koslowski (2005). For the implications of ever increasing life expectancy on this process, see Feeser-Lichterfeld (2008).

36 Many authors have pointed to this disadvantage bound up with the accumulation of individual social capital in the sense of promoting one's own career, including Portes and Landolt (1996, p19).

37 Besides, type B overlaps with human capital, because it includes the abilities of individuals. However, most authors who use an actor-oriented definition of social capital distinguish it from human capital (cf. Riemer 2005, p87). They state that the human capital explanation is that people who do better are smarter, more skilled, more attractive, etc. The social capital explanation is that people who do better have better connections (Burt, 1999, p48).

38 Written by Putnam as an introduction to his book *Bowling Alone* (Putnam, 2000). See also www.bowlingalone.com accessed 20 August 2007.

39 'Worse' in a qualitative, not a normative sense.

40 Measured, for instance, by the question: 'Generally speaking, would you say that most people can be trusted, or that you can't be too careful in dealing with people?' (Layard, 2005, p69).

41 Easterlin (2007, p29) takes this easy way out of the terminological quagmire when he writes: 'I take the terms "wellbeing", "utility", "happiness", "life satisfaction" and "welfare" to be interchangeable and measured by the answer to a question such as...: Taken all together, how would you say things are these days – would you say that you are very happy, pretty happy or not too happy?'.

42 These can only be rudimentary definitions. It would go beyond the scope of this study to define all these terms in accordance with the criteria listed in Chapter 2.

43 The examples given for the use of the term are: 'Such concern for our wellbeing was pleasing.' And 'the belief that every technological advance contributes to the well-being of mankind'.

44 The questions of measurement with objective indicators such as the 'Human Wellbeing Index' (Prescott-Allen, 2001) and subjective indicators are dealt with in the section 'Measuring well-being' in this chapter.

45 An example given is 'a society in which all cooperate and work for the welfare of all its members'.

46 An example given is 'cut-backs in health and welfare services'.

47 An example given is 'They were living off welfare.'

48 For example Headey and Wearing (1992); Diener (1994); Layard (2005). Höffe uses the terms 'well-being' and 'happiness' synonymously (Höffe, 2007b, p9).

49 For the definition problems of the term 'happiness', see Haybron (2000, 2007); Brülde (2007a, 2007b); Chekola (2007); and Griffin (2007).
50 Note that there are two happinesses: being happy and feeling happy. By contrast, there is 'well-being', but no 'well-feeling'.
51 For the relation between utility and standard of living, see also Bruni and Porta (2007) and Sen (2000).
52 Singer (1979), for instance, focuses on 'satisfaction of interests'.
53 I prefer 'need-fulfilment' to 'need-satisfaction' because the former has no sexual connotation.
54 These two authors have devised the most comprehensive theory of needs that I know. On needs, see also Birnbacher (1979); Max-Neef (1992, 1995); De-Shalit (1995, p5).
55 For the capabilities approach, see also Nussbaum and Sen (1993) and Sen (2000, p39).
56 Thompson (1980) tries to use this objection to state that we have no obligations to future generations at all. But this argument is untenable. For replies see Ahrens (1983, p2 et seq.); Birnbacher (1988, pp152–155); Partridge (2008); Page (2008); Wolf (2008).
57 Another of Mill's passages (1979, p9) can also be understood in two ways: 'no intelligent human being would consent to be a fool, no instructed person would be an ignoramus, no person of feeling and conscience would be selfish and base, even though they should be persuaded that the fool, the dunce, or the rascal is better satisfied with his lot than they are with theirs'.
58 In Mill's days, this was a knockout argument. The question of whether animals such as apes or pigs are also moral subjects on account of their needs, interests or pursuits was only seriously discussed much later; cf. Singer (1976a).
59 Version one of Mill's argument would only make sense to a certain degree if he were criticizing the fact that people *artificially* reduce their demands by using drugs or escaping from reality, for instance. The argument would then be: 'It is better to lead a demanding, but less happy life than a happy life that is causally maintained by ignorance or drugs (in the widest sense).' I deal with this in section 'Escaping from Reality' in Chapter 5.
60 In many cases, it may make more sense to calculate the median value instead of the average. Then, extreme preferences are even less relevant.
61 Sextus Empiricus (2002, Chapter 6). Another common name for this problem is the Munchhausen-Trilemma (see Albert, 1991, p15). See also Albert, 1971; Ernst, 2007, p20.
62 Try it yourself and you will see what I mean.
63 For more details, see Ott (2001, pp63–76 and 153 et seq. Ott uses his rejoinder in a different context.)
64 On category mistakes, see Ryle (1970) and von Savigny (1993, p90).
65 Definitely not Friedrich Nietsche, as anyone can see who reads his books.
66 Likewise Bentham (1907, p4) says: 'Is it [the principle of utility] susceptible of any direct proof? It should seem not: for that which is used to prove every-

thing else cannot itself be proved. A chain of proofs must have their commencement somewhere. To give such proof is as impossible as needless.'

67 However, he does not make the argument for asceticism as a social end as strong as possible. Instead, he ridicules it hastily.

68 Only in passing, we should note that, when Gautama Buddha writes: 'Happiness is impassiveness in the world, the overcoming of desire, the elimination of I-awareness' (cited in Höffe, 2007b, p87), then he does not mean 'happiness' the way we understand it, but as 'the final objective'.

69 Until today, philosophy keeps dealing with the tension between morals and happiness, see MacIntyre (1981); Taylor (1981); Spaemann (1989); Horn (1998); Seel (1999); Höffe (2007b); Nussbaum (2007); and Matravers (2007).

70 It is characteristic of Epicurus' teachings that he develops special forms of regulating needs in order to maximize pleasure and justifies a radical this-worldly orientation by arguing that the human soul dissolves upon death. Not eternal life, but tranquillity of mind (*ataraxia*) is his basic motivation. According to Epicurus, happiness can be attained in seclusion, in a garden far away from the state and its politics. The feasting and other excesses the Epicureans are said to have indulged in are probably merely slander. Epicurus (2007, p23) rather propagates the absence of displeasure as the greatest good. The following inscription is said to have been at the entrance to Epicurus' garden: 'Stranger, here you will do well to tarry; here our highest good is pleasure. The caretaker of that abode, a kindly host, will be ready for you; he will welcome you with bread, and serve you water also in abundance, with these words: "Have you not been well entertained? This garden does not whet your appetite; but quenches it".'

71 Kant (1968b, p515, A 13) says: 'The term *duty* does not refer to things everyone would want themselves; because duty is *coercion* to do something one does not want to do' (emphasis original). However, Kant does not say one has to renounce happiness completely to lead a moral life. He also says: 'Yet, although the principle of happiness and that of ethical practice are different, they are not *opposed*, and pure practical reason does not require *giving up* one's right to happiness, but only to *ignore* it whenever duties are concerned' (Kant 1968a, p217, A 166, emphasis original).

72 See also Sidgwick, who accuses the critics of utilitarianism of being unknowingly utilitarian themselves (Sidgwick, 1981, pp422–426). Birnbacher also points out that even non-utilitarian ethical systems contain sets of norms that partially comply with one version of utilitarianism or the other (Birnbacher, 1986, 31).

73 Mill (1979, p8): 'There is no known Epicurean theory of life which does not assign to the pleasures of the intellect, of the feelings and imagination, and of the moral sentiments, a much higher value as pleasures than those of mere sensation. It must be admitted, however, that utilitarian writers in general have placed the superiority of mental over bodily pleasures chiefly in the greater permanency, safety, uncostliness, etc., of the former – that is, in their

circumstantial advantages rather than in their intrinsic nature.' Prima facie, one could argue that Mill is stuck in a subjective hedonistic calculation in the style of Bentham. Even if Bentham has not distinguished between quantitative and qualitative pleasures, he explicitly pointed out that the duration (as well as intensity, etc.) of pleasure must be taken into account. According to Mill, one must distinguish between quantity and quality, but quality could then be converted into quantity. But isn't that nevertheless a fundamental deviation from Bentham's opinion?

74 For concepts of 'utilitarianism', see for example Rescher (1966); Smart (1973); Höffe (1974); Sen and Williams (1982); Glover (1990); Goodin (1995); Birnbacher (2002).

75 Sometimes, the terms 'descriptive vs. evaluative' are used instead of 'subjective vs. objective'. Erikson (1993, p77) explains that with descriptive indicators, the individual is asked to describe his resources and conditions. A typical question would be: 'How high is your monthly salary?' With evaluative indicators, the individual is asked to evaluate his conditions, for instance by saying whether she is satisfied with her salary. It should be added that in the descriptive approach, the information is usually not obtained from the individuals themselves, but from official statistics.

76 Usually, the questionnaires ask for 'happiness' or 'life satisfaction', not 'well-being'.

77 This is the view of, for example, Tännsjö (2007, p81 et seq.) and Layard (2005, p20).

78 This threshold seems to be at about $12,000 (€8200).

79 The 'hedonic treadmill' hypothesis was first formulated by Brickman and Campbell (1971). Studies have subsequently been undertaken, including Easterlin (1974); Duncan (1975); and Headey and Wearing (1992).

80 Beautifully described with Count Vronksy in Tolstoy's novel *Anna Karenina*, or in the story of *Don Juan*.

81 For many, a jackpot is a symbol of utmost happiness, a synonym for the fulfilment of all dreams. On the life of lottery millionaires after their sudden wealth, see Lau and Kramer (2005).

82 Recent research questions the view that the happiness of individuals cannot permanently increase or decrease, see Inglehart et al (2008, p265), with further references.

83 Layard (2007, p151) says that rivalry is in our genes. See also Easterlin (2007, p55).

84 A study focused on the UK revealed that a rise in wages of comparable workers reduces a person's job satisfaction as much as a rise in his own wage increases it (Clark and Oswald, 1996).

85 In economic terms, this is called the 'relative consumption thesis' (Duesenberry, 1949) or the 'interdependent preferences thesis' (Easterlin, 2007, p53).

86 Data from the World Value Survey at www.worldvaluessurvey.org/

87 An important database within happiness research comes from the World Value Surveys. To measure 'life satisfaction', a scale from 1 (not at all satis-

fied) to 10 (very satisfied) is used. 'Happiness' is assessed by using four categories: very happy, rather happy, not very happy, not at all happy. Often, a combined index is calculated.

88 The American Institute of Public Opinion (Gallup) asks: 'In general, how happy would you say you are – very happy, fairly happy or not happy?'. The General Social Survey asks: 'Taking all things together, how would you say you are these days – would you say that you are very happy, pretty happy or not too happy?'

89 Overviews such as Figure 5.8c, using the questionable method for different numbers of years, can be found in many scientific happiness studies. For instance Myers (1993) or Layard (2005) for the US, or Allensbach (2002, p35) for the years 1958–2001 for Germany. On the website www.worldval-uessurvey.org/happinesstrends/ it is possible to see such charts for various countries. Veenhoven (1993) uses these charts for 56 countries for the years 1946–1992. The first scientific interviews on happiness were carried out after the Second World War; therefore we have no information about earlier epochs.

90 A good description of the everyday life in past centuries can be found in Braudel (1981) or in the five-volume work *A History of Private Life*, edited by Ariès and Duby (1987, 1988, 1989, 1990, 1991).

91 Jared Diamond, in a surprisingly superficial analysis, contributed to this myth by generalizing that bushmen were taller and healthier than their successors, who were farmers (Diamond, 1992, Chapter 10).

92 Spontanous answers differ significantly from answers given after one hour reflection time.

93 According to other studies, 'having sex' ends up fourth on the list of activities that make people happy (Pieper, 2003, p24).

94 However, a portable MRI does not exist yet. Perhaps new methods of measuring brain waves will be developed over the coming decades.

95 Tännsjö (2007, p86) tries to counter the argument by saying that even Parfit would give a clear answer to the question 'How are you?', but this is a particularity of the English language. The answer to the equivalent question in French, '*Comment tu vas?*', might well be '*Comme ci, comme ça*', (partly so, partly so).

96 This subject gained wide public attention by the popular movie *Matrix*. But the matrix does not create a world in which all preferences are fulfilled, because human minds are not designed for permanent happiness, says the programmer of the matrix in the movie. At best, there is no unbearable suffering in the matrix. Nevertheless, one of the rebels, Mr Reagan, prefers this virtual world to reality.

97 The role game 'Second Life', for instance. Virtual realties have rapidly developed since Nozick wrote his lines, and they are booming.

98 The following section is an extension of Tremmel and Goetz (2007).

99 Elsewhere, he calls the HDI the standard for 'the widening of people's choices and the enrichment of their lives' (1995, p20).

100   In his remarkable study, Maddison (1995) determines the growth of the GDP per capita from 1820 to 1992. The data on the average life expectancy and the average number of school years prior to 1870 are based on his own calculations. For that purpose, the average increases of both partial indicators for the years 1870 to 1900 were calculated. Then, the data from 1820 to 1870 were extrapolated.

101   While Africa's HDI has increased, its WISP has dropped.

102   There are further indices, for example the Physical Quality of Life Index (Morris, 1979) or indices that include progress in security, intelligence (as measured by IQ tests) and mental health (Heylighen and Bernheim, 2000). The indicator systems of national sustainability strategies in dozens of countries should also be mentioned here. For instance, the German federal government published a Nationale Nachhaltigkeitsstrategie (National Sustainability Strategy) in April 2002. It defined sustainability on the basis of 21 indicators (Bundesregierung, 2002), from 'perspectives for families' to 'integration of foreign citizens'. However, for reasons of space, I will concentrate on the three objective approaches I consider most important.

103   See Morris (1979, p22), who also discusses criteria for indices for objectively measuring well-being.

104   For the intensity of the individual correlations, see Heylighen and Bernheim (2000, pp330–335); Easterlin (2001, p8, 2007, p45).

105   For the concept of QALYs, see for example Prieto and Sacristán (2003).

106   For the nature of risks in general, see Perrow (1984) and Renn (2008).

107   Already now, dangerous impacts are occurring in natural and social systems in certain regions due to rising mean temperatures. For example, some major Asian rivers' flows have changed due to Himalayan glacial melt. In the future, major changes in the Earth's frozen area, significant rises in sea levels, disruption of major sea-air circulation patterns, massive extinction of species, altered rainfall patterns and widespread changes to ecosystems are likely to occur (Hansen et al, 2008). The human costs of the greenhouse effect will mainly accrue in Southern countries; see also IFCC (2007).

108   For more, see www.globalzero.org accessed 14 April 2009.

109   The following passage is based on Müller (2008).

110   Looking back at our age, future historians must consider it absurd madness that some states – by no means all – have developed an arsenal of nuclear weapons that could wipe out mankind. Yet, some contemporary political scientists think it is owed to the allegedly always selfish behaviour of all states. They call this attitude 'realism'. From a scientific point of view, this definition (realism = orientation by selfishness) is inadequate, as explained in Chapter 2. Now, words define politics. Whoever wins the battle of definitions succeeds in the real world. Whoever controls language controls mankind. According to a Chinese proverb, the first thing Kung Fu Tse said he would do after having taken office was to 'surely rectify the terms'. Indeed, there have been attempts to manipulate key terms in almost

all scientific disciplines. But the way some political scientists use the term 'realism' to justify an extremely backward behaviour is a particularly negative example. Every sensible political scientist should do her or his best to end this act of language manipulation. Just say say 'selfishness' instead of 'realism'.

111 Because the stockpiles of the US and Russia account for 96 per cent of the world's nuclear weapons, these two countries should begin with deep reductions to their arsenals, while beginning a dialogue with other nuclear weapon states. The new US president, Barack Obama, announced his intention to make this a priority. In April 2009, he said: 'Just as we stood for freedom in the 20th century, we must stand together for the right of people everywhere to live free from fear in the 21st. And as a nuclear power – as the only nuclear power to have used a nuclear weapon – the United States has a moral responsibility to act' (www.thenational.ae accessed 13 April 2009). The new breathing space that will develop if North Korea and Iran can be stopped from getting nuclear capacity ought to be used. Otherwise, Brazil, Indonesia, Argentina, Vietnam, Malaysia, South Africa, Egypt, Nigeria, Venezuela, etc. will not be kept from following the path blazed by India, Pakistan and Israel.

112 And thus all research efforts that help us better quantify the different types of capital are absolutely welcome.

113 On this problem, see the anthologies Bayles (1976) and Sikora and Barry (1978); also Parfit (1976, 1982, 1987, 2000); Barry (1977); Birnbacher (1986, 1988; 2006a); Wolf (1995, 1996, 1997); Fehige and Wessels (1998); Arrhenius (1999, 2000); and Gosseries (2002).

114 In the second paragraph of the preface to his *A Fragment on Government* (1988), Bentham writes: 'It is the greatest happiness of the greatest number that is the measure of right or wrong.' This maxim is originally attributed to Hutcheson's Inquiry Concerning Moral Good and Evil (1728). In section III, 8, it reads: 'that action is best, which procures the greatest happiness for the greatest numbers; and that, worst, which, in like manner, occasions misery'. This maxim is an unholy admixture of two quite different principles which often point in different directions. Realizing this, Bentham dropped the misleading 'greatest number' part of the principle, replacing the original formulation with the more direct 'greatest happiness principle' in his later works.

115 For an at length discussion of the ethical implications of population policy, see Tremmel (2005a, pp101–189 and 2008).

116 Narveson already uses the word 'repugnant' for this case in 1973 in an essay for *The Monist* (vol 57, no 1), which is identical with Narveson (1976).

117 'For any possible population of at least ten billion people, all with a very high quality of life, there must be some much larger imaginable population whose existence, if other things are equal, would be better, even though its members have lives that are barely worth living' (Parfit, 1987, p388).

118 In parenthesis, it should be noted that the non-personal variant of maximizing 'utility on earth' could also include the utility of animals and plants.

119 The idea of sufficientism is to give greater weight to well-being changes that affect individuals below a certain well-being threshold (see Crisp, 2003, p762). This is an interesting position, but a different debate in which there are no misleading terms and concepts. To debate sufficientism in more detail would be a digression from my topic.

6 How Much to Sustain? The Demands of Justice in the Intergenerational Context

1 It is currently subject of some debate whether justice has to be 'relational' or can also be understood as 'non-relational' or alternatively 'non-comparative', see for example the anthology by Krebs (2000a). However, for the philosophic mainstream it is beyond dispute: 'Poverty is an evil but not itself an injustice' (English, 1977, p103).

2 If we consider animals as being moral objects, Robinson Crusoe could theoretically have a justice issue with non-human beings, for instance with some apes over the water resources on his small island.

3 Whether or not an roughly equal potential to harm each plays a role in the question of justice is discussed in section 'Justice as reciprocity' in this chapter.

4 In contrast to the concept of 'rights', the idea of 'justice' is very old. It already played a major role in the works of Plato, Aristotle and other philosophers. Cf. Gosepath (2004, p9).

5 Brian Barry (1989, pxiii) calls this theory 'justice as mutual advantage'. In my opinion this terminology is inappropriate and I later explain why.

6 The 'original position' (mistakenly also called 'natural position') is neither an early historical state of modern society nor a primitive near-natural lifestyle of certain groups of people, but a purely fictional thought experiment on contract theories. The factual situation, consisting of existing legal and state systems, is confronted with the 'original position' as an imagined situation without these systems. This construction was applied, for example, by Rousseau, Locke or Hobbes, with very different results.

7 The relationship between generations has been a topic of interest throughout history. Before the 1970s, however, the obligation of children to their parents was emphasized, and not the other way around. The Fourth Commandment in the Bible, 'honour thy father and mother', is repeated astonishingly often in the Old Testament (Dabrock, 2006, p108). For more on intergenerational duties in the Bible, see Derr (1980, pp41–44) and Auerbach (1995). For a comparison between the Bible, the Quran and the Talmud, see Agius and Chircop (1998) and Scherbel (2003).

8 If norms are developed under the auspices of impartiality, the thought model of only one impartial decider who – simultaneously or subsequently – identifies with all persons concerned (Lewis, 1946, p547; Brandt, 1955, 1959; Hare, 1982, p26; Harsanyi, 1982; Smith, 1991) is the second most important. Compared to the 'veil of ignorance' model, the 'impartial decider'

model has various advantages and drawbacks (see e.g. Brandt, 1979, pp224–245; Birnbacher, 2003a, pp413–424). As regards the latter, one key question is whether the decider should be considered rather like a just God (cf. Smith, 1776) or rather like a human being with certain characteristics (cf. Brandt, 1959, p173). A second key question is whether he should be 'benevolent'. Discussing the 'impartial decider' model in detail is beyond the scope of this paper. Rawls himself compared both models and came to the conclusion that the 'veil of ignorance' has a number of distinct advantages that make it superior (Rawls, 1971, pp148–149).

9 Rawls follows Hume (1975) in describing these circumstances for justice.

10 Of course, each one of the others may be benevolent enough to choose the smallest slice, leaving the person with the knife with a larger piece after all. But the method is a better guide to a fair division if we assume that the parties are self-interested (cf. English, 1977, p92).

11 Rawls (1971, pp153–156), argues against the 'expected value principle' and defends his view that the 'veil of ignorance' model will necessarily lead to a kind of maximin strategy. However, many philosophers agree that Rawls draws a wrong conclusion from his own sensible premises (see Daniels, 1975; Harsanyi, 1982, p47).

12 Rawls' (1971) passages on intergenerational justice (pp284–293) precede the final and central formulation of his theory of justice (pp303–304).

13 www.justiciadejusticias.com.ar/ accessed 19 January 2007.

14 According to Rawls (1971, p294), 'the different temporal position of persons and generations does not in itself justify treating them differently'.

15 This is true for the last three decades, from Barry (1973) to Dierksmeier (2006). In the intervening 33 years examples include Daniels (1975); Hubin (1976); English (1977); Birnbacher (1977); Routley and Routley (1978, pp166–173); Richards (1983); De-Shalit (1995, pp99–111); Paden (1997); Höffe (1998a, 1998b); Unnerstall (1999); Wissenburg (1999); Muñiz-Fraticelli (2002); and Veith (2006).

16 Also see Barry (1989, p193), who reiterates this critique.

17 See Buchholz (1984, p32) and Höffe (1998b). Rawls' theory also fails to address a mounting state debt, unequal returns on pensions and the unequal treatment of young and old people on the labour market.

18 Rawls' book was published in 1971, but its ideas had already been developed in the 1950s and 1960s (Barry 1989, p193), when research on need and happiness was still in its infancy.

19 It is not always clear which particular 'original position' model Rawls relates to. These three different models are usually identified in literature on the exegesis of Rawls' account. See Birnbacher (1977, pp388–396); Leist (1991, p349); Unnerstall (1999, p419); Veith (2006, pp119–122).

20 For instance, Rawls (1971, p287): 'But this calculus of advantages, which balances the losses of some against benefits to others, appears even less justified in the case of generations than among contemporaries.' Or, on page 293: 'We can now see that persons in different generations have duties and obligations to one another just as contemporaries do.'

21 Rawls acknowledges that this principle is stated independently by Jane English (1977, p98).

22 For critics, see Dauenhauer (2002); Dierksmeier (2006, p78); Wallack (2006, p91).

23 These two terms are used as synonyms by some writers, especially economists. I use 'rational' in a different sense than 'self-interested'. I call an actor 'rational' if he can clearly name his preferences and bring them into a consistent order (transitivity axiom). Self-interested behaviour serves to satisfy one's own interest, see Tremmel (2003c, pp46–54).

24 'Homo sapiens' is the collective name for 'homo sapiens neanderthalensis' and 'homo sapiens sapiens'. Here, we can disregard the anthropological dispute on whether the Neanderthal was already a human being. It would not influence our rationale if the time of the appearance of mankind was rescheduled backwards or forwards.

25 The number of generations is therefore exogenous in this model. Birnbacher takes another route by discussing how many generations should exist in an optimal world (1988, pp67–70). In his study, the number of generations is an endogenous parameter established by a rational universalist according to utilitarian contemplations on the sum of utility.

26 Sometimes the former aspect is not mentioned at all. Dierksmeier (2006, p73) describes the 'original position' as follows: 'One is to imagine all representatives who formulate the social contract and decide about basic matters of welfare distribution behind a veil of ignorance that obfuscates their view so they cannot find out about their future role in society.'

27 There is an absolute minimum for the HDI because life expectancy (which accounts for one third of the HDI) cannot sink below a certain level. Otherwise reproduction would not be possible and the species would simply become extinct.

28 Not sharing his knowledge or lying would not bring him any advantage, as will be shown later.

29 Historically, the HDI did not increase steadily but only very slowly for more than about 100,000 years. In the last 10,000 years, the increase was slightly larger, and only in the last centuries was it truly large. The HDI curve is therefore an exponential function rather than a straight line. Only for reasons of simplification, it is depicted as a straight line here.

30 The human race has been more or less ingenious and innovative throughout its entire history; the rate of innovations was never zero.

31 The wheel was invented by the Sumerians in Mesopotamia (modern Iraq) in the 5th millennium BC.

32 In the past most of these catastrophes were wars. In the future, ecological desasters might take the place of wars. Nevertheless, both must be avoided.

33 This important result is owed to the 'veil of ignorance'. If we call the maximization of well-being or benefit 'utilitarianism', then the representatives of all generations under the Rawlsian 'veil of ignorance' would not choose exclusively 'utilitarian' principles of intergenerational justice.

34 Especially G_1, which accumulates knowledge and makes inventions without having inherited anything.

35 Already in 1977, Birnbacher published two lexicographically ordered principles:

   '1   Maximize the expected value of the average of the average utility of the generations (respectively, minimize the expected value of the average of the average grief of the generations).

   2   Minimize the risk of drastic impairments for the less-advantaged generations in case you belong to the relatively least-advantaged generations by choosing out of two saving programmes, which are indifferent concerning (1), the one which helps the least-advantaged – according to their average utility – generation the most.' (Birnbacher, 1977, p396).

The first principle is rather similar to my principle. However, my example does not depend on the expected value, as the six participants can establish values in the parallel world with 100 per cent security. Assuming there are also insecurities in the parallel world, the expected value has to be applied.

36 What would it have cost to prevent the Second World War? Not much, in economic terms. Even today, at the dawn of the 21st century, the arms race accrues costs instead of saving them. At any rate, principle 1 obliges every generation to avoid disasters even if it actually does cost something to prevent them (for example, global warming).

37 English states that several *premises* of Rawls' reasoning would prompt the outcome that self-interested individuals in the 'original position' would choose not to save (1977, p91). One of these premises is that saving only transfers goods from earlier to later generations. According to English, this premise should be given up because children can save for their parents, too. She argues that the result that 'no saving would result' in model 2 is therefore unsubstantiated (p97). She thus arrives at the conclusion that saving would occur. However, English, unlike Rawls, uses the word 'generation' in a temporal manner, so there are some misunderstandings in her interpretation in his concept. Between non-overlapping generations, savings can indeed only be passed on from an earlier generation to a later one.

38 Teutsch (1985, p14) also believes this principle can largely be considered as accepted in the field of intragenerational ethics. Mill (1979, p45) says: 'Each person maintains that equality is the dictate of justice, except where he thinks that expediency requires inequality.'

39 See also Nielsen (1979) and Carens (1981) for strict egalitarianism.

40 By the way, that has nothing to do with equal human dignity. If two goldfish were concerned, we would feed them equally as well if we had no detailed information on their condition.

41 See BverfGE (German Federal Constitutional Court Decisions) 1, 14/52; also see BverfGE 4, 144 (155); 71, 255 (271), cited by Hesselberger (2000, p81).

42 According to Plato, this definition of justice stems from the poet Simonides (Plato, 1958, 331e–332c). It is also referred to as Ulpian's Formula, because

it was the Roman jurist who used it as a basis to coin the formula: '*Justitia est constans et perpetua voluntas ius suum cuique tribuendi*' (Justice is the firm and continuous desire to render to everyone that which is his due). See Ulpian (1999, I 1 pr.), cited by Gosepath (2004, p45). Ulpian's formula is universally applicable, but his contemporaries probably interpreted it in a conservative way, so it meant that each person has his own fixed, natural position in society. In antique or traditional societies, a person's rights and obligations depended on their position, social class or sex. This fatalistic view has fortunately and justifiably been abandoned in modern times.

43 The question of when to apply the principle of equal proportionality, when to apply a certain degree of proportionality, and when to apply other principles (for example 'the winner takes it all') is very complex and cannot be treated exhaustively here. Just think of the long dispute on whether a system of proportional representation or a majority vote system is more just.

44 A similar example was also used by Karl Marx (1875, p296). For 'justice according to performance', see in detail Miller (1976, 1989); Sher (1987); Riley (1989). For 'justice according to effort', see in detail Sadurski (1985) and Milne (1986).

45 However, even that is not undisputed. First, it was questioned by the argument of speciesism (Singer, 1979, pp48–71), and second, the dignity of embryos, foetuses or severely handicapped persons is strongly disputed. For the concept of dignity, see for example Böckenförde (1987); Bayertz (1996); Stoecker (2003); Gosepath (2004, pp128–175, especially 164 et seq.). Kavka (1978, p191 et seq.) discusses in which respects all humans are empirically equal and unequal.

46 For a comprehensive summary on 'equality of opportunity', see Arneson (2002) with further references. However, Arneson does not always distinguish clearly enough between 'merit' and 'talent'.

47 The 'level playing field' as a metaphor for 'equality of opportunity' was explicated by Roemer (1998) and Dworkin (2000).

48 They might both attend a boarding school with special emphasis on music or sports, or even a regular school. The nature of the pupil's talent shall not be specified here.

49 Example taken from Ott and Döring (2004, p92). They, however, advocate an egalitarian concept of intergenerational justice that I do not find convincing.

50 To operationalize this abstract principle for different policy fields, I have dealt elsewhere with intergenerationally just environmental policy (Tremmel, 2005a), finance policy (Tremmel 2005b; Boettcher and Tremmel, 2005), pension policy (Tremmel, 1997, 2003d, 2007b) and labour market policy (Tremmel 2007c). In this book, a general theory of generational justice is developed; therefore I will not go into these specific areas any further.

51 This is a secular point of view. Some religions and cults teach differently.

52 See Thompson (2002); Meyer (2003, pp17–26, 2004, 2005); Miller and Kumar (2007); Miller (2008); Howard-Hassmann (2008).

53 For the obligations of the present generation towards earlier generations, also see Kavka (1978); Baier (1980); Partridge (1981); Sher (1992); Simmons (1995); Mulgan (1999); Veith (2001, pp118–122); Ridge (2003); Gosseries (2004a); Haber (2004); Ulshöfer (2005); Bohmeyer (2007). For an early discussion, see Aristotle (2005, p24 et seq. 1100 a and b). Note that the 'non-identity problem' is also relevant for past evils, as Adams (1979, p53) points out: 'Since the least difference in events makes a different possible world, it follows that none of us actual individuals could have existed if any actual evil failed to occur.' For a detailed discussion of this question, see Morris (1984).

54 It is frequently claimed that this expression was first used in his main book *Leviathan*. However, it actually originates from the dedication of the work *De Cive* (Hobbes, 1994, p59). There, it only refers to relationships between states. But considering all his writings, there can be no doubt that Hobbes believes man's essential nature is competitive and selfish.

55 Hobbes (1985, p187) gives examples for this natural state, which is not only a thought experiment for him: 'I believe it was never generally so, over the world: but there are many places, where they live so now. For the savage people in many places of America, except the government of small Families, the concord whereof dependeth on natural lust, have no government at all; and live at this day in that brutish manner, as I said before.' This statement reflects the prejudices about Native Americans in Hobbes's days.

56 Hobbes's contemporary Descartes expressed it even more drastically: 'Hobbes alleges that all men are evil, or may at least act in such a way' (Hobbes, 1994, pxix).

57 The emancipatory aspect of Hobbes's concept is that man is able to solve the problems that, according to Hobbes, result from his nature by concluding a social contract and delegating authority to the state. He does not need heaven or hell, nor an external power to 'redeem his sinful soul'. There is no need to make him fear Judgement Day to keep him from living according to his egoistic impulses (cf. Baurmann, 2000, p7). Hobbes's work was therefore welcomed by the monarchy and fought by the Church in his days.

58 Bible, Exodus 21. Of course, today many enlightened societies do not behave anymore according to the maxim 'murder for murder, torture for torture'.

59 See Gouldner (1961); Barry (1989, pp211–241); Hondrich (2001, p187).

60 On the Golden Rule, see the Bible, Matthew 7 (12).

61 This is a revised and extended passage of Tremmel (2003c, pp18–23).

62 A standard example in decision theory, a subfield of microeconomics, goes like this: two elderly sisters have the tradition of going out to play bingo every time they meet. Each of them thinks the other enjoys it, but in fact, both of them would rather stay at home. But this example differs from the other examples because the two agents have insufficient information.

63 Without any problem, this maxim may also be extended to animals being capable of well-being.

64 On the general debate on 'homo oeconomicus', see Schelling (1984); Kirchgässner (2000); Baurmann (2000, p130); and Nelson (2006), with further references.

65 This optimism is expressed, for example, in de Mandeville (1968).

66 For an informative explanation of the 'vision of liberalism', see Baurmann (2000, pp4–41).

67 Exemplarily worked out in the essay *Tragedy of the Commons* by Hardin (1968). External effects are defined as follows: the utility or production function of economic subject X is influenced by the actions of economic subject Y to whom X has no contractual relations. X may also be a future person.

68 Today, many economists consider game theory the new core of microeconomics, see Harsanyi (1977); Feess (1997, p68).

69 Versions of this problem have been discussed in Laslett (1992, p46); Barry (1977, p270); Bickham (1981); Goodin (1985); Kymlicka (1990, p105); O'Neill (1993); De-Shalit (1995, pp87–111); Ott (2001, p130); Hösle (2003, p132); Mulgan (2006, pp24–54); Dierksmeier (2006, p80); Gardiner (2006, p154); Page (2007, pp99–131).

70 The term 'upstream/downstream problems' for such ethical problems was coined by Scherer (1990).

71 Muñiz-Fraticelli (2002, p21, emphasis original) states 'given this overlap, every person in the present generation can expect to depend on the generations that immediately follow to care for her in sickness or old age; call this the fact of *inevitable dependence*'.

72 'Apparently, many people's unwillingness to assume responsibility to remote future generations can be attributed to self-interest. More specifically, we assume that, by fulfilling our moral responsibility to our immediate descendants, we will be paid back in our old age, whereas we will not be able to reap what we have contributed to remote future generations' (Li, 1994, p5).

73 Surprisingly, this is also acknowledged by Gauthier (1986, p298 et seq.), although this author belongs to the Hobbesian tradition. However, his 'continuing contract argument' (Sauvé, 1995) fails in a world with egoistic people because this intergenerational contract is not a step-by-step business.

74 See, likewise Baier (1980). Alternatively, for De-Shalit, the principle of indirect reciprocity ('reciprocity in the sense of fair play', as he names it) is too vague to establish obligations towards future people (De-Shalit, 1995, p99).

75 Parfit (1987, pp487–490) is not so sure about this. Again, we enter metaphysical territory. It would be beyond the scope of this study to discuss different notions of death, after-life and reincarnation.

76 Of course, there are crisis regions where the HDI is much lower than in wealthy regions. For the comparison of generations, however, *average* members of each generation are taken into consideration.

77 Cf. also already Kant (1949, p6) and Addison (1968): '"We are always doing", says he, "something for Posterity, but I would fain see Posterity doing something for us"' (cited in Page, 2007, p99).

78 This may have been Rawls' original expectation. However, as already stated, in respect of the intergenerational context he recognized: 'it submits any ethical theory to severe if not impossible tests' (Rawls, 1971, p284).

79 As justice in the intragenerational context might be the oldest problem of political philosophy, a lot more could have been written here about it. But

that would have shifted the focus of this study, away from the intergenerational context. Good and helpful analyses of various further aspects of intragenerational justice are offered by, for example, Del Vecchio (1950); Pieper (1953); Brandt (1962); Perelman (1967); Honoré (1970); Miller (1976); Lucas (1980); Walzer (1983); Gauthier (1986); Lukash and Shklar (1986); Barry (1989, 1995); Dreier (1991); Young (1994); Höffe (1994b, 2001); Fraser (1997); Druwe and Kunz (1999); Krebs (2000a); Kersting (2002b); Koller (2003); Schmidtz (2006).

80 Examples are Scherbel (2003, p178) or Heubach (2008, p44), who states: 'Intergenerational justice is achieved if nobody is discriminated against because of his affiliation to a certain generation.' Other proponents of such an egalitarian standard of intergenerational justice are Ott and Döring (2004, p92) and Barry (1978, p243), who demands 'that the overall range of opportunities open to successive generations should not be narrowed'. Edith Brown-Weiss (2002, p5) advances an egalitarian account with regard to 'options (diversity), quality and access'. De George formulates the egalitarian maxim negatively. With regard to family generations, he says: 'Parents do not owe their children better lives than they had' (De George, 1980, p162).

81 Locke (1965, sec. 4, pp309 and 328–329) explains that men in the state of nature are moral equals and that God has given to them, in common, the use of the earth and its resources. He claims that, under these conditions, an individual may fairly appropriate land for his own use without belying the equal status of his fellows, provided that he (a) uses rather than wastes what he appropriates and (b) leaves 'enough and as good for others'. Locke justifies the latter condition on the ground that a person who appropriates a resource, but leaves enough and as good for others, leaves others as well off as they were prior to the appropriation. Hence, they are not injured by his act and have no complaint against him. Given that present and future generations have equal claims to the earth and its resources, Locke's analysis can be extended to apply to the intergenerational allocation of resources.

82 According to Tremmel (2003a, p34), 'Generational justice is achieved if the opportunities of future generations to satisfy their needs are at least as good as those of today's generation.'

83 By this general formulation, the principle can be applied to temporal, intertemporal and family-related generations. Distributions of well-being in the sense of need-fulfilment *within* a generation belong to the realm of intragenerational justice, not intergenerational justice (see Figure 1.2).

84 If no additional assumptions are made, for example that only one of the two generations is desperately in need of that resource.

85 For more detail on these two aspects see Tremmel (2005a, pp94–98).

86 For a nice formulation of the latter question, see Norton (2003, p423).

87 As mentioned, location in time is not a morally relevant feature of a person, determining his worthiness for considerations. This also applies to distant generations as long as their members have needs that are comparable to our needs.

88 This is emphasized in Unnerstall (1999), and justifiably so.

References

Adams, R. M. (1979) 'Existence, self-interest, and the problem of evil', *Nous*, vol 13, no 1, pp53–65

Addison, J. (1968) 'The Spectator, Friday, 20 August 1714', reprinted in F. D. Bond (ed) *The Spectator*, Clarendon Press, Oxford, pp592–595 (first published in 1714)

Adler, M. D. (2007) 'Economic growth and the interests of future (and past and present) generations: A comment on Tyler Cowen', *The University of Chicago Law Review*, vol 74, no 1, pp41–49

Adler, P. S. and Kwon, S. (2002) 'Social capital: Prospects for a new concept', *Academy of Management Review*, vol 27, no 1, pp17–40

Agius, E. (2006) 'Intergenerational justice', in Tremmel, J. (ed) *Handbook of Intergenerational Justice*, Edward Elgar Publishing, Cheltenham, pp317–332

Agius, E. and Chircop, L. (eds) (1998) *Caring for Future Generations. Jewish, Christian and Islamic Perspectives*, Westport, CN/Praeger/Adamantine Press, Twickenham

Ahrens, J. (1983) *Preparing for the Future. An Essay on the Rights of Future Generations*, Transaction Publisher, Bowling Green, OH

Albert, H. (1971) 'Ethik und meta-ethik', in Albert, H. and Topitsch, H. (eds) *Ernst: Werturteilsstreit*, Wissenschaftliche Buchgesellschaft, Darmstadt, pp472–517

Albert, H. (1991) *Traktat über kritische Vernunft*, 5th revised edition, Tübingen, UTB

Allen, T. (1994) 'The Philippine children's case: Recognizing legal standing for future generations', *Georgetown International Environmental Law Review*, vol 6, pp713–741

Allensbach (2002) *Allesbacher Jahrbuch der Demoskopie 1998–2002*, vol 11, edited by E. Noelle-Neumann, R. Köcher and K. G. Saur, München

Ariès, P. and Duby, G. (eds) (1987) *History of Private Life. From Pagan Rome to Byzantium*, vol 1, Belknap Press of Harvard University Press, Cambridge, MA

Ariès, P. and Duby, G. (eds) (1988) *History of Private Life. Revelations of the Medieval World*, vol 2, Belknap Press of Harvard University Press, Cambridge, MA

Ariès, P. and Duby, G. (eds) (1989) *History of Private Life. Passions of the Renaissance*, vol 3, Belknap Press of Harvard University Press, Cambridge, MA

Ariès, P. and Duby, G. (eds) (1990) *History of Private Life. From the Fires of Revolution to the Great War*, vol 4, Belknap Press of Harvard University Press, Cambridge, MA

Ariès, P. and Duby, G. (eds) (1991) *History of Private Life. Riddles of Identity in Modern Times*, vol 5, Belknap Press of Harvard University Press, Cambridge, MA

Aristotle (2005) *Die Nikomachische Ethik*, translated by O. Gigon, edited by R. Nickel, Artemis/Winkler, Zürich, Düsseldorf

Arneson, R. (2002) 'Equality of opportunity', http://plato.stanford.edu/entries/equal-opportunity accessed 4 January 2008

Arrhenius, G. (1999) 'Mutual advantage contractarianism and future generations', *Theoria*, vol 65, no 1, pp25–35

Arrhenius, G. (2000) 'Future generations: A challenge for moral theory', Dissertation for the Degree of Doctor of Philosophy in Practical Philosophy, Uppsala University, Uppsala

Atkinson, G., Dubourg, R., Hamilton, K., Munasinghe M., Pearce, D. and Young, C. (1997) *Measuring Sustainable Development: Macroeconomics and the Environment*, Edward Elgar Publishing, Cheltenham

Attfield, R. (1983) *The Ethics of Environmental Concern*, Blackwell, Oxford

Attfield, R. (1999) *The Ethics of the Global Environment*, Edinburgh University Press, Edinburgh

Auerbach, A., Gokhale, J. and Kotlikoff, L. (1991) 'Generational accounts: A meaningful alternative to deficit accounting', *Tax Policy and the Economy*, vol 5, pp55–110

Auerbach, A., Kotlikoff, L. and Leibfritz, W. (eds) (1999) *Generational Accounting around the World*, University of Chicago Press, Chicago/London

Auerbach, B. E. (1995) *Unto the Thousandth Generation. Conceptualizing Intergenerational Justice*, Peter Lang, New York/Frankfurt am Main

Axelrod, R. (1984) *The Evolution of Cooperation*, Basic Books, New York, NY

Bäcker, G. and Koch, A. (2003) 'Die Jungen als Verlierer? Alterssicherung und Generationengerechtigkeit', *WSI-Mitteilungen*, no 2, pp111–117

Baier, A. (1980) 'The rights of past and future persons' in Partridge, E. (ed) *Responsibilities to Future Generations. Environmental Ethics*, Prometheus Books, Buffalo, NY, pp171–186

Baker, W. E. (2000) *Achieving Success through Social Capital: Tapping Hidden Resources in your Personal and Business Networks*, Wiley & Sons, New York, NY

Bandman, B. (1982) 'Do future generations have the right to breathe clean air?', *Political Theory*, vol 10, no 1, pp95–102

Barrett, C. B. and Grizzle, R. (1999) 'A holistic approach to sustainability based on pluralist stewardship', *Environmental Ethics*, vol 21, pp23–42

Barry, B. (1973) 'The liberal theory of justice. A critical examination of the principal doctrines' in Rawls, J. (ed) *A Theory of Justice*, Oxford University Press, Oxford

Barry, B. (1977) 'Justice between generations', in Hacker, P. M. S. and Raz, J. (eds) *Law, Morality and Society. Essays in Honour of H. L. A. Hart*, Clarendon Press, Oxford, pp268–284

Barry, B. (1978) 'Circumstances of justice and future generations', in Sikora, R. and Barry, B. (eds) *Obligations to Future Generations*, Temple University Press, Philadelphia, PA, pp205–248

Barry, B. (1989) *Theories of Justice. A Treatise on Social Justice*, vol 1, Harvester–Wheatsheaf, London/Sydney/Tokyo

Barry, B. (1995) *Why Social Justice Matters?*, Polity Press, Malden, MA

Baurmann, M. (2000) *Der Markt der Tugend. Recht und Moral in der liberalen Gesellschaft. Eine soziologische Untersuchung*, 2nd edition, Mohr Siebeck, Tübingen (1st edition 1996)

Baurmann, M. and Kliemt, H. (1987) *Glück und Moral. Arbeitstexte für den Unterricht*, Reclam, Stuttgart

Bayer, S. (2004) 'Nachhaltigkeitskonforme Diskontierung. Das Konzept des Generation Adjusted Discounting', *Vierteljahreshefte für Wirtschaftsforschung*, vol 73, pp142–157

Bayertz, K. (ed) (1996) *Sanctity of Life and Human Dignity*, Reidel, Dordrecht

Bayles, M. D. (ed) (1976) *Ethics and Population*, Schankman, Cambridge

Bayles, M. D. (1980) *Morality and Population Policy*, Alabama University Press, Alabama

Becker, A. (2003) 'Generationengerechte Finanzpolitik', in Stiftung für die Rechte zukünftiger Generationen (ed) *Handbuch Generationengerechtigkeit*, Oekom, München, pp243–271

Beckerman, W. (1994) 'Sustainable development – Is it a useful concept?', *Environmental Values*, vol 3, no 3, pp101–209

Beckerman, W. (2003) *A Poverty of Reason. Sustainable Development and Economic Growth*, The Independent Institute, Oakland, CA

Beckerman, W. (2004) 'Intergenerational justice', *Intergenerational Justice Review* (English edition), vol 4, no 2, pp1–5

Beckerman, W. (2006) 'The impossibility of a theory of intergenerational justice', in Tremmel, J. (ed) *Handbook of Intergenerational Justice*, Edward Elgar Publishing, Cheltenham, pp53–71

Beckerman, W. and Pasek, J. (2001) *Justice, Posterity, and the Environment*, Oxford University Press, Oxford

Bentham, J. (1824) *The Book of Fallacies. From Unfinished Papers of Jeremy Bentham, By a Friend*, J. & H. L. Hunt, London

Bentham, J. (1907) *An Introduction to the Principles of Morals and Legislation*, Clarendon Press, Oxford (first published in 1780)

Bentham, J. (1988) *A Fragment on Government; The New Authoritative Edition by J. H. Burns and H. L. A. Hart*, Cambridge University Press, Cambridge (first published in 1776)

Berger-Schmitt, R. (1999) 'Human Development Report 1998', *Informationsdienst Soziale Indikatoren*, no 21, pp14–15

Bertrand, M. and Mullainathan, S. (2001) 'Do people mean what they say? Implications for subjective survey data', *American Economic Review*, vol 91, no 2, pp67–72

Bible (2004) Published by the German bishops, Calwer Verlag, Stuttgart

Bickham, S. (1981) 'Future generations and contemporary ethical theory', *Journal of Value Inquiry*, vol 15, no 2, pp169–177

Binmore, K. G. (2005) *Natural Justice*, Oxford University Press, Oxford

Binmore, K. G. (2006) 'Justice as a natural phenomenon', *Analyse & Kritik*, vol 28, no 1, pp1–12

Birnbacher, D. (1977) 'Rawls' Theorie der Gerechtigkeit und das Problem der Gerechtigkeit zwischen den Generationen', *Zeitschrift für philosophische Forschung*, vol 31, pp385–401

Birnbacher, D. (1979) 'Was wir wollen, was wir brauchen und was wir wollen dürfen' in Meyer-Abich, K. M. and Birnbacher, D. (eds) *Was braucht der Mensch um glücklich zu sein. Bedürfnisforschung und Konsumkritik*, Beck, München, pp30–57

Birnbacher, D. (ed) (1980) *Ökologie und Ethik*, Reclam, Stuttgart

Birnbacher, D. (1982) 'A priority rule for environmental ethics', *Environmental Ethics*, vol 4, no 1, pp3–16

Birnbacher, D. (1986) 'Prolegomena zu einer Ethik der Quantitäten', *Ratio*, vol 28, no 1, pp30–45

Birnbacher, D. (1988) *Verantwortung für zukünftige Generationen*, Reclam, Stuttgart

Birnbacher, D. (ed) (1993) *Glück*, Reclam, Stuttgart

Birnbacher, D. (ed) (1997) *Ökophilosophie*, Reclam, Stuttgart

Birnbacher, D. (1998) 'Aussichten eines Klons', in Ach, J. S., Brudermüller, G. and Runtenberg, C. (eds) *Hello Dolly? Über das Klonen*, Suhrkamp, Frankfurt am Main, pp46–71

Birnbacher, D. (1999) 'Quality of life: Evaluation or description?', *Ethical Theory and Moral Practice*, vol 2, no 1, pp25–36

Birnbacher, D. (2002) 'Utilitarismus/Ethischer Egoismus', in Düwell, M., Hübenthal, C. and Werner, M. H. (eds) *Handbuch Ethik*, Weimar, Metzler, Stuttgart, pp95–107

Birnbacher, D. (2003a) *Analytische Einführung in die Ethik*, DeGruyter, Berlin

Birnbacher, D. (2003b) 'Can discounting be justified?', *International Journal of Sustainable Development*, vol 6, no 1, pp42–51

Birnbacher, D. (2006a) 'Responsibility for future generations: Scope and limits', in Tremmel, J. C. (ed) *Handbook of Intergenerational Justice*, Edward Elgar Publishing, Cheltenham, pp23–38

Birnbacher, D. (2006b) *Natürlichkeit*, De Gruyter, Berlin

Blanchard, O. (ed) (1990) *The Sustainability of Fiscal Policy: New Answers to an Old Question*, OECD Economic Studies 15, OECD, Paris

Blanchflower, D. G. and Oswald, A. J. (2000) 'Well-being over time in Britain and the USA', *NBER working papers series*, no 7487, NBER, Cambridge, MA

Böckenförde, E.W. (ed) (1987) *Menschenrechte und Menschenwürde. Historische Voraussetzungen, säkulare Gestalt, christliches Verständnis*, Klett-Cotta, Stuttgart

Boettcher, F. and Tremmel, J. (2005) 'Generationengerechtigkeit in der Finanzverfassung', FRFG-Study no 1, www.generationengerechtigkeit.de/images/stories/Publikationen/artikel_studien/studie_finanzverfassung.pdf accessed 20 December 2007

Bohmeyer, A. (2007) 'Der moralische Status zukünftiger Generationen', *Intergenerational Justice Review / Generationengerechtigkeit!* (German edition), vol 7, no 4, pp16–19

Bomsdorf, E. (2004) 'Horizontale, vertikale und diagonale Gerechtigkeit. Anmerkungen zur Messung von Generationengerechtigkeit in der Alterssicherung', in VDR (ed) *Generationengerechtigkeit – Inhalt, Bedeutung und Konsequenzen für die Alterssicherung*, DRV-Schriften, Frankfurt am Main, pp85–93

Bond, M. (2003) 'The pursuit of happiness', *New Scientist*, no 2415 (online edition), www.newscientist.com/article/mg18024155.100-the-pursuit-of-happiness.html accessed 22 November 2006

Bourdieu, P. (1983) 'Ökonomisches Kapital, kulturelles Kapital, soziales Kapital', in Kreckel, R. (ed) *Soziale Ungleichheiten. Soziale Welt: Special vol. 2*, Schwartz, Göttingen, pp187–198

Bourdieu, P. (1986) 'The forms of capital' in Richardson, J. G. (ed) *Handbook of Theory and Research for the Sociology of Education*, Greenwood Press, Westport, CT

Bourg, D. (2006) 'The French constitutional charter for the environment: An effective instrument?', in Tremmel, J. C. (ed) *Handbook of Intergenerational Justice*, Edward Elgar Publishing, Cheltenham, pp230–243

Brandt, R. B. (1955) 'The definition of an "ideal observer" theory in ethics', *Philosophy and Phenomenological Research*, vol 15, pp407–413

Brandt, R. B. (1959) *Ethical Theory*, Englewood Cliffs, Prentice-Hall, New York, NY

Brandt, R. B. (ed) (1962) *Social Justice*, Englewood Cliffs, Prentice-Hall, New York, NY

Brandt, R. B (1979) *A Theory of the Good and the Right*, Clarendon, Oxford

Braudel, F. (1981) *The Structures of Everyday Life: The Limits of the Possible*, Collins, London (French original edition: *Les Structures du Quotidian*)

Brecht, B. (2004) *Die Dreigroschenoper*, Suhrkamp, Frankfurt am Main (first published in 1928)

Brehm, J. and Rahn, W. (1997) 'Individual-level evidence for the causes and consequences of social capital', *American Journal of Political Science*, vol 41, pp999–1023

Brickman, P. and Campbell, D.T. (1971) 'Hedonic relativism and planning the good society', in Apley, M. H. (ed) *Adaptation-level Theory: A Symposium*, Academic Press, New York, NY, pp287–302

Brock, D. (1993) 'Quality of life measures in health care and medical ethics', in Nussbaum, M. and Sen, A. (eds) *The Quality of Life*, Oxford University Press, Oxford, pp95–132

Brock, L. (1998) 'Umwelt und Konflikt im internationalen Forschungskontext', in Carius, A. and Lietzmann, K. M. (eds) *Umwelt und Sicherheit. Herausforderungen für die internationale Politik*, Springer, Heidelberg, pp39–56

Brown-Weiss, E. (1989) *In Fairness to Future Generations*, United Nations University and Transnational Publishers, Tokyo/New York, NY

Brown-Weiss, E. (2002) 'Intergenerational fairness and rights of future generations', *Intergenerational Justice Review* (English edition), vol 2, no 3, pp1–5

Brülde, B. (2007a) 'Happiness theories of the good life. Introduction and conceptual framework', *Journal of Happiness Studies*, vol 8, no 1, pp1–14

Brülde, B. (2007b) 'Happiness theories of the good life', *Journal of Happiness Studies*, vol 8, no 1, pp15–49

Bruni, L. and Porta, P. L. (eds) (2007) *Economics and Happiness. Framing the Analysis*, Oxford University Press, Oxford (first published as hardcover 2005)

Buchanan, J. (1975) *The Limits of Liberty. Between Anarchy and Leviathan*, University of Chicago Press, Chicago, IL

Buchholz, W. (1984) *Intergenerationelle Gerechtigkeit und erschöpfbare Ressourcen*, Duncker und Humblot, Berlin

Bude, H. (2000a) 'Qualitative Generationsforschung', in Flick, U., von Kardorff, E. and Steinke, I. (eds) *Qualitative Forschung. Ein Handbuch*, Rowohlt, Hamburg, pp187–194

Bude, H. (2000b) 'Die biographische Relevanz der Generation', in Kohli, M. and Szydlik, M. (eds) *Generationen in Familie und Gesellschaft*, Leske und Budrich, Opladen, pp19–35

Buhlmann, T. (2000) 'Zur Entwicklung der Lebensqualität im vereinten Deutschland', *Politik und Zeitgeschichte*, vol 40, www.bpb.de/publikationen/P3VSTZ,0,0,Zur_Entwicklung_der_Lebensqualit%E4t_im_vereinten_Deutschland.html accessed 23 November 2007

Bundesregierung von Deutschland (2002) 'Unsere Strategie für eine nachhaltige Entwicklung', April, Bundesregierung von Deutschland, Berlin

Burt, R. (1999) 'The social capital of opinion leaders', *Annals of the American Academy of Political and Social Science*, vol 566, pp37–54

Carens, J. (1981) *Equality, Moral Incentives and the Market*, Chicago University Press, Chicago, IL

Carnap, R. (1959) *Induktive Logik und Wahrscheinlichkeit*, Springer, Wien

Cassese, A. (1996) *International Law in a Divided World*, Clarendon Press, Oxford

Chekola, M. (2007) 'Happiness, rationality, autonomy and the good life', *Journal of Happiness Studies*, vol 8, no 1, pp51–78

Cincotta, R. and Engelmann, R. (2001) *Mensch, Natur! Deutsche Stiftung Weltbevölkerung*, Balance-Verlag, Stuttgart

Clark, A. E. and Oswald, A. J. (1996) 'Satisfaction and comparison income', *Journal of Public Economics*, no 61, pp359–381

Coleman, J. S. (1988) 'Social capital in the creation of human capital', *American Journal of Sociology*, vol 94 Supplement, pp95–120

Costa, P. T. and McCrae, R. R. (1988) 'Personality in adulthood: A six-year longitudinal study of self-reports and spouse ratings on the NEO Personality Inventory', *Journal of Personality and Social Psychology*, vol 54, no 5, pp853–863

Costanza, R. et al. (1998) 'The value of the world's ecosystem services and natural capital', *Ecological Economics*, vol 25, no 1, pp3–15

Costanza, R. (ed) (2001) *Einführung in die ökologische Ökonomik*, German edition, translated by H. Bruns, edited by T. Eser, J. Schwaab, I. Seidl, Lucius und Lucius, Stuttgart

Cowen, T. and Parfit, D. (1992) 'Against the social discount rate', in Laslett, P. and Fishkin, J. S. (eds) *Justice between Age Groups and Generations*, Yale University Press, New Haven, CT/London, pp144–161

Crisp, R. (2003) 'Equality, priority, and compassion', *Ethics*, vol 113, pp745–763

Csikszentmihalyi, M. (1990) *Flow. The Psychology of Optimal Experience*, Harper Collins, New York, NY

Cummins, R., Arita, B. and Baltatescu, S. (2006) 'The International Wellbeing Index: A Psychometric Progress Report', http://acqol.deakin.edu.au/inter_wellbeing/nov-dec/International-Wellbeing-Index.ppt accessed 23 November 2007

Dabrock, P. (2006) 'Rationierung von Gesundheitsleistungen aus Altersgründen? Perspektiven theologischer Ethik unter Berücksichtigung intergenerationeller Gerechtigkeit', in Brink, A., Eurich, J., Hädrich, J., Langer, A. and Schröder, P. (eds) *Gerechtigkeit im Gesundheitswesen*, Duncker & Humblot, Berlin, pp105–123

D'Agostino, F. (2003) 'Original position', *Stanford Encyclopedia of Philosophy*, http://plato.stanford.edu/entries/original-position// accessed 20 August 2008

Dahrendorf, R. (1971) *Homo Sociologicus*, Westdeutscher Verlag, Opladen

Dallinger, U. (2005) 'Generationengerechtigkeit – Wahrnehmung in der Bevölkerung', *Politik und Zeitgeschichte*, no 8, pp29–37

Daly, H. (1991) 'Elements of environmental macroeconomics', in Costanza, R. (ed) *Ecological Economics: The Science and Management of Sustainability*, Columbia University Press, New York, NY, pp32–46

Daly, H. and Cobb, J. B. Jr. (1989) *For the Common Good: Redirecting the Economy Towards Community, the Environment, and a Sustainable Future*, Beacon Press, Boston, MA

Daniels, N. (ed) (1975) *Reading Rawls*, Blackwell, Oxford

Daniels, N. (1988) *Am I my Parents' Keeper? An Essay on Justice between the Young and the Old*, Oxford University Press, Oxford

Däubler-Gmelin, H. (2000) 'Leserbrief', *Zeitschrift für Rechtspolitik*, vol 33, no 1, pp27–28

Dauenhauer, B. P. (2002) 'Response to Rawls', in Cohen, R. A. and Marsh, J. L. (eds) *Ricoeur as Another: The Ethics of Subjectivity*, State University of New York Press, New York, NY, pp203–220

Davidson, R. (2000) 'Affective style, psychopathology and resilience: Brain mechanisms and plasticity', *American Psychologist*, vol 55, pp1196–1214

De George, R. T. (1980) 'The environment, rights, and future generations', in Partridge, E. (ed) *Responsibilities to Future Generations. Environmental Ethics*, Prometheus Books Buffalo, NY, pp157–166

de La Mettrie, J. O. (1985) *Über das Glück oder das höchste Gut*, edited by B. A. Laska, LSR-Verlag, Nürnberg (first published in 1751)

Delattre, E. (1972) 'Rights, responsibilites, and future persons', *Ethics*, vol 82, pp254–258

Del Vecchio, G. (1950) *Die Gerechtigkeit*, 2nd edition, Verlag für Recht und Gesellschaft, Basel

de Mandeville, B. (1968) *Die Bienenfabel oder Private Laster, öffentliche Vorteile*, (English original edition: *The Fable of the Bees or Private Vices, Public Benefits*), Suhrkamp, Frankfurt (first published in 1714)

Derr, T. S. (1980) 'The obligation to the future', in Partridge, E. (ed) *Responsibilities to Future Generations. Environmental Ethics*, Buffalo, NY, Prometheus Books, pp37–45

De-Shalit, A. (1992) 'Environmental policies and justice between generations. On the need for a comprehensive theory of justice between generations', *European Journal of Political Research*, vol 21, pp307–316

De-Shalit, A. (1995) *Why Posterity Matters. Environmental Policies and Future Generations*, Routledge, London/New York, NY

Deutsche Bundesbank (1993), 'Zur Vermögenssituation der privaten Haushalte in Deutschland', *Monthly Report October*, pp19–32

Deutsche Bundesbank (2001) 'Zur langfristigen Tragfähigkeit der öffentlichen Haushalte – eine Analyse anhand der Generationenbilanzierung', *Monthly Report December*

Deutsche Bundesbank (2003) 'Die gesamtwirtschaftlichen Finanzierungsströme im Jahr 2002', *Monthly Report June*, pp29–49

Diamond, J. M. (1992) *The Third Chimpanzee: The Evolution and Future of the Human Animal*, HarperCollins, New York, NY

Diener, E. (1994) 'Assessing subjective wellbeing: Progress and opportunities', *Social Indicators Research*, vol 31, pp103–157

Diener, E. and Suh, E. (1997) 'Measuring quality of life: Economic, social and subjective indicators', *Social Indicators Research*, no 40, pp189–216

Dierksmeier, C. (2006) 'John Rawls on the rights of future generations', in Tremmel, J. C. (ed) *Handbook of Intergenerational Justice*, Edward Elgar Publishing, Cheltenham, pp72–85

Di Tella, R., MacCulloch, R. J. and Oswald, A. (1999) 'How do macroeconomic fluctuations affect happiness?', Harvard Business School, mimeo

Dobson, A. (2000) *Green Political Thought*, 3rd edition, Unwin Hyman, London (1st edition 1990)

Doyal, L. and Gough, I. (1991) *A Theory of Human Need*, MacMillan, Basingstoke

Dreier, R. (1991) 'Recht und Gerechtigkeit', in Dreier, R. (ed) *Recht – Staat – Vernunft*, Suhrkamp, Frankfurt am Main, pp8–38

Drewnowski, J. (1974) *On Measuring and Planning the Quality of Life*, Mouton, The Hague

Druwe, U. and Kunz, V. (eds) (1999) *Politische Gerechtigkeit*, Leske und Budrich, Opladen

Duesenberry, J. S. (1949) *Income, Saving, and the Theory of Consumer Behavior*, Harvard University Press, Cambridge, MA

Duncan, O. D. (1975) 'Does money buy satisfaction?', *Social Indicators Research*, vol 2, pp267–274

Dworkin, R. (1981a) 'What is equality? Part 1: Equality of welfare', *Philosophy & Public Affairs*, no 10, pp185–246

Dworkin, R. (1981b) 'What is equality? Part 2: Equality of resources', *Philosophy & Public Affairs*, no 4, pp283–345

Dworkin, R. (2000) *Sovereign Virtue*, Harvard University Press, Cambridge, MA

Easterlin, R. A. (1974) 'Does economic growth improve the human lot? Some empirical evidence', in David, P. A. and Reder, M. W. (eds) *Nations and Households in Economic Growth*, Academic Press, New York, NY, pp89–125

Easterlin, R. A. (1980) *Birth and Fortune. The Impact of Numbers on Personal Fortune*, Basic Books, New York, NY

Easterlin, R. A. (2001) 'Life cycle welfare: Trends and differences', *Journal of Happiness Studies*, vol 2, no 1, pp1–12

Easterlin, R. A. (2002) 'Is reported happiness five years ago comparable to present happiness? A cautionary note', *Journal of Happiness Studies*, vol 3, no 2, pp193–197

Easterlin, R. A. (2005) 'Feeding the illusion of growth and happiness. A reply to Hagarty and Veenhoven', *Social Indicators Research*, vol 74, no 3, pp429–443

Easterlin, R. A. (2007) 'Building a better theory of wellbeing', in Bruni, L. and Porta, P. (eds) *Economics & Happiness. Framing the Analysis*, Oxford University Press, Oxford, pp29–64

Eckersley, R. (2000) 'The mixed blessings of material progress: Diminishing returns in the pursuit of happiness', *Journal of Happiness Studies*, vol 1, no 3, pp267–292

Ederer, P., Schuller, P. and Willms, S. (2002) *Wieviel Bildung brauchen wir? Humankapital in Deutschland und seine Erträge*, Alfred Herrhausen Gesellschaft, Frankfurt am Main

Ederer, P., Schuller, P. and Willms, S. (2006) 'The economic sustainability indicator', in Tremmel, J. C. (ed) *Handbook of Intergenerational Justice*, Edward Elgar Publishing, Cheltenham, pp129–147

Ehmke, H. (1953) *Grenzen der Verfassungsänderung*, Duncker & Humblot, Berlin

Elliot, R. (1989) 'The rights of future people', *Journal of Applied Philosophy*, vol 6, no 2, pp159–169

El Serafy, S. (1988) 'The proper calculation of income from depletable natural resources', in Lutz, E. and El Serafy, S. (eds) *Environmental and Resource Accounting and their Relevance to the Measurement of Sustainable Income*, World Bank, Washington DC

Elster, J. (1989) *The Cement of Society*, Cambridge University Press, Cambridge

Engels, W., Sablotny, H. and Zickler, D. (1974) *Das Volksvermögen. Seine verteilungs- und wohlstandspolitische Bedeutung*, Herder und Herder, Frankfurt am Main/New York, NY

English, J. (1977) 'Justice between generations', *Philosophical Studies*, vol 31, pp91–104

Enquete Commission of the German Bundestag (Schutz des Menschen und der Umwelt) (1994) *Die Industriegesellschaft gestalten. Perspektiven für einen nachhaltigen Umgang mit Stoff- und Materialströmen*, Schutz des Menschen und der Umwelt, Bonn

Epictetus (2007) 'Stoische Lebenskunst', in Michel, S. (ed) *Glück. Ein philosophischer Streifzug*, Fischer, Frankfurt am Main, pp33–43

Epicurus (2007) 'Brief an Menoikeus', in Michel, S. (ed) *Glück. Ein philosophischer Streifzug*, Fischer, Frankfurt am Main, pp19–24

Erikson, R. (1993) 'Descriptions of inequility: The Swedish approach to welfare research', in Nussbaum, M. C. and Sen, A. (eds) *The Quality of Life*, Oxford University Press, Oxford, pp67–83

Ernst, G. (2007) *Einführung in die Erkenntnistheorie*, WGB, Darmstadt

Essler, W. K. (1970) *Wissenschaftstheorie. Vol. 1: Definition und Reduktion*, Alber, Freiburg

Estes, R. J. (2004) 'Development challenges of the "New Europe"', *Social Indicators Research*, no 69, pp123–166

Ewerhart, G. (2001) 'Bildungsinvestitionen, Bildungsvermögen und Abschreibungen auf Bildung', *Beiträge zur Arbeitsmarkt- und Berufsforschung*, vol 247, pp127–134

Feeser-Lichterfeld, U. (2008) 'Intergenerational justice in an extreme longevity scenario: Ethical issues in biogerontological endeavours', in SRzG (ed) *Demographic Change and Intergenerational Justice*, Springer, Berlin/New York, NY

Feess, E. (1997) *Mikroökonomie: Eine spieltheoretisch- und anwendungsorientierte Einführung*, Metropolis-Verlag, Marburg

Fehige, C. and Wessels, U. (eds) (1998) *Preferences*, de Gruyter, Berlin

Feinberg, J. (1973) *Social Philosophy*, Prentice-Hall, Englewood Cliffs

Feinberg, J. (1980) 'The rights of animals and unborn generations', in Partridge, E. (ed) *Responsibilities to Future Generations. Environmental Ethics*, Prometheus Books, Buffalo, NY, pp139–150

Fernández-Dols, J. and Ruiz-Belda, M. (1990) 'Are smiles a sign of happiness? Gold medal winners at the Olympic Games', *Journal of Personality and Social Psychology*, vol 69, no 6, pp1113–1119

Feuerbach, L. (2007) 'Glück und Moral', in Michel, S. (ed) *Glück. Ein philosophischer Streifzug*, Fischer, Frankfurt am Main, pp111–118, from 'Aus der nachgelassenen Studie Zur Ethik: Der Eudämonismus', in Schmidt, A. (ed) (1985) *Anthropologischer Materialismus: Ausgewählte Schriften*, vol 2, Ullstein, Frankfurt am Main/Berlin/Wien, p249; pp252–258

Field, J. (2003) *Social Capital*, Routledge, London/New York, NY

Fox, W. (1990) *Toward a Transpersonal Ecology: Developing New Foundations for Environmentalism*, Shambhala, Boston, MA

Frank, R. H. (2007) 'Does absolute income matter', in Bruni, L. and Porta, P. L. (eds) *Economics and Happiness. Framing the Analysis*, Oxford University Press, Oxford, pp65–90

Frankena, W. K. (1963) *Ethics*, Prentice Hall, Englewood Cliffs

Fraser, N. (1997) *Justice Interruptus. Critical Reflections on the 'Postsocialist' Condition*, Routledge, New York, NY/London

Frederick, S. and Loewenstein, G. (1999) 'Hedonic adaptation', in Kahneman, D., Diener, E. and Schwarz, N. (eds) *Wellbeing: The Foundations of Hedonic Psychology*, Russell Sage Foundation, New York, NY, pp302–329

Freud, S. (2007) 'Glück ist nur als "episodisches Phänomen möglich"', in Michel, S. (ed) *Glück. Ein philosophischer Streifzug*, Fischer, Frankfurt am Main, pp69–82

Frey, B. S. and Stutzer, A. (2001) 'What can economists learn from happiness research?', University of Zurich Working Paper no 80/CESifo Working Paper 503, www.cesifo-group.de/portal/page/portal/ifoHome/b-publ/b3publwp/_wp_abstract?p_file_id=5121 accessed 24 November 2007

Fukuyama, F. (1999) 'Social capital and civil society', www.ukzn.ac.za/undphil/collier/Chomsky/Social%20Capital%20and%20Civil%20Society%20-%20Francis%20Fukuyama%20-%20Prepare...pdf accessed 24 November 2007

Gardiner, S. M. (2006) 'Protecting future generations: Intergenerational buck-passing, theoretical ineptitude and a brief for a global core precautionary principle', in Tremmel, J. C. (ed) *Handbook of Intergenerational Justice*, Edward Elgar Publishing, Cheltenham, pp148–169

Garrod, G. and Willis, K.G. (1999) *Economic Valuation of the Environment*, Edward Elgar, Cheltenham.

Gauthier, D. (1986) *Morals by Agreement*, Clarendon Press, Oxford

Gewirth, A. (1982) *Human Rights. Essays on Justification and Applications*, University of Chicago Press, Chicago, IL/London

Glatzer, W. (2006) 'Quality of life in the European Union and the United States of America: Evidence from comprehensive indices', *Applied Research in Quality of Life*, no 1, pp169–188

Glover, J. (ed) (1990) *Utilitarianism and its Critics*, Macmillan, New York, NY

Godard, O. (2006) 'Justice ou Promesses pour les Générations Futures', *Intergenerational Justice Review* (French–German bilingual edition), vol 6, no 1, pp19–20

Godechot, J. (ed) (1979) *Les Constitutions de la France depuis 1798*, Garnier-Flammarion, Paris

Goklany, I. M. (2007) *The Improving State of the World*, CATO Institute, Washington DC

Golding, M. P. (1980) 'Obligations to future generations', in Partridge, E. (ed) *Responsibilities to Future Generations*, Promtheus Books, Buffalo, NY, pp61–72

Goodin, R. E. (1985) *Protecting the Vulnerable*, University of Chicago Press, Chicago, IL

Goodin, R. E. (1995) *Utilitarianism as a Public Philosophy*, Cambridge University Press, Cambridge

Goodin, R. E. (1996) 'Enfranchising the earth, and its alternatives', *Political Studies*, vol 44, no 5, pp835–849

Goodpaster, K. (1978) 'On being morally considerable', *Journal of Philosophy*, vol 75, pp308–325

Gosepath, S. (2004) *Gleiche Gerechtigkeit. Grundlagen eines liberalen Egalitarismus*, Suhrkamp, Frankfurt am Main

Gosseries, A. (2002) 'Intergenerational justice', in LaFollette, H. (ed) *The Oxford Handbook of Practical Ethics*, Oxford University Press, Oxford, pp459–484

Gosseries, A. (2004a) *Penser la justice entre les générations: De l'affaire Perruche á la réforme de retraites*, Éditions Flammarion, Paris

Gosseries, A. (2004b) 'Constitutionalizing future rights?', *Intergenerational Justice Review* (English edition), vol 4, no 2, pp10–11

Gosseries, A. (2005) 'The egalitarian case against Brundtland's sustainability', *GAIA*, vol 14, no 1, pp40–46

Gosseries, A. (2008) 'On future generations' future rights', *Journal for Political Philosophy*, vol 16, no 4, pp446–474

Gouldner, A. W. (1961) 'The norm of reciprocity', *American Sociological Review*, vol 25, pp161–189

Gowdy, J. M. and McDaniel, C. N. (1999) 'The physical destruction of Nauru: An example of weak sustainability', *Land Economics*, vol 75, pp333–338

Granovetter, M. (1973) 'The strength of weak ties', *American Journal of Sociology*, vol 78, no 6, pp1360–1380

Griffin, J. (2007) 'What do happiness studies study?', *Journal of Happiness Studies*, vol 8, no 1, pp139–148

Grütz, J. (1999) 'Generational Accounting – Buchhaltung für die Generationen: Einige Anmerkungen zu Vorgehen und Aussagekraft', *Soziale Sicherheit*, no 4, pp165–176

Gukenbiehl, H. L. (1995) 'Generation', in Schäfers, B. (ed) *Grundbegriffe der Soziologie*, Leske und Budrich, Opladen, pp89–90

Haber, J. A. (2004) 'Generationengerechtigkeit – einige Anmerkungen methodologischer Natur', *Intergenerational Justice Review* (German–Polish bilingual edition), vol 4, no 4, pp16–20

Haber, W. (2001) 'Ökologie und Nachhaltigkeit. Einführung in die Grundprinzipien der theoretischen Ökologie', in Di Blasi, L., Goebel, B. and Hösle, V. (eds) *Nachhaltigkeit in der Ökologie. Wege in eine zukunftsfähige Welt*, Beck, München, pp66–95

Haeberle, P. (2006) 'A constitutional law for future generations – the 'other' form of the social contract: The generation contract', in Tremmel, J. C. (ed) *Handbook of Intergenerational Justice*, Edward Elgar Publishing, Cheltenham, pp215–229

Halbfass, W. (2000) *Karma und Wiedergeburt im indischen Denken*, Hugendubel, Kreuzlingen/München

Halpern, D. (2004) *Social Capital*, Polity Press, Cambridge, MA

Hampicke, U. (1991) 'Neoklassik und Zeitpräferenz: der Diskontierungsnebel', in Berenbach, F. (ed) *Die ökologische Herausforderung für die ökonomische Theorie*, Metropolis-Verlag, Marburg, pp127–150

Hampicke, U. (2001) 'Grenzen der monetären Bewertung – Kosten-Nutzen-Analyse und globales Klima', in *Jahrbuch Ökologische Ökonomik*, vol 2, Metropolis, Marburg, pp151–179

Hanifan, L. J. (1920) *The Community Center*, Silver, Burdett & Company, Boston, MA

Hansen, J., Sato, M., Kharecha, P., Beerling, D., Berner, R., Masson-Delmotte, V., Pagani, M., Raymo, M., Royer, D. and Zachos, J. (2008) 'Target atmosphere CO_2: Where should humanity aim?' *The Open Atmospheric Science Journal*, vol 2, pp217–231.

Hardin, G. (1968) 'The tragedy of the commons', *Science*, vol 162, no 12, pp1243–1248

Hare, R. M. (1987) 'Moral reasoning about the environment', *Journal of Applied Philosophy*, vol 4, no 1, pp3–14

Hare, R. M. (1982) 'Ethical theory and utilitarianism', in Sen, A.K. and Williams, B. (eds) *Utilitarianism and Beyond*, Cambridge University Press, Cambridge, pp23–38

Harsanyi, J. C. (1977) *Rational Behavior and Bargaining Equilibrium in Games and Social Situations*, Cambridge University Press, Cambridge

Harsanyi, J. C. (1982) 'Morality and the theory of rational behavior'. in Sen, A.K. and Williams, B. (eds) *Utilitarianism and Beyond*, Cambridge University Press, Cambridge, pp 39–62

Hart, H. L. A. (1973) *Bentham on Legal Rights. Oxford Essays in Jurisprudence. Second Series*, Oxford University Press, Oxford

Hart, H. L. A. (1984) 'Are there any natural rights?', in Waldron, J. (ed) *Theories of Rights*, Oxford University Press, Oxford, pp77–90

Haumann, W. (2006) *Generationen-Barometer 2006. A survey by the Institut für Demoskopie Allensbach*, edited by FORUM FAMILIE STARK MACHEN, Verlag Karl Alber, Freiburg im Breisgau

Hauser, R. (2004) 'Generationengerechtigkeit, Volksvermögen und Vererbung', in Böhning, B. and Burmeister, K. (eds) *Generationen & Gerechtigkeit*, VSA-Verlag, Hamburg, pp29–44

Hauser, R. (2007) 'Soziale Gerechtigkeit in Deutschland – Zieldimensionen und empirische Befunde am Beispiel der Generationengerechtigkeit', in Empter, S. and Vehrkamp, R. B. (eds) *Soziale Gerechtigkeit in Deutschland: Eine Bestandsaufnahme*, Verlag Bertelsmann Stiftung, Gütersloh, pp136–167

Haybron, D. (2000) 'Two philosophical problems in the study of happiness', *Journal of Happiness Studies*, vol 1, no 2, pp207–225

Haybron, D. (2007) 'Life satisfaction, ethical reflection, and the science of happiness', *Journal of Happiness Studies*, vol 8, no 1, pp99–138

Headey, B. and Wearing, A. (1992) *Understanding Happiness: A Theory of Subjective Well-being*, Longman Cheshire, Melbourne

Held, M. and Nutzinger, H. G. (2001) (eds) *Nachhaltiges Naturkapital*, Campus-Verlag, Frankfurt am Main

Hesselberger, D. (2000) *Das Grundgesetz. 11. Auflage*, Bundeszentrale für Politische Bildung, Bonn

Heubach, A. (2008) *Generationengerechtigkeit – Herausforderung für die zeitgenössische Ethik*, V&R unipress, Göttingen

Heyd, D. (1992) *Genethics*, University of California Press, Berkeley, CA

Heylighen, F. and Bernheim, J. (2000) 'Global progress I. Empirical evidence for ongoing increase of quality-of-life', *Journal of Happiness Studies*, vol 1, no 3, pp323–349

Hobbes, T. (1985) *Leviathan*, Penguin Books, London (first published 1651)

Hobbes, T. (1994) *Vom Menschen. Vom Bürger*, edited by G. Gawlick, Meiner, Hamburg (first published 1642)

Höffe, O. (ed) (1974) *Einführung in die utilitaristische Ethik. Klassische und zeitgenössische Texte*, Francke, Tübingen

Höffe, O. (1994a) 'Tauschgerechtigkeit und korrektive Gerechtigkeit', in Grimm, D. (ed) *Staatsaufgaben*, Nomos-Verlags-Gesellschaft, Baden-Baden, pp713–737

Höffe, O. (1994b) *Politische Gerechtigkeit*, Suhrkamp, Frankfurt am Main

Höffe, O. (1998a): 'Einführung in Rawls' theorie der gerechtigkeit', in Höffe, O. (ed) *John Rawls: Eine Theorie der Gerechtigkeit. Klassiker auslegen*, vol 15, Akademie-Verlag, Berlin, pp3–26

Höffe, O. (1998b) 'Zur Gerechtigkeit der Verteilung', in Höffe, O. (ed) *John Rawls: Eine Theorie der Gerechtigkeit. Klassiker auslegen*, vol 15, Akademie-Verlag, Berlin, pp169–186

Höffe, O. (2001) *Gerechtigkeit. Eine philosophische Einführung*, Beck, München

Höffe, O. (2007a) 'Gerechtigkeit zwischen den Generationen', *Intergenerational Justice Review / Generationengerechtigkeit!* (German edition), vol 7, no 4, pp4–6

Höffe, O. (2007b) *Lebenskunst und Moral. Oder: Macht Tugend glücklich?*, Beck, München

Hohfeld, W. N. (1919) *Fundamental Legal Conceptions as Applied in Judicial Reasoning*, Yale University Press, New Haven, CT

Hondrich, K. (2001) *Der neue Mensch*, Suhrkamp, Frankfurt am Main

Honoré, T. (1970) 'Social justice', in Summers, R. S. (ed) *Essays in Legal Philosophy*, Blackwell, Oxford, pp61–94

Horn, C. (1998) *Antike Lebenskunst. Glück und Moral von Sokrates bis zu den Neuplatonikern*, Beck, München

Horn, C. and Scarano, N. (eds) (2002) *Philosophie der Gerechtigkeit*, Suhrkamp, Frankfurt am Main

Hörnquist, J. O. (1982) 'The concept of quality of life', *Scandinavian Journal of Social Medicine*, vol 10, no 2, pp57–61

Hösle, V. (1997) *Moral und Politik. Grundlagen einer politischen Ethik für das 21. Jahrhundert*, Beck, München

Hösle, V. (2002) 'Stellungnahme zur These Ist der Verbrauch nicht-erneuerbarer Ressourcen ein Unrecht an kommenden Generationen?', *Intergenerational Justice Review / Generationengerechtigkeit!* (German edition), vol 2, no 2, pp14–16

Hösle, V. (2003) 'Dimensionen der ökologischen Krise – Wege in eine generationengerechte Welt', in Stiftung für die Rechte zukünftiger Generationen (ed) *Handbuch Generationengerechtigkeit*, Oekom-Verlag, München, pp125–152

Howard-Hassmann, R. E. (2008) *Reparations to Africa*, University of Pennsylvania Press, Philadelphia, PA

Hubin, D. C. (1976) 'Justice and future generations', *Philosophy and Public Affairs*, vol 6, no 1, pp70–83

Hume, D. (1975) 'An enquiry concerning the principles of morals', in Selby-Bigge, L. A. (ed) *Enquiries Concerning Human Understanding and Concerning the Principles of Morals*, 3rd edition with text revised and notes by P. H. Nidditch, Clarendon Press, Oxford (first published in 1751)

Hunt, L. (2007) *Inventing Human Rights*, W.W. Norton & Company, New York, NY

Hutcheson, F. (1728) *An Essay on the Nature and Conduct of the Passions and Affections*, James & John Knapton, London

Inglehart, R. (1997) *Modernization and Postmodernization. Cultural, Economic, and Political Change in 43 Societies*, Princeton University Press, Princeton, NJ

Inglehart, R., Foa, R., Peterson, C. and Welzel, C. (2008) 'Development, freedom, and rising happiness', *Perspectives on Psychological Science*, vol 3, no 2, pp264–285

IPCC (Intergovernmental Panel on Climate Change) (2007) *Climate Change 2007: Impacts, Adaptation and Vulnerability*, Working Group II Contribution to the Fourth Assessment Report, Cambridge University Press, Cambridge (see also www.ipcc.ch)

Ishay, M. R. (2004) *The History of Human Rights. From Ancient Times to the Globalization Era*, University of California Press, Berkeley, CA

Jackson, A. (1996) 'Wrongful life and wrongful birth', *Journal of Legal Medicine*, vol 17, no 3, pp349–381

Jávor, B. (2006) 'Institutional protection of succeeding generations: Ombudsman for future generations in Hungary', in Tremmel, J. C. (ed) *Handbook of Intergenerational Justice*, Edward Elgar Publishing, Cheltenham, pp282–298

Johnson, L. E. (1991) *A Morally Deep World: An Essay on the Moral Significance and Environmental Ethics*, Cambridge University Press, Cambridge

Jonas, H. (1979) *Das Prinzip Verantwortung. Versuch einer Ethik für die technologische Zivilisation*, Suhrkamp, Frankfurt am Main

Jonas, H. (1980) 'Technology and responsibility: The ethics of an endangered future', in Partridge, E. (ed) *Responsibilities to Future Generations. Environmental Ethics*, Prometheus Books, Buffalo, NY, pp23–36

Jureit, U. and Wildt, M. (2005) 'Generationen', in Jureit, U. and Wildt, M. (eds) *Generationen. Zur Relevanz eines wissenschaftlichen Grundbegriffs*, Hamburger Edition, Hamburg, pp7–26

Kahneman, D. (1999) 'Objective happiness', in Kahneman, D., Diener, E. and Schwarz, N. (eds) *Wellbeing: The Foundations of Hedonic Psychology*, Russell Sage Foundation, New York, NY, pp3–25

Kahneman, D., Krueger, A., Schkade, D., Schwartz, N. and Stone, A. A. (2004) 'A survey method for characterizing daily life experience: The day reconstruction method', *Science*, no 3, pp1776–1780

Kamlah, W. and Lorenzen, P. (1967) *Logische Propädeutik oder Vorschule des vernünftigen Redens*, Bibliographisches Institut, Mannheim

Kant, I. (1949) *Idee zu einer allgemeinen Geschichte in weltbürgerlicher Absicht*, Verlag Öffentliches Leben GmbH, Göttingen/Hamburg (first published in 1785)

Kant, I. (1968a) *Kritik der praktischen Vernunft. Collected Works Edition. vol VII*, edited by W. Weischedel, Suhrkamp Verlag, Frankfurt am Main (first published in 1781)

Kant, I. (1968b) *Die Metaphysik der Sitten. Collected Works Edition. vol VIII*, edited by W. Weischedel, Suhrkamp Verlag, Frankfurt am Main (first published in 1797)

Kavka, G. S. (1978) 'The futurity problem', in Sikora, R. and Barry, B. (eds) *Obligations to Future Generations*, Temple University Press, Philadelphia, PA, pp186–203

Kavka, G. S. (1982) 'The paradox of future individuals', *Philosophy and Public Affairs*, vol 11, no 2, pp93–112

Kelsen, H. (2000) *Was ist Gerechtigkeit?*, Reclam, Stuttgart

Kern, K. (2004) 'Sozialkapital, Netzwerke und Demokratie', in Klein, A., Kern, K., Geißel, B. (eds) *Zivilgesellschaft und Sozialkapital*, VS Verlag für Sozialwissenschaften, Wiesbaden, pp109–129

Kersting, W. (2002a) 'Kontraktualismus', in Düwell, M. (ed) *Handbuch Ethik*, Metzler, Stuttgart/Weimar, pp163–178

Kersting, W. (2002b) *Kritik der Gleichheit. Über die Grenzen der Gerechtigkeit und der Moral*, Velbrück Wiss, Weilerswist

Keyes, C. F. and Daniel, E. V. (eds) (1983) *Karma: An Anthropological Inquiry*, University of California Press, Berkeley, CA

Kilian, E. (2000) 'Generation', in Ralf, S. (ed) *Metzler-Lexikon Kultur der Gegenwart. Themen und Theorien, Formen und Institutionen seit 1945*, Metzler, Stuttgart/Weimar, pp177–179

Kim, T. and Harrison, R. (eds) (1999) *Self and Future Generations*: An Intercultural Conversation, White Horse Press, Cambridge

Kirchgässner, G. (2000) *Homo oeconomicus. Das ökonomische Modell individuellen Verhaltens und seine Anwendung in den Wirtschafts- und Sozialwissenschafte*, 2nd edition, Mohr, Tübingen

Kissler, A. (2003) 'Die Ahnungsvollen', *Süddeutsche Zeitung*, www.sueddeutsche.de/sz/feuilleton/red-artikel1731/ accessed 28 August 2003

Knaus, A. and Renn, O. (1998) *Den Gipfel vor Augen. Unterwegs in eine nachhaltige Zukunft*, Metropolis-Verlag, Marburg

Kohli, M. (2006) 'Aging and justice', in Binstock, R. H. and George, L. K. (eds) *Handbook of Aging and the Social Sciences*, 6th edition, Elsevier, New York, NY, pp457–478

Kohli, M. and Szydlik, M. (2000) 'Einleitung', in Kohli, M. and Szydlik, M. (eds) *Generationen in Familie und Gesellschaft*, Leske und Budrich, Opladen, pp7–18

Koller, P. (2003) 'Soziale Gerechtigkeit. Begriff und Begründung', *Erwägen Wissen Ethik*, vol 14, no 2, pp237–250

Koller, P. (2007) 'Der Begriff der Gerechtigkeit', *Intergenerational Justice Review / Generationengerechtigkeit!*, (German edition), vol 7, no 4, pp7–11

Kopfmüller, J., Brandl, V. and Jörissen, J., Paetau, M., Banse, G., Coenen, R. and Grunwald, A. (2001) *Nachhaltige Entwicklung integrativ betrachtet. Konstitutive Elemente, Regeln, Indikatoren*, Sigma Verlag, Berlin

Koslowski, P. (2005) 'Gerechtigkeit zwischen den Generationen – Globale Perspektiven', in Tremmel, J. and Ulshöfer, G. (eds) *Unternehmensleitbild Generationengerechtigkeit – Theorie und Praxis*, IKO Verlag, Frankfurt am Main, pp187–206

Kraemer, R. A., Blobel, D. and von Raggamby, A. and Knoblauch, D. (2008) 'Demographic change and sustainability: A generational balance', in SRzG (ed) *Demographic Change and Intergenerational Justice*, Springer, Berlin/New York, NY, pp99–125

Krebs, A. (ed) (1997) *Naturethik*, Suhrkamp, Frankfurt am Main

Krebs, A. (ed) (2000a) *Gleichheit oder Gerechtigkeit? Texte der neuen Egalitarismuskritik*, Suhrkamp, Frankfurt am Main

Krebs, A. (2000b) 'Wieviel Natur schulden wir der Zukunft?', in Mittelstraβ, J. (ed) *Die Zukunft des Wissens*, Akademie Verlag, Berlin, pp313–333

Kymlicka, W. (1990) 'Two theories of justice (Review essay on Brian Barry's theories of justice)', *Inquiry*, vol 33, no 1, pp99–119

Kymlicka, W. (1995) *Multicultural Citizenship*, Oxford University Press, Oxford

Lamont, W. D. (1946) *The Principles of Moral Judgement*, Clarendon Press, Oxford

Landweer, H. (1996) 'Generationenkonflikte und Sachdifferenzen. Das Beispiel Frauenbewegung', *Transit*, no 11, pp87–100

Laslett, P. (1971) 'The conversation between generations', in Laslett, P. (ed) *The Proper Study. Royal Institute of Philosophy Lectures*, vol 4, Basil Blackwell, London, pp8–20

Laslett, P. (1992) 'Is there a generational contract?', in Laslett, P. and Fishkin, J. S. (eds) *Justice between Age Groups and Generations*, Yale University Press, New Haven, CT/London, pp24–47

Laslett, P. and Fishkin, J. S. (1992) 'Introduction. Processional justice', in Laslett, P. and Fishkin, J. S. (eds) *Justice between Age Groups and Generations*, Yale University Press, New Haven, CT/London, pp1–23

Lau, C. and Kramer, L. (2005) *Die Relativitätstheorie des Glücks. Über das Leben von Lottomillionären*, Centaurus, Herbolzheim

Layard, R. (2005) *Happiness. Lessons from a New Science*, Penguin, London

Layard, R. (2007) 'Rethinking public economics: The implication of rivalry and habit', in Bruni, L. and Porta, P. L. (eds) *Economics and Happiness. Framing the Analysis*, Oxford University Press, Oxford, pp147–169

Leist, A. (1991) 'Intergenerationelle Gerechtigkeit', in Bayertz, K. (ed) *Praktische Philosophie*, Rowohlt, Reinbek bei Hamburg, pp322–360

Lepsius, M. R. (2002) 'Generationen', in Greiffenhagen, M. and Greiffenhagen, S. (eds) *Handwörterbuch zur politischen Kultur der Bundesrepublik Deutschland*, Westdeutscher Verlag, Wiesbaden, pp162–165

Lerch, A. (2001) 'Naturkapital und Nachhaltigkeit – Normative Begründungen unterschiedlicher Konzepte der nachhaltigen Entwicklung', in Held, M. and Nutzinger, H. G. (eds) *Nachhaltiges Naturkapital*, Campus-Verlag, Frankfurt am Main, pp93–112

Levi, M. (1996) 'Social and unsocial capital: A review essay of Robert Putnam's Making Democracy Work', *Politics and Society*, vol 24, no 1, pp45–55

Lewis, C. I. (1946) *An Analysis of Knowledge and Valuation*, The Open Court Publishing Company, La Salle, IL

Lexis, W. (1875) *Einleitung in die Theorie der Bevölkerungsstatistik*, Trübner, Strassburg

Li, H. (1994) 'Environmental education: Rethinking intergenerational relationship', Ontario Institute for Studies of Education, Philosophy of Education, www.ed.uiuc.edu/EPS/PES-Yearbook/94_docs/LI.HTM#fn2 accessed 1 December 2007

Locke, J. (1965) *Two Treatises of Government*, Second Treatise, edited by P. Laslett, New American Library, New York, NY (first published in 1689)

Lorenz, E. N. (1963) 'Deterministic nonperiodic flow', *Journal of the Atmospheric Sciences*, vol 20, no 2, pp130–141

Lucas, J. R. (1980) *On Justice*, Oxford University Press, Oxford

Lucke, B. (2002) 'Stellungnahme zur These Ist der Verbrauch nicht-erneuerbarer Ressourcen ein Unrecht an kommenden Generationen?', *Intergenerational Justice Review / Generationengerechtigkeit!* (German edition), vol 2, no 2, pp14–16

Lukash, F. S. and Shklar, J. N. (1986) *Justice and Equality Here and Now*, Cornell University Press, Ithaca, NY/London

Lumer, C. (2002) 'Motive zu moralischem Handeln', *Analyse & Kritik*, vol 24, no 2, pp163–188

Lumer, C. (2003) 'Prinzipien der Generationengerechtigkeit', in Stiftung für die Rechte zukünftiger Generationen (ed) *Handbuch Generationengerechtigkeit*, Oekom-Verlag, München, pp105–123

Lüscher, K. (2005) 'Ambivalenz – eine Annäherung an das Problem der Generationen', in Jureit, U. and Wildt, M. (eds) *Generationen. Zur Relevanz eines wissenschaftlichen Grundbegriffs*, Hamburger Edition, Hamburg, pp53–78

MacDonald, M. (1984) 'Natural rights', in Waldron, J. (ed) *Theories of Rights*, Oxford University Press, Oxford, pp21–40

MacIntyre, A. (1981) *After Virtue. A Study in Moral Theory*, Duckworth, London

Macklin, R. (1980) 'Can future generations correctly be said to have rights?', in Partridge, E. (ed) *Responsibilities to Future Generations. Environmental Ethics*, Prometheus Books, Buffalo, NY, pp151–157

Maddison, A. (1995) *Monitoring the World Economy 1820–1992*, OECD Publications, Paris

Marx, K. (1875) 'Randglossen zum Programm der deutschen Arbeiterpartei', in Marx, K. and Engels, F. (eds) *Werke (1972).Vol 19*, Berlin, reprinted in Horn, C. and Scarano, N. (eds) (2002) *Philosophie der Gerechtigkeit*, Suhrkamp, Frankfurt am Main, pp290–298

Marx, K. (1959) 'Paris Manuscripts', in Marx, K. (ed) *Economic and Philosophic Manuscripts of 1844*, Foreign Languages Publishing House, Moscow (first published in 1932)

Marx, K. (1975) 'Das Kapital. Kritik der politischen Ökonomie. Vol 3' in Marx, K. and Engels, F. (eds) *Werke.Vol 25*, Dietz, Berlin (first published in 1894)

Maslow, A. H. (1943) 'A theory of human motivation', *Psychological Review*, vol 50, no 4, pp370–396

Maslow, A. H. (1954) *Motivation and Personality*, 2nd edition, Harper & Row, New York, NY/London

Matravers, M. (2007) 'Happiness and political philosophy: The case of Nancy Mitford versus Evelyn Waugh', in Bruni, L. and Porta, P. L. (eds) *Economics & Happiness. Framing the Analysis*, Oxford University Press, Oxford, pp184–195

Max-Neef, M. (1992) 'Development and human needs', in Ekins, P. and Max-Neef, M. (eds) *Real-life Economics: Understanding Wealth Creation*, Routledge, London, pp197–213

Max-Neef, M. (1995) 'Economic growth and the quality of life: A threshold hypothesis', *Ecological Economics*, vol 15, no 2, pp115–118

McLean, S., Schultz, D. A. and Steger, M. B. (eds) (2002) *Social Capital: Critical Perspectives on Community and 'Bowling Alone'*, New York University Press, New York, NY/London

Meadows, D. L., Meadows, D. H., Randers, J. and Behrens, W. (1972) *The Limits to Growth*, Universe Books, New York, NY

Meyer, L. H. (2003) 'Intergenerational justice', *Stanford Encyclopedia of Philosophy*, http://plato.stanford.edu/entries/justice-intergenerational/ accessed 20 March 2007

Meyer, L. H. (ed) (2004) *Justice in Time. Responding to Historical Injustice*, Nomos, Baden-Baden

Meyer, L. H. (2005) *Historische Gerechtigkeit*, de Gruyter, Berlin/New York, NY

Meyer-Abich, K. M. (1997) 'Ist biologisches Produzieren natürlich? Leitbilder einer naturgemäßen Technik', *GAIA*, no. 4, pp247–252

Mill, J. S. (1979) *Utilitarianism. With an Introduction by George Sher*, Hackett Publishing Company, Indianapolis, IN/Cambridge (first published in 1861) (German edition *Der Utilitarismus*, translated and edited by D. Birnbacher (1976), Reclam, Stuttgart)

Miller, D. (1976) *Social Justice*, Clarendon Press, Oxford

Miller, D. (1989) *Market, State, and Community*, Clarendon Press, Oxford

Miller, D. (2008) *National Responsibility and Global Justice*, Oxford University Press, Oxford

Miller, J. and Kumar, R. (eds) (2007) *Reparations. Interdisciplinary inquiries*, Oxford University Press, Oxford

Milne, H. (1986) 'Desert, effort, and equality', *Journal of Applied Philosophy*, vol 3, no 2, pp235–243

Moore, G. E. (1914) *Ethics*, Home University Library of Modern Knowledge, London (first published in 1903)

Morreim, E. H. (1988) 'The concept of harm reconceived: A different look at wrongful life', *Law and Philosophy*, vol 7, no 1, pp3–33

Morris, C. (1984) 'Existential limits to the rectification of past wrongs', *American Philosophical Quarterly*, vol 21, no 1, pp175–82

Morris, D. M. (1979) *Measuring the Condition of the World's Poor*, Pergamon Press, New York, NY

Motel-Klingebiel, A. and Tesch-Römer, C. (2004) *Generationengerechtigkeit in der sozialen Sicherung. Diskussionspapiere. No. 42*, Deutsches Zentrum für Altersfragen (DZA), Berlin

Mulgan, T. (1999) 'The place of the dead in liberal political philosophy', *Journal of Political Philosophy*, vol 7, no 1, pp52–70

Mulgan, T. (2002) 'Neutrality, rebirth and intergenerational justice', *Journal of Applied Philosophy*, vol 19, no 1, pp3–15

Mulgan, T. (2006) *Future People: A Moderate Consequentialist Account of Our Obligations to Future Generations*, Oxford University Press, Oxford

Müller, H. (2008) 'Zwischen Macht und Gerechtigkeit. Zustand und Perspektiven des nuklearen Nichtverbreitungsregimes', *Politische Vierteljahresschrift*, vol 49, no 3, pp425–437

Muñiz-Fraticelli, V. M. (2002) 'The circumstances of justice across generations' http://ptw.uchicago.eduMuniz02.pdf accessed 20 December 2007

Muñiz-Fraticelli, V. M. (2005) 'Book review: A. Gosseries "Penser la justice entre les générations: De l'affaire Perruche á la réforme de retraites"', *Ethics*, vol 115, no 2, pp412–415

Myers, D. (1993) *The Pursuit of Happiness*, Avon Books, New York, NY

Myers, D. (2003) 'Happiness', www.davidmyers.org accessed 20 January 2008

Nagel, T. (1979) *Mortal Questions*, Cambridge University Press, Cambridge

Narveson, J. (1976) 'Moral problems of population', in Bayles, M. D. (ed) *Ethics and Population*, Schankman, Cambridge, pp59–80

Narveson, J. (1978) 'Future people and us', in Sikora, R. and Barry, B. (eds) *Obligations to Future Generations*, Temple University Press, Philadelphia, PA, pp38–60

Nelson, E. and Robertson, G. (2001) 'Liability for wrongful birth and wrongful life', *ISUMA*, vol 2, no 3, pp102–105

Nelson, J. A. (2006) *Economics for Humans*, University of Chicago Press, Chicago, IL

Neumayer, E. (1999) *Weak versus Strong Sustainability*, Edward Elgar Publishing, Cheltenham

Nielsen, K. (1979) 'Radical egalitarian justice: Justice as equality', *Social Theory and Practice*, vol 5, pp209–226

N.N. (2006) 'Die Oase der Buren', *Der Spiegel*, no 52, 22 December, www.spiegel.de accessed 7 November 2007

Norton, B. G. (1987) *Why Preserve Natural Variety?*, Princeton University Press, Princeton, NJ

Norton, B. G. (1991) *Toward Unity among Environmentalists*, Oxford University Press, Oxford

Norton, B. G. (1992) 'Epistemology and environmental values', *The Monist*, vol 75, pp208–226

Norton, B. G. (1995) 'Why I am not a nonanthropocentrist: Callicott and the failure of monistic inherentism', *Environmental Ethics*, vol 17, no 4, pp341–358

Norton, B. G. (2003) 'Intergenerational equity and sustainability', in Norton, B. G. (ed) *Searching for Sustainability. Interdisciplinary Essays in the Philosophy of Conservation Biology*, Cambridge University Press, Cambridge, pp420–455

Nozick, R. (1974) *Anarchy, State and Utopia*, Blackwell, Oxford

Nozick, R. (1989) *The Examined Life*, Simon & Schuster, New York, NY

Nussbaum, M. C. (1992) 'Human functioning and social justice: In defense of Aristotelian essentialism', *Political Theory*, vol 20, no 2, pp202–246

Nussbaum, M. C. (2007) 'Mill between Aristotle and Bentham', in Bruni, L. and Porta, P. L. (eds) *Economics and Happiness. Framing the Analysis*, Oxford University Press, Oxford, pp170–183

Nussbaum, M. C. and Sen, A. (eds) (1993) *The Quality of Life*, Oxford University Press, Oxford

Nutzinger, H. (ed) (1996) *Naturschutz – Ethik – Ökonomie. Theoretische Begründungen und praktische Konsequenzen*, Metropolis-Verlag, Marburg

OECD (2007) 'Education at a glance', www.oecd.org/dataoecd/4/55/39313286.pdf accessed 20 January 2009

Oeppen, J. and Vaupel, J. W. (2002) 'Broken limits to life expectancy', *Science 296*, pp1029–1031

Offe, C. and Fuchs, S. (2001) 'Schwund des Sozialkapitals? Der Fall Deutschland', in Putnam, R. D. (ed) *Gesellschaft und Gemeinsinn: Sozialkapital im internationalen Vergleich*, Verlag Bertelsmann Stiftung, Gütersloh, pp417–506

O'Flaherty, W. D. (ed) (1980) *Karma and Rebirth in Classical Indian Traditions*, University of California Press, Berkeley, CA

Ohsmann, S. and Stoltz, U. (2004) 'Entwicklung der Rendite in der gesetzlichen Rentenversicherung', *Die Angestelltenversicherung*, vol 51, no 2, pp56–62

O'Neill, J. (1993) 'Future generations: Present harms', *Philosophy*, vol 68, no 1, pp35–51

Opaschowski, H. (2004) *Der Generationenpakt. Das soziale Netz der Zukunft*, Wissenschaftliche Buchgesellschaft, Darmstadt

Oposa, A. (2002) 'In defence of future generations', *Intergenerational Justice Review* (English edition), vol 2, no 3, p7

Opp, K. (2002) *Methodologie der Sozialwissenschaften*, Westdeutscher Verlag, Wiesbaden

Ostrom, E. (2000) 'Social capital: A fad or a fundamental concept?', in Dasgupta, P. and Serageldin, I. (eds) *Social Capital. A Multifaceted Perspective*, The World Bank, Washington DC, pp172–214

Ott, K. (1997) *Ipso Facto*, Suhrkamp, Frankfurt am Main

Ott, K. (2001) *Moralbegründungen zur Einführung*, Junius, Hamburg

Ott, K. (2003) 'Reflections on discounting. Some philosophical remarks', *International Journal of Sustainable Development*, vol 6, no 1, pp7–24

Ott, K. and Döring, R. (2004) *Theorie und Praxis starker Nachhaltigkeit*, Metropolis Verlag, Marburg

Paden, R. (1997) 'Rawls' just savings principle and the sense of justice', *Social Theory and Practice*, vol 23, no 1, pp27–51

Page, E. (2007) *Climate Change, Justice, and Future Generations*, Edward Elgar, Cheltenham

Page, E. (2008) 'Three problems of intergenerational justice', *Intergenerational Justice Review* (English edition), vol 8, no 1, pp9–12

Paine, T. (1996) 'Dissertation on first principles of government', in *The Writings of Thomas Paine. Vol III, 1791–1804*, collected and edited by M. D. Conway, Routledge/Thoemmes, London (reprint of the 1895 edition), pp256–277

Paley, W. (1826) *Principles of Moral and Political Philosophy*, T. & J. Allmann, London

Pappu, S. S. R. R. (ed) (1987) *The Dimensions of Karma*, Chanakya Publications, New Delhi

Parfit, D. (1976) 'On doing the best for our children', in Bayles, M. D. (ed) *Ethics and Population*, Schankman, Cambridge

Parfit, D. (1982) 'Future generations: Further problems', *Philosophy and Public Affairs*, vol 11, no 2, pp113–172

Parfit, D. (1986) 'Comments', in *Ethics*, vol 96, no 4, pp832–872

Parfit, D. (1987) *Reasons and Persons*, Oxford University Press, Oxford, 3rd revised edition (1st edition 1984)

Parfit, D. (2000) 'Gleichheit und Vorrangigkeit', in Krebs, A. (ed) *Gleichheit oder Gerechtigkeit? Texte der neuen Egalitarismuskritik*, Suhrkamp, Frankfurt am Main, pp81–106

Partridge, E. (1980a) 'Introduction', in Partridge, E. (ed) *Responsibilities to Future Generations*, Prometheus Books, Buffalo, NY, pp1–16

Partridge, E. (1980b) 'Why care about the future?' in Partridge, E. (ed) *Responsibilities to Future Generations*, Prometheus Books, Buffalo, NY, pp203–220

Partridge, E. (ed) (1980c) *Responsibilities to Future Generations*, Prometheus Books, Buffalo, NY

Partridge, E. (1981) 'Posthumous interests and posthumous respect', *Ethics*, vol 91, no 2, pp243–264

Partridge, E. (1990) 'On the rights of future generations', in Scherer, D. (ed) *Upstream–Downstream. Issues in Environmental Ethics*, Temple University Press, Philadelphia, PA, pp40–66

Partridge, E. (2007) 'Should we seek a better future?', www.igc.org/gadfly/papers/swsabf.htm accessed 4 January 2008

Partridge, E. (2008) 'Just provision for the future', *Intergenerational Justice Review* (English edition), vol 8, no 1, pp4–8

Pawlowski, T. (1980) *Begriffsbildung und Definition*, De Gruyter, Berlin/New York, NY

Pearce, D. and Turner, K. R. (1990) *Economics of Natural Resources and the Environment*, Harvester Wheatsheaf, London

Perelman, C. (1967) *Über die Gerechtigkeit*, C.H. Beck, München, reprinted in Horn, C. and Scarano, N. (eds) (2002) *Philosophie der Gerechtigkeit*, Suhrkamp, Frankfurt am Main, pp305–311

Perrow, C. (1984) *Normal Accidents. Living with High-Risk Technologies*, Basic Books, New York, NY

Pezzey, J. (1997) 'Sustainability constraints', *Land Economics*, vol 73, no 4, pp448–464

Pieper, J. (1953) *Über die Gerechtigkeit*, Kösel, München

Pieper, A. (2003) *Glückssache. Die Kunst gut zu leben*, Deutscher Taschenbuch Verlag, München (first hardcover edition 2001)

Pigou, A. C. (1932) *The Economics of Welfare*, MacMillan and Co, London (first published 1920)

Plato (1958) 'Der Staat (Politea)', in *Platon. Sämtliche Werke*, vol 3, Rowohlt, Hamburg

Plato (1971) *Gorgias*, translated by F. Schleiermacher, edited by G. Eigler, Wissenschaftliche Buchgesellschaft, Darmstadt

Pletcher, G. (1980) 'The rights of future generations', in Partridge, E. (ed) *Responsibilities to Future Generations. Environmental Ethics*, Prometheus Books, Buffalo, NY, pp167–170

Popper, K. R. (1945) *The Open Society and its Enemies*, Routledge, London

Popper, K. R. (1960) *The Poverty of Historicism*, Routledge, London

Popper, K. R. (1995) *Objektive Erkenntnis: ein evolutionärer Entwurf*, translated by H. Vetter, edited by I. Fleischmann, Hoffmann und Campe, Hamburg

Portes, A. and Landolt, P. (1996) 'The downside of social capital', *The American Prospect*, no 26, pp18–22

Posner, R. (1990a) 'Atommüll als Kommunikationsproblem', in Posner, R. (ed) *Warnungen an eine ferne Zukunft. Atommüll als Kommunikationsproblem*, Raben-Verlag, München, pp7–15

Posner, R. (1990b) 'Das Drei-Kammer-System: Ein Weg zur demokratischen Organisation von kollektivem Wissen und Gewissen über Jahrtausende', in Posner, R. (ed) *Warnungen an eine ferne Zukunft. Atommüll als Kommunikationsproblem*, Raben-Verlag, München, pp259–305

Prescott-Allen, R. (2001) *The Wellbeing of Nations*, Island Press, Washington DC

Prieto, L. and Sacristán, J. A. (2003) 'Problems and solutions in calculating quality-adjusted life years (QALYs)', *Health and Quality of Life Outcomes*, vol 1, www.pubmedcentral.nih.gov/picrender.fcgi?artid=317370&blobtype=pdf accessed 22 November 2007

Prim, R. and Tilmann, H. (1977) *Grundlagen einer kritisch-rationalen Sozialwissenschaft. 3rd revised edtion*, UTB, Darmstadt

Putnam, R. D. (1995) 'Tuning in, tuning out. The strange disappearance of social capital in America', *Political Science & Politics*, vol 28, no 4, pp664–683

Putnam, R. D. (1996) 'Symptome der Krise – Die USA, Europa und Japan im Vergleich', in Weidenfeld, W. (ed) *Demokratie am Wendepunkt. Die demokratische Frage als Projekt des 21. Jahrhunderts*, Siedler Verlag, Berlin, pp52–80

Putnam, R. D. (2000) *Bowling Alone. The Collapse and Revival of American Community*, Simon & Schuster, New York, NY

Putnam, R. D. and Goss, K. A. (2001) 'Einleitung', in Putnam, R. D. (ed) *Gesellschaft und Gemeinsinn: Sozialkapital im internationalen Vergleich*, Verlag Bertelsmann Stiftung, Gütersloh, pp15–44

Radermacher, F. (2002) *Balance oder Zerstörung. Ökosoziale Marktwirtschaft als Schlüssel zu einer weltweiten nachhaltigen Entwicklung*, Herold, Oberhaching

Raffelhüschen, B. (1999) 'Generational accounting: Method, data, and limitations', *European Economy, Reports and Studies*, no 6, pp17–28

Raffelhüschen, B. (2002) 'Generational accounting – quo vadis?', *Nordic Journal of Political Economy*, vol 28, no 1, pp75–89

Rakowski, E. (1991) *Equal Justice*, Clarendon Press, Oxford

Rat von Sachverständigen für Umweltfragen (2002) *Umweltgutachten 2002*, Langfassung. Bundestagsdrucksache, 14/8792, Berlin

Rawls, J. (1951) 'Outline of a decision procedure for ethics', *The Philosophical Review*, vol 60, no 2, pp177–197

Rawls, J. (1971) *A Theory of Justice*, Belknap Press of Harvard University Press, Cambridge, MA (German edition: Rawls, J. (1979) *Eine Theorie der Gerechtigkeit*, Suhrkamp Frankfurt am Main)

Rawls, J. (1993) *Political Liberalism*, Columbia University Press, New York, NY

Rawls, J. (1999) 'The idea of public reason revisited', in Freeman, S. (ed) *John Rawls. Collected Papers*, Harvard University Press, Cambridge, MA, pp573–615

Rawls, J. (2001) *Justice as Fairness: A Restatement*, Harvard University Press, Cambridge, MA

Regan, T. (1983) *The Case for Animal Rights*, University of California Press, Berkeley, CA

Renn, O. (2008) *Risk Governance. Coping with Uncertainty in a Complex World*, Earthscan, London

Rescher, N. (1966) *Distributive Justice. A Constructive Critique of the Utilitarian Theory of Distribution*, Bobbs-Merrill Co, Indianapolis, IN

Rest, A. (1994) 'The Oposa decision: Implementing the principles of intergenerational equity and responsibility', *Environmental Policy and Law*, vol 24, no 6, pp314–320

Richards, D. J. (1983) 'Contractarian theory, intergenerational justice, and energy policy', in MacLean, D. and Brown, P. G. (eds) *Energy for the Future*, Rowman and Littlefield, Totowa, pp131–150

Ridge, M. (2003) 'Giving the dead their due', *Ethics*, vol 114, no 1, pp38–39

Riemer, K. (2005) *Sozialkapital und Kooperation*, Mohr Siebeck, Tübingen

Riley, J. (1989) 'Justice under capitalism', in Chapman, J. W. and Pennock, R. J. (eds) *Markets and Justice*, New York University Press, New York, NY, p122–162

Roberts, M. A. (1998) *Child versus Childmaker: Future Persons and Present Duties in Ethics and the Law*, Rowman & Littlefield, Lanham, MD

Roemer, J. (1998) *Equality of Opportunity*, Cambridge University Press, Cambridge

Rolston, H. III (1974) 'Is there an ecological ethics?', *Ethics*, vol 85, no 1, pp93–109

Rolston, H. III (1988) *Environmental Ethics. Duties to and Values in the Natural World*, Temple University Press, Philadelphia, PA

Rolston, H. III (1997) 'Werte in der Natur und die Natur der Werte', in Krebs, A. (ed) *Naturethik*, Suhrkamp, Frankfurt am Main, pp247–270

Ross, W. D. (1930) *The Right and the Good*, Clarendon Press, Oxford

Routley, R. and Routley, V. (1978) 'Nuclear energy and obligations to the future', *Inquiry*, vol 21, pp133–179

Rupprecht, R. (1993) 'Lebensqualität – Theoretische Konzepte und Ansätze zur Operationalisierung', Dissertation, Friedrich-Alexander-Universität Erlangen-Nürnberg

Rürup, B. (2002) 'Generationenvertrag und intergenerative Gerechtigkeit', *Zeitschrift für Gerontologie und Geriatrie*, vol 35, no 4, pp275–281

Russell, Y., Kals, E. and Montada, L. (2003) 'Generationengerechtigkeit im allgemeinen Bewusstsein? Eine umweltpsychologische Untersuchung', in Stiftung für die Rechte zukünftiger Generationen (ed) *Handbuch Generationengerechtigkeit*, Oekom-Verlag München, pp153–173

Ryle, G. (1970) *Begriffskonflikte*, Vandenhoeck und Ruprecht, Göttingen

Sachverständigenrat zur Begutachtung der gesamtwirtschaftlichen Entwicklung (2004) *Jahresgutachten 2004/2005. Erfolge im Ausland – Herausforderungen im Inland*, Sachverständigenrat zur Begutachtung der gesamtwirtschaftlichen Entwicklung, Wiesbaden

Sadurski, W. (1985) *Giving Desert its Due*, Reidel, Dordrecht/Lancester

Sandvik, E., Diener, E. and Seidlitz, L. (1993) 'Subjective wellbeing: The convergence and stability of self-report and non-self-report measures', *Journal of Personality*, vol 61, no 3, pp317–342

Sauvé, K. (1995) 'Gauthier, property rights, and future generations', *Canadian Journal of Philosophy*, vol 25, no 2, pp163–176

Scanlon, T. M. (1998) *What We Owe to Each Other*, Belknap Press of Harvard University Press, Cambridge, MA

Scanlon, T. M. (2003) *The Difficulty of Tolerance. Essays in Political Philosophy*, Cambridge University Press, Cambridge

Schechler, J. (2002) *Sozialkapital und Netzwerkökonomik*, Lang (Hohenheimer Volkswirtschaftliche Schriften: vol 41), Frankfurt am Main/Berlin/Bruxelles/New York/Oxford/Wien

Schefczyk, M. (2009) 'Untangling historical injustice and historical ill', *Intergenerational Justice Review / Journal für Generationengerechtigkeit*, vol 9, no 1, pp4–8

Schelling, T. C. (1984) *Choice and Consequence. Perspectives of an Errant Economist*, Harvard University Press, Cambridge, MA

Scherbel, A. (2003) 'Die Begründung von Generationengerechtigkeit im Schöpfungsglauben der monotheistischen Offenbarungsreligionen', in Stiftung für die Rechte zukünftiger Generationen (ed) *Handbuch Generationengerechtigkeit*, Oekom-Verlag, München, pp175–197

Scherer, D. (1990) 'Introduction', in Scherer, D. (ed) *Upstream–Downstream. Issues in Environmental Ethics*, Temple University Press, Philadelphia, PA, pp3–18

Scherhorn, G. and Wilts, H. (2001) 'Schwach nachhaltig wird die Erde zerstört', *GAIA*, no 4, pp249–255

Schmähl, W. (2004) 'Generationengerechtigkeit und Alterssicherung aus ökonomischer Perspektive', in VDR (ed) *Generationengerechtigkeit – Inhalt, Bedeutung und Konsequenzen für die Alterssicherung*, DRV-Schriften, Frankfurt am Main, pp74–84

Schmidtz, D. (2006) *Elements of Justice*, Cambrige University Press, Cambridge

Schneider, W. (2007) *Glück*, Rowohlt, Reinbek bei Hamburg

Scholz, C., Stein, V. and Bechtel, R. (2004) *Human Capital Management – Wege aus der Unverbindlichkeit*, Luchterhand Verlag, Neuwied

Schopenhauer, A. (2007) 'Das Streben nach Glück – ein Irrtum', in Michel, S. (ed) *Glück. Ein philosophischer Streifzug*, Fischer, Frankfurt am Main, from A. Schopenhauer *Die Welt als Wille und Vorstellung I/II*, Zürich Edition, works in 10 Volumes, Zürich (1977)

Schuller, P. (2003) 'Nachhaltigkeitsindikator von Deutschland Denken', PowerPoint presentation, 27 November 2003, Berlin, unpublished

Schüttemeyer, S. (1998) 'Generation', in Dieter, N., Rainer-Olaf, S. and Suzanne, S. (eds) *Lexikon der Politik*, vol 7, Politische Begriffe, Directmedia Publ, München, pp211–212

Schwartz, T. (1978) 'Obligations to posterity', in Sikora, R. and Barry, B. (eds) *Obligations to Future Generations*, Temple University Press, Philadelphia, PA pp3–14

Schwarz, N. and Strack, F. (1991) *Evaluating One's Life: A Judgment Model of Subjective Wellbeing*, edited by ZUMA (Zentrum für Umfragen, Methoden und Analysen) and GESIS (Gesellschaft Sozialwissenschaftlicher Infrastruktureinrichtungen e.V.), ZUMA, Mannheim

Schwarz, N. and Strack, F. (1999) 'Reports of subjective well-being: Judgmental processes and their methodological implications', in Kahneman, D., Diener, E. and Schwarz, N. (eds) *Well-Being: The Foundations of Hedonic Psychology*, Russell Sage Foundation, New York, NY, pp61–84

Schwarze, R. (2003) 'Für und Wider der Diskontierung. Abschied von einem Grundpfeiler der Wirtschaftswissenschaften?', *Intergenerational Justice Review / Generationengerechtigkeit!* (German edition), vol 3, no 2, pp16–18

Scitovsky, T. (1976) *The Joyless Economy: An Inquiry into Human Satisfaction and Consumer Dissatisfaction*, Oxford University Press, Oxford

Seel, M. (1999) *Versuch über die Form des Glücks*, Suhrkamp, Frankfurt am Main (1st hardcover edition 1995)

Sen, A. K. (1985) 'Well-being and freedom', *The Journal of Philosophy*, vol 82, pp185–203

Sen, A. K. (1999) *Development as Freedom*, Oxford University Press, Oxford

Sen, A. K. (2000) 'Der Lebensstandard. Hamburg: Europäische Verlagsanstalt/Rotbuch Verlag' (English Original: 'The standard of living'), in MacMurrin, S. (ed) (1986) *Tanner Lectures on Human Values*, vol VII, Cambridge University Press, Cambridge

Sen, A. K. and Williams, B. (1982) *Utilitarianism and Beyond*, Cambridge University Press, Cambridge

Sextus Empiricus (2002) *Grundriss der Pyrrhonischen Skepsis*, Suhrkamp, Frankfurt/Main

Shapira, A. (1998) 'Wrongful life lawsuits for faulty genetic counselling: Should the impaired newborn be entitled to sue?', *Journal of Medical Ethics*, vol 2, pp369–375

Sher, G. (1987) *Desert*, Princeton University Press, Princeton, NJ

Sher, G. (1992) 'Ancient wrongs and modern rights', in Laslett, P. and Fishkin, J. S. (eds) *Justice between Age Groups and Generations*, Yale University Press, New Haven, CT, pp48–61

Shiffrin, S. H. (1999) 'Wrongful life, procreative responsibility and the significance of harm', *Legal Theory*, no 5, pp117–148

Shoham, S. and Lamay, N. (2006) 'Commission for Future Generations in the Knesset: Lessons learnt', in Tremmel, J. C. (ed) *Handbook of Intergenerational Justice*, Edward Elgar Publishing, Cheltenham, pp244–281

Sidgwick, H. (1981) *The Methods of Ethics*, Hacket Publishing Company, Indianapolis, IN (first published in 1874)

Sikora, R. and Barry, B. (1978) *Obligations to Future Generations*, Temple University Press, Philadelphia, PA

Simmons, A. J. (1995) 'Historical rights and fair shares', *Law and Philosophy*, vol 14, no 1, pp149–184

Simon, J. L. (1998) *The Ultimate Resource 2*, Princeton University Press, Princeton, NJ

Singer, P. (1976a) *Animal Liberation*, Cape, London

Singer, P. (1976b) 'A utilitarian population principle', in Bayles, M. D. (ed) *Ethics and Population*, Schankman, Cambridge, pp81–99

Singer, P. (1979) *Practical Ethics*, Cambridge University Press, Cambridge

Singer, P. (1984) *Praktische Ethik*, Reclam, Stuttgart

Smart, J. C. C. (1973) *Utilitarianism: For and Against*, Cambridge University Press, London

Smith, A. (1991) *Wealth of Nations*, Prometheus Books, Amherst (Great Minds Series) (1st edition 1776)

Sölle, D. (1975) 'Die Hinreise. Zur religiösen Erfahrung. Texte und Überlegungen', Kreuz Verlag, Stuttgart

Solow, R. M. (1992) *Growth with Equity through Investment in Human Capital*, G. Seltzer Distinguished Lecture Series, Minnesota

Solum, L. B. (2001) 'To our children's children's children: The problems of intergenerational ethics', *Loyola of Los Angeles Law Review*, vol 35, no 1, pp163–234

Spaemann, R. (1989) *Glück und Wohlwollen*, Klett-Cotta, Stuttgart

Stark, W. (1952) *Jeremy Bentham's Economic Writings*, vol I, Allen & Unwin, London

Steffens, G. (2004) 'Editorial', *Polis*, no 3, p1

Stein, H. (2004) *Anatomie der Vermögensverteilung: Ergebnisse der Einkommens- und Verbrauchsstichproben 1983–1998*, Sigma, Berlin

Steinvorth, U. (2007) 'Generationengerechtigkeit', *Intergenerational Justice Review / Generationengerechtigkeit!* (German edition), vol 7, no 4, pp12–15

Stern, N. (2007) *The Economics of Climate Change. The Stern Review*, Cambridge University Press, Cambridge

Stoecker, R. (ed) (2003) *Menschenwürde. Annäherung an einen Begriff*, ÖPV & HPT, Wien

Strack, F., Argyle, M. and Schwarz, N. (eds) (1991) *Subjective Wellbeing: An Interdisciplinary Perspective. International Series in Experimental Social Psychology*, Pergamon, Oxford

Strasser, M. (1999) 'Wrongful life, wrongful birth, wrongful death and the right to refuse treatment: Can reasonable jurisdiction recognize all but one?', *Missouri Law Review*, vol 64, pp29–75

Strauss, W. and Howe, N. (1991) *Generations. The History of America's Future*, Quill, New York, NY

Strauss, W. and Howe, N. (1993) *13th Generation. Abort, Retry, Ignore, Fail?*, Vintage Books, New York, NY

Sukhdev, P. (2008) 'The economics of ecosystems and biodiversity. An interim report of the European Communities', http://ec.europa.eu/environment/nature/biodiversity/economics/pdf/teeb_report.pdf accessed 26 June 2008

The Talmud (2007) Weltbild, Augsburg

Tännsjö, T. (2007) 'Narrow hedonism', *Journal of Happiness Studies*, vol 8, no 1, pp79–98

Taylor, C. (1981) *Sources of the Self*, Harvard University Press, Cambridge, MA

Taylor, P. W. (1981) 'The ethics of respect for nature', *Environmental Ethics*, vol 3, no 3, pp197–218

Taylor, P. W. (1986) *Respect for Nature. A Theory of Environmental Ethics*, Princeton University Press, Princeton, NJ

Teutsch, G. M. (1985) *Lexikon der Umweltethik*, Vandenhoeck und Ruprecht, Göttingen

Thomä, D. (2003) *Vom Glück in der Moderne*, Suhrkamp, Frankfurt am Main

Thompson, J. (2002) *Taking Responsibility for the Past*, Polity, Cambridge

Thompson, T. (1980) 'Are we obligated to future others?', in Partridge, E. (ed) *Responsibilities to Future Generations. Environmental Ethics*, Prometheus Books, Buffalo, NY, pp195–202

Thomson, D. (1991) *Selfish Generations? The Ageing of New Zealand's Welfare State*, Bridget Williams Books, Wellington, NZ

Thomson, D. (1992) 'Generations, justice, and the future of collective action', in Laslett, P. and Fishkin, J. S. (eds) *Justice between Age Groups and Generations*, Yale University Press, New Haven, CT/London, pp206–236

Tremmel, J. (1997) 'Wie die gesetzliche Rentenversicherung nach dem Prinzip der Generationengerechtigkeit reformiert werden kann', in Gesellschaft für die Rechte zukünftiger Generationen (ed) *Ihr habt dieses Land nur von uns geborgt*, Rasch und Röhring, Hamburg, pp149–240

Tremmel, J. (2003a) 'Generationengerechtigkeit – Versuch einer Definition', in Stiftung für die Rechte zukünftiger Generationen (ed) *Handbuch Generationengerechtigkeit. 2nd revised edition*, Oekom-Verlag, München, pp27–80

Tremmel, J. (2003b) 'Positivrechtliche Verankerung der Rechte zukünftiger Generationen', in Stiftung für die Rechte zukünftiger Generationen (ed) *Handbuch Generationengerechtigkeit. 2nd revised edition*, Oekom-Verlag, München, pp349–382

Tremmel, J. (2003c) *Nachhaltigkeit als politische und analytische Kategorie. Der deutsche Diskurs um nachhaltige Entwicklung im Spiegel der Interessen der Akteure*, Oekom-Verlag, München

254 A Theory of Intergenerational Justice

Tremmel, J. (2003d) 'Generationengerechtigkeit und Rentenbesteuerung', in Manfred, R. (ed) *Integriertes Steuer- und Sozialsystem*, Physica-Verlag, Heidelberg, pp421–436

Tremmel, J. (2003e) 'Generationengerechtigkeit aus ökonomischer Sicht. Abdiskontierung – die ökonomische Sicht der Zukunftsbewertung in der Diskussion', *Intergenerational Justice Review / Generationengerechtigkeit!* (German edition), vol 3, no 2, pp19–21

Tremmel, J. (2004a) 'Generationengerechtigkeit – eine Ethik der Zukunft', *Natur und Kultur. Transdisziplinäre Zeitschrift für ökologische Nachhaltigkeit*, no 1, pp45–64

Tremmel, J. (2004b) 'Is a theory of intergenerational justice possible? A response to Beckerman', *Intergenerational Justice Review* (English edition), vol 4, no 2, pp6–9

Tremmel, J. (2004c) '"Nachhaltigkeit" – definiert nach einem kriteriengebundenen Verfahren', *GAIA*, vol 13, pp26–34

Tremmel, J. (2005a) *Bevölkerungspolitik im Kontext ökologischer Generationengerechtigkeit*, DUV Verlag, Wiesbaden

Tremmel, J. (2005b) 'Verankerung von Generationengerechtigkeit in der Verfassung', in *Aus Politik und Zeitgeschichte*, no 8, pp18–28

Tremmel, J. (2006a) 'Introduction', in Tremmel, J. (ed) *Handbook of Intergenerational Justice*, Edward Elgar Publishing, Cheltenham, pp1–19

Tremmel, J. (2006b) 'Establishment of intergenerational justice in national constitutions' in Tremmel, J. (ed) *Handbook of Intergenerational Justice*, Edward Elgar Publishing, Cheltenham, pp187–214

Tremmel, J. (2006c) 'Einwände gegen Generationengerechtigkeit – und ihre Widerlegung', in *Intergenerational Justice Review / Generationengerechtigkeit!* (French–German bilingual edition), vol 6, no 1, pp4–8 (in French pp9–12)

Tremmel, J. (2007a) 'Der Schleier der Unwissenheit. Eine empirische Studie zu präferierten Geburtsjahren', *FRFG-Study 2/2007*, www.generationengerechtigkeit.de/images/stories/Publikationen/artikel_studien/studie2_2007_final.pdf accessed 20 December 2007

Tremmel, J. (2007b) 'Generationengerechte Rentenpolitik', *FRFG-Study 1/2007*, www.generationengerechtigkeit.de/images/stories/Publikationen/artikel_studien/studie_generationengerechte_rentenpolitik.pdf accessed 20 December 2007

Tremmel, J. (2007c) 'Ungleichbehandlung von Jung und Alt in Unternehmen', in Aβländer, M. S., Suchanek, A. and Ulshöfer, G. (eds) *Generationengerechtigkeit als Aufgabe von Wirtschaft, Politik und Gesellschaft. Tagungsband zur DNWE-Jahrestagung vom 7.-8.4.2006*, Rainer Hampp-Verlag, Mering, pp127–143

Tremmel, J. (2008) 'An ethical assessment of the legitimacy of anti-natalistic birth policies', in Tremmel, J. (ed) *Demographic Change and Intergenerational Justice. The Implementation of Long-term Thinking in Political Decision-Making*, Springer, Berlin/New York, NY, pp137–159

Tremmel, J. (2009) 'Der Schleier der Unwissenheit. Eine empirische Studie zu präferierten Geburtsjahren. Teil 2', *FRFG-Study 1/2009*, Forthcoming

Tremmel, J. and Goetz, O. (2007) 'Steigende Lebensqualität und Generationengerechtigkeit', *Intergenerational Justice Review / Generationengerechtigkeit!* (German edition), vol 7, no 4, pp20–26

Tremmel, J. and Ulshöfer, G. (eds) (2005) *Unternehmensleitbild Generationengerechtigkeit – Theorie und Praxis*, IKO Verlag, Frankfurt am Main

Tremmel, J., Laukemann, M. and Lux, C. (1999) 'Die Verankerung von Generationengerechtigkeit im Grundgesetz – Vorschlag für einen erneuerten Art. 20a GG', *Zeitschrift für Rechtspolitik*, vol 32, no 10, pp432–438

Tugendhat, E. (1993) *Vorlesungen über Ethik*, Special Edition, Suhrkamp, Frankfurt am Main

Ul Haq, M. (1995) *Reflections on Human Development*, Oxford University Press, Oxford/New York, NY

Ulpian (1999) *Institutionen*, UTB, Heidelberg

Ulshöfer, G. (2005) 'Generationengerechtigkeit bei Unternehmen – eine theologisch-wirtschaftsethische Perspektive', in Tremmel, J. and Ulshöfer, G. (eds) *Unternehmensleitbild Generationengerechtigkeit – Theorie und Praxis*, IKO Verlag, Frankfurt am Main, pp227–238

UNDP (United Nations Development Programme) *Human Development Report 2006*, UNDP, New York, http://hdr.undp.org/en/reports/global/hdr2006/ accessed 30 November 2007

Unnerstall, H. (1999) *Rechte zukünftiger Generationen*, Königshausen & Neumann, Würzburg

UN Population Division (2003) *World Population in 2300*, UN Publications, New York, NY

van Dieren, W. (ed) (1995) *Mit der Natur rechnen: der neue Club-of-Rome-Bericht; vom Bruttosozialprodukt zum Okosozialprodukt*, Birkhäuser, Berlin

Vaupel, J. W., Schnabel, S. and von Kistowski, K. (2006) 'Möglichkeiten und Grenzen demographischer Prognosen', in Bertelsmann Stiftung (ed) *Demographiemonitor. vol 2: Handlungsoptionen im demographischen Wandel*, Verlag Bertelsmann Stiftung, Gütersloh, pp35–59

VDR (Verband Deutscher Rentenversicherungsträger) (2004) *Generationengerechtigkeit – Inhalt, Bedeutung und Konsequenzen für die Alterssicherung*, DRV-Schriften, Frankfurt am Main

Veenhoven, R. (1993) *Happiness in Nations: Subjective Appreciation of Life in 56 Nations 1946–1992*, Erasmus University Press, Rotterdam

Veenhoven, R. (2005) http://worlddatabaseofhappiness.eur.nl accessed 23 June 2007

Veenhoven, R. (2007) 'Happiness in hardship', in Bruni, L. and Porta, P. L. (eds) (2007) *Economics and Happiness. Framing the Analysis*, Oxford University Press, Oxford, pp243–266

Veith, W. (2001) 'Solidarität der Generationen', in Baumgartner, A. and Putz, G. (eds) *Sozialprinzipien. Leitideen einer sich wandelnden Welt*, Tyrolia-Verlag, Innsbruck/Wien, pp107–124

Veith, W. (2006) *Intergenerationelle Gerechtigkeit. Ein Beitrag zur sozialethischen Theoriebildung*, Kohlhammer, Stuttgart

Vernon, R. (2003) 'Against restitution', *Political Studies*, vol 51, no 3, pp542–557

Vernon, R. (2009) 'Intergenerational rights?', *Intergenerational Justice Review / Journal für Generationengerechtigkeit*, vol 9, no 1, pp8–12

Vlastos, G. (1984) 'Justice and equality', in Waldron, J. (ed) *Theories of Rights. Oxford Readings in Philosophy*, Oxford University Press, Oxford

Vokey, D. (2001) *Education for Intergenerational Justice:Why should we care?*, Ontario Institute for Studies of Education, Philosophy of Education, www.ed.uiuc.edu/eps/PES-Yearbook/94_docs/VOKEY.HTM accessed 25 December 2004

von Brück, M. (2007) *Ewiges Leben oder Wiedergeburt? Sterben, Tod und Jenseitshoffnung in europäischen und asiatischen Kulturen*, Herder, Freiburg im Breisgau

von Savigny, E. (1980) *Grundkurs im wissenschaftlichen Definieren*, 5th edition, Deutscher Taschenbuchverlag, München

von Savigny, E. (1993) *Die Philosophie der normalen Sprache: eine kritische Einführung in die ordinary language philosophy*, Suhrkamp, Frankfurt am Main

von Wright, G. H. (1963) *The Varieties of Goodness*, Routledge, London

Waldron, J. (1984) 'Introduction', in Waldron, J. (ed) *Theories of Rights*, Oxford University Press, Oxford, pp1–20

Waldron, J. (1992) 'Superseding historic injustice', *Ethics*, vol 103, no 1, pp4–28

Wallack, M. (2006) 'Justice between generations: The limits of procedural justice', in Tremmel, J. C. (ed) *Handbook of Intergenerational Justice*, Edward Elgar Publishing, Cheltenham, pp86–105

Walzer, M. (1983) *Spheres of Justice: A Defense of Plurism and Equality*, Basic Books, New York, NY

Weber, M. (1904) 'Die Objektivität sozialwissenschaftlicher und sozialpolitischer Erkenntnis', in Winkelmann, J. (ed) (1988) *M. Weber: Gesammelte Aufsätze zur Wissenschaftslehre*, Mohr, Tübingen pp146–214

Weimann, J., Hoffmann, A. and Hoffmann, S. (eds) (2003) *Messung und ökonomische Bewertung von Biodiversität: Mission impossible?*, Metropolis-Verlag, Marburg

Weston, B. and Bach, T. (2009) 'Recalibrating the law of humans with the laws of nature: Climate change, human rights, and intergenerational justice', policy paper forthcoming from Vermont Law School and The University of Iowa in March 2009, www.vermontlaw.edu/x4128.xml, accessed 13 April 2009

Westra, L. (2006) *Environmental Justice and the Rights of Unborn and Future Generations*, Earthscan, London

Wilson, E. O. (1984) *Biophilia*, Harvard University Press, Oxford

Wilson, E. O. (1992) *The Diversity of Life*, Belknap Press of Harvard University Press, Cambridge, MA

Wilson, E. O. (ed) (1998) *Biodiversity*, National Academy Press, Washington DC

Wissenburg, M. (1999) 'An extension of the Rawlsian savings principle to liberal theories of justice in general', in Dobson, A. (ed) *Fairness and Futurity*, Oxford University Press, Oxford, pp173–198

Wissenschaftlicher Beirat beim Bundesministerium der Finanzen (2001) *Nachhaltigkeit in der Finanzpolitik: Konzepte für eine langfristige Orientierung öffentlicher Haushalte*, www.bundesfinanzministerium.de/Anlage9127/Gutachten-zurÿNachhaltigkeit-in-der-Finanzpolitik.pdf accessed 30 January 2008

Wolf, C. (1995) 'Property rights, Lockean provisos, and the interests of future generations', *Ethics*, vol 105, no 4, pp791–818

Wolf, C. (1996) 'Social choice and normative population theory: A person-affecting solution to Parfit's mere-addition paradox', *Philosophical Studies*, vol 81, no 2–3, pp263–282

Wolf, C. (1997) 'Person-affecting utilitarianism and population policy; or, Sissy Jupe's theory of social choice', in Fotion, N. and Heller, J. C. (eds) *Contingent Future People: On the Ethics of Deciding Who Will Live, or not, in the Future*, Springer, Dordrecht, pp99–122

Wolf, U. (1990) *Das Tier in der Moral*, Klostermann, Frankfurt am Main

Wolf, C. (2008) 'Justice and intergenerational debt', *Intergenerational Justice Review* (English edition), vol 8, no 1, pp13–17

Woodward, J. (1986) 'The non-identity problem', *Ethics*, vol 96, no 4, pp804–831

World Bank (2004) 'Measuring social capital. An integrated questionnaire', *World Bank Working Paper*, no18, edited by C. Grootaert, D. Narayan and V. N. Jones, http://povlibrary.worldbank.org/library/view/11998 accessed 13 August 2007

World Commission on Environment and Development (1987) *Our Common Future*, Oxford University Press, Oxford

Young, H. P. (1994) *Equity in Theory and Practice*, Princeton University Press, Princeton, NJ

Zapf, W. (1984) 'Individuelle Wohlfahrt: Lebensbedingungen und wahrgenommene Lebensqualität', in Glatzer, W. and Zapf, W. (eds) *Lebensqualität in der Bundesrepublik*, Campus Verlag, Frankfurt am Main/New York, NY pp13–27

Index